TAIL ENDS OF THE FIFTIES

THE THIRD IN A TRILOGY OF AVIATION MEMORIES

COMPILED AND EDITED

BY

PETER CAMPBELL

CIRRUS ASSOCIATES

PUBLISHED BY:
Cirrus Associates (S.W.),
Kington Magna,
Gillingham,
Dorset,
SP8 5EW UK.

ISBN 0 951 5598 9 3

PRINTED IN ENGLAND BY:
The Book Factory,
35-37 Queensland Road,
London,
N7 7AH.

PHOTO SCANNING BY:
Castle Graphics Ltd.
Nunney,
Nr. Frome,
Somerset,
BA11 4LW.

DISTRIBUTORS:
Cirrus Associates (S.W.),
Kington Magna,
Gillingham,
Dorset,
SP8 5EW.

COVER PHOTOS:
Cloud background: Peter Campbell.
Tails: T.L. Peter Amos, T.M. via Sandy Sproule, T.R. Peter Amos,
B.L. Alf Jenks, B.M. Ginger Bedggood, B.R. Peter Amos.

EDITOR'S ACKNOWLEDGEMENTS

I would like to acknowledge with grateful thanks the help of the following persons and organisations, in purely alphabetical order, without whom this book could not have been completed (once more, I hope I've not forgotten anyone!).

Air Officer Commanding and Commandant of the Royal Air Force College Cranwell, Peter Amos, Ambrose Barber, Ginger Bedggood, Lewis Benjamin, Ronald "Dickie" Bird, Maurice Brett, British Aerospace, Jean Buckberry, Chris Button, Dugald Cameron, James Campbell, David Chalmers, Noel Collier, Jack Da-Costa, Chris Dearden, David Elliott, John Farley, Dick Flute, Tim Foster, James Gilbert, John Havers, Alf Jenks, Neil Jensen, Geoffrey Jones, Margaret Lloyd, Roy Mills, Ministry of Defence, Col. (Retd.) John Moss, MC, MRAeS, Roy Nerou, David Ogilvy, Charles Oman, Arthur Ord-Hume, Chris Parker, Geoffrey Pitt, Nick Pocock, John Pothecary, Richard Riding, Edwin Shackleton, Sandy Sproule, John Teasdale, Lord Trefgarne, John de Uphaugh, Stan Ward.

CONTENTS

DEDICATIONS

It is very sad to have to record the passing during 1998 of yet two more experienced flyers who have contributed to previous books in this trilogy about flying in the 1950s.

RANALD PORTEOUS

Arthur Ord-Hume writes:

Ranald Porteous (1916-1998) – An Appreciation

Last year's book *"More Tails of the Fifties"* was blessed with a delightful contribution by Ranald Porteous. Now it seems hard to accept that Ranald is no longer with us.

His skill at flying, his charming ways, and his humour have been stilled forever. A whole generation grew up watching him throw Austers around the sky and land other aeroplanes on a wheel and a wingtip. And a still earlier generation watched him demonstrating ultralights such as the Luton Buzzard, the Ding-Bat and the Currie Wot at air shows around the land. But it was his love of the little Chilton Monoplane that we shall probably remember most . . .

Ranald Logan Porteous was born on March 25th 1916 at Alva, near Stirling in Scotland. Both his father and his grandfather were Provosts and the family business concerned the manufacture of tweed. His father died when Ranald was nine years old, and by the time a career choice had to be made the tweed business had been pitched into the young but capable hands of his older brother Alan and Ranald had set his sights on the skies.

After an education at Canford he went to the de Havilland Technical College at Hatfield where he met many contemporaries who would play a part in his later career including Alexander Reginald "Reggie" Ward and the Hon. Andrew W. H. Dalrymple, who later founded Chilton Aircraft, and Eric Watkinson and Cyril W. Taylor who built the Ding-Bat.

At the age of 22 he made the maiden flight in the Chilton and began an involvement with this little machine, evolved from the unbuilt TK.3, which was to continue well into postwar years. Besides doing all the test-flying, he amassed more than 300 hours in G-AFGH.

In 1937, after training at Montrose and Driffield, he joined the Reserve of Royal Air Force Officers to fly Harts and Harrows, but a call from another ex-DH friend, Geoffrey Alington, took him to Air Tours at Gatwick flying the Short Scion, Desoutter and Falcon Major.

Between times he acted as junior test pilot to Philips & Powis (Miles) at Reading but at the outbreak of war in 1939 he was sent to Rhodesia in charge of Training Command, a position he held until 1945.

Now with the rank of Squadron Leader, peacetime brought him back to the Chilton monoplane, and in 1947 he won the International 100 km Class 1 Closed Circuit Record in that machine.

A spell as CFI and secretary to Derby Aero Club led in 1948 to the invitation to join Auster Aircraft as chief test pilot, taking over from George Norman Snarey, the former Spitfire production test pilot who earlier still had learned his skills with Harald Penrose at Westlands. At Auster's Rearsby factory and airfield, Ranald tested virtually every new type, aided eventually by Les Leetham.

Long delivery flights were also part of the job. Taking an Aiglet to India earned him an unusual reward. Invited to take part in a crazy-flying competition in the 1951 International Air Rally he won the prize outright.

For the SBAC Farnborough show, Ranald created a classic aerobatic manoeuvre. This was a time when RAF pilots were demonstrating jets in a fairly dramatic way and Ranald decided that he could do at least as well. So was born his extraordinary 'avalanche' manoeuvre for his Auster Aiglet Trainer. It was half a loop at the top of which was a flick-roll from inverted back to inverted. It gained the popular name 'top-knot' and entered RAF flight training manuals as "The Porteous Loop."

After the event he commented that while the faster boys began their demonstrations at Reading and finished at Winchester, at least his show took place in one small piece of sky immediately above the runway where everybody could see him. He was a perfectionist in the art of the precise and concise display.

One-wheel landings, landing off (and in) a turn, tailwheel 'wheelie' runs with the nose held high – all were stunts at which Ranald excelled and the majority were inspired by his favourite among the Auster types, the Aiglet Trainer. But stunting was not restricted to Rearsby products: many will recall Ranald's habit during the 1940s of landing Miles Messengers on one wheel with a wingtip brushing the ground.

He raced Chiltons and missed no opportunity to fly them. He would start up the black-and-white 'FSV, then walk round and pick up the tail to walk it out to take-off point so as to save tailskid metal.

In addition to test-pilot, he became Auster's sales director in 1956.

With the formation in 1960 of Beagle Aircraft, Ranald was appointed official Beagle test pilot. His expert input, however, was not appreciated, and his firm belief that the 242 should be put into production rather than the 206 was ignored. He grew increasingly unhappy with the setup.

In July 1968 Beagle was taken over as a wholly government-owned company. Under the command of a managing director who had no aviation background, staff-cutting culled Ranald as well as a number of others who represented the skill-kernel of the business.

The collapse of Beagle came despite repeated warnings from, among others, George Miles, who knew that the direction of the business was totally wrong.

In January of 1969 Porteous moved to Scottish Aviation at Prestwick to take up the position of sales manager and, later, director of marketing. Following the final collapse of Beagle in 1969-70, the Bulldog export order and RAF contract was taken over by Scottish Aviation. Ranald was closely involved not only with the supply of the Bulldog to the Swedish Air Force but also the Jetstream programme.

Industry was in a period of turmoil and when, in 1977, Scottish Aviation became part of British Aerospace, Ranald left to join Britten-Norman at Bembridge on the sales side. He stayed until his retirement in 1981.

In retirement at his Scottish home he indulged himself in his love of sailing, writing poetry and, once a year, driving south to go shooting at Bisley in the Canfordians' team. He suffered a heart attack at the end of October 1998 and died peacefully on November 5th.

My own personal recollections began in the halcyon days of the 1930s when I was a lad admiring this dapper young man flying with great precision at Myles Bickerton's little airfield at Denham. Years later I flew with him on test flights and played Number Two on a couple of delivery trips.

Only last year we stood in Ann Harington's back garden at Woking and watched a hot-air balloon struggling to avoid treetops, and we laughed heartily at the paradox of altitude and the age-old problem of not having sufficient beneath you. We had many laughs together over the years.

For his dear wife, Susan, and son, Bruce, let us always remember the happy times. He would certainly have preferred it that way.

ERIC BELL

Peter Amos writes:

Eric Bell (1927-1998) – Some Unforgettable Memories

I was first introduced to Eric by Julian Temple during one of the Brooklands Fly-Ins in 1996, and was very pleased to meet a 'kindred spirit.' Eric had worked for Vickers at Weybridge for many years before his retirement, and during conversation I soon found that we both shared a common interest in light aeroplanes and had known the same people at Croydon in the late forties and early fifties.

After this first meeting, Eric joined the Miles Aircraft Collection and would often telephone me in the evening after he had received the latest Miles Magazine to tell me he was so pleased to discover that we had both known "old so-and-so" and other personalities who had flown from Croydon in those halcyon days so long before.

I was also surprised to find that Eric must also have been the only aircraft design draughtsman in the country who had actually flown to Brooklands – to work! This unique event apparently occurred in the fifties when there had been a public transport strike and he had obtained special dispensation to fly his Puss Moth G-AHLO there from Croydon; those were the days when design draughtsmen were really appreciated.

After his retirement, Eric regularly attended the Vickers' 'Old Boys' gatherings at Brooklands, and often related many tales of these (including some stories about his one-time boss George Edwards, whom he greatly admired); for some time I had been trying to get him to commit these to paper so, when he rang me early in 1998 to let me know that he was not well, I was deeply shocked.

Although I had only known Eric for two years it seems much longer: he was so full of life, a real aviation enthusiast. When I heard that he had passed away in May, I found it hard to take in – no more lovely stories to read, no more wonderful telephone calls . . .

PREFACE

by

Peter Campbell

It is always sad to record the passing of friends, but tempus fuges relentlessly; however, no one could deny that Ranald and Eric thoroughly enjoyed their lives in flying, and survived into happy retirement.

In 1908, less than five years after the Wright Brothers' first flight, *"The New York Times"* began an editorial thus:

"Flying machines, one and all, have quickly illustrated the adage of our youth: 'What goes up must come down.'"

Nevertheless we can perhaps draw some comfort from a recent Lloyd's of London comment that it is 25 times safer to travel by commercial airlines than by car. Many people perceive smaller aircraft as being less safe but, statistically speaking, is there any evidence that this is so? After all, any air crash will always make the headlines. It is a sobering thought that, whereas the statistics for 1997 show that only 1,226 people died in airline accidents, about half a million people die in accidents on the roads of the world each year, most of them unreported. Every activity carries *some* risk; but long live the science, sport and art of flying, along with the deep satisfaction that it provides.

This is the third and final book in our trilogy about flying in the immediate postwar period until the early sixties. I have counted the total number of authors contributing to the series and there are well over sixty of them! I am so very grateful to each and every one for taking the trouble to record their memories of those times and now share them with us. Hopefully this series of books will provide a permanent record of what flying – and indeed life in general – was like nearly half a century ago.

The annual series of "Great Vintage Flying Weekends," (where our books are launched) continues on, and each year I notice that the event is better attended. Bigger doesn't always mean better, but I am determined to try to preserve the relaxed garden party atmosphere of fifties' events. In 1999 I am grateful to have had a lot of extra help, and the organising team has been extended to include, in addition to David Dowell, Ian Turner and Terry Knight of Kemble Airfield Management Ltd, John Farley, Terry Booker and Keith Preen, all of whom are experienced in the organisation of aviation events. I am also encouraged that so many owners and operators of British-built classic and vintage aeroplanes seem to regard our event as one that it is worth their while turning out for.

I hope you will enjoy this book just as much – or more – as the two that have preceded it.

FOREWORD

by

Lord Trefgarne

As the twentieth century and second millennium come to an end, it is so good to have an opportunity to pause and look back at events and achievements of the past, including of course comparatively recent times. So this third volume about aviation in the fifties is most timely.

The fifties marked the end of the line for World War Two technology including, above all, the piston engine. So the stories and reminiscences so vividly conveyed in the following chapters of this book, and indeed the previous ones, do truly provide an account of the end of an era. And all this barely a generation since the Wright brothers changed the course of history at Kitty Hawk.

Within a few months of my writing these words the new millennium will be with us. Let us remember with pride the achievements of those who have gone before. Let us only hope that in fifty years' time our successors will look back with equal approbation to the achievements of today.

CHAPTER 1

ANOTHER VIEW

by

David Ogilvy

[NOTES ON THE AUTHOR: David Ogilvy was born in 1929. He was a pilot in the RAF from 1947 until 1952, when he accepted a post at Elstree as CFI/Manager; this led to Directorships of the London School of Flying, the Midland School of Flying and Derby Aerosurveys. He became General Manager of the Shuttleworth Collection in 1966, and an Independent Aviation Advisor & Consultant in 1980. He is currently Executive Chairman of the Aircraft Owners' & Pilots' Association and Chairman of the General Aviation Awareness Council.

He was joint founder of the Vintage Aeroplane Club in 1951, and was a regular participant in air races between 1950 and 1956. He became involved in flying displays for some forty years from 1951, first as a participant and later also as an organiser.

He has written 14 aviation books and is currently a member of the CAA's Operations Advisory Committee, National Air Traffic Management Advisory Committee, General Aviation Safety Council, CAA's General Aviation Consultative Committee and other bodies. He was awarded the OBE in 1996 "for services to aviation." He is a fellow of the Royal Aeronautical Society. – Ed.]

Those of us who were around on the flying scene in the fifties were very fortunate. Contrary to much-spread and ill-informed opinion, there were far, far more aeroplanes around then than there are today. Yet, despite the vast numbers, no one made a fuss over crowded airspace and all users tended to get along without trying to grab chunks of the sky as their own protected patches. The only pieces of crowded airspace today are artificially created through the use of choke points and various corridors. When there were lots of aircraft in the air, we spread ourselves widely and all was well. It would have been impossible to accommodate all the flying into today's cramped corners.

To put this all into perspective, we must go back to long before most of us were born: to April 1918. Then the Royal Air Force had a strength of 23,500 aeroplanes. Today the RAF, the Royal Navy, the Army Air Corps, the commercial air transport industry and general aviation (GA) all together have little more than two-thirds of that figure. The UK airlines have a mere 800 aircraft in total, with GA as the largest sector with about 10,000. Even with recent cutbacks the Services have considerably more aircraft than the commercial operators.

This sets the scene for comparisons between the fifties and the late nineties. Many people earn their livings today by seeking ways to keep aircraft apart. Some argue that this has come about because of the vast speed differentials between the fastest and slowest machines, but has that differential really grown so much since the fifties? To answer that we must go back to the numbers.

Today the RAF has about 200 Tornados; Harriers, Jaguars and Hawks amount to another 176 aircraft, bringing the total number of fast jets to considerably fewer than 400. RAF trainers – Bulldogs and Tucanos – fall below 200. At 800 in total, the airlines have only about 50 more aircraft than they had 15 years ago. Who would believe that when we hear the bleats about crowded skies?

Now let us return to the title theme for this publication. 2,900 Meteors and about 2,000 Vampires were built for the RAF. Prior to this, 4,200 Tiger Moths and 1,200 Magisters had entered service in the UK. For several years Meteors and Tiger Moths in very considerable numbers shared the sky, with three auxiliary fighter squadrons and seven Reserve Flying Schools in the London area alone. The speed differential was not so different from today, for as early as 1945 a Meteor had established a world speed record of 606.25 mph. The only real difference was in numbers: then, the sky was well loaded with aeroplanes. Today it is uncannily empty.

Now to the civil scene. In the fifties there were 14 civil aerodromes along the south-east coast between Ramsgate (closed) and Christchurch (also gone): today there are six. The various users shared the airspace without divisions: well I remember flying along the south coast in a civil Magister (officially known as a Hawk Trainer III), to be overtaken by a flight of RAF Vampires. As the formation passed, the leader gave a salute followed by a clearly matey wave. I returned both. This was a recognised practice at a time when we saw and met aeroplanes frequently. Then, on the commercial side, Bristol Freighters crossed the Channel with their mixed loads of cars and passengers at a frequency that would shame any commercial operator today: in the 10 years to 1958, Silver City Airways completed 125,000 flights – or an average of 35 services a day, winter and summer.

So this is the set-up in which I had the good fortune to find myself. I had been fortunate enough to train as a pilot in the RAF at a time when throughput was minimal – just after the second World War – and I enjoyed the aeroplanes of the day, from Tiger Moth to Mosquito and Meteor. Although many people enjoy flying and many others have deep-rooted interest in aircraft, relatively few are seriously interested in both, but I was in that strange category of person who was unable to leave aeroplanes alone. So, even whilst in the RAF, I did a spot of part-time club instructing in a decrepit Taylorcraft Plus D from a field at Bourne End, and in a slightly healthier Piper Cub from the very pleasant grass aerodrome known as Gatwick Airport.

My main interest, though, was in vintage aircraft. The late Doug Bianchi, founder of Personal Plane Services, which is still extant today at Booker, was based in a couple of huts at Blackbushe, which was occupied mainly by Lancastrians, Yorks, Vikings and DC-3s, for at that time there were a lot of commercial air transport aircraft around. (CAA records show that there were about 20% more certificated civil aircraft in the medium to heavy categories than there are today.) Doug, though, ran a small engineering company for light aircraft and, on my first visit, he had just made airworthy a 1935 Miles Falcon G-ADFH. I stepped off my stalwart 125 cc BSA Bantam, marched in and asked if I could fly it! Not only was the answer "yes," but within a few days we had agreed that I could enter it in the 1950 Daily Express Air Race from Hurn (Bournemouth). When that day came to pass, things went well at first, but unfortunately a broken oil pipe necessitated a rather rapid forced landing on the (now long defunct) airport at Portsmouth. Nevertheless, it opened the door to the air racing world and strengthened my appetite for more.

Soon after this I thought we should form an association for owners and pilots of ageing aeroplanes. I wrote to *"Flight"* and by sheer co-incidence my letter was published on the same day as one appeared in *"The Aeroplane"* (then a weekly competitor) from Ron Gillman, who had similar ideas. We joined forces, with Ron – a senior Captain with the then British European Airways who was part owner of a 1930 Avro Avian G-ABEE – becoming Chairman. As very much his junior, I became Honorary Secretary. We called the new body the Vintage Aeroplane Club.

We had formed the club, but now we needed action. We decided that membership would be open to owners or pilots of aircraft types that had been out of production since before the start of the second World War – so Tiger Moths, Magisters, Austers and Proctors were not on the list. To test the water, we publicised our first meeting at White Waltham and we attracted 12 assorted and genuine vintage machines. This sufficed to encourage us to go ahead.

It was one thing to invite owners to come along with their pride and joy possessions, but what could we do for the larger number of enthusiasts who wanted to fly real aeroplanes but who were unable to afford their own kit? Of these I was one. We tracked down a 1933 Avro Club Cadet, G-ACHP, and pooled our meagre resources to buy it and obtain a new Certificate of Airworthiness – for a combined total of £150.

The Cadet was a delight to fly. The nearest comparison flying in the UK today is the Avro Tutor in the Shuttleworth Collection – which also, I

15

assure you, is a pilot's aeroplane. Originally the Cadet had been powered by an Armstrong Siddeley Genet radial engine, but in the mid-thirties Airwork Limited at Heston remotored four examples to take Gipsy Majors: G-ACHP was one of these. Although the uncowled radial would have had a stronger vintage appeal, the Gipsy was an untiring and reliable workhorse that served us well. With ailerons on upper and lower wings, reasonably effective brakes, adjustable seats and rudder pedals and roomy cockpits for two, G-ACHP offered most features that a pilot would want.

From time to time we hear about people who take unfair advantage of situations in which they find themselves. In retrospect, perhaps I was guilty of that, for as Honorary Secretary I had control of the Cadet's operations and decided not only that it should be entered in a few air races, but that the Hon. Sec. should fly it. My reasoning at the time – if, in fact, I bothered to reason – must have been that this was a just reward for doing almost all the club's chores, which included organising meetings, day-to-day correspondence, writing, rolling off (on a hand-turned duplicator) and despatching regular newsletters and all the other tasks that fall to one or two pairs of hands in a voluntary organisation. However, I did pay for my flying – at the going rate of £2.10.0 (£2.50) per hour.

The Vintage Aeroplane Club held several flying meetings and a few semi-public small displays. Barely any money changed hands and people participated for the sheer pleasure of being involved with vintage aeroplanes. Vivian Bellamy turned up with his privately-owned and privately-restored Gloster Gladiator G-AMRK (now in the Shuttleworth Collection), Neville Duke or one of his test pilot colleagues attended with the Hawker Tomtit G-AFTA (also now at Old Warden), Clem Pike came along with de Havilland's original 1925 Cirrus Moth G-EBLV and there were many others. The atmosphere was healthy and the peak performance was a day on which the Hawker trio of Tomtit, Hart G-ABMR (now grounded in the RAF Museum) and Hurricane G-AMAU (now PZ865 of the RAF Battle of Britain Memorial Flight) managed to remain in line abreast formation despite the vast differences in comfortable operating speeds.

Perhaps the club's most ambitious venture was to stage the Chiltern Hills Air Races, based on Denham. We ran these for two years and the entry for the West London Trophy was a veritable "what's what" of notable historic aeroplanes. Nowadays, with a greater respect for ageing engines and the airframes that follow them, I would not support the idea of belting these machines to their limits, but perhaps the truly postwar era with its protection of everybody from everything had not become fully established and the same applied to aeroplanes; we just enjoyed what we were able to do. The Chiltern Hills entries included such notable aircraft as the Hawk Speed Six, Falcon Six, Hawk Major, Leopard Moth, Spartan Arrow, Blackburn B.2, Club Cadet and Cirrus Moth. This was the last occasion on which these historic names assembled collectively on the racing start line.

The Vintage Aeroplane Club had a short but very active life. Volunteers to fly were numerous, but volunteers to work were few; this is one thing that has not changed over the years! The Chairman – who was a worker – needed to resign due to other pressures and I had left the RAF to earn my keep as CFI/Manager at Elstree, often on a six-and-a-half-day week, so with no willing successors we decided to wind up the organisation before it ran itself down. Nothing quite like it has happened since, but it sowed the seed of interest in and activity with historic aircraft which, in very different form, is alive and healthy today. If we can make no other claim, we ran the first-ever events that were restricted rigidly to genuine vintage aeroplanes. It was hard work but it was great fun and – perhaps selfishly again – I added about 20 types to my logbook entries!

For much of my life I have had the good fortune that when one thing slips away another looms on the horizon. Shortly before the demise of the VAC I was asked if I would like to 'foster' the famous Comper Swift G-ABUS "Black Magic." This was negotiated by Ron Paine, who was my immediate boss in the Derby Aviation/Air Schools Group and who was well established as a racing pilot in his Miles Hawk Speed Six G-ADGP. The Swift's owner was reluctant to part with it, but was too old to fly and sought someone who would operate, maintain and fly it, paying all expenses, but handing it back in due course. This called for no capital outlay and I jumped in before anyone else could come round the corner.

The Swift, with its uncowled Pobjoy 5-cylinder radial engine (in this case a 90 hp Niagara in place of the original 75 hp 'R') was in complete contrast to the Cadet. It was small, had a fixed tail skid and no brakes, and gave very little forward view, and what little it offered was lost through oil deposits on the windscreen. What missed the screen covered one's goggles. Although originally there was a small luggage space, this had been sealed up and lost in the quest for maximum performance for racing; so overnight stays called for using pyjamas and washing kit as substitutes for the seat cushion. Keeping the fuel tank topped up was an essential pre-flight feature, for if the level was less than about half, as soon as you were established on a steady climb the engine would stop until you shoved the nose down, when it would pick up again. At low level that was not a happy practice.

The Pobjoy engine was an interesting device. It cruised at about 2,800 rpm and could build up easily to about 3,200, but a drastic reduction gear brought the massive propeller down – I believe, from memory – to about 1,300. The result was that, from the outside, it purred with a noise reminiscent of a Singer sewing machine. Not once did it fail me on mechanical grounds, despite my belting it in every available air race for four years, but in the King's Cup Race in 1955 an oil pipe burst and the system's entire contents escaped all over and inside the aeroplane in a matter of a few seconds. An instant and completely blind landing ahead turned out to be comfortably in the middle of Coventry airport.

If all this sounds like a form of hell, in practice it was great: those moments on the starting line, watching the Moths and other 'slower coaches' being flagged away at their allotted times following careful calculations by the handicappers, the tense waits for the 'off' and the knowledge that seconds lost at this stage may never be recouped, the rush to get round the first scatter point and onto the first full leg of the course. Then there are many variables: a really steep pylon turn minimises the distance to be covered, but that benefit can be lost due to the resulting loss of airspeed; getting low on an into-wind leg may improve ground speed due to the (usually) reduced wind strength, but there might be a lot of turbulence, necessitating speed-losing control movements; gaining height for a leg that is downwind may be beneficial, but possibly only if the leg is sufficiently long to justify a loss of airspeed on the climb . . . However, whatever series of actions one takes the throttle remains wide open and it is important to check engine behaviour under stressful conditions which it was not designed to endure.

When a race has several laps of the same circuit, it is easy to become confused when overtaking a slower machine or being overtaken by one of the back markers, for depending on speed differentials, the slowest types may need to be overtaken twice by the fastest. Despite seven years on the scene, I won only one main event, the Grosvenor Challenge Trophy Race at Newcastle in 1951, flying the Avro Cadet, but I realised that I was unable to compete with the wealthy brigade who spent considerable sums on fine-tuning their mounts. I was there for the atmosphere and the enjoyment, but shortly before withdrawing from the fray I was pleased to have third place in the King's Cup in a very close finish.

Again, a fresh opportunity arose. This was before I returned "Black Magic" to its owner, although already I had decided to hand it back – with due gratitude.

One evening the phone rang and with his customary crispness Ron Paine said: "Sit down. Listen. Do you want to fly a Mosquito again?"

I gasped, and before I could gather my wits he added: "Well, yes or no?"

For about four years I had flown mainly Austers and Magisters with an occasional venture on a Gemini light twin, but enthusiasm took control and I replied: "Yes, of course."

Derby Aviation (predecessor of today's British Midland Airways) had gained a contract with Spartan Air Services of Ottawa, Canada, to acquire and convert ten ex-RAF Mosquitoes for air survey work. As I was the only pilot on company strength with type experience, I was on to a good thing. Arrangements were made for me to have an hour's refamilarisation on a dual-control Mosquito T.3 with the RAF's Home Command Examining Unit at White Waltham and then I was on my own. The work involved fetching the long-stored machines from the RAF Maintenance Unit at Silloth in Cumberland and flying them to the (now defunct) grass airfield at Burnaston. As far as I was aware, no one had flown a Mosquito in or out of Derby before and the B.35 was a heavier beast than the T.3, but after a few orbits I summoned my out-of-practice courage and decided to try a landing. Fortunately all went well with this and the many subsequent flights, except on one occasion when I needed to abort a take-off due to an unmanageable swing. This was easy to achieve: insensitive opening of the throttles guaranteed a frightening outcome!

This was an amazingly – but enjoyably – busy time, often spending mid-week days at Derby and, whenever possible, returning to Elstree to manage training activities there. The work at Burnaston included air-testing the converted Mossies (and, occasionally, when the weather was good and the mood was right, finding an excuse to recheck some feature on an extra flight) and later flying them to Prestwick, leaving them there for a more courageous person to ferry across the Atlantic. There were other interesting projects to vary the theme, including the first trial flights with a magnetometer trailing behind an ageing Anson 1 (G-AMDA), with its hand-wound undercarriage system. When not flying, I was put to work on several administrative tasks, including design and preparation of the timetable brochure for Derby Aviation's first daily scheduled service to and from Glasgow. Boredom was not on the menu.

Perhaps one of the most useful experiences that I was able to gain at this time – and I was still in my twenties – was the opportunity to be involved in a broad band of aviation activity. Although I found difficulties in balancing flying, management and general administration, for one of these always stepped in the way of another, I learned quickly that time spent in the cockpit can be developed into related uses: by the age of 25, before the Mosquito ventures, I had been captured for a seat on the Pilotage Committee of the Association of British Aero Clubs, which was one of the forerunners of today's Aircraft Owners and Pilots Association. After a few years serving on that earlier body I was asked to write and produce a new version of the Handbook of Flying and Ground Training which for a time was the standard manual for civil flying instructors. Perhaps surprisingly, I am not in the habit of looking back too frequently, for there are more than enough problems and projects today to be tackled on behalf of general aviation. I admit, though, that I was very fortunate in at least two ways: I entered aviation when a lot of people were flying a lot of aeroplanes, when there was very little if any division between the various aviation sectors and when a generally pleasant atmosphere existed. None of this, though, would have meant so much to me if I had not had the good fortune to have numerous interesting opportunities placed on my plate.

Did I have any regrets or frustrations? Well, I had a very strong desire to fly a Hornet – that snappy successor to the Mosquito – with its handed propellers that would enable a smart take-off without 'losing' it through swinging. The opportunity very nearly arose on at least two occasions, but the chance never quite materialised. If that is my only regret, then, I hear you say, I am very fortunate. I agree.

CHAPTER 2

EAST ANGLIAN ESCAPADES

by

Stanley Ward

[First published in his autobiography "Tales out of Flying School"]

EAST ANGLIAN FLYING SERVICES LTD AT IPSWICH AIRPORT

By an extraordinary coincidence it happened that a company called East Anglian Flying Services Ltd, which operated passenger services from Southend Airport, re-opened Ipswich Airport at Easter in 1954, just as the Cambridge Reserve Flying School closed. Their lease required that they should provide facilities for flying training at the Airport so I did not waste too much time in notifying my availability, and I was duly appointed instructor, but more of that later.

The company had taken over the lease in 1953 from Ipswich County Borough Council who were the owners. The place was quite derelict by then and a considerable amount of work was required in getting it up to the standard required for a passenger terminal and for licensing as a public aerodrome. This task was in the hands of Dan Burgess, a man with an undisclosed number of operational tours in Bomber Command during the war, as well as considerable experience as a commercial pilot in general aviation and on scheduled passenger services, to say nothing of a stint of flying Halifax ex-bombers on the Berlin Airlift.

One of nature's gentlemen and one of the calmest men I ever met, Danny directed and worked as leading hand in demolishing, rebuilding, concreting, joinering, rewiring, plumbing, painting and decorating, pulling out hundreds of gorse bushes, ploughing and sowing, to say nothing of the enormous administrative task in getting an airport operational for scheduled passenger services. Even then if there was a shortage of pilots on the airline, Danny would drive off to the base at Southend to take an airliner full of passengers to the Channel Islands.

After the re-opening and the start of services, Dan remained as manager and airline pilot with which he combined a task he loved, of farmer to the 160 acres put down to the production of corn, sugar beet and potatoes, all of which helped to make Ipswich one of the few financially viable airports at that time. I have frequently seen waiting passengers and friends in a packed lobby move out of the way of a filthy driver who had come off a farm tractor parked just outside the airfield entrance doors. Little did they realise that this man was the pilot of the aeroplane some of them were about to board, and that he had come in with just enough time to have a shower and change into his immaculate blue uniform with its four gold rings at the cuff – and thus he would appear minutes later to pass through the same crowd in the opposite direction. Similarly, on the arrival flight to night-stop ready for the first flight outbound next day, the resplendent Captain would within minutes be in his working clothes doing a bit of weeding to the garden area in front of the terminal building.

East Anglian Flying Services Ltd started operations to and from Ipswich with four de Havilland Rapides, fabric-covered, twin-engined biplanes, seating eight passengers in four seats on each side of a central gangway leading from the door at the rear to the nose of the aircraft where there was a single seat for the pilot – the total crew. At this time Ipswich had no radio facilities nor approach aids although the aeroplanes were fitted with radio communication and primitive navigation aids. It followed that in really bad weather they could not get any nearer than Southend, which was the company's base.

There was no such luxury as a loo or in-flight refreshments, indeed they did not even carry an hostess. The normal procedure was that the ground hostess at Ipswich would check the tickets, weigh the luggage, lead the passengers out to the aeroplane, put them into the seats, fix their lap straps, and then get out and wait by the door. Then, and only then, the pilot would stroll out, climb aboard, and pausing only to check that the hostess had closed the door from outside, he would walk up the gangway to take his seat.

The story goes that, on one occasion, Captain Frank was on his way between the fully-occupied lines of seats, four on each side, when he was hailed by a male passenger, who was an acquaintance, with a "Hello Frank," to which he offered a courtesy "Hello," hoping thus to end the conversation in the interests of the time-keeping. But it was not to be because the fellow continued: "Nice to see you again, Frank. Are you better now? Feeling quite well? No more fits?" The effect on the other passengers, who were not in the jesting mode, is not recorded.

It was not long however before Ipswich had ground-to-air radio on a fixed company frequency, to provide two-way communication with approaching and departing airliners, so that the office could be advised by the pilot that he would be there in five minutes or so. He could also ask for an unofficial weather report and suggest that he could do with a sandwich, or "Be quick with getting the passengers off and on – things are getting a bit fraught timewise." Later on, direction-finding equipment was installed, the airport obtained a public radio frequency, and a licensed air traffic controller was appointed to provide homing and descent facilities with full radio-telephony communication – big stuff!

The first real improvement in aircraft into Ipswich was the purchase in 1955 of the first of six de Havilland Doves – very modern-looking, low-wing, twin-engined, ten-seater monoplanes with nosewheel undercarriage which was, wait for it, retractable! Chatting to the Chairman's wife shortly after this, I was amazed to hear her say that she was not as happy in these because she always feared that the wheels might not come down when required.

*   *   *

THE "HONEYMOON EXPRESS"

I don't suppose that I will ever forget the day when we had no less than three happy couples waiting for the 'Honeymoon Express,' which was the 18.30 flight, a Dove, on a Saturday to Jersey. At that time the flying club shared an office off the lobby with the ground hostess or receptionist, so I was on the spot.

The lobby was packed with the jolly parties from the receptions who had arrived an hour before the scheduled time of take-off; many were a bit pickled, all were very happy and boisterous. Ominously, no aeroplane had arrived by 1800 hours, but Maureen, the ground hostess, had no great difficulty in parrying the many queries. At 18.30 she had to announce that there was a slight delay, and fortunately their good humour enabled most of them to find a joke in it. At 1900 hours we had to telephone Southe⸱ [1] operations, only to learn that the Channel Islands were 'closed in' and they had problems, but would get an aeroplane to Ipswich as soon as they could.

Maureen announced another half-hour delay and then explained to me that she had a date, so would I mind holding the fort for her? It was not my job, but I had to be there anyway because I had club aeroplanes flying until dusk. By 1945 hours the passengers and their guests were becoming a bit restless, some were clearly suffering from hangovers caused by earlier consumption and long abstention. Demands were made for me to telephone somebody, but I knew that this was useless – I could by now make up the stories to explain non-arrival as well as the people at Southend could: "There has been fog all day in Jersey and no aeroplanes have been able to get in until late so there is a big backlog of passengers at Southend from earlier flights who had to be got away first; your turn will come. We cannot help the weather and we don't have blind landing facilities yet." At 2030 hours I could not hold them off any longer, but the call to Southend brought the anticipated comments with the continued assurance that the aeroplane would be coming, and a gentle reprimand about the cost of telephone calls to Southend. I badly needed a pee but dare not run the gauntlet of the hostile mob between the office and the loo.

It must have been nine o'clock when the dreaded telephone call came from Southend: "Regret no flight tonight into Ipswich. Advise passengers that they will be accommodated on an aeroplane at 0900 hours tomorrow." How do you gather enough courage to face all these people with such news after their wait since 5.30, with six of them at the start of their honeymoon? The company were no fools – if the passengers had been moved to Southend they would have commenced their journey and the company would have had to find them accommodation for the night, but these people had not started so they had no claim. And I was the unfortunate, really only a bystander, who now had to explain it all.

There was no other course, so here we go: a brief announcement with apology and regret, then a quick return to the haven of the office. A good theory, but you do not get away that easily: you are followed by unhappy bridegrooms, weeping brides, disappointed friends, but most violently, the best men determined to prove their worth in those appointments. Some actually beat me on the chest with their clenched fists and I remember mentally thanking my protector that I had refused to allow them to use the non-public club bar because their tempers might have been even more inflamed by the additional alcohol.

Nobody got hurt, physically anyway, but I was saddened by the whole affair as much as any of those more directly involved. And these included an elderly couple, with the tearful lady pleading: "What are we going to do? I threw out the last of the bread and milk just before we left home." It was really nobody's fault, except perhaps that they should have abandoned much earlier the attempts to get an aeroplane to Ipswich – in trying to avoid disappointment they had increased the distress.

I was able to do a bit more to help on Saturday the 9th of August 1958 when the morning flight, a Dove from Southend scheduled to return to Southend, failed to appear. Two passengers, Mr & Mrs Paul Walter, were relying on this to connect with their midday flight to Bergen, Norway, by Lapair. A telephone call to Channel Airways at Southend revealed that in the chaos caused by the previous day's bad weather, they had no aeroplane to send up.

The agony of all this was explained to me by Maureen, the ground hostess, asking if there was anything I could do to help them. There was not enough time to get them there by any other means than flying, and all I had was a non-radio Auster with no self-starter, no baggage space, and a third seat which required the passenger to sit across the aeroplane behind the two front seats! But that was nothing compared with the legal difficulties in view of the fact that I, with no commercial licence, would be carrying scheduled service passengers who had paid their fares. I thought that I should not do this without higher authority, so I rang the boss and explained the problem, but this was a wasted phone call because he just did not want to know anything about it. I was on my own, with the passengers who were now in real danger of losing their holiday flight to Norway.

Southend air traffic control cleared me by telephone, to follow the usual procedure of circling a point to the north of the airfield until they gave me a green Aldis lamp signal which would be permission to land. There was some difficulty in getting the suitcases into the rear cockpit and then getting the lady into her seat just in front of them – I did not dare to do a weight-and-balance calculation because I knew that this would show us to be outside both weight and balance limits. This may appear a little irresponsible, but it wasn't really, because I knew my Auster well enough to be able to tell before we got airborne whether or not it would be controllable.

We taxied on to the apron at Southend just as the passengers were boarding the Lapair flight. Mr Walter leapt out and ran across to speak to the loading staff – and their holiday was saved. My face must have had a slightly worried expression as I unloaded Mrs Walter and their suitcases, because this was all happening just below the windows of the control tower, and I still had to book in and out.

But nothing untoward happened, and I received a letter dated 10th August from Paul Walters at the Victoria Hotel, Bergen, saying that no words could express his thanks for my kindness and service, and he waxed a little lyrical as follows:

"There was a good fellow named Ward,
From Ipswich to Southend he soared
To enable a stranger to board
Another plane bound for the Nord."

Well it's nice to be appreciated!

Ipswich was however looking up as an Airport. The Doves were followed in 1957 by the Bristol Freighter, a monster converted to carry 40 passengers, in 1960 by the Douglas DC-3 (Dakota) and in 1965 by the HS.748, a really modern propjet with good short take-off and landing capability. We were in good company because a development of the 748 came into service with the Queen's Flight of the RAF as the Andover.

In 1962 East Anglian Flying Services Ltd had become Channel Airways Ltd and Ipswich was providing feeder flights to Southend to meet their scheduled services to Rochester, Portsmouth, Ostend, Rotterdam, Jersey and Guernsey. Other aircraft owned and operated by Channel Airways from Southend, and later, Stansted, included Vikings, Viscounts, a DC-4, a BAC 1-11 and a Trident. By 1971 the fleet totalled 21 airliners and Channel was concentrating a lot of its capacity on inclusive holidays to Malta, Majorca, Barcelona and Rimini.

*   *   *

DISPLAY FLYING

It was in 1959 that I started giving aerobatic and crazy-flying displays at both civil and RAF shows, variously called 'At Homes,' 'Galas,' 'Open Days,' 'Fetes' or 'Battle of Britain Days.'

Our Auster G-AGXP was by now semi-aerobatic, which meant that although it was a standard Autocrat, it was fitted with strengthened seats and was thus authorised to do loops, stall turns, steep turns and spins. Using a bit of artistic licence I was able to turn this into a reasonably entertaining display which, when operated from an airfield, would include some slapstick humour on the ground before the flying started.

The show took two forms – depending on whether the site was an airfield or overhead a school or village fete or somewhere that could not include the take-off. In the latter, it was largely a matter of formal aerobatics with a bit of crazy cavorting, all carried out within a very small radius and at quite low level so that the crowd could enjoy a close-up view of this comparatively quiet and definitely slow aeroplane.

From airfields, it took the form of a comedy act in which, under one disguise or another, I 'stole' an aeroplane and then demonstrated how I was unable to fly it. Few pilots watching this act for the first time would have believed that an Auster was capable of doing what they were seeing – one CFI wrote to me suggesting that this was even more robust than Ranald Porteous demonstrating the aerobatic Auster – and Ranald was Auster's chief test pilot. But I suggested that what I was showing were merely demonstrations of what some students do to long-suffering instructors.

An item like this soon catches on in the flying world, and I found myself in demand for flying displays in all parts of the country. Obviously I could not run a flying club in my spare time while spending every weekend somewhere else, so I had to restrict this sort of thing mainly to the local area, but even then the frequency soon rose to some 12 to 15 shows per season.

Being a bit of an exhibitionist, I enjoyed the whole thing very much – the disguises included a French peasant onion seller, a Russian VIP, a patient in the Flying Doctor Service, and even a prisoner escaped from a local prison: all of these sweating under a long black beard and a black beret or a black Grecian lambskin hat.

The format involved a very good friend, Roy Wilks, who was in each case announced as the pilot of the aeroplane. He might for example be taxying out to do a demonstration flight when he would stop somewhere in front of the crowd and, with a display of very bad airmanship, would leave the engine running while he got out to inspect the tailwheel for some supposed fault – as the commentator would explain. Meanwhile, what looked like a French onion seller (because he had a black beard, wore a beret and had a string of onions hanging from the handlebars of his bicycle) would pedal on to the runway and around the aeroplane. When I was an escaped prisoner the act was similar except that the dress would be prison garb complete with arrow heads.

In either case, the commentator would demand that the interloper be restrained immediately – but not before I had time to fall off the cycle and get into the aeroplane on the passenger's side. For the 'Flying Doctor Service,' Roy would taxi the aeroplane out in front of the crowd while two ambulancemen came through the crowd carrying a stretcher with a drip feeding into my arm from a bottle of gin. They had some difficulty in getting me into the right-hand seat, so the pilot would similarly get out, this time to help to load the passenger, and the aeroplane would move off as he was returning via the tail to his seat. The routine was the same with the Russian VIP except that it all started with the black-bearded visitor being paraded in an open car before the crowd, prior to his having to be helped by the pilot.

The various introductions always led to the same thing while the tension was being worked up with varying degrees of competence by the commentators. In each case, the aeroplane would move off before the pilot could get back to his seat – generally he was just by the tail so the only thing he could do was to go down full-length and grab the tailwheel, and Roy, bless him, made it all look so realistic by hanging on to be dragged along grass, mud or even tarmac until he had seemingly done all he could to stop the runaway aeroplane.

The take-off involved many of the blunders student pilots have faced me with as an instructor, plus a few that I had thought up to make it a bit more exciting. Anyway the commentator would be stirring it up by advising the crowd that this untrained person would never be able to land it.

The show would continue with the aeroplane cavorting all around the airfield, including specialities like the very slow fly into wind – even going backwards on some occasions when the wind was strong enough – and a heavily-ruddered flat turn downwind over the crowd, giving them the impression that the aeroplane was travelling sideways. Rolling around would continue with the Auster gradually gaining height to fifteen hundred feet where it would do one or two clumsy aerobatics before it fell off the top of an excruciatingly bad loop and dropped into a spin from which the recovery was made along the runway, and clearing the ground with only a few feet to spare. No real danger here because the apparent recovery could be delayed deliberately for a short time after it is effective.

After that, up to five attempts would be made to land, including downwind and flapless, a high hold-off with a late recovery at the stall, an enormous bounce with recovery about thirty feet up, and a wheel landing with the aeroplane rocking violently from one wheel to the other and wingtips only a few inches from the ground. The final one would generally be from a full-flap, steep, side-slipping approach turn to land on one wheel while still in the turn, and, if the wind were not too strong, we would end up with a controlled ground-loop.

I did these shows all over the place including twenty-one consecutive years at Seething near Bungay, and inevitably there were some funny incidents. I once asked a policeman who was on duty at a show if he would be good enough to 'arrest' me after landing, only to get a forceful explanation as to what his duties were – and these did not include "playing bloody games." On another occasion Anglia Television showed a bit of this hair-raising flying in their news programme and blamed Roy Legge for it, while ignoring his excellent, more formal, aerobatic display at the show. Bill Wix, who was the delightful and unflappable officer in charge of the crash truck, once commented that the crew enjoyed my contribution, and he claimed that my display was clearly the most exciting. "As a matter of fact," he said, "we always start the engine as you come on!"

At Sleap in Shropshire, we had some difficulty with a nitwit of a commentator. I had tried unsuccessfully to brief him before the show (alas, he knew it all), but he did have a written description of the act. So imagine my amazement as I heard him tell the 45,000 crowd, just as Roy was taxying out, that someone had stolen an aeroplane: I was in fact still hiding behind a shed with my beard and bicycle waiting for the aeroplane to get into a suitable position for my entry!

At Seething I had one of the two real scares of my life as a stunt pilot when, after a gliding stall-turn in an Auster, I found myself pointing vertically down at 500 feet with no airspeed, and a joystick that felt like a piece of wet spaghetti. At that moment it seemed that nothing would alter the attitude of the aeroplane, or its flight path towards the ground. Afterwards, I could not remember whether or not I had opened the throttle – but somehow, the aeroplane had rounded out before reaching the ground, and the show went on.

I was a bit naughty on one occasion at Ipswich in that, during the display, I added an item which seemed to offer a bit of heart-stopping excitement for the crowd – quite contrary to my normally highly disciplined procedure – and it was outrageously impolite to the comm-entator. This was at a time before the building of the bridge over the river Orwell, and perhaps before I had learned of the danger of departing from your own set programme. With the Airport having an elevation of 128 feet above sea level, and the river close by, there was a fairly steep escarpment that I could disappear behind.

If the throttle is closed sharply, the engine produces a loud bang through the exhaust, so I employed this at about 200 feet along runway 32, in front of the crowd, thereby creating the impression that the engine had blown up. From there I was able to glide down to the left towards the river which was on the other side of the airfield below the crowd's line of sight – and that is where the aeroplane disappeared from their view. As soon as I was below the level of the cliff I opened the throttle again and turned the Auster left down-river, and then left again across the shore-line keeping low, out of sight and hearing, until I was in line with the trees on the threshold of runway 32.

Meanwhile, poor old Ron was left stranded: being the good comm-entator that he was, he kept going, deliberately building up the tension that something awful had happened to me, except that now he was not sure that this was still make-believe. Then, just as he was considering alerting somebody the Auster appeared over the trees – it could only have taken me four minutes to get round to that position at low level, but it was a very long four minutes to Ron and the crowd. I never did that again.

It was at Seething at such an air show in 1968 that I stopped smoking – actually at 15.30 on Sunday the 30th of June, since when I have been able to look smugly down on, and express my sympathy for, those who still have to smoke – there can be nobody worse than the ex-smoker – but it was really all very simple.

Having just finished my display I parked the Auster and walked over to join club members who were watching from the privileged position of a special enclosure. Friend John was standing there so I picked on him to scrounge a cigarette from. As he lit it for me, his dishy blonde girl friend, Penny, looked across with what I hoped was a warm admiring gaze and said quite innocently: "I should think you need a cigarette after that."

I don't know what it was, maybe I took it as an insult to my manhood or an implication that I needed a fix or something, but my reaction was simply that if it appeared that I had to have a cigarette to help me recover after a display flight then it was time that I gave one of them up. So I threw the cigarette away, and continued showing off in aeroplanes for many more years.

Another amusing incident at Seething followed my 21st show there. A young lad, who perhaps should not have been in the area of the 'display aircraft,' came up to me as I was fiddling with the Auster after my display and said: "You know, Mr Ward, you ought to think about altering your disguise: you have used that beard so often here that the people don't believe that the aeroplane has been stolen, because they know it is you!" Such is fame.

As a civilian pilot I took part in a number of Battle of Britain displays at RAF Stations, but without doubt the funniest one was at Coltishall in 1969. George Black, former leader of Treble-One Squadron with its famous 16 Lightning formation team, was Wing Commander Flying at this Operational Conversion Unit, and he wrote asking me if I would like to consider doing my stolen Auster show at their display on the 20th of September.

A show-off like me was being given the chance to display in front of about 100,000 people – wouldn't I just! A change of format for this occasion seemed reasonable to me so details of this were submitted by letter and telephone to George, along with a request for the cooperation of their commentator. Both were approved with no difficulty.

Don Peacock was happy that I should use his home-built Luton Minor at any time – this was a tiny single-seat monoplane with a modified Volkswagen engine. The idea was that announcements would be made over the Tannoy that this aeroplane was so easy to fly that, later in the day, volunteers from the crowd would be invited to come forward and fly it, even if they had never flown before. If the selected person made a success of this, he or she would be invited to fly an Auster; and if this was satisfactory then the next offer would be the opportunity to fly a Lightning jet fighter.

The RAF commentator entered fully into the spirit of the thing, working up a great interest in the item by his many advance references to it, so that when the time came to invite volunteers to come forward, I was nearly killed in the rush! The officials had some difficulty in selecting a black-bearded gentleman.

There followed an immaculate display of flying in this lovely little aeroplane, including some low-level work close in along the line of the huge crowd, so that everyone had to agree that I should be given the opportunity to fly the Auster.

It was in fact a Taylorcraft Plus D owned by Eric Stephenson of Colchester, substituting for the club Auster because my employers were unwilling to provide the insurance cover required by the RAF. You could hardly blame the Company – they were after all in the business of selling flying to passengers of their airliners, or to students who were learning to fly. The top men in the Company did not get to know too much about the shows that did not require the extra insurance, but they had to be approached about the RAF requirement, and not surprisingly they did not think that a slightly-crazy flying act in one of their aeroplanes would be the best advertisement for their services, especially if it were to have an accident at such a public event.

Anyway we were quickly settled into the Taylorcraft which was, up to this moment, definitely classified as a non-aerobatic aeroplane: the antics which followed departed from this if one accepts the official description of an aerobatic as "any sudden change of speed or direction," because there were a few of those.

However, my slightly alarming standard display was much enjoyed, but nobody could have been surprised when the commentator stated with regret that it had been decided that the pilot would not be invited to fly the Lightning.

What most of the people, except George, did not know, was that with his 16 Lightnings steaming away at the end of the runway waiting to take-off, I muffed the last crazy approach to land, and had to go around again before landing – 20 seconds behind schedule!

Earlier, I described one of the two scares of my stunt-flying career when I misjudged things a bit at Seething. The other happened at Felixstowe during a Battle of Britain fly-past and display when I was slotted in between an RAF Comet transport and a Phantom – both fairly big irons, one before and one after the little civilian non-radio Auster. I had four minutes to entertain the large crowd collected on the beach and the promenade south of the pier. Clearly, time was important – I had to be around waiting for the Comet to do his stuff while keeping well out of his way, but not far enough to allow the crowd to get bored while I struggled to get into position at 80 mph. Any time lost would have to come out of my four minutes before the Phantom would take over at about 500 mph.

Now all of this is very tricky – without radio you had to watch your watch, watch the Comet in case he over-ran or under-ran his time, watch where you are, then watch your watch and look out for the Phantom while you are tearing the guts out of the aeroplane and yourself in front of the crowd and at low level over the sea.

Being ultra-careful, I normally flew all such shows solo so that the aeroplane was as lightweight as possible, and I did not have to worry about anyone throwing up over me, falling on me or otherwise distracting me, but on this occasion it seemed that to have an assistant with a watch and a pair of eyes would be a positive asset. Bernard Daniel had a feeling for aerobatics and he could count numbers, so he was the partner I selected, and he jumped at the opportunity.

So off we went near to the appointed time heading towards Felixstowe, with four eyes searching the sky trying to spot the Comet in, as they say, good time: the timing was perfect – it was the flying that caused the trouble, and then only to the two of us. Once again it was the low-level stall turn that caused it – not a gliding one this time, at least it was not intended to be a gliding one because I went into it from sea level with full power and lots of speed, but I had misjudged the extra weight of Bernard – normally my aeroplane was very light because there was only me and only just enough fuel to do the show, which often started and finished on an airfield.

But here we were, a bit heavy with Bernard and extra fuel for the return flight and a possible hang-around, so that we lost speed a little more rapidly than usual in the vertically upwards part, with the result that when I ruddered into the yaw which should have put us vertically downwards, we were going very slowly. So slowly that the change of attitude from upwards to downwards was delayed enough to starve the engine of fuel from the gravity-fed system. That was a pity because the propeller was now slowing down, and I knew that it would not get any encouragement to go faster until either the aeroplane speeded up in the dive or the fuel started flowing again with the change of attitude.

This probably sounds all very technical and unexciting, but it wasn't to us because as the propeller slowed to the point that we could see the individual blades, we were faced with the possibility that it might stop. If we had a self-starter it would have been only a small problem at 500 ft, and the fact that we did not have a self-starter would have been no problem at all if we had been over an airfield, even at 500 feet. But we were over the sea, and the beach and promenade were well covered with people – beyond them was a row of hotels and funfairs. If we had to come down, it followed that we had only the sea.

Of course, it didn't happen: don't ask me why not – we hadn't time to pray. Somehow the nose of the aeroplane went down far enough for our speed to increase sufficiently to keep the propeller windmilling until the fuel started to flow again as we pulled out of the dive, and we were back in business. The dry mouths, shaking hands and white faces were not visible to the crowd as we completed our four minutes without further incident.

Generally speaking, display flying is not really dangerous provided that the pilot maintains a firm personal discipline, keeps well in practice, and never does anything that he has not tried out before. Many an item can be made to look dangerous for the effect – for example, the recovery from a spin can be made to look as if there was only a few feet left at the bottom of the recovery dive by delaying the moment and rate of the pull-out.

Personal discipline is required to resist the temptation to add something that has not been thoroughly practised at high level where an accurate assessment of height loss can be made: a sudden desire to add something to an old routine in the belief that, because you are bored with it, the crowd will also be finding it dull, can lead to excessively exciting additions that had not been intended.

* * *

PARACHUTING

Auster 'NHZ had doors that could be jettisoned. It was not expected that we as civilians would ever need to jettison the doors – we did carry parachutes – but when 'HZ was in the RAF during the war, aircrew wore parachutes and you couldn't get out of an Auster in flight unless you could get rid of the door.

I am telling you all this because one day in 1959 along came David Hall, a keen parachutist and instructor in parachuting. At first, all he wanted was an aeroplane to jump out of, and 'HZ filled the bill. That appeared to be quite reasonable except that my licence did not have an endorsement allowing me to drop parachutists. To obtain this I had to fly for three drops under the supervision of a duly authorised observer, and David was an authorised observer, so the EAFC got into the para-dropping business.

David did a number of drops over the airfield much to the joy and excitement of spectators, but occasionally I had to drop him at public displays of one sort or another. It was at one such at Martlesham Heath that I had the nasty shock of seeing a failure – one shroud line had become caught above the canopy causing what is called a split periphery, and the canopy blossomed in two mounds.

This causes a higher rate of descent, but the real danger is that the line might burn through the canopy with fatal results. There was some fear that opening the chest-mounted reserve parachute could cause a tangle with the main, but it had to be done. Fortunately it opened clear and he came down quite safely on the reserve chute with the main hanging down below him.

It was not long before other parachutists came along, and following this, even quite sane folk wanted to have a go. With 'HZ it was possible to carry two droppers if they were authorised to operate without supervision – one would sit on the down-folded seat-back to my right beside the door-hole, while the other would be in the rear ready to take the first one's place as soon as he had gone. This was quite satisfactory except that our well-loved engineer, Jack Squirrel, complained bitterly about the damage being done by the parachute packs chafing the door surround during the departures.

Student jumpers could only be flown one at a time, because David in the rear seat would have to act as Jumpmaster directing me where to go and supervising the student as he positioned himself outside the aircraft on the entry step. He would have to give the dreaded order to "GO." In those days even the first drop was in 'free-fall' with the student having to open the parachute by pulling the rip-cord – whereas today such drops use a static line which automatically pulls the cord as the parachutist leaves the aircraft. After the drop I would turn the aeroplane sharply to

33

the right so that David could observe the opening and the subsequent behaviour of the student. Then generally, David would re-position me for his own jump; parachutists appear to hate to land in an aeroplane although I suspect that the real reason is that it would be foolish to waste the opportunity to parachute by coming down in an aeroplane.

I had been teaching son Robert to fly, largely facilitated by the generosity of Frank Waller who donated his aeroplane for the purpose. But the parachuting bug got him and he transferred to that. The minimum age was 17, so after all the ground training with David, Rob had to wait for his birthday, the 26th August 1960, when a large company, including the press, assembled to witness the event. Of course, I had to fly the aeroplane with David as Jumpmaster, and a happy time was had by all except his mother who had a hanky-screwing time until the lad had landed safely. The whole thing attracted extensive press coverage, fortunately not including the party which followed in the club bar.

Rob continued parachuting and reached the level where he could do exhibition drops at air shows. It was unfortunate that we had to give a fine demonstration of the 'sea breeze' effect at Ipswich airport; it was on the 28th of May 1961 during the flying display at a public 'At Home' at Ipswich. I had taken off with Rob from runway 32 towards the north-west. He acted as his own Jumpmaster and we duly dropped a marker from which he was able to observe the wind effect, and from that work out the best position to leave the aeroplane in order to land in front of the crowd.

I repositioned for the run-up, and he jumped at the selected point. As I circled overhead to observe his descent it became clear that he was not going to land in front of the crowd, in fact, he was not going to land on the airfield. Unfortunately this side of the airfield is bounded by a large housing estate which could be nasty with its two-storey roofs and cables on poles. So it was a relief to see him land in the roadway between two rows of houses, and he had got to his feet before I lost sight of him in the mass of people who had suddenly appeared.

My experience of the winds that blow at Ipswich Airport told me at once what had happened – the 'sea breeze' had arrived and had given us a change of wind speed and direction. This was soon confirmed by the windsock which was now indicating a brisk breeze from the south-east. It follows that I landed on runway 14 – in exactly the opposite direction from my take-off! The simple fact is that on sunny days early in the year, the surface of the land warms up faster that the surface of the sea; this causes the air warmed by contact with the land to rise, and cold air in contact with the water to flow in over the land to replace it. Unless the prevailing wind at the time is similar to the direction of this 'sea breeze,' there will be a sudden change in the wind speed and direction over the land near to the coast.

I was acutely aware of these changes at Ipswich Airport when considering sending students off on early solo flights because the time of its happening could not be forecast with any accuracy, and with our aeroplanes being non-radio it was not possible to advise the student of a wind change after take-off. It follows that I was vexed that I had overlooked this possible change during the para flight, but fortunately, apart from some gravel rash, Rob was not hurt and no damage had been done. He did another jump later in the afternoon to show that he had not been frightened off. When I went to view the scene of the landing the next day, I found (i) that with the maze of cables around these houses he had been perhaps more than lucky to miss them all, and (ii) that the children in the street had adopted a craze of parachuting with knotted handkerchiefs attached to all sorts of loads being thrown into the air.

CHAPTER 3
CUBBING THROUGH THE RYE
by
Chris Dearden

Forty-five shillings (£2.25) an hour for a Piper Cub may well raise a wry smile now – which has got the awful pun out of the way! But even in May 1950 it was an attractive proposition and still bearable when it snook up to fifty shillings.

As I've said before, and say again, I was already finding the cost of "Maggie"-flying a touch on the heavy side, so I was interested to hear of a newly-formed club operating Cubs from Gatwick; I soon got myself over there and joined. Well, sort of. It's just the truth that it operated only in daylight which dissuades me from calling it a fly-by-night outfit.

One example will suffice. The club secretary, Nick, decided we should have a lapel badge. Being the foolish young draughtsman that I was I volunteered to do the necessary design work, make the working drawing, the master copy for the photo-etching process, and fix it all up with the supplier. So far so dandy. When the job was done Nick set about selling the badges for half a crown (12p) a time, but said he'd let me have mine for two shillings (10p). Generous, or what? More than that, when the supplier needed paying Nick made himself 'unavailable for comment.' Muggins was left holding the bill and eventually found himself on the wrong end of a solicitor's letter. They reckoned that I (not the club) was liable and would have to pay – or else. And that's how I became the owner of one very expensive badge – which (happily) I've long-since lost.

Back to more pleasant things. Gatwick in the early fifties! It was a quiet little grass 'drome where I could meander in on my creaking bicycle, past the old racecourse grandstands, round the peri-track and not see another living soul (there were indeed people beavering away in sundry offices and hangars, but they were invisible). It seemed nothing ever moved there, not even the windsock. The place was pervaded by an enchanting air of limpness – yes, and skylarks too!

The Cubs, leased out by A.J. Walter, lived in a blister hangar over towards the north-western corner, next door to the wartime control tower which was still in use then. Since the 'drome was officially open there had to be luckless bods on duty in the tower, though they'd little to control except their own boredom. I used to go up there to check out: "I'm just off in Cub 'IYX for half an hour's local. Anything to look out for?" Nothing! There never was. In the absence of radio it was all conveyed by personal contact. Hurrah for that!

I cherish the memory of the time I poked my head round the door only to have them practically grab me by the lapels and hoink me into the room (cartoon style) and say: "Don't rush off just yet! Come in! Sit down! Have a cup of tea! Talk to us!" It really happened. I wonder what would happen if I got within a hundred metres of the control tower today. Methinks they'd set ye dogs on me and ask a lot of nasty questions, probably at gun-point. Tea and sympathy would be nowhere in the equation. That's progress for you!

. Talking of which: in more recent years I was having a snack in one of the cafeterias at the 'new' Gatwick when a nostalgic thought hit me hard enough to make me comment to the people to whom I'd been chatting at the table. "Gosh!" I said brightly. "I've just realised that where we're sitting now used to be right on the approach to the field, at just about this height. So I used to fly Piper Cubs smack through the middle of this lot." Their disinterest was total. Blanksville! Oh well, some you lose! As a wit once remarked: "Nostalgia isn't what it used to be."

In those olden times, though, when there was living contact, after I'd taxied out and done my cross-wind checks, one or other of the bods in the tower would solemnly stroll out onto the balcony and flash me a green on the Aldis – a whimsical piece of theatre considering there was nothing else in sight, hadn't been all day and was most unlikely to be (not literally true but near enough). Still, it gave them in the tower an object for living and it amused me. On take-off we'd exchange waves as I went by. We laughed at a lot of simple things in those dreamy days.

Of specific days I well remember Saturday the 19th of August 1950 in Cub 'IYV. I'd promised to take my workmate, George, for a trip to Bembridge – for no particular reason. During the preceding week, though, the Press had published word of a polio scare on the Isle of Wight, and had advised all non-essential visitors to stay away. George wasn't worried for himself but was rightly concerned not to take his kids back an unwelcome present. I made a few facetious remarks about doubting my own ability to find the Isle of Wight and suggested Lympne as an alternative.

Lympne it was then. That was an easy one from Gatwick: follow the railway up to Earlswood, a daring cross-country dash to Nutfield, follow the railway to Ashford, then right hand down and Lympne should be straight ahead. At least, it was going to be either Lydd, Lympne or Hawkinge. Luck was with me. We hit Lympne. (Hawkinge was then occupied by the WRAF. But I was never going to be that lucky!)

On arrival at Lympne we were directed to park up by the Flying Club. The people there received us kindly enough though with a certain reserve, a smiling tolerance. George and I were evidently not quite . . . um . . . er, the . . . um . . . er, type of chaps they were accustomed to entertaining at the club. I mean to say, a tatty draughtsman and a lathe operator . . . Well, you know how it is, old boy!

We made our escape on the bus into Hythe. It was part of our day out, anyway. A trip to the seaside was quite a novelty to George. In those days a working lad was lucky if he had a serviceable bike, never mind a car.

It was while we were at Hythe that I sensed trouble. I began to feel queasy. I started to sweat. Vision began to go grey and to close in to a letterbox slot. Oh hell! The rapid onset of a migraine. They seldom give warning.

What to do? I knew full well what I should do but didn't dare do it. Flying club secretaries are not generally noted as being among the world's great philanthropists. "It'll cost you, Chummy" is more their style (though it has been known for one to offer as much as a 2p discount on a badge!). It was the possible cost of keeping the Cub overnight that I didn't dare think about. Besides, there'd be complications in getting messages to our respective families. Then the cost of a night's accommodation. . . . Not on! So I just said blandly that I thought it was time we made tracks for home. George was easy about it.

By grace of the railway from Folkestone I found Ashford and turned on to the main flog up the line to Nutfield. And flog it was! A brisk wind had come up during the afternoon and it was smack on the nose. Gatwick seemed an awfully long way away and unconsciousness ominously close.

My misery was compounded by the dim sight of a goods train puffing up the line; a ratty old tank engine with a long line of rusty-looking trucks. And he was overtaking us by about five knots. I might not have minded so much had it been "The Flying Scotsman" or "The Orient Express" or something with a bit of style. But a branch-line goods! Oh, the pain! Oh, the ignominy!

However, things took a turn for the better just then. George, who'd opted to ride in the front seat, shouted back to me: "Do you think I could, er, like . . . ?" The message was clear enough.

I thought "Oh! yes *please*," but said: "Sure. Have a go if you like." Leaning forward as best I could I pointed and shouted over the din: "Put that hand on *that* bit. That hand on *that* bit. Your feet on *those* bits down there. Keep *that* needle pointing there, and *that* one pointing there. Keep us about this far to the right of the railway, and let me know when you see somewhere that looks like Nutfield."

He sat there, transfixed in the position I'd dictated, grinning like he was chuffed out of his skull to be flying an aeroplane. And a very good fist he made of it. Was an automatic pilot ever so welcome? Good old George!

For my part I slumped back and was quietly sick into my handkerchief while silently praying for an early death (migraine victims will understand that the remark isn't quite as flippant as it may seem;

one can feel very ill indeed). But I didn't convey my death-wish to George as I thought it might lower his morale.

So we flogged on, and on . . . At Nutfield I relieved George of his command and he thanked me profusely for having let him have a go. It really should have been the other way about. I shall never know whether it was the sight of home or whether someone upstairs was looking after me but the migraine let go as suddenly as it had struck. Full vision returned and, aside from the usual feeling of having just passed through a mincing machine, I was as right as ninepence (in old money!).

In the extreme north-eastern corner of Gatwick, between the inner and outer peri-tracks, there was a patch of grass as smooth as the traditional billiard table and plenty big enough to take a Cub in a significant headwind. I made for it. If I say it myself (as shouldn't) I accomplished what was technically the best landing I ever made; didn't even feel the touchdown. Like smooooth, man!

*   *   *

Now, headwinds! While it was true, in spirit, to speak of nothing moving at Gatwick, not even the windsock, in reality there were naturally days when the sock seemed determined to have a life of its own. February the 18th 1951 was such a day. A wild and woolly westerly tumbled across the open expanse of the 'drome.

Today I'd hesitate even to go out on foot in such a wind. But in '51 I was full of green bravado, and I'd promised my friend Ron I'd take him for a trip round come the weekend. This was it!

"Probably be all right," I said to him. "Let's get over there and have a gander, anyway."

I was greeted at the hangar by the chief mechanic, who delivered me a cautionary lecture about how A.J. Walter himself had tried to take a Cub out that very morning and had at once stood it on its nose, smashing the prop, and that if I did likewise it'd cost me a minimum of forty quid – about six weeks' wages for me.

"Of course, it's entirely up to you," he added laconically. "You can take 'LVR – if you like." He'd issued a challenge!

"I'll chance it," I said. Idiot!

Regrets were soon gnawing at me. Taxying out, downwind, was a dicey business and I did my crosswind checks as I went because I even less fancied parking side-on to that wind. A crumpled wing would likely have cost a mite more than forty quid. My friends in the control tower cooperated, giving me an instant green so that I could turn straight into wind. And we were flying even before I'd got the throttle fully open. If memory serves we were already above 1,000 ft as we crossed the western perimeter. No waving to them in the tower *that* day!

We stooged around over Horley at 1,500 ft while Ron played the routine game of "Spot my house" and "Can we circle it?" 'LVR was prancing about like a flea in a sandpit, but that was no big deal – just go slack on everything and let the inherent stability sort it out. In due time I slacked-off the power and wallowed uncertainly down to circuit height at Gatwick (this was no time to get academic about the 2,000 ft rejoining ritual).

To my dismay, but not complete surprise, I found conditions quite a bit rougher down there than they had been higher up. I guess we were getting among the 'surf.' My earlier bravado ebbed out of sight and, for the first time, I felt really frightened. It was nearly time to panic. With a mere twenty-three solo hours to my name I began seriously to doubt my ability to cope with the situation. If not panic, then what? What else was left?

As I settled onto a short final I must have been mulling over the options, because I suddenly snapped out of it and realised that not only were we much too low but the 'drome wasn't getting any closer. 'LVR was simply sinking on the spot and going no place. . . . Full gas and climb to be sure of clearing the railway. . . . What? Approaching to land in a full-power climb? A likely story! It was more than likely, it was true. I was making a right box of kippers of it. If the Devil Himself had knocked on the cabin door just then and offered me salvation in return for my soul I think I'd have done business with him – I think!

Yet once again someone must have been keeping a loving eye on me. We'd cleared the railway, were safely across the peri-track and down to hold-off height. I heaved a sigh (just a little one) and did a juggling act with stick and throttle as 'LVR got slower and slower. Dead stop; just hovering again. Common sense, and the feel on the controls, told me we still had flying speed. Aerodynamically we were still going forwards and downwards. In relation to the ground, though, we'd started going upwards and backwards. Just for a moment the wind dropped and so did 'LVR. Miraculously, in response to a blip of throttle, she fell quite gently – but still going astern. But at least we were down. No we weren't! We were at about six feet again and still reversing. And down again. And up again. And so on.

The hangar was plumb upwind of us, so even the most cautious attempt to taxi in simply resulted in another take-off – and another landing. Rather despairingly I glanced across and saw the rotten sod mechanics fairly falling about in a state of near-hysterical merriment at the sight of this pantomime with the bucking bronco. At last they took pity and came hounding out to drape themselves variously over the rear fuselage and wing struts. And thus ingloriously adorned I taxied in.

"Why didn't you land it over here, nearer the hangar?" the chief mechanic asked reprovingly.

I treated him to a jaundiced look and a short burst of humourless laughter. "Because," I said, "it was all I could do to land in the right field without being pedantic about which *bit* of the field."

But secretly I was quite chuffed. Once 'LVR was safely handed over – and therefore no longer my responsibility – I glowed with an after-the-event smugness. I suppose such things matter to you when you're young and prone to a he-who-dares mentality!

As for Ron, who'd never flown before, he'd thoroughly enjoyed the whole thing and seemed to think that aeroplanes always landed backwards.

*　　*　　*

Of course there were other less thought-provoking flights, each one, no doubt, enthralling in its time but now forgotten, except as a few figures and scrawled words in a dusty old log book. . . . '12.11.50, Cub, 'IYX, 30 mins, local.' What was the purpose behind that one? And who was with me? Gone now. Or: '16.12.50, Cub, 'IYX, 25 mins – About 4 in of snow on field.' What lunatic motive made me want to fly in such conditions? An insubstantial pageant faded.

Yet I remember the one on 23.9.50. Our revered club secretary had decreed that we should host a Tea Patrol, and I was detailed to defend the north-eastern sector in 'IYV. I spent a pleasantly uneventful hour or so swilling back and forth over the Redhill area. In the event we had only one solitary visitor. But glory be, it was a Magister! Sorry to say I can't remember either the registration or whence it came. However, I *do* remember the way the disillusioned crew regarded us with an understandable measure of disdain and winged away just as soon as good manners would allow. The rest of us sat around glumly for a short while longer before we too went home. There was a lot of tea left over!

The club – I use the term laughingly – folded some time around the middle of '53, though I continued to hire Cubs direct from A.J. Walter. On the second of April '55, in 'JDS, I made my final sortie, and at 1555 hours my Cubbing days at Gatwick ended.

I went on to the Tiger Moth 'MNN at Redhill, and that dreamy little field at Gatwick went on to greater things. And greatness devours idealism.

CHAPTER 4
BETTER TO BE BORN LUCKY THAN RICH
by
David Chalmers

[NOTES ON THE AUTHOR: Was educated at Cranleigh School and the de Havilland Aeronautical Technical School. Served in the Royal Air Force as a pilot with Nos. 38 and 42 Squadrons. Later, 27 happy years with British European Airways and its successor, British Airways. Long love affair with the magic that was the de Havilland Aircraft Company and its products. Privileged to be one of the fortunate pilots entrusted to fly Brian Woodford's de Havilland collection of classics at Wessex Aviation & Transport Ltd. Long-time gliding enthusiast with gold and diamond badges. Lives now in the Cotswolds where he shares a private airstrip and keeps his Robin DR.400 (G-BSVS). – Ed.]

My family home, when war came, was London and my father, expecting the bombing, took the lull in hostile activity, known as the "phoney war," to move his family to the relative safety of Kent, whilst he stayed on in the City as a GP awaiting his call to arms. Settled in Caterham, my brother attended a secondary school whilst I was making friends of my own age at a local junior school, hence by the time the Battle of Britain started I was in a group of impressionable small boys who revelled in watching, and collecting, items falling from the air battles above. Probably stemming from that exciting period, my sole goal in life when grown up was focussed to a life with aeroplanes.

Thankfully my immediate family came through the war and returned to a bomb-damaged house in which I had to find room for a collection of precious artefacts scrounged from various crash sites. During the autumn of 1950 my father was taken seriously ill, needing a major operation, and a locum doctor entered the practice to take his place during conval-escence. This new doctor soared in my estimation when I discovered he had a private pilot's licence, and one glorious summer day in 1951 he took me to the Redhill Flying Club where he was a member. The scene was intoxicating with colourful characters all around and endless green grass on which the Club's aircraft, three Magisters and two Auster Autocrats, were coming and going. How well I remember the detail of that day and my first-ever flight (in an Autocrat) down to Shoreham for tea. At Shoreham our Auster was parked alongside two Tiger Moths both looking resplendent in Brooklands Aviation colours. Later, there was the totally magical flight back to Redhill in the calm evening air – I was completely hooked and to this day my enduring passion is grass airfields and aeroplanes of that period.

With the summer holidays over I returned to my boarding school in Surrey to hear the wonderful news that the Hawker Aircraft Company were moving out of Langley and had bought the nearby ex-RAF airfield of Dunsfold. My boyhood dreams were already centered on a film star called Mitzi Gaynor and the equally curvaceous Hawker P.1052 and P.1081. *"Flight"* magazine was forecasting that something even more exciting was planned by Sydney Camm and his team at Kingston. This new Hawker fighter prototype was the P.1067 (WB188) and it first flew from Boscombe Down on the 20th July 1951. Naturally all this was kept secret, but shortly after our return to school from the summer holidays I was thrilled to see the prototype (painted duck-egg green) regularly flying at low level seemingly around our playing fields! Looking back I realize that in fact this was Neville Duke working up his display sequence for that month's SBAC display at Farnborough. Nine months later on the 24th June 1952 the local area was shaken by a double explosion, quickly followed by that goose-pimpling sound of the new fighter pulling out of a dive overhead. Such was our first-hand experience of the "breaking of the sound barrier." Chuck Yeager was ignored: we had our own home-grown hero in Neville Duke who was making history in the sky overhead. How could an already air-minded youth concentrate on those school subjects that could have so little relevance to a future pilot or aircraft designer, when such intoxicating sounds were to be heard outside?

Free time was spent cycling to Dunsfold where I had discovered a spot well-hidden in the bushes near the northern taxiway to runway 07 from which to observe and take photographs. All this made the heart beat pretty fast, as to get to my vantage point I had to pass large notices threatening dire things to anyone guilty of tresspass against the Official Secrets Act. The school darkroom was to witness the making of enlargements which even today cause me to reflect on my youthful folly! My immediate aim was to arrange an official visit to the flight line at Dunsfold so I founded a school aviation society, complete with printed notepaper, on which I penned letters to the various test pilots at Dunsfold. Both Frank Murphy and Frank Bullen were persuaded to come to the school to give talks and must have reported back to the boss favourably, as one day four of us squeezed into a master's Morris Minor for a trip to the airfield where Bill Bedford (then deputy CTP) gave us a quick tour of a black hangar where the Hawker Tomtit (G-AFTA) and Hurricane (G-AMAU) were housed – not exactly secret stuff but we did get to see the second Hunter prototype (WB195). Bill Bedford never tired of fielding all our questions and I will always remember his great kindness and good humour.

Under the banner of the school aviation society I sent letters to the various British aircraft constructors and to the RAF asking for information on careers and the school certificates required for acceptance to training. Doubtless these organisations received many such requests from schoolboys, yet the response in information and photographs was marvellous. Naturally my goal was to fly in the RAF but my parents (and schoolmasters) were adamant that this was not a fitting career and that I should first train for a "proper job." Perhaps with hindsight this was understandable so soon after the war, but it made me see red and led to a rift between myself and my peers whilst strengthening my resolve to prove them all wrong! Sadly as my schooldays were coming to an end two things happened which affected my future plans: firstly I fell down a quarry (out of bounds), giving myself a big fright and a spell in hospital, and secondly my father was now dying from cancer. My family was naturally distressed and in my remorse I promised to forgo my ambition to fly in the Service until I had attained another career to fall back on.

Now, totally captured by the aviation bug, I attended a series of interviews with the aim of gaining an appenticeship within the aircraft industry. The day came when I went to Hatfield to be interviewed by de Havillands and fate played me a huge slice of luck. Arriving by train at Hatfield station I was in need of lunch to fortify myself for the afternoon's grilling so, dressed in my best suit, I entered the Station Hotel only to find the dining room full. Seeing a table with only one occupant I asked if I might sit in the vacant seat. Over lunch I mentioned to my companion that I was on my way to Manor Road and Astwick Manor and could he direct me. It transpired that he worked for de Havillands and would be pleased to drop me off on his way back to the office. All my pre-interview nerves vanished instantly when, once outside the hotel, I realized that my "lift" was to be in a Jaguar XK 120 and that my lunch companion was Desmond de Villiers, Chief Test Pilot of the de Havilland Propeller Company. The car journey was all too short but I must have prattled on about how I too wanted to be a pilot, with the result that Desmond said that if my interview finished on time I could have a flight in a Percival Pembroke he was due to fly later. Wow! What luck!

My interview that afternoon was with Sqn. Ldr. Bob Reeve, Principal of the de Havilland Aeronautical Technical School, and Saul-Brown, who was the Chief Education Officer. Both men, though charming, were unimpressed with my grades in GCE, especially as I wanted to follow the course in aircraft design. Perhaps my enthusiasm won the day for I was accepted on condition that I re-sat two subjects, including Physics, via night school at St. Albans College of Further Education. I would have accepted any condition so long as I could be on my way and not miss that promised flight in the Pembroke.

I have no recollection of any problems with security on gaining entry to the Manor Road site of de Havilland Propellers but I have the most vivid memories of the sights and sounds of Hatfield Aerodrome at this zenith of activity. The smell of aviation was all around: petrol, kerosene, slurry on hot metal and new mown grass, and I felt already part of the Company as I found my way to the test pilots' offices. Apprentices often flew on certain test flights as part of their training so there was no great surprise as I announced my mission. That flight (only my second) took me above the clouds for the first time and the beauty of the evening sunlight reflecting off cumulus clouds almost overshadowed the thrill of being on a "test flight." Looking now at my indentures of apprenticeship I see that my training started on 30th August 1954 and that I was paid £2.7s.6d a week, though my now-widowed mother had to pay fees of £80 a year.

First-year engineering students were accommodated in Sherrards, a hostel adjacent to the school's workshops. From the very first day firm friendships were made amongst the students, for we all shared this passion for aeroplanes, things mechanical and the making of them. The students' car park was an amazing sight with a motley collection of motor bikes, owner-designed "specials," a huge old Lagonda, Bond mini-car and one out of place brand-new MG TF. Every night seemed to be party night, much to the consternation of a Mr & Mrs Heath who ran the hostel but who must have seen it all before. This was no place for the seriously studious and yet I knew come the autumn I had to sit those beastly exams again, otherwise my stay in this paradise would come to an abrupt end.

The early days at Astwick Manor were devoted to the acquisition of metal working skills. First one took a chunk of ½ in. mild steel and converted it by hacksaw, file and emery paper to a perfect square. When this had eventually passed the most critical inspection by Mr Duffey, one side was stained blue and then marked out in anticipation of cutting out a perfect square hole in the centre. Next, the would-be engineer had to file yet another square to fit the hole any side to any side. Mr Duffey was hard to satisfy and I had countless items rejected before being allowed to progress to the next fitting exercises.

Despite all our youthful enthusiam we were all so aware of the problems facing the de Havilland Aircraft Company in 1954, for tragedy had struck that January when a Comet 1 (G-ALYP), having departed Rome, mysteriously crashed into the sea off the island of Elba with the loss of all passengers and crew. All remaining Comets were minutely inspected, as were the various theories including sabotage and catastrophic engine failure. Full commercial services were resumed in March, but in April disaster struck again when another Comet (G-ALYY), also having departed Rome, disappeared near Naples not far from the crash site of the first. The coincidence was almost unbelievable that these two aircraft should have crashed within a few miles of each other. Comets were immediately grounded, the Royal Navy were tasked with locating and retrieving wreckage from the seabed, whilst the Air Ministry instructed the scientists at Farnborough to immediately institute a full investigation into the causes of the accidents. A huge water tank was constructed to take a complete Comet fuselage for pressure-testing whilst the rest of the structure was subjected to the stresses and strains of the equivalent of thousands of hours of flight. Meanwhile the Royal Navy was overcoming huge difficulties and succeeding in raising essential parts of the aircraft which were sent to Farnborough to be identified and then placed in their correct relative positions within an airframe reconstruction. The Comet at that time held a four-to-five-year lead for Britain in the commercial airliner market and orders had been received from Canada and France, with most of the world's major airlines taking options on the forthcoming Comet 2 with Rolls Royce Avon engines.

As apprentices we remained convinced that the great Company of which we were now proud members would quickly overcome this setback and that many of us would go on to work for de Havilland for the rest of our lives. For me, rather selfishly, my major concern was that the Company was prudently making economies, including the withdrawal of sponsorship for apprentices to learn to fly with the London Aeroplane Club at Panshanger, with the result that the club had restructured as the North London Aero Club. However lack of funds has never stopped any young man desperate to be a pilot from getting airborne, and soon all my spare time was to be spent at Panshanger doing any odd job, a dedication that was to be rewarded by occasional dual training in the Tiger Moths G-AHIZ and G-ANOH, resulting in a first solo on 15th May 1955.

The workshops at Astwick Manor, where apprentices learnt their basic craft skills, were historic in that the prototype Mosquito (W4050) had been assembled under their roof in 1940 when the buildings had been sited at Salisbury Hall, near London Colney. Following successful completion of this first year, in which we had covered fitting, sheet metal work, machining and mechanical drawing, we apprentices moved on to a "sandwich course" system where our time alternated between technical school and the many different departments within the main factory.

The Comet investigation had eventually revealed that the pressure cabin had suffered a catastrophic structural failure due to fatigue of the metal structure. This was caused by over-stressing on the corners of the square windows and particularly the roof-mounted direction-finding aerials. With the knowledge gained re-design partly consisted of replacing the whole length of the window panel with one of much increased strength with special reinforcements round all cut-outs for doors, windows and hatches.

Comet 2 production progressed slowly as the new drawings were awaited from the design and stress offices, with the result that the shop floors were overmanned, thus the various benevolent chargehands under whom I worked often turned a blind eye on my frequent periods of absenteeism to seek flights in the huge variety of aircraft then on test from Hatfield. The Engine and Propeller divisions of the Company all had their own individual sites within the aerodrome boundaries and with them their flight offices. My early friendship with Desmond de Villiers soon led to flights with several other test pilots, particularly "Fizz" Waters, Chris Capper and Pat Fillingham in aircraft as diverse as a Beaver Series 2 (G-ANAR) powered by an Alvis Leonides to the Short Sperrin (VX158) which in 1957 was being used as flying test-bed for the de Havilland Gyron. However, of all the dozen different types in which I flew, a Mosquito and the Sea Venom (WK379) stand out. The Sea Venom was my first jet flight and a total revelation, for from that moment on I knew that I had to make every endeavour to gain entry to the Navy or Air Force for pilot training.

The Heron prototype (G-ALZL) was used as the test pilots' hack to commute between the other de Havilland facilities of Christchurch and Chester, so whenever possible I would skip my factory work to go along, in the knowledge that most pilots would use me as a poor form of autopilot!

A bombshell hit the industry and indeed the Royal Air Force on April 4th 1957 when the (Conservative) Defence Minister, Duncan Sandys, stood up in the Palace of Westminster and announced that manned military aircraft were to be considered obsolete and that even bombers would be replaced by the Thor and Blue Streak ballistic missiles! Of all the many foul-ups made by politicians when meddling in aviation matters this was surely the most damaging to our country's defence and wealth. By a strange irony Roly "Bee" Beamont had, that very day, made the first flight of the English Electric P.1. This insane policy change immediately led to the cancellation of the Hawker P.1121, Saunders Roe 177, Fairey Delta fighter and the Avro 730 supersonic bomber. Although de Havilland were the lead contractor in developing the Blue Streak ICBM, they also had in mock-up stage a supersonic interceptor designed to use the Gyron and carry their own Firestreak infra-red guided missile.

Looking back as the new millennium nears I could weep for our designers and engineers who were denied, during the 1950s, so many chances to lead the world, purely by changes in political whim.

It was clear to me that as the Royal Air Force contracted their need for aircrew would lessen, and consequently initial entry would get ever more difficult, but so long as the chance remained then I must take it. Firstly I persuaded the Company apprentice supervisor, Mr Dillon-Godfrey, to sponsor me on an Outward Bound course in the Lake District; this was closely followed by healthy summer working on a farm in Devon during harvest time. Early in 1958 I was invited to the Aircrew Selection Centre in Hornchurch and here during the course of the two days' aptitude assessment I managed to persuade the panel and the medics that I was worth being giving the chance to train as an RAF pilot.

The first my poor mother knew that I had decided to abandon engineering training was when I phoned to say that I was joining No. 1 Initial Training School (ITS) South Cerney on the 28th May 1958. Officer training of that period was a tedious bind to be endured, but public school and the outward bound course were worse and, however unpleasant the situation, I always reminded myself that as long as I kept my nose clean then flying training was next.

Later that year on August 19th I reported to No. 2 FTS at Royal Air Force Syerston as a 'sprog' Acting Pilot Officer, soon to meet Flt. Lt. Sargent who was to be my instructor on the piston Provost. I had been wisely warned not to mention that I had any previous flying training, but it must have proved a distinct advantage at this *ab initio* stage, for any failure to meet the required standards meant a swift return to civvy street. My abiding memory of Flt. Lt. Sargent was his penchant for covering the inside of the Provost's canopy with chinagraph diagrams, then demonstrating superbly the exercise of the day. The Provost was a delight to handle and I soon made rapid progress to the solo exercises, thanks to excellent instruction, luck and a sound grounding in aerodynamics. I finished top of the No. 136 Course and with 130 hours in my log book moved on to the de Havilland Vampire T.11, up the Fosse Way at RAF Swinderby.

Swinderby was a shock and those remaining on the course were left in no doubt that the Air Force had a large surplus of pilots and any lack of discipline or failure to keep up with the course would mean immediate suspension from flying training. Despite my achievements on the Provost I was soon struggling to keep up with the pace of events in a Vampire, with the result that in my mental confusion I was over-controlling. Adding to my personal problems was a young instructor, just fresh from Central Flying School, ex-ground attack and a total hooligan who seemed determined to frighten me into submission. Needless to say when my macho friend put me up for a solo check with the chief instructor I failed and was returned for another dual session in the circuit. Weekly, our course numbers seemed to get smaller due to "wastage" and often I felt I was hanging on by a thread. Instrument flying that had been so easy in the Provost suddenly became a big problem and I became my own worst enemy as I contemplated failure in the "white card" rating test.

Luck again came to my rescue in the form of a Royal Navy exchange instructor who, in the course of just one flight, sorted me out and immediately put me up for that first instrument rating which thankfully I passed. How I wish I could meet Lt. Thompson RN again and thank him for his patience and skill on that day. Formation flying went well and was always exhilarating; a good three-ship formation detail was often followed by a tail-chase which could go from 30,000 ft right down to the deck. This was just what I had joined the Air Force to do and each trip was followed by an intense feeling of well-being.

However another hurdle loomed in the shape of the low-level navigation test and here I thought my luck had run out as I was to drawn to fly with the examiner holding a feared reputation for failing as many students as he could. That flight deserves an article all to itself for, despite careful preflight planning, I soon believed myself hopelessly lost. Despite the rising panic inside my bone-dome I continued to fly my flight plan and turning whenever it was required. Eventually the silent frosty figure in the right-hand seat ordered a diversion to a new target. I took a wild guess based on little more than intuition and cranked the Vampire onto yet another new heading, shortly after which my examiner spoke again with the dreaded words: "I have control."

Without a further word he then climbed up and amused himself by doing a sequence of medium-level aeros before returning to Swinderby. An almost violent rejoin for a fighter break and landing was completed without a single word being spoken (to me) and so it continued until we were in the debriefing room when, to to my sheer amazement, he shook my hand saying: "Congratulations on a well-planned flight and hitting the target right on the nose."

'Scuse? What did I just hear? From near-failure, thanks to a fair chunk of luck, I had nearly reached the end of my "wings" course and with it the end of the fabulous fifties that took me from schoolboy to jet pilot. Another forty-plus years of sheer pleasure from flying and the love of aeroplanes lay ahead but that, as they say, is another story.

CHAPTER 5

SYWELL REMINISCENCES

by

Chris Parker

[NOTES ON THE AUTHOR: Chris Parker saw the aviation world of the 1950s mainly through the many hours spent with his father at Sywell aerodrome. Parker senior (Arthur, universally known as "Artie") held various engineering positions with Brooklands Aviation and the Northamptonshire Aero Club, and passed his own passion for aeroplanes on to his growing son.

Chris learned to fly in the mid-sixties on Austers (at Sywell, of course), and has amassed some 3,000 hours to date – all "flying for fun." Together with wife Mavis he is involved in running the Jodel Club and the Sywell Aero Club, and in looking after and flying Norman Spiller's Messenger G-AKIN; as well as shouldering these responsibilities he joined the PFA's Executive Council in 1998. – Ed.]

It is rather difficult for anyone to be certain of their earliest memories, but mine have a decided aeronautical flavour. I'm sure that I would have been taken to Sywell aerodrome (never referred to as an "airfield," always the "aerodrome" or "'drome") as a babe-in-arms, but can't claim to recall any such occasions; what I can remember, however, is being lifted by my father into the rear cockpit of a Tiger Moth to have my photograph taken. The evidence survives, and it is noted as being the summer of 1947, when I was three years old.

To explore the reason for my being in that Tiger at Sywell, I'd like to digress a little into much earlier years – back to Edwardian Farnborough in fact. There, another father and son (my grandfather and father) enjoyed time together. Grandfather was a "horse man" and was involved in providing the horse-drawn fire-fighting facilities for the Balloon factory and later the Royal Aircraft Factory. My father had recollections of seeing Cody's aeroplanes at Farnborough, and photographs of the great man have survived in the family collection. This early and undoubtedly exciting exposure to the then very new world of flying impacted father greatly, and in 1919 at the age of sixteen he entered the Royal Air Force as a raw recruit. Shortly after reaching LAC status in 1922, he set sail in HMS *"Glengorm Castle"* for the Middle East and Baghdad bound for 8 Squadron, their DH.9As and the job of the world's first use of air power for peace-keeping. The life of an LAC in those formative years included flying duties as air-gunner and bomb-aimer. His life and adventures in Mesopotamia are a story in their own right for another time.

He left the RAF in 1927, shortly after returning to the UK from Mesopotamia, and joined the flight department of the Hawker company at Brooklands. There he enjoyed the next eight years involved in the service trials and introduction of the Tomtit and, primarily, the Hart series. His log book records a flight with George Bulman in the prototype Hart in July 1928 (the month of the type's first flight) – the entry reads "Brooklands local – 22 thousand – cold"!

In 1935 he was tempted by an offer from locally-based Brooklands Aviation to join them and relocate to their newly-formed flying school at Sywell in Northamptonshire to look after a growing fleet of Tiger Moths. Brooklands Aviation, under the dynamic leadership of ex-Royal Flying Corps pilot Captain Duncan Davis, was quick to exploit the business opportunities of the time; they had taken over the flying side of the Northamptonshire Aero Club in the early 1930s, and soon after (in partnership with Sywell Aerodrome Ltd) expanded their base there and taken on a contract to train RAF Volunteer Reserve pilots as part of the service's rapid expansion plans.

From 1935, until that 1947 day when I took my place in a DH.82A for the first time, father was heavily involved in the engineering side of what became 6 E & RFTS at Sywell (and wartime satellite, Denton) with a fleet of Tiger Moths which grew to some 120 aircraft at peak.

Having explored the reasons for my having a high concentration of aviation blood in my veins, let's roll forward into Sywell of the 1950s. A good starting point is the 21st anniversary of the Northamptonshire Aero Club, marked by a grand reunion and Flying Display held at Sywell on May 21st 1949. I was a seasoned nearly-five-year-old and can recollect being affected by the excitement of the occasion, all very new to me. The impressions of that day are indelible: the noise of many aeroplanes manoeuvering on the ground and in airborne formation, picnic food, a public address system, excited conversations in the crowd, the fresh-cut grass smell, brilliant spells of sunshine, the breeze, the sense that it was all somehow "important." This sense of anticipation and sensory pleasure from flying events has stayed with me throughout my life. The 1949 Sywell show was to an extent a celebration of the end of a long and drab decade of wartime and early postwar life, and it was also a chance for many of those who had worked at or flown from Sywell since its early days in 1928 to get together once again. Aerial attractions included Tiger Moth formation-flying by instructors of Sywell's 6 RFS in their silver-with-yellow-band liveried aircraft, parachute dropping from Dakotas, some sizzlingly low runs from "Timber" Woods in a Sywell-overhauled Mosquito, Auxiliary Squadron Spitfire formation demonstrations, Ranald Porteous "one-wheeling" in an Auster Autocrat fitted with the odd-ball Goodyear castoring undercarriage, vertical flight performed by an early

Saro Skeeter (probably the first time that most of those present had seen a helicopter), and tranquil silent flight by a new Olympia sailplane built by furniture manufacturers Elliots of Newbury.

An additional "act," carrying on with a long Sywell tradition of speciality items, was the magnificent "Sywellicopter." This incredible creation was manned by a six-strong crew, bearing an uncanny resemblance to the Marx brothers, who boarded their machine after a rousing send-off from their admirers, then bounded and whirled their way around Sywell's green acres, fortunately failing to become airborne. Being of too-tender years to grasp that this was a "spoof" I can recall being somewhat terrified by the device and the accompanying proceedings, and puzzled when sweep brushes and other paraphernalia appeared from several orifices (presumably attempts by the intrepid occupants to provide locomotive assistance to their steed!). The instigators of this piece of wonderful light relief were the indomitable Linnell brothers, Geoff and Jack, who were the first to land on the fields that became Sywell in their Cirrus Moth back in 1927, and who were the leading lights of Sywell's social and Club scene from those formative days until their retirements from flying in the early 1960s.

Sywell in 1949, and into the early 1950s, continued the momentum of the various aviation activities which had originated in the late prewar days and during the wartime period. The aircraft of the Northamptonshire Aero Club had reverted to the prewar red, black, and silver livery of parent Brooklands Aviation and included Tiger Moths G-ADIA, 'HMM and 'HMN, together with newly purchased Auster Autocrats G-AIBR, 'JRB and 'JDW. For a short period Brooklands also had as part of the fleet some Proctors and Rapides for air-taxi work, but this activity fairly quickly died away. One Rapide, G-AJHO, remained however, being used by directors of the company as executive transport and for occasional joyriding duties and Club outings (happy days!).

My own first flight, etched permanently in my memory, was at the age of six with a primary school chum, on the occasion of his birthday, and was with the then Aero Club CFI, Leslie Hilditch, in his favourite Auster G-AIBR. The first living beings I saw from the air (from the sideways-facing rear seat in the Autocrat as she chugged over Sywell's eastern boundary in the still early morning air) were our local postman, George Denton, pedalling his bike in his normal laboured fashion along the lane pursued by his black-and-white mongrel "Scamp." I didn't stop talking about that flight for days afterwards, and on the next few birthdays for the two of us we repeated the exercise. Our school, as it happened, was in Sywell village, no more than 300 yards from the aerodrome boundary and, in addition to having the teacher's words frequently and pleasurably drowned out by the music of the Merlins equipping the Mosquitoes which Brooklands Aviation were overhauling, we could hop over the boundary wall to get a close look at what was going on during our breaks from lessons.

In addition to the Aero Club activities, by the early '50s private aviation had firmly re-established itself, and Sywell had a growing contingent of what were referred to then as "the Private Owners." I had acquired an ancient box-Brownie camera and began to record photographically the locally-based aircraft, as well as visitors of interest. For the record, amongst the locals were the Linnell brothers' collection of Messengers G-AIDK and G-AIEK (flying today as Monty's "RG333"), Gemini G-AKER, and Comper Swift G-ABUS (currently with Roger Bailey); Derek Crouch's Messenger G-AJFC and Gemini G-AJWC; the Spiller brothers' Messenger G-AKIN (raced by "Johnny" Spiller on occasion, and maintained in airworthy condition to the present day by his younger brother Norman); "Johnny" Spiller's Proctor G-AHFK (extensively raced by him, and a Kings Cup winner in 1959); Kurt Weininger's Messenger G-AHXR (ex-Regent of Iraq's Baghdad-based YI-HRH) and several Austers and Tigers. At the time in question, all these aeroplanes were tucked cosily into one blister hangar, remaining in use today as the base of March Helicopters, and many were the rainy winter's days when I would pass contented hours just mooching about amongst them, and sitting in the various cockpits, flying them all in my imagination (I'd never heard of James Thurber's Walter Mitty then, but that's who I was!).

The RAF side of flying training lasted until the disbanding of the Volunteer Reserve in 1953. All the Sywell activities continued to be run by Brooklands Aviation, and included the Tiger Moths of 6 RFS, replaced in 1950 by Percival Prentices, and supplemented for VR continuation flying by a small number of Ansons and Oxfords, plus the separate 4 BFTS equipped with Chipmunks providing ab-initio training in response to the demands created by the Korean war. The VR aspect meant that a lot of weekend flying took place, enabling me in school term time to be there with my father. Most of my time was spent helping push and pull aircraft around, which I thoroughly enjoyed, but I must have been something of a nuisance to my father and others who (presumably) had to keep an eye on me to prevent me disappearing under an undercarriage or through a propeller.

Non-aviation memories of the time included the village children's Coronation Tea in 1953 which was held in one of the guard rooms – such was the close linkage between aerodrome and village in those days; the details escape me other than my eating too much and feeling sick afterwards.

My side of the aerodrome was the Aero Club and Private Owner facilities in the south-east corner of the site, and I would happily come and go on my bike (school was nearby and home only a mile away). The repair factory hangars occupied the south-west and western areas, and were not readily accessible. Many of the aeroplanes coming and going were easy to see however, and always provided something of interest. Early in the war Brooklands Aviation started repair and overhaul of Wellingtons, and this particular activity continued until the last aeroplane was completed in 1952, after over 1,800 had been through Sywell. In the early postwar period Mosquitoes, Harvards, and Berlin Airlift Dakotas were all handled and, for a short time, Vampires, although Sywell's grass was not really suitable. The Vampire work was soon transferred to newly-opened Brooklands Aviation facility at Little Staughton, near Kimbolton. The work which did continue at Sywell throughout the 1950s however was the overhaul of Vickers Valettas and Varsities, and these were often parked in abundance around the boundaries and available for my inspection. When on flight-test these larger aircraft generally used the longest 03/21 direction, and the flight path passed directly over our aforementioned school, providing many pleasant distractions from the daily pursuit of the three "R"s. The only drama I can recall was on a day when storm activity caused a rapid 180° wind-shear whilst a Valetta was landing, resulting in it overrunning into the side of a hangar: no serious injuries resulted but the general excitement kept the village agog for a few days afterwards.

Back to my main interest – the private flying. From the mid-1950s onwards I spent increasing amounts of time helping rather than hindering in the day-to-day activities, all the normal 'gopher' tasks including aeroplane manhandling, refuelling, oil replenishment, cleaning and chock-pulling. As a reward I got to do increasing amounts of passenger flying. Much of this was in the rear seat of Autocrats with various Club pilots, both on local trips and visits to other nearby clubs – Leicester East was a favourite. The sideways rear seat in the Autocrat provides an uninterrupted view over the tail – an unusual aspect but one I enjoyed on take-off and which reminded me of the film shots often taken looking rearwards during carrier based operations! By dint of hanging around long enough and looking sufficiently forlorn I got many trips in other types; these included a lot of back-seat flying in Messengers and Geminis, some memorable racing practices in the Proctor with Johnny Spiller at ultra-low-level and around friendly farmers' buildings used as turning points, and some memorable jaunts in the Brooklands Rapide with Eric Grieve, sitting behind him in the cockpit area on the fold-down W/Ops seat whilst he cruised around the local area keeping his hours up and his currency on type.

An interesting diversion was the founding at Sywell around 1955 of the Northamptonshire Gliding Club. I took to joining in with their activities, which provided some exciting moments including landing in adjacent fields with the gliders being manhandled back onto the aerodrome over the hedges. Nearly all their operations were winch-launched, which caused moments of alarm, generally when non-radio powered traffic elected to land or take off in directions which crossed the cable paths; happily no disasters occurred. There was a little aerotowing, however, as locally-based Kurt Weininger had somehow persuaded the ARB to clear the installation of a tow-hook on his Messenger, and this seemed to work out reasonably well. There was one memorable occasion when, at the end of a long day's glider operations conducted from a launch point at the furthest corner of the aerodrome, Kurt offered those with no other transport a taxy-ride back to the distant hangars in the Messenger. All those present (about 5, including yours truly, plus various paraphernalia including tow-ropes) squeezed in on top of each other and Kurt set off. His exuberance (or lack of judgement) quickly overcame him, however, and he proceeded to get the Messenger airborne and (as only a Messenger can) cruise at a few feet altitude and about 35 mph around the boundary and alight practically in the hangar doorway. This incident came to mind some years later when I saw at the RAF Museum some wartime Miles colour film showing a similar number of people cramming into a Messenger to demonstrate its load-carrying capabilities as a contender for ship-launched anti-submarine duties carrying depth charges or other heavy armaments.

The gliding club's operations eventually became incompatible with other traffic activities at Sywell, and they moved away. One of these activities was the establishment of a Derby Airways service to the Channel Islands operated by Dakotas and Miles Marathons, established in the late '50s, and running for a couple of years or so. It was all a fairly informal business, with the Aerodrome Restaurant (the ex-prewar Club House) used as a "terminal," and the "airliners" pulling up on the grass outside for the embarking and disembarking passengers to wander in and out, often having their photographs taken beside the aircraft in the process.

Other happenings which come to mind include the UK tour around 1956 (I believe organised by Harold Best-Devereux) of a very early Druine Turbulent, F-PHFR. Being used only to aeroplanes sized from Tiger Moths upwards, this seemed impossibly small to me, as it probably did to most of those present. It was demonstrated by its pilot, also flown by the Club's CFI, and categorised by my father as having a "pop-bottle" engine – I don't think he believed anything smaller than a Cirrus Minor to be worth considering. The message of the future value of such diminutive aeroplanes began to filter through, however, and the following year, the second Sywell Popular Flying Association Rally was held. Harold Best-Devereux was at the helm in an Edgar Percival EP.9 and a veritable gaggle of Frenchmen appeared (eventually) in more Turbulents, Jodels and Minicabs. I recall Harold setting off in the EP.9 to locate and liberate from adjacent airfields (some occupied by the USAF) several whose navigational abilities were a little deficient. John Blake was in evidence, recorded on camera squeezing into a Minicab with Jean Barritault, and also producing for the occasion a commemorative menu with such delights as "Gardan" Peas, Fromage Jodel and Birch-Ply Biscuits. It was to be some 12 years later in 1969 that the present series of annual PFA Rallies started at Sywell.

Much has been written in this series of books of the Tiger Club, and Sywell was a regular venue for their displays. There was a very enthusiastic Sywell contingent of the Club led by local pilot the late Charles Boddington, who went on to form his own flying circus, the "Barnstormers," and whose son Matthew continues the family tradition currently. For me, a visit by the Tiger Club was to be anticipated and savoured, the whole enterprise being a bustle of activity and colour and general excitement.

Sywell's superb "Art Deco" Aero Clubhouse, opened in 1934, had been extended for its wartime and early postwar role as Sergeants' and Officers' messes, lecture rooms, and administrative facilities. Following the service run-down, the Aero Club was re-established, and in 1958 the core of the building was refurbished and officially reopened to the public as the "Airport Restaurant." The opening ceremony was performed by Group Captain Douglas Bader, at that time working for Shell's aviation department, who arrived in his Gemini 7 (Gipsy Major 10 engines), G-AMGF, and was joined by another wartime ace AVM Johnny Johnston. The Northamptonshire Aero Club retained a wing of the building as its Clubhouse, and summer Sunday afternoons, with a vista of visiting aircraft (Geminis, Messengers, Tigers, Austers) and tea on the lawn were evocative of the golden prewar days. Photographs and films of these occasions, right up to the early sixties, show the gentlemen universally attired in jackets and ties, and the ladies in summer dresses, gloves, and (in many cases) hats.

An annual Club event was the Sunday "At Home" which regularly followed the King's Cup Air Race (then generally flown on a Saturday at Baginton). These "At Homes" attracted visitors from far and wide, including representatives of the Air Racing community, and service types such as Army Austers and RAF Communications-flight Ansons. As a bit of general interest and excitement the "At Homes" featured a landing competition – not the "spot landing" we are used to today but one involving landing *over* a rope barrier held aloft on poles, and then touching down nearest to it. This naturally encouraged some hair-raising techniques. On one occasion I remember an AOP 6 certainly hitting the ground nearest the barrier, but unfortunately flattening the undercarriage in the process!

That little incident reminds me that undercarriage-bending was a relatively common occurrence following heavy landings on the Club's Autocrats used for *ab initio* training. Rectification was quickly accomplished with replacement legs however, damage rarely being transferred to the fuselage structure.

The availability of imported American aircraft from the late fifties onwards didn't initially have much impact on the Tiger Moth and Auster fleet of the Northants Aero Club. However at the turn of the decade the Club's proprietors, Brooklands Aviation, yielded to pressure from the members for something a little more appealing than the Autocrats for touring and obtained a second-hand Tripacer, G-APZY. I enjoyed a number of trips in this aeroplane as ballast, particularly when members being checked out on it were having its 'loaded' performance demonstrated to them. It seems odd now to recall that the exclusively tailwheel-trained Club pilots of that era regarded the nosewheel Tripacer as a 'hot ship,' needing careful conversion to master the tricycle undercarriage configuration!

One of Sywell's many aviation "characters" of the period that I haven't so far mentioned is the late David Lloyd. David was a very wealthy man (a family member of the Stewarts & Lloyd's steel-making enterprise), but always a true gentleman in his dealings with people from all walks and stations of life. His flying started back in the 1920s with the Auxiliary Air Force; he was a friend and contemporary of Richard Shuttleworth, and in the Battle of Britain distinguished himself as a Fighter Controller at Tangmere. I first remember him through his flying at Sywell of Tiger Moths – Club machines and his own all-red G-AIXD. All flights by David were events not to be missed – his control over the Tiger in all attitudes and at all airspeeds (often very low) was legendary – every flight was in effect an exhibition of crazy flying! This was truly prewar *joie de vivre* and freedom from control living into the 1950s and 1960s. David's style finally ran foul of the regulated and rather soulless approach to airfield operation in the 1970s. I was very fortunate to have known him since childhood, and in later years to be able to gain my initial Tiger Moth experience by flying his beautiful aeroplane.

The Sywell scene was further enlivened at the end of the fifties by the arrival of the Grantair company (a subsidiary of Cambridge-based Grant-chester Garages) – destined unfortunately to last for only a couple of years before ceasing trading. My father joined Grantair to provide licensed engineering coverage, and I continued to spend much weekend and after-school time helping out with whatever hangar tasks came my way and scrounging rides whenever possible. Grantair maintained, hired and sold a variety of light aircraft, but of great interest to me were the latest US imports that they handled, including the first examples I had seen of the Cessna 175 Skylark, Piper Comanche, Super Cub and Caribbean, plus a gaggle of the more familiar Tripacers. I can recall thinking that the Cessna 175 in particular was the "bee's knees" with its technicolour paint scheme, smart upholstery, smooth ride over Sywell's ridge-and-furrow, and vibration-free engine – a great improvement on the tooth-rattling Austers! An additional attraction was that whereas the dual controls were religiously removed by CFI Leslie Hilditch from the Club Austers and Tigers for non-instructional flights, in Grantair's Cessna and Pipers they were left in. This enabled me to accumulate some unofficial stick time and whet my appetitie to go on to obtain a PPL; I had to wait a further eight years to afford this however, even at the £3 per hour then being charged!

Grantair was not without its characters, and those that come to mind include general Manager Bob Hampshire, who went on to a senior role with Rolls Royce Motors at Crewe when they took on the licence manufacture of Continental aero engines, joyriding pilot Bill Rushworth, who aspired to the flight deck of one of Derby Airways' Marathons, general engineering dogsbody Paget Bellin who had a Tiger Moth (G-ARMS) prepared for him by Rollasons for a planned flight to the Cape and whose eventual fate I cannot recollect and, last but not least, one Cliff Piper who progressed eventually from flying everything and attacking anything with a spanner for Grantair to a long and distinguished airline career, followed currently in retirement with stewardship of the PFA's Pilot Coaching Scheme.

To round this story off, we can run into the very early 1960s. In 1961 and 1962 "Shackleton Sales Weekends" were held at Sywell. These were promoted by the long established W.S. Shackleton aviation enterprise and were showcases for all that was latest in the light aeroplane world. The ending of import restrictions in 1958 had opened up a whole new world of available aircraft, particularly the products of the American and French industries. Optimism was running high, and the events promoted the wares of a wide array of manufacturers and importers – truly happy and exciting times. Even de Havilland was still an active constructor, displaying the latest in the Dove range. Aerial views of the 1962 event show the aerodrome fairly well covered in visiting and display aircraft – shades of PFA rallies to come in much later years – the largest of which was Luton-based Keegan Aviation's executive DC-4 (I don't think they sold many!)

The Shackleton organisation's links with Sywell had been strengthened over the two years or so preceding the Sales Weekends as the company had been acquired by Raymond Way in 1960. Raymond Way Motors was a well-known North London motor trading business, and its aviation activities were already Sywell-based. These activities were merged with Shackletons and an aircraft sales operation, trading as Shackleton Aviaton, ran at Sywell until the late 1960s when it moved on to Coventry.

My involvement with Sywell continues to the present day – but nothing really rivals that colourful, free-from-regulation, never dull decade of the fifties!

CHAPTER 6
HEATHROW MEMORIES AND THEN SOME
by
Dick Flute

I reckon that a love of aviation could easily be registered as a classified drug: so many people get hopelessly addicted when in bodily contact with it, and it gives extraordinary pleasure. Who could disagree with that? Yet, despite the addiction, most of us continue happily without any detriment to our health, although maybe the same cannot be said about our wallets!

For me, how did it all begin? My parents moved to a house close to the southern edge of London (Heathrow) Airport when I was seven, in 1954, and it wasn't long before I was smitten with the long-recognised 'spotter' condition and soon became a bad case. It took many years, involving treatment from college life, exposure to girls especially, and 'close contact' therapy with healthy unafflicted friends and colleagues before a partial cure was effected.

But I am certain that aviation, as an affliction, is never completely cured, like the time after our marriage ceremony (in Caxton Hall which I and my Australian bride thought was pretty good going, although my mother-in-law would have preferred St. Paul's Cathedral!). On our short cash-starved honeymoon, I took my new wife on a trial lesson from Stapleford Tawney aerodrome in a PA-28 "Cherry-Tree"; this was en route to the bridal suite in a modest hotel near Steeple Bumpstead, transported in our half-timbered Elizabethan-style Morris Traveller.

Concerning the flight in the PA-28, I desperately wanted to impress, but little did I know that, back in Australia several years before, my wife had already jumped thirteen times out of aeroplanes with a parachute, whilst I was still anxious to know what happened when you had the yoke or stick in hand and feet placed on the rudder bar. The truth is that I really believed that a flight in a small aeroplane was one of the best presents you can give anyone. Twenty five years later with my own Private Pilot's Licence, I haven't changed my mind on that.

I'm a hopeless case, stricken down by aviation. Since getting my PPL the door to the boundless possibilities of aviation have opened and I've tried to grab some of them with both hands. I've flown into or from more than one hundred and eighty two airports, aerodromes and farm strips, and experienced some element of control in over fifty types, many solo. Although most were single-engined aeroplanes, some highly aerobatic and a couple on floats, I've also flown a couple of twins (one land, one amphibian), a hot-air balloon (logged as a training flight), and two microlights (one three-axis single-seater a couple of times), plus at least

TOP: Comper Swift G-ABUS after David Ogilvy's forced landing in the 1955 King's Cup Air Race, fortunately in the middle of Coventry Airport. David Ogilvy is on the extreme right, and Ron Paine is nearest to the aircraft.
Photo: via David Ogilvy.
BOTTOM: Mosquito CF-HMT on the approach at Derby (Burnaston). The cyclist seems quite unperturbed!
Photo: by courtesy of "Flight International" Quadrant House picture library.

TOP: Crazy flying in Autocrat G-AIZY by Stan Ward in a fifties Ipswich air display.
BOTTOM: The pilot (possibly Dan Burgess) of East Anglian's Dragon Rapide G-AEMH at Ipswich waits for the ground hostess to close the door before taking off on a scheduled flight – probably about 1954.
Photos: Stan Ward.

Parachutist Robert Ward and father Stan Ward at Ipswich with Auster V
G-ANHZ – probably 1960. Photo: via Stan Ward.

TOP: Chris Dearden and Gwen Bull just back from Beachy Head in Cub G-ALVR on the 14th October 1950 (smoking near an aeroplane was not *verboten* in those days, it seems!). Photo: D. Hollingsbee.
BOTTOM: In 1955 David Chalmers was taught in Tiger Moth G-ANOH at Panshanger. Photo: via David Chalmers.

POPULAR FLYING ASSOCIATION -
- - SECOND NATIONAL RALLY

Sywell Aerodrome

14–15 Sept: 1957

MENU

Melon Emeraude
-
Flétan Poche Roche
Sauce Evra
-
Dindon Druine et Porc P.F.A.
Sauce Havraise
Le Stuffage
-
Pommes d'Atterrissage
Beraud Beans – Sauce Favriel
Gardan Peas
-
Salade de Berck
Maraschino
-
Fromage Jodel
Birch Ply Biscuits
-
Café Sphinx
-

The dinner menu at the P.F.A.'s Second National Rally at Sywell, 1957.
Original drawing by John Blake, via Chris Parker.

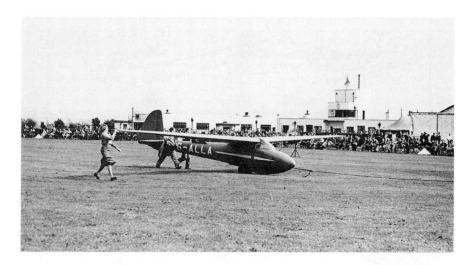

TOP: Olympia 1 G-ALLA at the Sywell Air Show in 1949.
BOTTOM: An aerial view of the 1962 W.S. Shackleton Sales Weekend, held on the 14th & 15th April.
Photos: via Chris Parker.

two memorable glider flights. All with just over four hundred hours in the log book. Unfortunately my best helicopter flight (one of four, all as a non-paying passenger) can't be told here, as it comes outside our 1950s remit. It's a shame, as it was truly remarkable.

My smallest (and slowest) type in which I soloed was a single-seat Letov Sluka (first flight single-seat and first flight in a microlight), my largest the AN-2 with James Black (one of my many aviation heroes), out of Popham. Going through the pre-take-off checks I discovered ten or more 'passengers' seated in the cabin. I have no idea how they got there, and after shutting down they'd all disappeared! I hope they're all still laughing about it. Fastest was a Jet Provost (thirty minutes) out of Lydd, a 50th birthday present from my wife. This will never be forgotten: the owner and I enjoyed ourselves so much he gave me ten minutes extra for nothing – and at around (I think) about £1,000 per flying hour true operating costs for the owner/pilot, that'll give you some idea how much we were enjoying it!

These flights have taken place in fourteen different countries ranging from Norway to Greece, Hungary, Spain and Australia, the USA and Bahamas. On top of all this I've talked myself (one of the privileges of gaining a PPL and knowing a few ATPL pilots), into several "white-knuckling" jump-seat arrivals in types like the Boeing 737 to 767, Tri-Star and even a Saab 2000!

I like to meet people and make friends, especially in aviation. For example, through a arbitrary meeting at Alençon aerodrome in northern France, I quickly made a friend of an ex-British Airways 747 captain by simply helping to push his tail-dragger C.152 back onto the small hard-standing apron prior to departure. I kept in touch and this chance encounter resulted, several years later, in a Cathay Pacific 747 jump-seat ride into Hong Kong (the 'old' one) on a crystal clear night!

Looking back it's hard to determine *when* my love of aviation really got going. The *why* of it might be easier: my father was in the RAF during the 'Last Big European Disagreement' and my mother was in the WAAF (with a Polish Lancaster squadron in Yorkshire) during the same period. These days I'd dearly love to know the 'why and how' behind seeing a air-to-air photo of my father flying a Harvard solo in Africa, although he was officially 'only' a Flight Engineer. Looking back it seems safe to assume I was brought up with a family 'background hum' attuned to aviation, also because I had two uncles heavily involved in flying.

One flew Dakotas for BOAC after his service career but gave up flying fairly early on. But I still vividly remember him telling me of a wheels-up landing somewhere in Africa or the Middle East. Upon reporting their predicament to ATC the controller responded with: "So you're suspended in the air," to which my far more practical uncle replied: "Until our bloody fuel runs out." It ended well with lots of screeching and sparks but nobody hurt. He was also on the flight which resulted in the fitting of chains to the tailwheels (or 'rear wheels') of BOAC Daks which dragged along the ground after landing to earth any build-up of static. This came about after one poor unfortunate (from memory I'm sure he said it was a stewardess) was killed by the discharge fitting the steps to a Dakota after landing from a long flight through bad weather.

My second uncle, Tommy Gibbs, had a far more illustrious career. We don't meet often but since I got a PPL he's told me some astonishing stories. During the second World War he was a Mosquito 'Pathfinder' pilot and he still doesn't talk of those times. After the war he also joined BOAC but quickly transferred to BEA to spend more time with his family. Starting on Daks he also had an (inevitable?) wheels-up landing, then progressed to Viscounts. He was Captain on the famous complete-hydraulic-failure-after-landing flight into Malta which resulted in the Viscount being embedded in the base of the control tower. Everybody else got out almost unscathed but he was trapped. Early opinions from the rescue team suggested that they should cut his legs off and haul his torso out. Knowing he was only slightly injured he very sensibly refused this drastic offer and around four hours later emerged with (only?) cuts and bruises! He went on to captain Comet 4Bs and ended his career flying Tridents.

But I must tell my favourite story of his which concerns a Dak flight to Lisbon in inclement weather when the wind (westerly or sou'-westerly) had increased in strength, although they didn't know this. His navigator had plotted a point of descent and they dropped down through cloud to emerge in a valley with mountains close by on either side! Climbing back up into the overcast he strongly advised his navigator to plot a generous course bound to descend way out to sea, after which they'd fly back to Lisbon at low level. It now occurs to me that this kind of incident might account for most airlines insisting that flight crew wear white short-sleeved shirts but only with very dark-coloured trousers.

At the tender age of seven in 1954 (I'm reminded, writing this, of the Jesuit claims regarding the significance of this age), my parents moved to a new house just south of London (Heathrow) Airport directly in line with runway 23. Incidentally, my oft-visited grandparents' home was just north of RAF Hendon, still quite active, though mainly with ATC gliders at weekends. At that age and for many, many years to come one thing was always clear in my mind: to pilot any kind of aeroplane, glider to airliner, was something distinctly divorced from anything I could ever hope to achieve. Childhood fantasies had me sitting at the controls, taking command and so on, but I knew it was just that – a fantasy.

When the wind was strong from the south or sou'-sou'-west, especially at night it seemed, heavily burdened Constellations, Super Constellations and Starliners (the best-ever-looking airliner), DC-4s, Stratocruisers perhaps, certainly DC-6s and DC-7Cs, flew out clambering for every foot of height, straight over our house, shaking it. Instead of sleeping (impossible!) I'd pull the bedroom curtains apart and sit crouched down at the window sill marvelling at the prodigious power of these pounding engines spitting flaming exhausts, struggling for every foot of altitude. Kids love noise and those beauties had it in abundance.

It was a wondrous and starkly romantic scene for a youngster. Even at that age I knew that these pilots, with their flight engineers, radio operators, navigators and cabin crew were embarking, as often as not, on a battle with the weather involving huge and frightening primaeval forces and unknown elements at some stage of their flight. At the time those aircrews were mostly equipped with 'cutting-edge state-of-the-art' technology and probably felt very confident. Imagine if they were told of the capabilities, performance and facilities a two-person crew in command of a 747-400 has at their disposal these days? Would or could they believe it?

It was also about that time when big films depicting military heroism were emerging, like *"The Dam Busters," "Battle of the River Plate"* etc., which emphasised that there were individuals prepared to sacrifice their life for a better and greater cause. In my mind, the crews of these airliners were doing little less than that. Only now, of course, I've got to include the passengers and their stoical (resignation?) ability to sit in these machines and take everything thrown at them.

I've one minor claim to fame: my mum worked for Hunting Clan (at Heathrow) and won seats in a draw for family seats on one of their Britannia troop carriers (with sensible rear-facing seats) to the Biggin Hill Air Fair, culminating in a display slot upon departure with all of us on board. For me the whole day and experience was fantastic, barely believable, and I 'lunched out' on it for weeks after, boring stiff and putting-off (even alienating) my best friends at school with endless accounts of this "magic" and "amazing" one-off flight.

I think my first-ever flight was in a Auster, sitting in the back (elated but really wanting a front seat), on a Pleasure Flight purchased by my parents from Weston-super-Mare. It didn't last long, maybe fifteen minutes (felt like fifty seconds), but I still strongly remember the elation coupled with fear as the world I thought I knew so well quickly dropped away, to be quickly replaced with a fantastic landscape completely unfamiliar but slightly recognisable. The approach to land, for the first time ever, was quite beyond belief. The runway looked stupidly short and the approach angle of the Auster seemed insanely steep. Sat strapped into the back seat, quite alone, there was nothing to be done but accept my fate. The fact that the pilot somehow managed to level out and plonk the Auster down with a few rumbles and bumps on the grass runway left me bemused because I was still alive. And unhurt! I'd been transported in broad daylight 'over the moon.'

I've never ever seen myself as a dare-devil type but the audacity we (a few select friends) had in concocting our apron and hangar raids on Heathrow by bicycle seems fantastic when looking back. We'd decided the optimum number was two, and it now seems I was nearly always one of the main instigators attempting a raid. I must have been extremely gullible but on the other hand the temptation to get really close and even inside an aeroplane was almost impossible to resist.

In those days there were several wicket-gates in the perimeter fence for people employed on the airport to use (to walk or cycle to work was very common – few could afford cars), and we used these. Making use of all available cover, like sheds and offices (Nissen type or prefab), we nearly always succeeded in our objective. We were often chased by airport police but usually escaped or evaded them. A bicycle is a formidable weapon amongst closely-spaced buildings. When we were caught we'd get a stern dressing-down and often reacted with consummate cheek, charm and clarity of knowledge. For example, when caught we were often asked if we realised how dangerous it was to be on a runway. I distinctly remember answering on several occasions saying something like: "Please sir, we were on an apron, not the runway or even the taxiway." It says a lot for the forbearance of those police officers because we were never reported, and neither were our parents informed.

So, what did we see? I remember being surprised when a Pan Am engineer insisted we took our shoes off and don little soft 'bootees' to walk inside one of their immaculate (and new) Boeing 707s. Afterwards I was stunned when he shoved an engine and saw it rocking. The cowlings were removed and the engine mounts sat in a simple lateral 'H'-shaped channel with a big cast block at the forward end. Only two or three bolts resisted reverse thrust. It was 'an education.' He told us (I can't remember it exactly): "You see, son, an aeroplane has to be simple, strong and flexible, but only where it matters."

Field Aviation was a prime target and the engineers there (bless them!) were very tolerant of our 'raids.' We saw inside a great variety of airliners and the distinct smell of their hangars and usually stripped-out airliners lingers to this day. Of note we were shown through the Shell executive Airspeed Elizabethans, astonished by such sumptuous arrangements, but always eager to get into the cockpit or flight-deck. One incident stands out: Field's had removed all four old engines and installed four new engines into an immaculate, polished-skin, DC-4 belonging to a Luxembourg airline serving South Africa. Their other aircraft was a Lockheed Constellation. We cycled up on the apron after school just as the flight engineer was about to test-run the engines, and he invited us on board. I wonder if he realised what a thrill that was. He left the small starboard hatch behind the flight-deck open so we could crouch there and be just a few feet away from the shrieking, pounding engines and propellers. From time to time we'd join him on the flight deck and he'd explain what he was doing and what was coming next. He ran the engines up individually, in outboard and inboard pairs, and every combination available. But the whole four at full chat was exhilarating almost beyond belief. The sheer volume of noise, and the aircraft shuddering and vibrating, resisting thrust against brakes, is one of the key moments I'll never forget.

On a quieter but no less satisfying note was an especially daring raid, deeper than any before, to the Cunard-Eagle hangars. Upon arriving and making our request we were told to 'stand by' and we expected that the airport police would soon arrive. Instead a very important-looking man invited us onto the flight-deck of one of their Bristol Britannias and sat us, in turn, in the Captain's seat and explained very thoroughly how to fly this magnificent airliner and how everything worked. Arriving home and telling of our adventures my father (why didn't he give me a severe telling off?) seemed both surprised and perplexed. From my description (he'd worked for Cunard-Eagle), he was certain we'd been 'entertained' by no less than the managing director, Harold Bamberg! I sincerely hope this was true, because it's a lovely memory to the tolerance of the 'big' men in aviation in those days.

Avro Yorks landing, the dysfunctional 'spit-farting' cacophony as the throttles came back, amused us no end. We watched the first Air France Breguet Deux Ponts freighters taking off, a simple procedure – gently accelerate to flying speed over at least 1.5 miles and retract the undercarriage. The curvature of the earth took care of the climb-out. We watched the first Boeing 707s and DC-8s land and take off later, usually trailing long plumes of black smoke, and watched enthralled by the staggering take-off performance of the Convair 880s and 990s.

Sitting on the approach to runway 27 Left in the summer holidays we were treated to a huge range of disparate airliners queuing in, six or more visible at any time. It was especially enjoyable when the wind was up. Daks, Viscounts, DC-6s and 7s, Comets, 707s and DC-8s, and the rest, waggling their wings intent on making a good landing. On one day we (I and my spotter friends) were almost wiped out by huge chunks of ice which smashed into the ground around us, falling from a BEA Viscount. It seems incredible now that none of us were hit. It was high summer and I took a couple of large pieces home. We'd got the registration and in the evening, on getting back from work, my father immediately telephoned BEA to tell them that the de-icing boots on that Viscount weren't working. We'd thought it to be a bit of unusual fun.

At some point, probably around the early 1960s, Heathrow relaxed their prohibition against General Aviation movements. I clearly remember, looking through the perimeter fence by telescope, watching a most improbable sight. Tracking across the vast expanse of Heathrow was a 'Follow-Me' Land-Rover leading a similar-sized Piper Tri-Pacer out to take off from runway 27 Left. It's an indelible memory, the Tri-Pacer appeared to lift off the massive runway almost immediately. My log books have long been lost, but I still wonder which Piper Tri-Pacer it was and who was flying it.

It's funny how for every memory dredged up five more surface. So I'm going to add a few more and see what happens. At the end of one early Biggin Hill Air Fair I was sauntering, in company with my best friend at that time, Mike Parker, who later became, and still is, a highly regarded aeronautical engineer (and still a very good friend), towards the threshold to runway 03 when departing aircraft were using the reciprocal 21. During the air show three Mosquitos had performed a sedate and constrained display. Realising the Mosquitos were about to depart we halted short of the threshold. Beyond the end of runway 21 at Biggin Hill is a long low valley. The Mosquitos took off, and with virtually nobody watching except us two youngsters, they stayed low and performed a line-astern slow roll down through the valley into the setting sun. That's one hell of a memory.

Another couple of memories concern how quickly and quietly old aeroplanes crash. One was at Rochester, an air show beset by bad weather, when Tiger Moth 'CDC was still going to display its low-level 'crazy-flying' slot. I turned away for some reason and looked back to see a heap of crumpled aeroplane before us. I believe the pilot was not seriously hurt. On another occasion, also with Mike Parker, we were touring by foot the aircraft to be seen at Farnborough, when we looked back at the main display runway and saw a small tangled mess on it. We later learned this was the remains of a Bristol Bulldog. Again, it seemed at the time unbelievable, but the pilot survived.

As we got older and bolder our parents let us strike out by bicycle to aerodromes further afield. Later on, day trips by bicycle to Gatwick especially were common, which seemed to present a never-ending array of rare and unusual types and registrations. One weekend about six of us planned to stay overnight. It resulted in one of the most memorable and evocative sights I've ever seen. The air was still and frosty and to the east the sun was rising and to the west the sky was still dark with stars clearly visible. A Spanish Super Constellation started up, typically clouding the terminal with huge wreaths of smoke, taxied out to the west and took off into the sunrise. Banking left it departed downwind and disappeared into the clear dark starlit sky.

Reading the previous two books in this series, (the word 'reading' seems pathetically inadequate to convey the pleasure involved), I've noticed a curious omission in descriptions of late fifties/early sixties air displays involving the Tiger Club (except briefly in Vol.2) – the arrival of the tiny, pert and spectacular Cosmic Wind. It probably comes outside the strict remit of these books but I hope I'll be forgiven for wishing to mention it. As kids we loved it arriving, usually second-perfect at low level and at a seemingly searing speed, and then scorching around the sky like a wasp that had just stung itself. Most of its wild gyrations were accompanied by heart-stopping cackles and coughs as the engine seemed to die on anything much outside straight and level flight. I'm exaggerating of course, but that little aeroplane was very exciting to watch, a firm favourite.

In this series of memories much has been made of how flying in the fifties, the relative freedom and so on, has disappeared forever. As a latecomer PPL I'm really in no position to do so but I'd still like to disagree a bit! Factually it has, of course, but emotionally I'm sure large lumps still survive and I'd like to give an example involving small memories but all the better for it, I hope. This story involves a Cessna 150, which will probably result in huge groans, but it really can be a fun aeroplane to fly. And anyway, for pilots in my position, especially from a financial point of view, getting access to something involving dope, fabric and wood is nigh-on impossible unless you build it yourself.

Quite a bit of my flying (in the '90s) involves operating out of a superb farm strip west of Cambridge. As often as not nobody else is around. It's all down to you, the pilot, to exercise the discipline required to conduct a safe flight. These days most of Norfolk and Suffolk is completely free airspace, nearly all the military bases have long since closed and at weekends the couple that survive have their MATZ (Military Air Traffic Zones) suspended.

Together with my friend Guy Browning (of Concorde TCAS fame), also a PPL, we arrived at the strip on one occasion intent on flying to a small aerodrome in Norfolk. Guy took the outward leg and on the way we decided to play with the ADF, little knowing that the alternator had failed so we were flying on a dying battery; strangely, the low-voltage light failed to illuminate. We found our destination eventually, without realising the reason why the ADF appeared to be unreliable. Upon leaving we found the battery totally flat. What to do?

It was my leg and I thought we didn't need anything electrical to get back. Just an engine that worked and 'full and free' controls. Guy thought about it but agreed. We found someone to swing the prop, my first experience of this, and it was a hard job to get the Continental going. After all, it wasn't designed to be hand-swung. Eventually, after we'd probably given up, to be honest, the engine caught and we taxied out, did the few checks remaining, and took off. I loved it and I'm sure Guy did too. No radio, no beacon, no flaps, just the two of us navigating along free as a bird into the setting sun, basically depending only on the Continental engine to keep humming away. We found the farm without any difficulty and – feeling a bit exuberant might have helped – managed to get a flapless 'greaser' onto the long thousand-metre grass runway, stopping, even in the still air, in well less than 500 metres. We 'booked-in' and left a note saying the alternator was u/s and the battery totally flat. And I drove home feeling very well satisfied.

I suspect the microlight community and PFA home-builders and pilots are also keeping the concept of flying freedom very much alive. Flying from one farm strip to another, we rarely use the radio except to tune it into a frequency which, hopefully, will provide us with assistance should an emergency arise. There's still a lot of free and open sky and farm strips and aerodromes which rely on the 'honour' system to book in and out and put the landing fee (if applicable) into a small box if you're visiting out of hours.

I've attempted to prove that the "spirit of flying in the fifties" is far from finished. Let's do all we can to keep things that way!

CHAPTER 7

A LESSON FROM JAN ZURAKOWSKI

by

Timothy R. V. Foster

[NOTES ON THE AUTHOR: Timothy Foster made his first solo in "Maggie" G-AITN at Croydon in 1955, aged 17. He moved to Canada in 1956 and obtained his airline transport licence, writing and publishing the Fostair Instrument Course the while. He moved to New York in 1974 and bought a Piper Comanche 250, which resulted in him writing "The Aircraft Owner's Handbook," a best-seller. He returned to the UK in 1986, where he continues to work as a writer, with over 20 books to his credit.

Incidentally, during the early fifties Tim and I were at school together at Lancing College (overlooking Shoreham Airport) and it is him I must thank for introducing me seriously to the world of aeroplanes back in 1952. – Ed.]

A favourite hangout of the fifties for me was the Farnborough air show put on by the SBAC – the Society of British Aircraft Constructors. Farnborough was where I saw, over the years, the Hawker Hunter piloted by Neville Duke break the sound barrier, the enormous eight-engine Bristol Brabazon with Bill Pegg at the controls, the appealingly ugly Saro Princess flying boat, the Avro Vulcan escorted by three little mini-Vulcans (Avro 707s), the DH Comet jetliner flown by John Cunningham, and Ranald Porteous doing strange things with an Auster Aiglet Trainer.

One particularly memorable display was that put on by Jan Zurakowski, Gloster's chief test pilot and a wartime Polish fighter pilot in the RAF, doing something called 'Zurabatics.' He would take a Meteor, which had a jet engine on each wing, climb it vertically, then throttle back one engine while going to full power with the other. The Meteor rotated like a Catherine wheel about its vertical axis, which was parallel to the ground, since the aircraft was going straight up. Most impressive.

A few years later, Zurakowski moved to Canada to test-fly the Avro Canada CF-105 Arrow, the first Canadian supersonic aircraft (maiden flight, March 25th 1958). The Arrow was eventually cancelled in a cost-cutting binge and Zurakowski retired, settling in a Polish-Canadian enclave called Barry's Bay, Ontario, about 130 miles north-east of Toronto, in the boondocks.

I moved to Toronto in 1956, with my PPL in my pocket. I got my commercial licence in 1961 and was married the same year. Now my new wife, Julie, née Chapeskie, was from the same Barry's Bay. Her brother,

69

Andy, was the local doctor and a keen private pilot and fisherman. His goal was to have a seaplane so he could go and fish in untouched waters. Being an enterprising fellow, he decided to build one himself – a homebuilt.

He bought a set of plans from one Volmer Jensen of California for a two-seater amphibian, the VJ-22 Sportsman, with the engine mounted on a pylon above the wing as a pusher. To save construction costs, the idea was to use the wings from an Aeronca Champion or Chief, a two-seater high-wing, and Andy came up with an undamaged set from an old wreck.

The fuselage/hull was made of mahogany plywood and spruce, covered in fibreglass. Construction took about two years. Since the Canadian Department of Transport required that the first ten hours flown in a homebuilt be carried out by a pilot with at least 150 hours flying time, Andy had a problem: he only had about 70 hours. I had about 665 hours, so he asked me if I'd do the first ten hours, which, of course, means also doing the first ten minutes – like the bit that's never been flown before!

Like, be a test pilot! Well, alright! That sounds like fun! I was 26. It would be cool (this was 1964).

As luck would have it, a few months earlier, having earned my instrument and multi-engine ratings, I acted as co-pilot with a friend, who had just bought a new Beech Baron, on a trip from Toronto to Los Angeles.

Pete Silverman was a very wealthy young man and decided to shoot some of the works on the best light twin $150,000 could buy. He asked me to advise him: I recommended a Baron. I specified the avionics and we ended up with the finest Baron in the world for that time – 1963, CF-PAS. All Collins avionics, HSI, RMI, de-ice boots and prop slingers.

We flew to LA in three hops on October 11th, 1963 – Toronto-Chicago (2 hours 25 minutes), Chicago-Tucumcari NM (4 hours 55 minutes, including 30 minutes night) and TCC-Van Nuys (north LA) (4 hours 50 minutes, all at night). We left Toronto just after noon Eastern time and touched down about 16 hours later in LA at one thirty in the morning Pacific time.

I had called Volmer Jensen, who lived in LA, in advance to set up a demonstration flight in his original Sportsman, N7902C. On October 13th we met up at San Fernando airport and I had a 20-minute flight. I had never flown an aircraft with a high-mounted pusher engine before. This configuration results in a slight idiosyncrasy in flight. In a conventional aeroplane with the engine in the nose, when you reduce power the nose drops, which is good, because that naturally tends to maintain speed. And when you increase power, the nose rises. In a pusher with a high thrust line, it's the other way around. Throttle back, nose rises. Add power, it drops. But you get used to it. So that's what it's like.

October 16th we flew the Baron back to Toronto, again in three hops. VNY-Denver (a l-o-o-o-o-ng way, 900 miles, especially when you have to take a pee one hour out! It took five hours. Three of those were on oxygen at 16,000 feet [mountains, you know]. The last four hours were a progression of agony. It never occurred to me to use a barf bag as a urinal!), DEN-Rockford, Illinois (4 hours 10 minutes, all at night) and RFD-Toronto (2 hours 35 minutes, all at night), arriving home at 4.45 am, Eastern daylight time. Since we left LA at 11.20 Pacific time, the trip took 14 hours 25 minutes.

So I was well primed for the test flight of Andy's Sportsman. This took place seven months later. Since I was not rated for water-flying, the testing was done from an airport. Fortunately, just a few miles from Barry's Bay is Bonnechere, a huge wartime emergency airstrip, with a 6,600 x 200 foot concrete runway and virtually no traffic. Andy had trailered the aircraft out to the airfield from his garage the week before and assembled it at the strip.

The night before he had carried out the 'weight and balance,' a complex procedure involving putting the whole aircraft (which weighed 1,500 pounds) on three weigh-scales (one for each wheel), weighing it, and then doing some very complex calculations to determine if the aircraft's centre of gravity was within design limits. All appeared correct.

On May 15th, 1964, at 6.10 pm, in the calm of early evening, I started CF-PNC up the first time. It had a 100 hp engine equipped with an electric starter: hand-swinging a rearward-facing prop mounted on an engine on a gantry three feet above the wing was not the answer.

Oil pressure OK. Fuel flow good. No significant drop in RPM at 1,800 when each of the magnetos was turned off, one by one. Full-power run-up against the chocks. RPM 2,700. Throttle back to 1,200, apply carburettor heat and see the expected drop in revs. There's not much else you can do to delay making it actually move. Pretty soon you have to deliver, and fly it.

But not tonight. First, there are the taxi tests.

I waved away the chocks and started gently moving forward. There was no air traffic. I taxied to the nearest end of the runway, did the famous TTMFFGHH, looked around and lined up.

I gently eased the throttle open and applied rudder to keep it straight. I increased taxying speed to about 30-40 mph. I opened her up to full power and eased the stick to neutral from fully back. The tail rose properly. All seemed well. I throttled back and coasted to a stop. First taxy test OK.

71

There was no wind, so I turned around at the other end of the runway, took a good look all over (no control tower) and repeated the exercise. And again, and again.

I taxied back to the tie-down area and shut down. Andy had this huge grin on his face. I felt pretty good, too. He wanted to inspect the aeroplane and make sure everything still looked unharmed. Andy took the engine cowling off and checked all the lines and cables. Everything was still connected. No leaks, no problems.

It was still quite light, so I took her out again for some more taxy tests up and down the runway. This time, as the speed built up at full power, I gently lifted her off the runway and flew down it at about ten feet altitude for a little way, then I reduced power and let her land.

Quite comfortable. I turned around at the end and ran the exercise again. Another gentle lift-off.

Well, I wasn't going to fly tonight for real. It was almost 8.30 pm and soon it would be dark. I taxied back and helped a still-grinning Andy tie her down for the night.

One of Julie's sisters, Noel, was getting married this weekend. You can imagine how popular Andy and I were dealing with our private set of priorities in the face of a Polish-Catholic wedding in a family of seven grown children. Old man Chapeskie sort of owned the town, too.

The groom was an Englishman, David Hopkins. I had introduced him to Noel. He and I were not Catholics, but we sort of played the party line. I've never seen so many nuns. The best man was a school chum of David's (they both had the decency to go to Harrow and Oxford) – a baronet. So here's this 25-year-old young man, with his wife, and they're Sir John and Lady something-or-other. Barry's Bay had never seen anything like it.

At the ceremony, Sir John (not his real name) performed the traditional English habit of reading smutty telegrams. The one I remember was: "If an apple a day keeps the doctor away, what will a pear do at night?" I loved it. The nuns didn't though. Nobody laughed. David was torn between guffawing loyally at his best man's jocule and displaying an image of propriety as befits one joining the super-devout Chapeskie clan. He ended up holding his breath. Everyone else just looked uncomfortable.

That probably explains why we only did one testing session that day, from 5.55 to 7.10 pm. "Several flights down runway," says my logbook. "'Nuff said," says I.

The next day we were rid of all this wedding nonsense and we got down to some serious aviating. After a few more repeats of the previous tentative flying activities and one last check, it was time: 7.30 pm (the air is nice and calm in the evening). First full flight. As the end of the runway passed under me, I addressed the fact that I would now have to turn the aircraft. The problems were: (a) the runway was now behind me and (b) the rudder didn't seem to be too effective. Apply lots of rudder and you get very little yaw, either way. Now you don't need a load of rudder to turn an aircraft, but you do like it to be effective. I gently banked her to the left and brought her around 180° to downwind. Alright, but not great. There certainly wasn't going to be any problem getting her back on the ground, but the feel of the rudder control was undesirable. So the approach and landing were fine. I taxied in and Andy looked ecstatic. I told him about the rudder problem.

"It's not a disaster, but I don't want to fly it again until we figure it out," I said.

"Let's talk to Zurakowski." Being the doctor, Andy knew everybody.

He told me about Zurakowski having retired to a nearby lodge in the hills.

I was stunned. "*The* Jan Zurakowski? I used to watch him at Farnborough when I was a kid! Wow!!"

We drove the few miles down dirt roads to Zura's place and Andy introduced me. He was very friendly and keen to help. I explained the problem and asked him what it looked like to him.

"It sounds like it's tail-heavy. Have you done the weight and balance?"

Andy said: "Yes. C. of G. was within limits."

"Better check your numbers."

"That's it?"

"That's where I'd start."

We thanked him and left.

He was correct, of course. Andy and I went through the numbers very carefully (this was before pocket calculators). There it was. A simple error in addition. The aircraft was tail-heavy. The Centre of Gravity was actually behind the design aft limit. We calculated what it would take to correct it. Eleven pounds of lead in the nose!

So we got some weights and installed them up front, ahead of the rudder pedals, then we reweighed everything and did the calculations again.

We did them thrice and each time they came out the same, now within limits.

The next morning I flew it again. It was beautiful! What a difference! I did a series of flights and gained more knowledge about the aircraft. Nothing too hairy, just a lot of take-offs and landings. By the end of the visit, the VJ-22 had logged seven hours and fifteen minutes. Andy and I thanked Zurakowski and I headed back to Toronto.

I returned a couple of times and checked Andy out in it. Then I left him to his own devices. A few months later he removed the engine, installed a more powerful 125 hp model and turned it around so it faced the front. He also enlarged the fin and rudder, making them more effective. The aircraft became a delight to fly with no further need for lead in the nose.

A year later I spent several hours flying it off the local lake with Andy. Sheer bliss! There's that moment just before you touch down on the water when you detect that it's one foot from your bottom and you are doing about 60 mph, then it kisses the water. I did one hour just literally taking off from the lake, climbing to 50 feet, cruising along a bit, turning a few degrees and landing, doing it again and again, probably 30 or 40 times in the hour. An unforgettable delight.

Two years later Andy got fed up with the poor load-carrying capacity of the Sportsman and he sold it and bought an old Republic Seabee – a four-seater amphib. big enough to sleep two. On the delivery flight the buyer of the Sportsman ran out of fuel, crashed and wrote it off. No injuries, though. But no aeroplane can fly for long without fuel. Here endeth the lesson.

CHAPTER 8

THE 1953 CRANWELL PASSING OUT PARADE

by

Peter Campbell

*[I gratefully acknowledge the cooperation of the Air Officer Comm-
anding and Commandant of the Royal Air Force College, Cranwell, not
only for the loan of photographic negatives but also permission to
reproduce part of an article which first appeared in the* "Journal of the
Royal Air Force College" *for November 1953. – Ed.]*

It was obligatory at Lancing College, where I was at school from 1951-55,
to join the Cadet Force, starting off for the first year in the Army section.
Apart from the inevitable drill practices, instruction on how to clean
uniform buttons and belts with Duraglit and pulling a piece of 'four-by-
two' through the barrel of a ·303 rifle, we were occasionally given duties
on the outdoor shooting range, which more often than not meant being
sent to the receiving end of the range with instructions to hold up a
pointer on a long stick to indicate which part of the target had been hit (if
anyone managed to be that accurate!). Another frequent detail was to
march to the top of nearby Boiler Hill (a local trig point) and learn how to
identify local geographical features from a large map before it was
snatched from your hands by the gusting winds. While Friday afternoons
passed fairly quickly this way, it was possible after a year to join the Air
Force section instead, and this made life a lot more interesting, as we
were taught things I considered useful, like meteorology, principles of
flight and aircraft recognition. I was made Flight Sergeant in charge of
the Cadets during my last year at school, although I suspect that this may
have been a case of "Hobson's Choice" for the CO, Bill Dovell.

A few days later, at the end of the summer term, we were all sent off
to Camp at RAF Cranwell. My diary records the list of things which we
were told to pack: kitbag, groundsheet, emergency ration card, Service
Record book, extra pair of shoes, extra pair of trousers, coat, towel, soap,
toothbrush, toilet paper, change of underclothing, pair of gym-shoes,
swimming trunks, running vest, running shorts, knife, fork, spoon and
drinking mug. This medley was all sent by rail addressed to: Cadet
Campbell, Lancing College Contingent, CCF Summer Camp, c/o RAF
Station, Cranwell, Lincolnshire.

We went to Cranwell by train directly from school, arriving on the
26th July. I can remember that, as could only be expected, we were kept
pretty busy, but that the food and accommodation were not at all bad,
considering. In accordance with standard forces procedure we had been
ordered to salute any officer we should pass, and after a confusing

incident the first afternoon shortly after leaving the NAAFI mess I had to remember that in future I should be sure to hold my cutlery and mug in my *left* hand!

On our second full day at Cranwell, the 28th July, a very important event took place at the College, although at the time I was not able to appreciate its full significance, except that I gathered it was the annual Passing Out parade. Now, after some research all of forty-five years later, I know that it was indeed the annual Passing Out Parade, but made even more of a special occasion because, being Coronation Year, the Duke of Edinburgh had graciously agreed to attend.

So it was that the 28th July turned out to be one of the most serendipitous days of my young life. Despite changeable weather a large number of aircraft descended on Cranwell South airfield, and to my surprise and delight we were allowed to wander around them all, quite unmolested, during lunchtime and the early afternoon.

Although most of the aircraft were service types, I remember discovering tucked away amongst the larger aircraft the Autocrat G-AJIE and the Miles Nighthawk G-AGWT (flown in by its owner, Wing Commander Grece). However, it is a pity that, out of all the records that I have kept since I first started 'spotting' in 1952, this event proves to be the only one where I have only very incomplete details of the aircraft present, as the grubby bit of paper that I recorded them all on must have been mislaid many years ago.

It has always been in my mind to try and obtain more information about this event. Recent correspondence with Jean Buckberry, the librarian and archivist at Cranwell, has revealed that there are no official records available detailing the aircraft attending on that day; in fact the only records that exist are an article which appeared later that year in the official College magazine and a number of photographic negatives. I was granted permission to quote from this article, and also to use any of the negatives I wished; and so I eagerly awaited the set of some seventy negatives to arrive so that I could resolve some of the identities of the attending aircraft. But in reality it was of course the Duke who was the centre of attention on that day, not the aircraft, and the pictures taken reflect that; nevertheless I was able to directly confirm the identities of some of them.

Then, by checking and cross-checking my other records, I have done my best to produce as near a complete list as possible. At least the *numbers* of each type present are correct, although their *identities* are for the most part deduced rather than known for certain. In the list that follows, serial numbers *not* followed by an asterisk are the only ones known for certain.

AIRCRAFT THOUGHT TO HAVE ATTENDED THE PASSING OUT PARADE AT CRANWELL ON THE 28TH JULY 1953

J/1 Autocrat	G-AJIE
Chipmunk:	WD373, WK353, WK363, WK565, WG566, WK516, WK518, WK556, WK557, WK559, WK560, WK561, WK562, WK567, WK568, WK569, WK570, WK581, WK586, WP844, WP845, WP853, WP854, WP855, WP859, WP860, WP862, WP866, WP869, WP903, WZ865, WZ874 (mostly part of the College fleet)
Anson:	PH698*, TX154, TX173*, TX256*, VM308*, VM315*, VM317*, VM330*, VM361*, VM378*, VM408*, VV257, VV258*, VV294*, VV325*
Canberra:	WH650*
Dakota:	KN446*, KP208*
Devon:	VP958*, VP961 (the Duke of Edinburgh's aircraft), VP963*, VP966*, VP968*, VP974*, VP975*, WB534*
Harvard:	ET 271*,FS752 (coded AH), FT354, KF703
Meteor 4:	RA368 + 7 more unidentified
Nighthawk:	G-AGWT
Oxford:	LB410*
Proctor 4:	NP178*
Shackleton 2:	VP287*, WB822*, WL751*
Spitfire:	EP770*
Valetta:	VL282*, VX576, VW820*, WD168*
Varsity:	WF419*

During our stay we were also given flights in the College's Chipmunks (I flew in WK556 & WK567). In 1953 I had only ever flown once before (in a Dominie at Lee-on-Solent in 1950) and so aerobatics was an entirely new experience for me; I remember that loops were actually quite enjoyable once you got used to them, but that barrel rolls, which seemed to be this particular pilot's *pièce de resistance*, had me feeling queasy for the rest of the day.

On the last of our three days we were taken by coach for a quick visit to Skegness. At the time I knew that there was an aerodrome at Boston, so was very disappointed to see nothing as we went past. It was just as well that I didn't know about the existence of Ingoldmells aerodrome at Skegness, or I would have felt let down twice as much!

The article commemorating the royal visit appeared in the "*Journal of the Royal Air Force College*" for November 1953, and read in part as follows:

"THE VISIT OF H.R.H. THE DUKE OF EDINBURGH TO THE COLLEGE, JULY 1953

There could have been no more fitting a close to a Royal Term than the visit to Cranwell on 28th July of Marshal of the Royal Air Force His Royal Highness The Duke of Edinburgh, K.G., P.C., K.T., G.B.E., who honoured the College with his presence at the passing-out parade of No. 59 Entry and No. 10 (E. & S.) Entry.

Fitful though the summer of 1953 had been till then, the day itself proved warm with a noticeable touch of dampness in a wind which persisted throughout the morning. As the time approached for the march on of the Cadet Wing, grey clouds began to heap in the west and rain seemed, momentarily, to threaten. But a sky that was all but covered fifteen minutes before His Royal Highness drove through the Main Gates had almost cleared by the time the Inspection was over. Once again Cranwell's extraordinary good fortune with the weather held. This was an April day in high summer.

In many ways the occasion of the visit of His Royal Highness was remarkable. Coming as it did at the end of a term that had been punctuated by loyal preparation for the Coronation, one might have expected an air of strain within the College, an air that might very easily have been communicated not only to staff but also, imperceptibly, to the many guests and spectators who came to Cranwell to witness the parade and to participate in the ceremonial. Taut nerves might have betrayed their presence in over-organisation and elaborate and unnecessary preparation. But, if memory can be trusted in the comparisons it automatically makes with former occasions of the moment, it was with a minimum of fuss and with tremendous élan that the College received the Royal Visitor. The crowds, one noticed, outside the gates took up their position in an orderly manner without official assistance of any sort, and inside one could plainly see in the parade itself an air of confidence and buoyancy of spirit which made this occasion unique. Was it for this reason that an Old Cranwellian, a member of No. 46 Entry, was heard to remark after the ceremony that this had been the best passing-out parade he had ever seen?

His Royal Highness arrived at Cranwell in a Devon aircraft flying his own personal standard. As it came to rest outside Air Traffic, His Royal Highness could be seen at the controls with his flying instructor, Flight Lieutenant C. R. Gordon, in No. 2's position. . . .

With the parade in review order the Colour and escort marched on under its ensign. . . . This was a dramatic moment before the pause that heralded the arrival of His Royal Highness and, even as the band played the traditional 'Greensleeves,' the Colour caught the wind and unfurled, flapping heavily.

Punctually at 1058 hours His Royal Highness arrived at the west flank of the parade ground and was escorted to the saluting base by the Commandant and other officials. The parade then greeted His Royal Highness with a triumphal fanfare played on this occasion on the seven silver trumpets recently presented to the College. The Royal Salute followed, majestically, and at this moment, high above the parade, His Royal Highness's personal standard was broken at the masthead. As the last strains of the National Anthem died away, Flight Cadet Under Officer Cock stepped forward and reported in a firm, strong voice to His Royal Highness that the Queen's Colour and Cadet Wing were now ready for inspection. Hardly had Flight Cadet Under Officer Cock completed his report when His Royal Highness began to descend the steps of the saluting base. He halted for a fraction of a second, it seemed, on the imperative "Sir!" and then quickly moved across the parade ground with the parade commander to begin his inspection of the Wing.

From afar it was difficult to pick out the faces of those to whom His Royal Highness spoke in the course of his progress down the ranks, but it was observed that he paused for a long time in conversation with several senior cadets before reaching the Colour party. The Colour itself, ensign and escort clearly caught His Royal Highness's attention: and subsequently as he passed down the rest of the super-numerary rank, he stopped with a jerk more than once to speak to certain senior cadets, among them Senior Flight Cadets Organ and Butt. He had many questions, also, for the recipients of Coronation medals and for cadets from overseas.

After the inspection the Cadet Wing formed close column on the west flank in preparation for the march past, first in slow time and then in quick. Hardly had the order "Close order" been given and dressing taken up to a drum roll when a Meteor carried out an unrehearsed flypast to the south-west of the parade ground. Coordination between the band and the parade was excellent and, though there appeared to be a certain amount of exaggerated movement in the rear and left of the parade as dressing was taken up before the slow march past, there was an unusual sprightliness in the way commands were obeyed by the parade: bearing, generally, was very good, and the marching was firm, confident and full of the pride of Service.

At this point, the climax of the parade, the sun came out. It picked up the whites, greys, yellows and blues in the Royal Standard. The Cadet Wing reformed line and advanced in review order, halted and presented arms in a second Royal Salute. The presentation of awards then followed. For this His Royal Highness descended once more from the saluting base. As the Assistant Commandant, Group Captain E.D.McK. Nelson, read out the names of the winners of awards, so each stepped smartly up to His Royal Highness. The Sword of Honour went to Flight Cadet Under Officer Cock, the Queen's Medal to Flight Cadet Under Officer Henderson, and the Medal of Honour to Flight Cadet Under Officer N.A. Parker.

The presentations over, His Royal Highness moved to the saluting base and delivered his inspiring Address.

The ceremony was now reaching its close. The Colour was marched off, as tradition demands, up the steps into the College and, as tradition also demands, the passing-out entries followed slowly up the same steps into the Entrance Hall, now commissioned officers of the Royal Air Force.

Watched by His Royal Highness the Band played the Cadet Wing off parade. The echo of the boom and crash of drums and cymbals from the west flank wall suddenly reminded spectators that the parade ground was almost empty. From behind the College itself came the words of command of a new senior term dismissing the squadrons for the first time and it was at this moment, from an easterly direction, that a second intruding Meteor flew in accidental salute over a now empty parade ground. . . .

At 1230 hours His Royal Highness The Duke of Edinburgh arrived on the tarmac to inspect the Flying Wing Parade. The Commandant presented Wing Commander I.N. MacDougall, Officer Commanding Flying Wing, and Wing Commander G.W.J. Cozens, Officer Commanding Technical Wing. His Royal Highness then passed slowly down the long line of officers, NCOs and airmen drawn up by squadrons in front of their aircraft. Squadron Commanders presented their officers to His Royal Highness who evinced in conversation a keen interest in flying and in the Royal Air Force. Few Long Service medals, post-war campaign stars or proficiency badges escaped his attention. At the conclusion of his inspection His Royal Highness drove slowly back along the tarmac to the accompaniment of cheers from the Flying Wing. The Royal car then returned to the College by a route which led through the East Camp. This gave the married families an opportunity of expressing their loyalty and their appreciation of the Royal visit. . . .

The senior under officers and under officers of No. 60 Entry were presented to His Royal Highness and, in the company of No. 60 Entry, he watched the fine flying display given by four Meteors of No. 203 A.F.S. led by Flight Lieutenant A. Lang of No. 16 Entry . . .

The flying display over, His Royal Highness returned for a brief moment into the College to sign the Visitors' Book, and re-emerged as flight cadets and spectators closed in to bid him a loyal farewell. As his car drove off a great cheer went up from all assembled on the parade ground and the Orange, a cheer which the waiting crowds outside the gates took up as His Royal Highness's car passed down the Sleaford road on its way to the airfield. On the airfield the officers who had piloted the Meteors in the flying display only fifteen minutes before were presented to His Royal Highness, his last official act before his departure.

The door of the Devon aircraft stood open. His Royal Highness took his leave of the Commandant and members of the Royal Party, mounted the steps and disappeared from view in the fuselage of the aircraft. A few moments later he was seen once again in the pilot's seat of his aircraft and it was minutes only before he was airborne."

CHAPTER 9
FROM BOTH SIDES:
SOME PERSONAL MEMORIES
by
John Havers

[NOTES ON THE AUTHOR: Born at Southminster, Essex, in 1927, his earliest memory of aviation is seeing a large formation of aircraft one summer (about 1933) which was likely the Royal Air Force annual Air Exercises. A family move to Great Dunmow in 1934 saw the nearest air activity at North Weald followed later by Debden. The second World War changed all that. Armed with the "Aeroplane Spotter," he was appointed in 1940 – together with his friend David Wallace – school spotter and 'stood to' whenever an air raid warning occurred. Surrounded by airfields and aviation it was no wonder the 'bug' was taken. After Army service his first professional job in aviation from September 1948 was with the Ministry of Civil Aviation at Croydon airport, which lasted six months. He then joined the Air Registration Board, remaining with them until absorbed by the Civil Aviation Authority in 1972, and continuing until retirement in 1987. An interesting and varied career which included management of the annual United Kingdom Airworthiness Course held at the University of Kent. A founder member of Air-Britain for whom he has been over many years the specialist in Near and Middle East civil aviation. – Ed.]

From the above you will know that much of my working life was involved with the regulatory side of civil aviation and so despite being an enthusiast, almost for ever, it was not always desirable or convenient to keep notes because of a possible conflict of interests. The ramblings that follow have been resurrected by consulting old diaries and notes, but mostly from memory of events which even now are all too clear, in an attempt to tell something of what was happening in the 1950s both from a personal and professional point of view. The coincidences and connecting events, often years apart, which play such a part in ones' memories, are also included. One area so often neglected is the individual contribution made, particularly by engineers, to the development of aviation and so many names appear throughout this narrative – no, it is not name-dropping, just that without these people aviation would have never got off the ground.

My working life at the Air Registration Board (ARB) during the 1950s was concerned with the approval of Maintenance Schedules, a department led by the indefatigable Ted Tonkin, well known for ingenious ideas for these essential documents. These were required for all operators, be they BOAC or BEA, charter companies, one-man joyriding concerns or flying clubs which operated for 'hire or reward.' Many colourful people visited our offices, then in Brettenham House just off the Strand in London, who, if you listened to them long enough, were going to change the whole face of air transport and succeed where others had failed. Some did of course and much of the success of UK air transport today can be traced back to the difficult days of the 1950s.

This then brought me into contact with these very individual people, many of them 'characters,' who came mostly from the engineering side of aviation. Some that come readily to mind are Ray Aspden (Eagle Aviation), Bob Batt and Charles Murrell (Aviation Traders), Tommy Atkins (Channel Airways), Jack Humphries (Silver City Airways), Frank Horridge (Dan-Air), Tom Chandler (Jersey Airlines), W.A. Wilkinson (Scottish Airlines), J.A. 'Mac' McTaggart (Skyways), Russell Whyham (Air Navigation & Trading), Tom Howie (Autair), Norman Monnick-endam (Tradair), Bill Meacock (William Dempster), Wally Bateman (Morton Air Services), Keith Belcher (BKS), Eric Holden (Don Everall), Marion Kozubski (Independent Air Travel), A.S.K. "Buster" Paine (Airwork), Bill Richardson (Transair), Pete Palmer (Orion Airways), Bill Kelly (Air Couriers) – later a colleague, D.M. 'Ginger' Ebbutt (Trans-World Charter) and Sid Leicester (Olley Air Service). Among the characters from the 'lighter' end of aviation was Norman Giroux, who had operated joyriding from Southport sands since long before the second World War. Every year prior to Easter he would travel down to London by taxi in order to get his schedule re-approved. I always regret not managing to get to Southport to take up an offer of a ride in his Fox Moth.

Away from the working day opportunities to fly came along, mostly from Croydon, with among the highlights my first landing at Heathrow on 24th June 1950 in Rapide G-AGUF of Island Air Services flown by Ray Rendall. This was on a positioning flight to begin a weekend of joyriding, so familiar at Heathrow in those days. Undoubtedly the top of the list was Short Sealand G-AKLO, in which, along with Don Conway, I went to Rochester on the 16th June 1951. Winning the toss of a coin, which was a bit unfair because Don had negotiated the trip, I got the right-hand seat and en route the pilot, Don Tanton, asked if I had ever landed on water. The answer being negative we proceeded to do a touch-and-go on the Medway before landing at the airport. (An interesting follow-up came in 1987 shortly before retirement when, after visiting Rochester to view the Sunderland G-BJHS, in my mail I found a book on Britannia Airways presented to me by Frank Bateman on behalf of the UK Operators Technical Group, of which I had been CAA secretary. The first page I opened had a picture of Don Tanton whom I had not heard of in all those years!) G-AKLO was the European and North Africa demonstrator which late in 1952 went to Shell and was operated in the Far East. Another pleasant trip was in Moth Minor G-AFNI with Don Chubb on the 23rd August 1952 to Redhill to visit the Experimental Flying Group, during which Ian Forbes made what was said to be the first flight of Heath Parasol G-AFZE following its being re-engined with a Bristol Cherub III.

Before leaving these flight reminiscences, here is one more from early 1960. With the introduction of British prop- and pure-jet aircraft in the first five years of the decade, flying opportunities did come along, for amongst the development flying was a requirement to complete some 200 hours of route-proving. On many of the flights two seats were allocated to ARB staff and my first was on the Vanguard, originally scheduled for 12th March 1960 to Copenhagen or Dusseldorf, but which slipped to 30th April when we went to Gibraltar. (My colleague on this trip, Cyril Page, had last flown in a Bristol Bombay over the Western Desert in 1942!) This was the time when Gibraltar saw regular visits from Viscounts of BEA (such as G-ANHD) or Airwork (such as G-APNE). Based there with the Royal Air Force were Canberras and Shackleton 2s; a number of Luftwaffe Lockheed T-33s were also to be seen.

Airfield visits and attendance at various aeronautical events are the spice of life for any enthusiast and I was no exception. The regular Saturday morning visit to Croydon usually produced something new and it would take more than this chapter to list all at that time regarded as interesting. The awe-inspiring sight of the Bristol Brabazon G-AGPW flying by at Farnborough in September 1949, only days after its first flight, became even more impressive when viewed at Heathrow on the 25th June 1950 on its first landing away from Filton, for flights over London. For this you were taken on a coach tour around the aircraft and as a reporter noted at the time: "It took me two-and-a-half minutes to walk once round the 130-ton Brabazon." We didn't get the chance and had to wait until Farnborough of that year. This year is the 50th anniversary of the Brab's first flight.

Equally impressive was the sight of Saunders-Roe Princess G-ALUN making its majestic fly-by at Farnborough in 1952, "dominating the proceedings," it was said in some press reports. While cruising on the Solent the next summer a much closer view was possible when it was seen moored at East Cowes, while the other two Princesses, G-ALUO and G-ALUP, were seen beached and cocooned at Calshot Spit. It is interesting to reflect that at the time of its Farnborough debut I was not to know that two members of the Princess flight crew of eleven, particularly Dick Wraith but also Dick Stratton, would subsequently figure in my life.

My first attendance at a King's Cup Air Race, which in June 1951 was held at Hatfield, proved something of a disaster in that the weather was dreadful. With David Crook, then a colleague and in recent years Membership Secretary of Air-Britain, we travelled by Green Line coach from Marble Arch clutching an entrance ticket by courtesy of Harold Best-Devereux. To race was impossible; there were plans to run it at the SBAC Show in the September, but eventually it was abandoned for the year. Despite the appalling conditions with a cloud base of about 500 ft some 20,000 people turned up; some remarkable flying took place by the Patrouille d'Étampes in their Stampe SV-4Cs Nos. 7, 10, 677 and 678, Prince Cantacuzene in his Jungmeister EC-AEX and Frank Murphy in Sea Fury T.20 VX828. 1953 proved to be a better year when the race returned to the South, taking place at Southend.

Before the advent of monitoring aircraft movements by VHF radio so much depended on the 'Mk. 1 eyeball' which brought with it rumours of unusual sightings which were frequently disbelieved but usually turned out to be true. When Convair B-36s were first reported the sound alone was sufficient to identify them, once described as like a formation of 'doodlebugs.' Many were the early mornings when I awoke at about 6 am to hear one or more climbing out over South London from bases in East Anglia; the first had arrived at Lakenheath in January 1951. The finest – and never to be forgotten – sight of these huge aircraft was a formation of three low over London on the 1st July 1951 en route for a fly-by at the Paris Air Show.

An airfield full of wartime memories for me, as we lived close to it, was Great Dunmow; I saw it built by the US Army engineers and avidly followed the 9th Air Force Maurauder operations and later RAF Stirling/Horsa activities including 'Operation Varsity,' the crossing of the Rhine. In the '50s, during visits to my parents, a walk on the former airfield evoked memories of those opening scenes in that great film "Twelve O'Clock High" and so during Easter 1952 it was with some surprise that I saw a USAF C-47 making approaches and touch-and-go landings. It was said to be assessing old wartime airfields for future USAF needs, but in that part of Essex it was Wethersfield that had already been chosen and lengthened to take, during that summer, the 20th Fighter Group F-84Gs. Great Dunmow saw a further spell of activity in the late '50s when the Great Easton Flying Group used it to operate their Auster J/1 Autocrat G-AGVG.

Another memory of this period is of the Aircraft Recognition Society. At one time meetings were held at the Royal Aeronautical Society in Hamilton Place, London, but later just off the Strand in the Covent Garden area. Here enthuiasts met and talked as well as testing their skill in the art of aircraft recognition. By the mid-1950s it had lost something of its interest, which left a gap for those wanting to meet in central London, and so the advent of the London Society of Air-Britain, meeting for the first time under the direction of Charles Cain at Caxton Hall on the 2nd February 1955, was most welcomed; this continues today. For many years until recently, Charles Oman provided varied and interesting meetings.

The DH 106 Comet 1 had been around since its first flight on 27th July 1949 and evoked as much interest as the Concorde still does today. John Cunningham was frequently in the news with record out-and-return flights in one day, so it was important to witness the arrival from Johannesburg of the first commercial service into Heathrow on the 6th May 1952. My notes say it passed over my house at 07.32 and was G-ALYP, later tragically lost off Elba in January 1954.

It is strange how one loss can solve the mystery of an earlier one. During the extensive underwater salvage operations in an attempt to solve this and other Comet accidents wreckage was recovered which was obviously not from "YP." What it did solve was the disappearance of the R.A. Brand and Co. Ltd Lockheed 14 G-AKPD, which failed to arrive at Rome in October 1948. At the time there was speculation that it had been forced to land in Yugoslavia, that Capt. Thornton Hall, crew and passengers were being held to ransom, that it had been seized by Israeli agents. The newspapers haven't changed!

It was remarkable what one could observe from the office window of the aeronautical activity over London by audacious use of the neck, but the real thing had to wait until lunch-time; then a walk over Waterloo Bridge (usually with Norman Walter, a veteran prewar spotter, as well as with Peter Noyes or Colin Mugford, both dedicated enthusiasts) followed by a circuit of the former 1951 Festival of Britain site would bring you to the helicopter pad located on the base of what was once the Festival dome. Here regularly was the Evening News Westland S-51 G-ANAL, while others could include Royal Navy Sikorsky S-55 WV221 and Bristol 171 G-AMWH. It was with considerable surprise that our quiet stroll on 5th May 1953 was shattered by Auster Autocrat G-AGYD emerging from under Waterloo Bridge and proceeding up-river under a few more! We were later to learn from the evening papers that this was Major Chris Draper, the "Mad Major," showing he could still do what he had previously achieved in 1931.

"Can you swim?" was the question posed in the office one morning in 1953. The answer being in the negative, I was told: "You are just the chap we are looking for." Shades of the kind of question you got when serving King and Country, but this time for a much more serious reason. Airwork Hermes G-ALDF, flying at the time as WZ841 on a military trooping flight, was forced to ditch in the sea off Trapani, Sicily on 25th August

86

1952 with loss of life, which it was considered was possibly due to the lifejackets then in use not being suitable. As a result it was decided that the ARB, in conjunction with the Institute of Aviation Medicine, should test those available, and so the 25th September 1953 found me about to jump in the swimming pool, more like a Roman bath I remember, beneath the RAC Club in Pall Mall. As a non-swimmer it was my job to don the early Kapok-filled life vest or modern RFD or Frankenstein lifejackets, jump in the pool and see what happened! On hand to pull me out if things went wrong were John Pardoe, Walter Bolsover and Jim Templeton of ARB, while S/Ldr D.G.V. Whittingham and Surg./Lt. J.S.P. Rawlins of the Institute observed what went on. An interesting experience, followed by a pleasant lunch at the Club!

By the summer of 1954 our first-born, Richard, was considered old enough to enjoy the pleasures of a seaside holiday and so we went to Ramsgate; quite why it was chosen is lost in the mists of time but it could have been because the Ramsgate brochure had a prewar picture of a Short Scion on the cover! Passing Manston we observed that the USAF were still in residence there but were not prepared for what was to come. Sitting on the beach we regularly saw the Autocrat G-AIRC and Messenger G-AHZS of Air Kruise (Kent) Ltd operating joyrides from the small prewar Ramsgate Airport, but then one afternoon came Boeing B-47 12193 low over the beach on approach to Manston followed quickly by six others, as well as KB-97s, F-86s, C-119s and T-33s. Heaven indeed for the aircraft spotter, especially when there were more on successive days, but less so for those wanting a quiet holiday.

RAF Battle of Britain Displays were as usual a must and for September 1954 it was a nostalgic return visit to RAF Debden with my brother Reg. My first visit here had been for the Empire Air Day display in 1937 followed by many 'over the fence' viewings throughout the second World War. Referring to brother Reg's account of the day in *"Air-Britain Digest"* I am reminded that the airfield then housed the Empire Radio School operating Lincoln RF341 "Mercury" as well as a number of Anson T.22s. On display were examples of the Auster, Canberra, Chipmunk, Dakota, Meteor, Neptune, Oxford, Provost and Vampire. Joyriding was provided by Morton Air Services Consul G-AIAH and Olley Air Service Rapide G-AGWP.

By the mid-1950s some change of direction came about, not only from a work point of view, but having had a very general interest in all things aviation it was felt that some specialisation was necessary and so, encouraged by that doyen of all enthusiasts, A.J. Jackson, research was undertaken into the history of the Miles Aerovan, and from that developed a life-long interest in civil aviation in the Near and Middle East. Jacko's wonderful knack of convincing you almost anything is possible is best illustrated by my suggesting we needed in the Air-Britain publication *"British Civil Aviation News"* a column to investigate the fate of many British aircraft sold abroad; his answer was: "You could produce a 'Sleuths' Corner'," and so it was born, and ran for several years. What we owe to "Jacko," or "A.J.J." as he was so often known, is immeasurable, as is our debt to so many others.

CHAPTER 10

PIONEERING SEARCH AND RESCUE

by

Lt. Cdr. John Sproule RN

[This chapter was originally published in "Aeroplane Monthly" for May 1982, and I am grateful for permission to reproduce it here. I also very much appreciate the help given by Sandy Sproule (John's son), who suggested its inclusion and very kindly supplied a copy of the article along with some appropriate photographs.

To many air show enthusiasts of the fifties, Lt. Cdr. Sproule will probably be best remembered for his unique flying displays, which included such bizarre items as a low-flying witch on a broomstick suspended under a S.51 Dragonfly; what would have ensued in the case of an engine failure at low altitude does not bear thinking about! – Ed.]

I joined the Fleet Air Arm as a pilot in 1940 from the design office of Airspeed Ltd at Portsmouth, on the strength of my 'A' licence (the equivalent of the present-day Private Pilots' Licence). I had obtained this on Avro Avians under a prewar Government-sponsored cheap flying scheme called the Civil Air Guard; so my flying experience on aeroplanes was minimal. I had, however, over 200 hrs on gliders – and perhaps in those dark days when the Battle of Britain was at its height, their Lordships were not being too choosy! As an amateur pilot it was splendid to discover that in those days the Royal Navy had a much more enlightened attitude to corrected vision for aircrew than the RAF. I had my interview medical and a flying test in a Magister aircraft, all in one day, and in no time at all I was wearing the uniform of a Sub Lieutenant (A) RNVR, spectacles and all!

I had a very varied wartime career, ranging from flying Proctor aircraft at Worthy Down to a transfer to the RAF to instruct on large military gliders. When hostilities ceased, I returned to the Royal Navy where I gravitated into the quite unique job of flying a special glider for scientific purposes from the carriers *"Pretoria Castle"* and *"Illustrious."* The base for these rather odd activities was to be Royal Naval Air Station, Gosport.

RNAS Gosport was then the home of a number of tasks, ranging from the training of aircraft handlers on a dummy carrier deck on the airfield to the development of torpedoes for dropping from aircraft. But by far the most interesting activity, as far as I was concerned, was the arrival of a number of Sikorsky R.4 helicopters. 705 Sqn had not long been formed and was commanded by Lt. K. Reed RNVR, who was one of the first

Naval helicopter pilots trained in the USA. The squadron soon settled down to pilot conversion courses and various odd jobs such as photography and radar calibration.

The Sikorsky R.4, powered by a Warner Scarab radial piston engine of 140 hp, was the first helicopter to be produced in series anywhere in the world. Developed in the USA by Igor Sikorsky from his prototype VS-300 machine of 1939, it established for the first time the now classic helicopter configuration, i.e. the large single lifting rotor at the front with the small vertical one at the rear to counteract the engine torque. True, the Sikorsky R.4s of 705 Sqn were neither capable nor equipped to do much more than fly, and most of the jobs the machine did at Gosport, apart from pilot training, could have been done equally well and more cheaply with a Tiger Moth. Nevertheless, the Sikorsky R.4 was a genuine helicopter and with it the FAA began to acquire the rotary wing expertise which has now become almost a Naval tradition. The formation of 705 Sqn at such an early stage in the development of the helicopter, when its potential was so uncertain, was indeed a far-sighted move on the part of someone in the Navy's corridors of power.

In those early days, FAA pilots were inclined to regard the helicopter course at Gosport as a bit of a come-down after flying Seafires and Corsairs and the like, but it was perfectly plain to me, at any rate, that helicopters were the coming thing. Needless to say, I pulled all possible strings to organise myself onto the list for the helicopter conversion course – known in those days as "Special Miscellaneous Air Course No. 20" – SMAC 20. Eventually I was successful, and one afternoon in December 1948 I wobbled off in a rotary-winged aircraft on my own for the first time. Then, just as with pupils today, it took a little time to master the trick of coordinating the additional and somewhat different controls of the helicopter, after flying conventional fixed-wing aircraft. By and large, however, a well-rigged Sikorsky R.4 was a remarkably pleasant aircraft to fly and, apart from a few crudities by modern standards, a present-day helicopter pilot would soon feel at home in this most inspired machinery of 35 years ago.

In 1950 I was offered a permanent commission in the RN and appointed Lieutenant Commander Flying at Gosport. I was delighted to be given the chance to stay on in the Navy, and as master of one of the most historic airfields in England. I felt greatly honoured to be following in a multitude of illustrious footsteps. In addition, I was well placed to continue to fly 705 Sqn's helicopters whenever one was available.

The final phasing out of the R.4 did not bring Naval helicopter activity to an end – far from it – as by the time the machines were worn out and the supply of spares was exhausted Westlands of Yeovil had acquired the licence to build the more advanced Sikorsky S.51. This machine, with a single Alvis Leonides radial piston engine of 550 hp, could carry a crew of two and, at a pinch, two passengers. But the most important thing from the Naval point of view was that it embodied a hydraulic winch with some 70 ft of flexible cable and a hook. With the introduction of this machine the proposition was to dispense with attendant destroyers for aeroplane guard duty in aircraft carrier operations; and, of course, to carry out rescue duties at Naval Air Stations.

The S.51 was a much bigger helicopter than the R.4, but as the first models had fabric-covered blades and the pilot had no mechanical help in controlling the large rotor, the machine has distinct ideas of its own as to where it wanted to go! Flying the early S.51s, or Dragonflies as they came to be known, was a muscular business, and it was with considerable relief that the Navy took delivery of Westland's improved versions with metal-covered blades and hydraulic servo-controls. This latter feature made the new machine much easier to fly.

In due time my tenure of office at Gosport came to an end and, after a most enjoyable year of seafaring in small ships in the Mediterranean, I did a helicopter refresher course and was checked out as competent to fly the Dragonfly. Thus qualified I was appointed in 1953 as C.O. of the newly-formed Search and Rescue Flight at RN Air Station Ford, near Arundel in Sussex. I confess that at the time I was not too pleased to be confronted with SAR duties, which sometimes dwell rather heavily on the sadder aspects of aviation. In a short time though, I discovered that I had been given the best flying job in the peacetime FAA. Ford was an excellent Naval Air Station to serve in as it was pleasantly situated and flying took precedence over anything else: from the Captain down, everyone flew aeroplanes. The weekends were busy and remarkably lively too, as Ford was the base of a keen RNVR squadron which operated Fireflies with great gusto, consumed large quantities of beer and sang very coarse songs.

The SAR flight at Ford consisted of the two S.51s, another pilot besides myself and two aircrewmen, and our base of operations was the Air Traffic Control building. The sea was only a minute's flying time away and our parish extended roughly from Selsey Bill to the west as far as Beachy Head to the east, and of course as far to seaward as the range of our helicopters would allow.

The air traffic controllers were a cheerful crowd and as the SAR office was in their midst we spent most our standby time looking over their shoulders, and listening in to the radio chit-chat which goes with all flying operations. In this way we were often able to anticipate trouble as it developed and to be already airborne when the emergency arose.

On taking over the SAR Flight, I had lost no time in getting down to a programme of training, so that both crews could perfect the technique of hoisting bodies out of the sea on the winch under all circumstances and generally cope with anything which might arise. Being the boss, I reserved the right to choose my permanent aircrewman, and in teaming up with Chief Petty Officer S. W. Lock, a telegraphist/air gunner of great experience, I rapidly found out that I had chosen the best helicopter aircrewman in the business. Lock was small and wiry, fast on the *"Daily Telegraph"* crossword, and an expert navigator and signaller. In a very short time he had resurrected the ancient but excellent device called the Bigsworth Board which had gone out of service with the Swordfish, and had taken over the intensive training of the second aircrewman in its use. As Lock had no more faith in radio communication at low altitude as navigational aid than I had, I was delighted to find that with the splendid Bigsworth Board and Lock's eye for windspeed and direction from the appearance of the sea, we could navigate independently with considerable accuracy.

At first there was a complete lack of the most simple ancillary equipment for the rescue operations; this applied even to the strop on which survivors were hoisted, and to begin with we had to make our own from hemp rope. Some time before, however, Lock had designed and made an excellent article out of parachute webbing padded with rubber and, as this was both practical and easy for a half-drowned survivor to understand and put on, we adopted his design. It is still standard equipment today.

Shortly after establishing ourselves at Ford, we were issued with the double-lift harness which had just been developed at Gosport for the recovery of inanimate survivors. The idea was for the helicopter aircrewman to be lowered by the pilot into the sea to grapple with the helpless survivor, secure him in a strop, and bring him up into the hovering aircraft. This sounded very simple, but we soon found out that the scheme had snags in the two-crew Dragonfly, for as soon as the pilot began to lower his aircrewman – his only friend and helper – he disappeared from view beneath the aircraft. To deal with this, the Dragonfly winch had been equipped with a drum with a length of telephone cable wound on it, to enable the aircrewman to keep up a running commentary, so that the pilot could lower or hoist as required. It is a fact of life, however, that salt water and electricity are bad partners, so, in nine cases out of ten, as soon as the aircrewman encountered the sea there was a spluttering noise and thereafter dead silence. For all the pilot knew when he began to hoist, he could be bringing up his faithful aircrewman with the winch cable wound round his neck! At Ford we developed a technique in which the pilot paid out a considerable length of cable and sidled off to one side to observe the antics of his aircrewman in the water. This was a partial solution but there was also a matter of corpses. Being endowed with some imagination I could see very clearly that sooner or later we might be called upon to recover a deceased person or parts thereof for identification.

One afternoon CPO Lock and I were discussing the matter, and it occurred to me that, as we were by then pretty expert in placing the helicopter's rescue hook just where we wanted it, it might be possible to trawl a corpse out of the water in some kind of net or scoop and proceed ashore with it at a decent distance below the aircraft. Lock agreed with this idea with understandable enthusiasm, and I immediately sketched out a frame of 1 inch steel tubing, about 5 ft square, to be suspended on four cables from the helicopter hook. In a very short time our Mark 1 rescue net was hanging from the ceiling of our crew room, and CPO Lock, being a true sailor, was busy stringing the frame with cod-line and tying a lot of complicated knots. That afternoon we spent an hour dropping a five-gallon oil drum, half-filled with water, into the sea off Climping beach, and dabbling our prototype net in the water to fish our dummy "victim" out. We soon added a small drogue or sea anchor, fastened to the rear of the net by a length of cod-line. This latter feature – in the first instance a child's plastic beach bucket with the bottom cut out – was intended to enter the water first and keep the net facing the right way. Trials soon proved our improved model was working perfectly and drums and live volunteers had been lifted successfully in varying seas. This, therefore, was the solution to the two-crew Dragonfly double-lift problem, and at Ford we proposed to fly henceforth with our net rigged permanently to the side of the aircraft as the first means of sea recovery. In due course the Admiralty endorsed our efforts, and our Mk.4 net – in reality a very obvious device – became standard equipment in all SAR flights at sea and ashore.

One lunchtime I happened to be airborne on one of our regular "warming up the engine" local sorties when air traffic called me up with the news that a Firefly flying ashore from a carrier out in the Channel had developed engine trouble and a ditching appeared imminent: we were therefore invited to head for sea on an intercepting course. It happened that Commander Baldwin, the Commander Air, was also airborne for his weekly trip in a Vampire, and being very much faster he soon located the Firefly about six miles off Littlehampton. Very shortly I was relieved to spot the two aircraft flying low over the water and we had a grandstand view of the Firefly ditching. With the Dragonfly fairly rattling along at maximum speed, I made encouraging remarks on the radio to its worried pilot. Within 30 sec of immersion a very surprised Lt. Foulkes RN was in our net and being winched up to the helicopter where, cold and wet, he sat shivering until we delivered him to the front door of the sick bay at Ford; to this day I get a Christmas card from him each year.

This sort of thing made for the greatest keenness among everyone connected with the helicopters at Ford, and the maintenance crews would willingly work long hours to ensure that we always had serviceable aircraft. As most of the flying was over the sea, often as much as 30 miles from land, we had reason to be grateful. In my two years at Ford we never had as much as a spit out of the Alvis Leonides engines, or in-flight airframe trouble of any kind. And of course our Ford-designed gadgets, which we introduced from time to time, made us all feel that we were a pretty sharp outfit. The Sproule net is still in use for its original rather macabre purpose, and a very similar device, complete with drogue, was used by the US Navy on the retrieval of the Apollo astronauts. Nowadays with much larger SAR helicopters, capable of carrying three crew, the double-lift method of recovery has become the standard drill. The pilot flies the helicopter and the navigator lowers the aircrewman onto the victim in the water and keeps the pilot informed of events as they occur underneath the aircraft. A lot less dicey than in the old two-crew Dragonfly days.

In addition to the net, I designed a special carry-cot stretcher for the recovery of injured personnel from ships, which was quite a success. We also did some trials with a scheme I devised for automatically securing a helicopter to the deck of a rolling ship at the moment of landing, by spearing a metal grid let into the deck of the ship with a vertical harpoon member located on the belly of the aircraft. Numerous people from Admiralty and elsewhere came to see demonstrations of a mock-up installation, but the harpoon we made in station workshops was before its time in 1955 and nothing came of it. I am happy to say, however, that a similar scheme is incorporated in the Lynx helicopter in current RN service, so perhaps I was on the right track after all. This seems to be borne out by the fact that in 1978 I was awarded £5,000 for the invention by the Ministry of Defence Awards to Inventors Committee.

A great many of our alarms and excursions at Ford were to go to the aid of yachtsmen in distress in various ways and, though we did achieve success in quite a number of genuine military aircraft emergencies, we were always delighted to help civilians. Apart from the real live practice it gave the SAR flight, it kept down the number of letters of complaint the station received about aircraft noise.

After my two years at Ford, I was lent to the Ceylon Air Force to show them how to operate their two S.51 Dragonflies; this was followed in 1957 by command of 700H Flight at Lee-on-Solent to carry out the first intensive flying trials of the new Whirlwind Mk.7 helicopter. We spent a most enjoyable summer putting in flying time in these machines all over the south of England and developed a routine of flying from one large swimming-pool-equipped mansion to the next, on the basis that if the engine did expire as it was expected to do, we might as well be near to luxurious hospitality and the possibility of being entertained by a bevy of beautiful daughters! Alas, our engine kept running without serious falter for the whole of the trials.

After a spell at sea with the SAR flight in HMS *"Albion,"* I formed 701 Sqn again at Lee-on-Solent as the parent squadron for all the ships' helicopter flights, and to carry out general fleet requirement work and special trials. In the latter capacity we were called upon to investigate the night rescue capability of the Whirlwind, and on the night of December 2nd 1957, in company with Lt. Simpson RN, I had the misfortune to get myself disorientated near the water in a layer of mist about a mile off Calshot. We splashed into the sea on all fours, and with the sound and sensation of being beaten about the ears by someone wielding a gate-post, the rotor broke up close above our heads and we rolled over into very cold water. I emerged from the cockpit at what seemed to be a great depth and on reaching the surface was joined by Simpson who, in leaving the aircraft, had torn a hole in the seat of his immersion suit. This excellent garment kept me nice and dry, but my companion in distress had a very cold bottom indeed when we were picked up by a Calshot motor boat about an hour later. This was an alarming experience and we were saved by the light on my Mae West. But out of evil cometh good, for I was convinced that had we been carrying some sort of signal pistol in our lifejackets, we could have been picked up in a matter of minutes. Some time afterwards, as a direct result of this ditching, I was able to find the little German-made Miniflare projector and design a pack for it, which is now standard on all aircrew life-jackets. I can say with deep conviction that in aeronautical matters in general, there is absolutely no substitute for personal experience!

My last two years in the RN were spent at the Ministry of Supply in the department responsible for developing helicopters, but I still managed to keep in helicopter flying practice at Lee-on-Solent; but the time came when I could spin it out no longer. One afternoon in October 1960, I found myself switching off the engine of a beautiful navy-blue Mk.22 Whirlwind, once Prince Philip's private steed, and sadly listening to the engine ticking and crackling as it cooled down. In a week's time I would be a civilian again with Service flying a thing of the past.

What a privilege it had been to fly as a pilot in the Royal Navy. And what fun to have been in on the helicopter game when it was new. And what luck for a gadgeteer like myself to have found such scope!

CHAPTER 11

WHEN I WAS A LITTLE LAD

by

Geoffrey Pitt

[NOTES ON THE AUTHOR: Geoffrey Pitt MBE, MCIT joined BOAC in the early forties, working at Leuchars, Croydon, Northolt and Heathrow.

In 1947 he joined Harold Bamberg and worked closely on the concept and development of Eagle Aviation, progressively with the operation of Halifaxes, Yorks, Vikings, DC-7Cs, Viscounts, Britannias and 707s engaged on charters, trooping, scheduled services and package tours.

After thirteen years with Eagle he decided on a change of course and in 1960, eight years before the tragic collapse of British Eagle, became General Manager in Britain for Aer Lingus, with responsibility for all the Irish Airline's commercial activities in this country.

He became a founding member of the British Airports Authority, and from this he was headhunted to be Director of Cunard Line with responsibility for the marketing of the Line's ships, including the new QE2. – Ed.]

I certainly wasn't born with a silver joystick in my hand (perhaps 'control wheel' would be more tactful!), but sort of drifted into Commercial Aviation because it was the best thing on offer at the time.

My originally chosen career path was as a Civil Engineer and I was duly articled to the Borough Surveyor of Tynemouth, in Northumberland. This was great fun, but to be truthful either I wasn't clever enough or else the wartime bombing was a hazard to serious studying – let's settle for a bit of both.

While at Tynemouth I took part in the local Home Guard and, before you go dashing off with sneers *à la* "Dad's Army," let me hasten to assure you we were very serious, able and in actual combat. We were linked to the local Regulars on Ack-Ack duty, looking after 60 Projectors which all sent off two rockets, each timed to go off at a predetermined height together and so wipe enemy aircraft out of the sky.

One night we were credited with a victory and I shall never forget the sight of the blazing bomber going down into the North Sea and silhouetting Cullercoats Church. No feeling for the lives lost. Not many Home Guard can claim Active Service.

After Duty we used to breakfast with the Regulars: sausage, bacon, eggs and about a pound of kidneys which I adore. Afterwards home to Mum who had saved half a kidney for me. I didn't dare tell her.

Tiring of Civil Engineering and having had it drummed into me that one must look for a permanent job with a Pension, I consulted Whittaker's Almanac for ideas, coming up with Customs, BBC and someone I had never heard of called British Overseas Airways Corporation. Heaven knows what they were or what they did.

Anyway, BOAC were the only ones to send me a rail pass to London for interview so I found myself in the Airways Terminal before Mr Webb, Traffic Superintendent – and then had a good weekend with friends in London.

Within a very short while an offer came as Traffic Clerk at the princely wage of £2-10s a week and a posting to somewhere in Scotland called Leuchars.

Thus started an association with Civil Aviation that was to last for 30 years and take me through BOAC, BEA, International Airways, Eagle Airways, Aer Lingus, Overseas National and finally BCal.

Such research as I was able to do established Leuchars on the Fife Coast; I thought it must mean flying boats and be pronounced "Loo-Kars." We learn, given time.

I duly reported, having found digs in nearby St. Andrews, and found myself with a good crowd including Station Manager Alfie (A.A.) Pigg, STO Jock Murray and such stalwarts as Ron Davis, Harry Crowther, Hugh Drummond *et al*. Hugh was no mean artist and I still have some very good black & whites he did of St. Andrews above my desk as I write. Most of this crowd went into BEA. Jock embarrassed me no end some years later by asking *me* for a job.

Among our visitors was a management trainee, a very exalted position; he even had a better uniform than a humble traffic clerk like me. This was Jimmy Wilson: we struck it off together and have been firm friends ever since, 55 years so far. Indeed he was my best man. He stayed with BOAC for a whole career while I chose to move around. We still meet once a month to chew the aviation fat.

Captains' names that I remember are Clive Houlder, David Longden, Mike Carroll and Nigel Pelly (yes, he of Chamberlain's 1938 appeasement visit to Hitler in Munich fame).

What was BOAC doing in the height of the war at Leuchars? The simple answer is: "Running a 'civilian' Service to Stockholm" – Sweden having remained neutral. What even I in my aviation ignorance immediately spotted as unusual was the sort of aircraft used – Mosquitos, yes, the ubiquitous "Mossie" which we all knew as fighter-bombers, reconnaisance etc. BOAC's were in camouflage with civilian markings (e.g. G-AGGE, 'GF & 'GG). Two crew, Captain and R/O/-Navigator. 500 kilos of cargo in a cage in the bomb bay and one passenger sitting rearward facing on the floor forward of the bomb bay, all dressed up in flying suit and helmet with an intercom to the cockpit, a box of sandwiches and a Thermos of coffee. Entry was an awkward twist up through the open bomb-doors with firm instructions to keep feet clear as the doors were closed. This route was used for important freight such as ball-bearings and VVIP passengers, such as the British Ambassador and Malcolm Sargent to mention two specifically. Oh! and also the British Ambassador's Secretary, Peggy Epps, who was delayed a week so she and I had a good time together.

The Mossies flew direct, taking about three hours: several were lost.

As winter came and there were longer hours of darkness C-47s were added to the fleet. With long-range tanks in the cabin they had range to go right up over northern Norway to avoid the enemy. One made a rough landing at Bromma and the front passenger broke his nose against the tank. He didn't think it was funny.

Also at this time we had Lodestars in BOAC wartime colours but flown by Royal Norwegian Air Force pilots in BOAC uniform. They flew to Bromma to bring back Norwegians who had escaped across the border into Sweden. They were carried 20 at a time, sitting on mattresses on the floor of the Lodestar.

It was interesting later on to see several of these RNAF pilots coming into Croydon as DNL (Norwegian Airline) Captains. I particularly remember Piltingsrud, Schonning and Giortz.

When the Norwegian refugees arrived at Leuchars they were shipped off to the local nick at Cupar until the following day, when they were transferred to Jurby, Isle of Man, for internment and release to the Services when their credentials had been proven. It was a good scrounge for us lads to fly with them over to Jurby, collect a few eggs (unused sick buckets made very good containers) and come home again. Eggs were in very short supply on the mainland at the time.

During all this activity at Leuchars, ABA (Swedish Airlines) were flying DC-3s into Dyce (Aberdeen). They were all decked out in neutral markings, lights and an almost 'dayglo' orange paint. Some time later it was interesting to see some of these aircraft coming into Croydon, first day in complete orange, next day with some removed overnight, until in about a week there was a pristine silver fuselage and wings.

ABA suffered several losses on this route due to enemy action despite all the neutral markings, and eventually gave up.

BOAC's part is quite well written up in a Stationery Office book which came out just after the war and called *"Merchant Airmen."* I did read a book about Dyce which detailed the ABA part but made scant mention of what went on at Leuchars.

It had been on my schedule for years to get to the Mosquito Museum at St. Albans and see how much is there about the BOAC Mossies; I finally managed it in 1998. The people there were very receptive to my tales of the BOAC Mosquitos and the destinations to which passengers and freight were carried. I also found that they also have there the Hornet Moth on which I later learnt to fly, G-ADOT.

Very shortly after VE Day BOAC closed down at Leuchars and we all got transferred to Croydon which was of course very new to me. By this time I was a Cargo "Expert" and banished to 'C' Hangar to handle the goods. At this stage I didn't spend a lot of time in the famous terminal but did manage to get on the roof one day and was fascinated to find the Flight Schedule for 3rd September 1939 still pinned up there for the spotters of the day.

Also, nosing around the back of 'C' Hangar I found a number of DH Flamingos crated up to go to BOAC in Egypt; they never went. Later on they were revived by British Air Transport (BAT) out of Redhill and one of my first jobs with an 'Eagle-ish' hat on was to charter one to take Stewart Granger and Elizabeth Taylor to Nice for a (then) illicit weekend. I also had the great fortune to fly to Le Bourget and back in Flamingo G-AFYH on the 2nd August 1947.

A lot of the Cargo Traffic we were handling at Croydon was food parcels from grateful Americans for us poor starving Brits. These parcels had come transatlantic by flying boat to Foynes, transferred thence to Rinneanna (which became better known as Shannon), then on into Croydon. Of course Customs had to have them all opened for inspection by very willing BOAC Traffic Staff and I do seem to remember a certain amount of tasting used to go on.

At this time it was great fun and of great serious interest to experience the postwar start-up of commercial aviation again. I have already mentioned ABA coming in but also DDL, DNL, KLM, Sabena ("Such a Bloody Experience, Never Again"?) Air France, TAP, Alitalia, Iberia, Railway Air Services. The latter inherited some Ju.52s in war reparations or something similar, three-engine monsters with corrugated fuselages. Air France also had some odd aircraft.

But no return of the might of Imperial Airways' HP.42s and the like; I believe they were all destroyed in wartime. I feel my education is incomplete somehow!

During this time preparations were being made for the start-up of BEA, or as it was at first, the European Division of BOAC. Northolt was to be the base and I got posted there fairly early on. I hated it and campaigned to get back to Croydon. I eventually succeeded but only for a very short while, because it was then back to Northolt again, through some strange juggling, on a temporary posting which meant I collected very generous allowances: in fact I have never been better off in my life in terms of spare cash.

So much so that I decided to learn to fly and went to the Herts & Essex Flying Club at Broxbourne. Here I had the great good fortune to have Dennis (D.A.D.) Cather, the Chief Instructor, as my mentor. The aircraft, as I have mentioned earlier, was a very gentlemanly closed-in Hornet Moth, G-ADOT. I tried a Tiger Moth one day when Dennis was away and didn't like that at all – very draughty.

One day Dennis and I were flying in G-ADOT fairly sleepily; I had the controls, when I heard the engine pop. Looked over at Dennis, who was gazing out the window, so I guessed it was OK. Then it happened again and I was getting a bit scared, so I looked across at Dennis again and noticed he had the Instructor's intercom mouthpiece in his hand and was gently banging it against the side of the cabin. I have asked myself for ever after whether it was deliberate or accidental, as he swore.

Dennis had a fiery, but very nice, Canadian wife, Tiny. One day in the bar in a fairly happy moment I shot a stream from a soda syphon across at her. Quick as a flash the contents of her beer glass were on their way over to me. I'll swear the two streams crossed in mid-air.

Then disaster struck at Northolt as far as I was concerned. Air France insisted on transferring to the very new Heathrow. BEA were their agents, BOAC in turn were *their* agents. So, some mugs had to go to LHR; BOAC did the work, BEA took the kicks, and as for complaints BOAC took no notice of us.

This was the mud and caravans time at Heathrow. Fumes from the paraffin heaters in the caravans gave us all the most awful styes in our eyes.

Dear old Heathrow didn't have much to commend it in those days, but two plusses stand out from those days. The W.H. Smith bookstall had export priority and you could get *"Flight"* there. And on one fine day the first Transats were due in and one could see the two aircraft concerned circling the horizon until the due time to land for all the waiting dignitaries.

This AF/BEA/BOAC mess was so unpleasant – the mud wasn't nearly as bad – that I decided to make a move and saw a job as Senior Traffic Officer with International Airways at Croydon advertised, went for it and got it. And so I was able to return to my beloved Croydon.

International was a wonderful name, whoever thought that up deserved some credit. The Company had the most strange ownership, Mr Burton, a hotelier from Bournemouth. GM was Jock Bonner who I understood to have been a prewar barnstormer. Traffic Superintendent was Ron Phelps, pilots were Stan Ainger, Mike Sproule and Peter Siegel. Aircraft were three Consuls (G-AHXP & G-AIIS, I don't recall the third), also a Gemini which was rather revolutionary at the time, G-AIDG.

Croydon was fascinating, with the old terminal completely revived and with a great many charter companies represented. Olley Air Services were on one side, newly-formed Morton Air Services on the other. It was a sad day for Gordon Olley when Sammy Morton, his prewar chief pilot, walked across the hall and announced he had bought the Company.

· Just now I was looking at a couple of photos I took of a BOAC York about to take off from Croydon, and they made my hair stand on end! The Yorks used to fly in to Croydon quite regularly from either Hurn or Aldermaston for servicing and/or mods to be made. To take off they used to start from right down by 'C' Hangar, completely empty of load and with, reputedly, an eggcupful of fuel in the tanks. There was only one pilot allowed to do these flights.

I inadvertently rocked the boat a bit; having been very conscious in BOAC/BEA about uniforms and stripes I put up the three stripes of an STO, only to find this was greatly ahead of everyone else. Peter Eskell of Mortons was very cross with me.

Prewar aviation names were in abundance, Jim Mollison was quite frequently to be found in the bar. Monique Agazarian was around and doing joyrides in a Rapide; she later switched to Heathrow. Can you imagine *that* happening today, joyrides from Heathrow?

Jock had a daily morning coffee date with Maurice Houdret in the bar. One day Jock was out when Maurice called, so I was invited. I wondered why the attendant poured the coffee and then turned his back to us; when I tasted it I realised it had been well laced with brandy.

Jock started doing some joyriding in our Gemini and it was quite a sight to see him resplendent in a pale blue Captain's uniform walking out to fly the Gemini. One day he came back into the office showing us a shilling tip a little old lady had given him. I said he should have given it back, but he counselled that that would have injured her pride; he was right of course.

Occasionally I was given the job of driving Jock's beautiful Triumph Dolomite up to the Quality Inn in Regent Street to meet his cousin for coffee. Going back I noticed that the rear was always heavily laden so something illicit was taking place. But I didn't care as long as I got to drive the Triumph – I was only about 23 at the time.

Phelps soon left and I became Traffic Superintendent. We had no business and the pilots didn't think much of the way Jock was running things, so I was delegated to write accordingly to Burton. He sent the letter straight to Jock so that didn't do much good.

After four months of idling the door burst open one day and another charter company asked if we could do a flight to Nice immediately. We got Stan away within an hour. Before he went I had the presence of mind to suggest he asked the one passenger when he was coming back and whether we could carry him.

Stan came back with the answer that the passenger's travel arrangements were made through Mr Bamberg of Liaison Travel in Fleet Street. I dug out a phone number, made contact and got the job.

Some weeks later I was minding my own business in the office on a Saturday morning when a tall young blond guy came in, introduced himself as Harold Bamberg and offered me a job; this I took and worked for Harold for the next 13 years (apart from a brief spell when we fell out).

Early on in the days of Eagle, when they operated Yorks out of Bovingdon, I recall that the chief pilot, "Pancho" Villa, used to blip the throttles on finals as a message to his wife in their caravan underneath that he was home and it was time to put the kettle on! It was also "Pancho" who made the very last flight of the Berlin airlift in the Halifax G-AIAP. Later, when I asked him how he managed to arrange it, he confided that he had 'snagged' it until everyone else had gone! That was one story that wasn't mentioned in the 1998 TV programme to commemorate the 50th anniversary of the airlift!

And so I saw the start of Eagle Aviation, which later became Eagle Airways, then British Eagle Airways. I was with them through the Berlin Airlift, worldwide charters, Cas-Evac from Korea, military contracts, the start of scheduled services (Belgrade!), also the start of package tours and the sell-out to Cunard to form Cunard-Eagle.

Cunard took fright at the first snag and sold back. I have always thought that Cunard, as a transatlantic leader on the sea, wasted their opportunity to follow up and make progress in the air travel business as well. But it wasn't to be.

Eagle lasted until 1968 when, very sadly, it all went to the wall. I had left in 1960 for pastures new in Aer Lingus.

CHAPTER 12

A VIEW FROM THE REAR

by

Margaret Lloyd

[NOTES ON THE AUTHOR: Born Margaret Barnes in Rossendale, Lancashire. Educated Bacup & Rawtenstall Grammar School and Slade School of Fine Art, Oxford and London Colonial Service wife in Nigeria. Joined BOAC in 1952 as Margaret Taylor. Married Glyn Lloyd in 1954, BOAC Radio Officer. Emigrated to the US in 1967. Since 1976 President of Lloyd International Media, independent representatives of American educational publishers to American schools overseas. Son Jon Taylor a partner in the business. – Ed.]

At the end of 1951 I was teaching in a boarding school for girls in the Scottish borders, having left my Colonial Service husband in Nigeria. My almost-three-year-old son Jon was in classes with me. In January he was to go to a boarding school in Edinburgh for children whose parents were abroad, or be sent back to Nigeria. I was searching for a job which would pay more and allow me to spend time with Jon. I remembered the Hermes stewardess on the flight back from Kano, who had told me a little about her working conditions, which allowed about a third of the time spent away on a trip off duty on return to the UK. I had enjoyed my flights in the Hermes and Wayfarer in Nigeria, and still remembered the exhilaration of a flight at Sir Alan Cobham's air display in Scarborough when I was about seven years old.

I wrote to BOAC and was summoned to London for an interview with Leslie Pace in Personnel. He was very understanding of my situation, said they had no vacancies, but to keep in touch and let him know "if my marital situation changed." A couple of months later he wrote to say BOAC would be interviewing for stewardesses in Glasgow because passengers like the Scottish accent, and would I like to come along. As a Lancastrian with a few Oxonian vowels I was not optimistic, but was one of four selected from 200 applicants. At that time PanAm had strict height and weight requirements, but BOAC only specified 'a reasonable relationship between height and weight' which covered a multitude of sizes and we all qualified. A rider was added to my letter of employment saying that I must never fly on West African routes because of my marital situation, which was fine by me.

I joined BOAC on May 2nd 1952, the day the Comet first flew. Training for catering crew was in an old convent in Heston and lasted 8-10 weeks. There were eight on our course, two stewardesses and two stewards added to the four of us. Training was a cross between finishing school and boot camp; exams every Friday, and off the course if you failed. I recently found my course notebook, packed with information about the structure of the Corporation: duties of a stewardess – must have strong arms and legs, and be of an agreeable disposition at all times; service must be modelled on that given by Club servants in exclusive residential clubs in London; jungle, arctic and desert survival (anything the monkey eats you can eat); ditching procedures; the will to live; how to address the Queen and lesser dignitaries; the importance of cleanliness and good grooming; how to deliver a baby in an aircraft aisle.

Serving bottle tops with a spoon and fork to our instructors in a mock-up cabin was an ordeal: they would knock their water glass over, complain about the food, insult you and enjoy behaving like the most obnoxious passengers one could meet in those days. Flight Attendants today have to deal with far worse behaviour. On the last Friday we were each interviewed and given words of advice; I was told I was too radical and we were all told we wouldn't last more than six months – the average length of a stewardess's service at that time. Little wonder we celebrated excessively that night.

We had some choice as to which fleet we could join. Most of the girls chose Stratocruisers; I chose Argonauts because I wanted longer trips to give me ample time to visit Jon in Edinburgh. The Argonaut was a DC-4 made by Canadair with four Rolls Royce Merlin engines. It held 40 one-class passengers and there was a semi-circular lounge in the rear which was very popular. The crew consisted of Captain, First Officer, Navigator, Radio Officer, Chief Steward, Second Steward and the Stewardess.

My first trip was a 14-day to Hong Kong. The catering crew had to report to one of the many pre-fab buildings at London Airport 3½ hours before take-off. The Chief Steward was in charge and the Second Steward and the Stewardess counted blankets, linen towels, and checked all the catering equipment; the Chief Steward was in charge of the bar. Both the Chief Steward and the Captain wrote reports on us each trip, and one could be 'snagged' for anything perceived as less than perfect behaviour, or incomplete equipment. Counting used linen towels was one of our more unpleasant duties, as was dealing with airsickness, far more prevalent before aircraft could fly above the weather.

Crew rosters ensured that you never flew with the same crew although occasionally there would be one familiar face on a crew, at an airport, or crew hotel. The only time I met one of my fellow trainees was when changing crews somewhere in the East. I remembered her as not too large of bosom, but she got off the aircraft looking more like Jayne Mansfield or Dolly Parton.

Noticing that I couldn't tear my eyes away from this sudden change of silhouette, she said: "Och, it's terrible – I've got one of those inflatable bras and I'm forever having to let them down or blow them up when I'm flying."

My physics master would have enjoyed seeing the light finally dawn.

"Boyle's Law!" I exclaimed.

"Who's he?" she asked.

"The volume of a given mass of gas varies inversely as the pressure when the temperature is constant," I parroted, understanding it for the first time.

It was emphasised during our training that we females must not expect to be treated differently just because we were women. Doors would not be held open for us, we must learn to pay our share at the bar, and accept the fact that crew conversation was usually about flying, second-hand cars and sex, in that order. They did not tell us that we would be teased continually until we passed some invisible boundary and were accepted as *bona fide* stewardesses.

My first taste of what was in store was before we took off from LAP on my first trip. The Chief Steward sent me to the flight deck to ask the Captain if the golden rivet was on board. I never did find out what it was, the answer was always: "We can't fly without it."

Briefing was done without a microphone in those days. I'm glad to note that the wording of the life-jacket briefing has been changed. It was an exercise in self-control to say: "Pull the red knob smartly downwards" with one of the stewards sitting in the rear lounge pulling faces and making rude gestures.

In Bahrain the crew took me to a nightclub full of Arabs watching belly-dancers. One of the Arabs approached the crew and asked if I were for sale. Naturally they said I was, and negotiated a price of five pounds, providing they could drop me off on the way back. Fortunately I knew we weren't coming back through Bahrain, so in spite of the convincing sales pitch, I knew it was a joke – and also learned my market value.

In Dhaka I was sent back to the terminal to find 16 unaccompanied Russian children before we could take off. Needless to say, they didn't exist, but the passengers enjoyed the joke.

The worst 'joke' was on a trip to Rome. The Captain sent for me. He had a navigation chart on his knees, withdrew his hand from his crutch area holding a pair of dividers which he placed on the map, saying: "Twice as big as Sicily."

I don't think the rest of the crew heard this, but I shot off the flight deck with a burning face. Today I would have said: "What a pity. I was looking for Norway."

Anxious to 'stand my corner' I would try to buy a round of drinks when the crew got together for a drink after a flight. "Buy us a beer in Karachi" was always the response. When we returned via Karachi I found out it was the most expensive place to buy beer on the route – and they still wouldn't let me pay.

Before landing in Hong Kong I was invited to watch the landing from the flight deck. Recently I read an article about the excitement of landing in Hong Kong, high-rises on either side of the approach – that was after the 'new' runway had been built out into the harbour, and before the new airport opened. In the fifties you could literally count the blades of grass on the rocky mountain pass the aircraft had to weave through to land. Take-off was equally challenging: full power, brakes off, sharp turn as soon as airborne at the end of the runway. I don't recall any accidents there in that period, quite a tribute to the skill of those pilots.

On one of my early trips the Chief Steward asked me what year I was born, and gave me a sovereign dated 1927, telling me that it would bring me luck, and to always have it with me when I was flying. I used to keep it in my handbag in a tiny leather envelope. These were the years of the gold rackets, and aircrews were natural couriers for various Oriental gentlemen, although I never suspected it until a steward was caught and jailed in Calcutta. I just thought it was a happy coincidence that the generous steward happened to have a sovereign from the right year.

After a few months the leg-pulling stopped; but on one trip from the Gulf a British man travelling with an Arab in full dress introduced himself as the British adviser to the ******** Government, and his companion as the Sheikh of ********.

As we were always told when VIPs were on board, I assumed the Steward had set this up and said: "And I'm the Queen of the Fairies," went back to the galley and said: "Very funny" to the Steward. Unfortunately they were who they said they were, but last-minute passengers.

Looking back over 40 years, memories pop up of unforgettable characters, phrases, sights and sounds. The flight-deck crew were usually in their thirties, ex-RAF, and because of their experiences and the type of aircraft they had flown, rather different from today's aviators. I remember one of the crew remarking to another as we were flying East: "A Comet's gone in," a phrase I didn't understand. It was the first Comet crash near Calcutta. Pat Rawlinson, the stewardess on that flight, was a girl I had been to school with who had recently joined BOAC.

"Stewardesses are either looking for something or running away from something," said one navigator. I fell heavily into the second category. He also said: "Stewardesses are either poppets or popsies."

"Hospitality is like a pot: if you take something out, you must put something back in – but it doesn't have to be the same pot," explained one captain after I had said I would never be able to repay all the hospitality we received in many places ("bring the girl").

Sights: the Alps rising up like a wall in Northern Italy; Mediterranean islands looking like pieces of a jigsaw puzzle; acres of jungle in South East Asia; but most of all the clouds, stars, sunrises, sunsets and skyscapes, which are an everyday feast for the eyes in the air.

Music: 'Volare' still brings back memories of Rome; 'The Blue Tango' is Tokyo during the Korean War. 'Some Enchanted Evening' is Kano.

During the 'flu season in Japan many people wore face masks. One captain would land and take off from Tokyo with an S.T. looped from ear to ear. Another insisted on eating on GMT and was breakfasting in the evening by the time we got to Tokyo.

Having been brought up by three maiden aunts I enjoyed male company, so in many ways this was an ideal job, and one difficult to reproduce in other walks of life: three weeks in close contact with six men rarely seen again. In Rome or Hong Kong I could wander alone, but there was always company available if wanted. In Basra the crew would relax at the pool at the Port Club; in Rome we could spend the day at one of the beaches – Ostia, Fregene, or Castel Fusano if it was too hot for sight-seeing. Although I was never a good team player, I was very comfortable being part of a crew. I respected all of them, and was usually treated with care and consideration. Many of the stewards were gay ("queer" in fifties slang), excellent at their job and good fun to fly with. I only remember one steward (non-gay) who gave me a hard time, bossed me round and had his own ideas of the duties of a stewardess, one of which was that she had to be first off the aircraft with the passengers trailing behind like a school crocodile. Most of all I remember the humour, and the pleasure of relaxing after a long rough flight with a drink before falling into bed.

In those days of long flight-legs and delays caused by engine changes or bad weather, sometimes it would be 24 hours from getting up to going to bed. On those occasions we received a letter from the Fleet Captain "to be placed in our personal file," along with any complimentary letters from passengers.

Flying from Austin to Detroit via Memphis last week was a marked contrast to the fifties. Detroit was closed by bad weather for a few hours, but it took more than two days to restore efficiency. As crews are paid more when the engines start, airlines prefer to keep them on the ground rather than stacked waiting to land. Union rules restrict the hours crews can be on duty. Detroit was full of mountains of luggage, and people sleeping on every available surface: no free meals, and certainly no free hotel rooms. Different times, at any class of service.

There were opportunities for romance but no pressure, and as men gossiped as much as women I learned about "the easy six," girls who were reputed to sleep around. These were pre-pill days, so promiscuity was rarer. One First Officer christened me "Cobwebs," but as most of the men were married and anxious to get "home to Mum," or as the charmer with the dividers put it: "Knees under Mum's bum," I wasn't tempted and preferred their friendship. Going 'down the route' was an escape from everyday life and its problems for me – and probably for many others.

Interesting passengers were another bonus: politicians, potentates, business men, Queen's messengers – one of whom did beautiful embroidery to pass the time – and with long flights we had time to sit and chat. Not as many women flew in those days, and most were accompanying or joining their husbands. There were few tourists. One female passenger on a flight to Hong Kong had a ten-month-old son, Andrew, and she was obviously unaccustomed to doing anything for him. During the night-stop in Rangoon I looked after him and made many scathing remarks to myself about Colonial wives who had so many servants they couldn't even make a cup of tea. At Kai Tak the woman's husband came to thank me for "helping Jill and Andrew – she only picked him up from the orphanage the day before." Both Jill and her husband, John, had been prisoners of the Japanese and were unable to have children when they married after the war. John and Andrew are now dead, but Jill, now in her nineties and living in Hampshire, is still a dear friend. So much for first impressions.

1953 was a vintage year: the Coronation of Elizabeth II, the conquest of Everest by Edmund Hillary, and I think we also won the Ashes. In April I was rostered for a trip to West Africa, Argonauts having taken over that route from the Hermes. I called the office and mentioned the rider in my contract and was told that I had been hired for worldwide service. So I went. In Kano our crew played snooker with another crew. Our First Officer, Arthur Grant-Jones, an unlikely Cupid, introduced me to Glyn Lloyd, the Radio Officer on the other crew. They had both been with British South American Airways and I had already seen what a close-knit group ex-BSAA crews were. Whenever two or more got together talk was of pisco sours in favourite watering holes, buying perfume in Dakar to sell at great profit in Brazil, local characters they met every trip, their famous Star girls, as BSAA stewardesses were known – and sometimes the Berlin airlift.

In any event, I found what I wasn't looking for. In spite of the difficulties in getting to know each other when were both flying, and we never flew on the same crew – we managed, and were eventually married in June 1954. To the surprise of our friends and families, it lasted for 43 years.

In January 1954 another Comet crashed off Elba after taking off from Rome. For several months after that, pieces of it were collected at Ciampino airport. I remember seeing the tail section intact and neatly severed, and feeling glad that my ditching position was in the Argonaut tail lounge so I might survive a crash equally intact. Putting the pieces of the Comet together at Farnborough eventually proved that explosive decompression caused the crashes.

At some time in the same period an Argonaut stewardess on her first trip was stuck to the loo when the bottom flew off. The aircraft had to reduce height before she could get up – a nasty experience. Soon after that a Stratocruiser window blew out over the Atlantic. A quick-thinking steward slapped a tray in the hole, which held the pressurisation until the aircraft descended. After that crews joked that: "On Strats they use a tray to fix the pressurisation – on Argonauts they use the stewardess's ass." Dated humour, not p.c. today. But it was funny at the time.

After Glyn and I were married we knew that we would not be allowed to fly on the same crew. In October I was posted to Constellations and did a conversion course to learn where everything was. My first trip was scheduled for Sydney, which would be the first time I had crossed the equator. I couldn't decide which clothes to take, packed my case and unlocked it at the last moment to put in a 'little black dress'. We had a full load, mostly men, including Denis Compton travelling with one of the MCC to a Test Match in Australia. There was one woman on board, Mrs Monk with two small daughters and a ten-month old baby, Winston. Her husband had been killed in a Constellation which had crashed in Singapore a few months previously. After his death Mrs Monk had gone back to the UK, but couldn't settle there and was returning to Australia. The crew had a letter asking us to take care of her, especially during landings.

As we prepared to land at Karachi we suddenly climbed again and proceeded to circle the airport. Apparently the main wheels had come down, but not the nosewheel. The control tower shone a light on us to make sure that it really had not descended and was not just a failure of the indicator light. A few sedate dives failed to budge it. After an hour or so using up fuel we told the passengers to prepare for a belly landing. We removed the Exit windows and door, took all belongings off the racks, stacked them in the loo, and showed them how to brace for the landing. It was dark, very noisy without the windows and door, but all the passengers were very calm. Mrs Monk asked me where I would sit for the landing. She was in the front and when I told her I would be in the rear, she asked me to take Winston so that perhaps one of the children would survive.

The Captain did a beautiful landing on the grass alongside the runway, guided by car headlights. I handed Winston out to the waiting ground hostess, Mrs Monk and the girls followed and everyone got out as if the whole thing were an exercise. (I learned that you don't need a chute for a belly landing – the ground is right there.)

We landed about 10.30 pm and at midnight it was my 27th birthday. Before the landing I had taken my sovereign out of my handbag (which was left on board with everyone's personal possessions) and put it in my bra. At breakfast the next morning the crew joked that it must have been my sovereign that had saved us all. I suddenly remembered where I had put it, ran back to my room to check where it had fallen when I undressed. The maid had put it on the bedside table. Nothing left on the aircraft was stolen. The Pakistanis treated us as charmed beings, and even touched us for luck. The euphoria disappeared later that day when the chief BOAC ground engineer, Jack Watson, was killed when an improperly-placed jack caused the Constellation to fall on him. We all attended the funeral a couple of days later, me in my black dress, and all of us wondering: "Why him and not us?"

In accordance with Corporation policy the whole crew was suspended, pending an investigation. We were to return to London on the first BOAC aircraft coming through. Glyn was the Radio Officer on the Argonaut which picked us up. It took the combined persuasive powers of both Captains to convince me that I could 'slip' with his crew in Rome, and return to London with him. I know that I did so, but don't remember much about it, or the next few weeks. I do recall that Glyn took me to see Kay Kendall in "Genevieve" and I cried, for the first time since Karachi, through the whole film. I remember getting out of the night train from Edinburgh after visiting Jon, and telling the engine driver that the wheels on my carriage were loose and about to come off. The only time I saw the crew again was when we were summoned to Stratton House a few months later to be presented with Certificates of Commendation by Sir Miles Thomas.

I had periodic check-ups with Dr Sibbald, the BOAC doctor, and he wouldn't clear me for flying. Eventually he sent me to a psychologist in Harley Street who asked for my life story, listened to me for over an hour, and although it seems far-fetched, started me on the road to recovery. He told me he had an appointment in Glasgow the next day, and would be taking the night train, because he was afraid of flying. He advised me to learn to drive and to type, and to forget about being a stewardess. If I had been the pilot, there was some point in 'getting back on the horse,' but not for me.

In his report he wrote: "The procedure in these cases should be abreactive treatment via injections of sodium pentathol to relive the crash and get rid of the fears that were not expressed at the time. But in Mrs Lloyd's case I think it would bring up a whole lot of things which are far better left buried." An unlikely phrase on this side of the Atlantic.

I gradually realised that it wasn't flying that I feared, but of having to be 'brave' again. Next time I would be first off. All our friends were aircrew who had suffered far worse experiences in the war and I was ashamed of making so much fuss about a mere belly-landing. Dr Sibbald was a great support during this time, and eventually I was invalided out, with a pension of four pounds, twelve shillings and sixpence a year. After a couple of years I flew to the States to visit friends and to see how I felt. I still remember the exhilaration of roaring down the runway. I didn't know any of the crew but when we came in to land at Idlewild one of them came and sat with me and held my hand – I still don't know how he knew, but it was very comforting.

In my present life I fly constantly, sometimes with British Airways, and occasionally write to Robert Ayling to complain about BA's sexist advertising or those ghastly new tails.

Looking back, I realise that those few years I spent in BOAC had the most influence on my life: since recovering from Karachi, every day has been a gift. When I had an hour expecting to die, as so many stewardeses had done in those years, I had no regrets about that I *had* done, only about what I *hadn't* done. When I start worrying about trivia, I remind myself that I had 45 bonus years, including a very good marriage. A book has just been published here called *"The Greatest Generation"* about those who served in the second World War. I still feel privileged that I got to know a few of them.

CHAPTER 13
DENHAM REMEMBERED
by
Roy Mills

When I joined Denham Flying Club in 1953 it was still coming to terms with the change from the prewar flying club and aerodrome (which had been patronised by only very wealthy people) to the postwar era, where people who had learned to fly during the war were now the majority of the membership. When I joined the club it had a large membership of ex-service personnel; Derek Wright ("Wilbur") and his deputy, Sqn. Ldr. Eddie Hewitt DFC were the CFI and deputy CFI respectively. "Tiny" Pantlin, Eric Pope (both ex-RAF) and Eric's wife Yvonne were part-time instructors. Other members included Ron Gillman, who at that time was chief pilot with BEA, "Panda" Watson, Jim Scarlet, an ex-Airframe Mechanic and Peter Heywood who had instructed at Booker during the war. He was now a schoolteacher during the week. There were others but time has eroded the memory. The overall atmosphere was more like an overcrowded crew room, with Andrea the club secretary and bookings clerk adding the feminine touch. At times we would have to vacate the clubroom to escape the heady aroma of her Chanel No. 5.

This atmosphere was just what I wanted. Having been turned down by the RAF, rubbing shoulders with these guys and learning to fly might give me the second chance I desperately wanted.

Regardless of the weather I would drive to Denham on my motor-bike, have my lesson and listen and learn as much as I could from them. I learned to fly on a Taylorcraft Plus D which had two very endearing features: it was uncomplicated and enjoyed the cheapest hourly rate of the club fleet. At the time I was learning to fly I was employed as a junior technician at £6-6s a week out of which I had to pay my way at home and run the motor-bike. My lessons went well and in 13 hours I went solo. After twenty hours I had consolidated my solo flying and had done the short solo cross-country, Westcott-Wallingford-Denham, together with a trip on my own to Shoreham via the tower at Heathrow and the almost non-operational Gatwick. Such dual nav. exercises I had done comprised telling the instructor the way home and how to work out a flight plan. Ground instruction was to read the Private Pilot's Handbook, which contained everything you needed to become a private pilot, from met. to nav. to air law. I still have it and occasionally refer to it when the old grey matter lets me down.

One particular afternoon I was off work for "time off in lieu." The Taylorcraft was booked by a RAF instructor on extended leave who wanted to keep his hand in. Eddie suggested to him he might like a passenger and he agreed. He had booked the aeroplane for two hours and wanted some cross-country flying. He was not very talkative, and other than asking for take-off, climbing and cruising speed and RPM, said nothing. About 15 minutes after take-off we were passing Eton playing fields and he pointed out that was where the Battle of Waterloo was really won. Then he altered course about 30 degrees to starboard, and 15 minutes later he made another turn to starboard. Every now and again he would ask me to find some feature on the map. Ten minutes later he turned to port by about 45 degrees and flew on, followed by another course alteration to starboard. About another 20 minutes later he suddenly turned 180 degrees and asked me for a heading home.

He maintained the heading I had given him without any deviation. After a while I began to recognise some of the features around the local area and I knew my heading was fairly close to the mark. Then I could see Denham on the nose. He joined the circuit and let down on the dead side. On the downwind leg he asked me for the approach speed and I told him 60 mph. As he turned finals he reduced the speed to 50 mph and the Taylorcraft really lost height. We touched down with an almighty bounce and he calmly announced a go-round. On the downwind leg he again asked for the approach speed and promptly reduced to 50 with the same resulting bounce. After a fourth go-round, I suggested that it might be better if I landed the aeroplane. I was curtly told that he had X thousands of hours instructing at Cranwell and Y thousands of hours as a navigator and he would land the aeroplane if it was the last thing he did. From his previous attempts this looked a distinct possibility. Finally he made it down with only a small bounce and we taxied in. As we got out of the aeroplane Eddie said that he hoped I had not been doing the landings. My pilot paid his bill and departed. This had been two valuable lessons, one in navigation and the other in sticking to the numbers in the handling notes.

In those days few light aircraft carried radio, neither did a large number of recreational airfields. PPO was the form. The only navaids as far I recall were NDBs for use by the airlines and the services. The club had the Chatham area forecast each day but for cross-countries you had to book a route forecast with the forecaster at Heathrow 12 hours ahead of the time of your flight. If there was any doubt about the forecast you could obtain the latest actuals from en route airfields and your destination. The best navaid was the mark one eyeball and British Rail, which was still operating steam locomotives; these could be seen for miles, and made life a lot easier. I should point out that in those enlightened days the controllers at Heathrow were more than happy to have private pilots overfly the tower, provided they phoned to give an approximate ETA. Their attitude was that it was far safer to have a light aeroplane over the tower at 1,500 feet where they could see both it and the passenger traffic either just taking off or landing. Usually they came out on the balcony, put the binoculars on you, and having identified you gave a cheery wave. How we have progressed!

The hub of the Club's social life revolved around the Hawk's Ridge restaurant. Every fortnight or so, somebody would think up an excuse for a party. The dos usually really got going at about 8 pm and went on into the late small hours. Quite often our genial host, "Pop" Young, would keel over behind the bar and someone would take over running it, but "Pop" never lost any money as a result of his passing out. Quite often Margaret and I would arrive at home just ahead of the milkman, which meant flying was out for Sunday, not only because of the lack of time between bottle and throttle but through a lack of funds. Despite these boozy interruptions, I was making good progress towards getting my licence.

All that I now needed was my qualifying cross-country, GFT and the written exams to complete my 30-hour course. Then the CFI noticed that I had not done spinning. That would have be done before anything else. I booked the lesson on a "Maggie" with Eddie as Instructor. On the day in question Eddie hired me one of his parachutes for 5/- to cover packing, and briefed me how to use it and how to land, should the occasion arise. "Maggies" had acquired a reputation of occasionally failing to recover after three turns of a spin. This 5/- was in addition to the cost of £3-5s per hour. The club loaned me a flying suit and leather helmet with Gosport tubes. Eddie helped me into the harness and jokingly pointed out that this would be the only time he would put his hands between my legs to reassure me.

I waddled out to the "Maggie" like a penguin and with difficulty clambered into the rear cockpit. Eddie checked that the harness was really tight and then briefed me on the exercise and the emergency drill if the "Maggie" decided not to recover. If after three turns the "Maggie" had not recovered he would tell me to bale out; if I had not done so by four turns, he would say goodbye and jump. We were to climb to 5,000 feet just beyond Princes Risborough, where we would carry out the spinning exercise. Following a clearing turn he demonstrated a three-turn spin to the right, recovered, did one to the left and then climbed back to 5,000 feet. After another clearing turn it was my turn to demonstrate how to initiate a spin and recover after three turns. Fortunately the "Maggie" behaved itself; the exercise was carried out successfully and I felt the exhilaration of watching the earth gyrate below me. When we landed, I got out of the aeroplane, unbuckled my parachute harness and walked back to the club with it over my shoulder with the air of a real pilot. Such was my confidence in Eddie, I am sure I would have done exactly what he said, had it been necessary.

During my qualifying cross-country, I had the privilege to meet Viv Bellamy for the first time, when he signed my chit to say I had carried out the circuit and landing satisfactorily at Eastleigh. Some years later we would meet again when I bought the Currie Wot G-APWT from him and, later, a selection of wing ribs when it got broken.

Once I had my licence, I felt I could afford to branch out and widen my experience. My first conversion was on a J/1 Auster. One Sunday morning I had 'GXG booked for a check-out and was trying to get the hang of raising and lowering the flaps without doing myself and aeroplane a mischief. The aeroplane had a mag. problem and while I waited, I had a chat with the aerodrome 'lad' Brian Dunlop, instead of doing the usual "brakes on," "petrol sucking-in," "set" and "contact." This was the beginning of a friendship that has endured over the last 45 years and is still going strong. Every weekend he would cycle from his home in Hounslow to Denham, get club aeroplanes out of the hangar and taxi them over to the club, and ensure that they were all fuelled up and ready to go on the ensuing bookings. He started this when he was only twelve and his enthusiasm has not abated some 45 years on. After an engineering apprenticeship, a stint with the RAF and several airlines, he has become the training captain of British Aerospace in Washington DC.

At the end of this chat I returned to the Club room to await the J/1. An Irishman called Phil was working out his flight plan for the Westcott-Wallingford trip, watched by Eric Pope. Brian had taxied the J/1 up to the club and Eddie and I did a running change. After several attempts to operate the flaps correctly, I decided that I would give it a rest and have another go in the afternoon if a slot was available, which it was. The bill paid for this lesson and another booked, I walked across the car park to the Hawk's Ridge restaurant for a cup of tea and a sandwich.

When I returned, Eric was looking across the airfield in anticipation of the "Maggie's" return; it was about 15 minutes late. In the Clubroom members were talking as only pilots can, with their hands flailing. Andrea had topped up the Chanel and the atmosphere was heavy, to say the least. I still had to wait for an hour before my next attempt to master the J/1 and I listened in and picked up some useful bits of lore. The phone rang and the volume of the chat lowered as Andrea took the call, but it was only somebody making a booking. By now the "Maggie" was 30 minutes overdue. The phone rang again: as Andrea took the call, the volume again dropped, but it was only another booking. By now the Clubroom was beginning to look and sound like a scene from a Battle of Britain film. Each time the phone rang the conversations hushed – yet more bookings.

Just before 1500 hrs the phone rang again and the room became silent. The "Maggie" had almost certainly run out of fuel and was on the ground somewhere: this was the call we had been expecting. The caller was bellowing down the phone and we could all hear his invective. It turned out that Phil had landed at Bovingdon, where the Air Training Corps was holding the Hertfordshire Wing parade. The parade was expecting the OC of the Wing to arrive by air. As the "Maggie" came to a halt and Phil switched off the engine, the band struck up the National Anthem. Although he was Irish, he considered he was every bit an Englishman, having served in the RAF during the war. He got out of the cockpit, stood to attention on the walkway of the wing and promptly fell off. Officers and cadets rushed to his aid and the band petered out. It was only when he asked them where he was that they realised he was not the CO they were expecting. The Anson carrying the VIP was on finals and the parade commander ordered the "Maggie" to be pushed away out of sight, together with Phil, until the parade was over. This was the reason why there had been no call earlier. The voice at the other end of the phone demanded to speak to the CFI and, despite Wilbur apologising, insisted that the CFI should fly over to Bovingdon with a can of fuel and escort the unfortunate Phil back home. Brian produced a jerrycan of juice and off he went.

My next trip produced more torture for the J/1 and I decided that I would call it a day before I went bust. When I got back to the club Wilbur was tearing one almighty strip off Phil and told him in no uncertain terms that he would have to do more dual cross-countries before he was allowed off on his own again. Outside the club I was preparing to ride home when Phil came out. He looked very dejected as he went over to his big Velocette and I spoke to him. This was the beginning of another life-long friendship which was abruptly terminated when he was killed in a flying accident some years later.

With 50 hours solo and several types in my logbook I decided to approach the RAF for another attempt at becoming a service pilot. A motor-bike accident some three months previously had left me with a good deal of backache and a slow reflex in my left knee. An X-ray revealed that as a result of the accident I now had a slight curvature of the spine, and that was the end of any hope of service flying.

Despite the disappointment I was determined to continue flying. Phil and I discussed the idea of forming a group. Brian knew where there were aeroplanes for sale and we chased after them. One he put us onto was a Gipsy Moth on an RAF field up in the Midlands. Phil's work as insurance assessor took him round the country and he made arrangements to have a look at it while he was out on a job. The Moth was immaculate, had been regularly looked after by RAF personnel, and was roped off in a corner of a hangar. The owner had a large mess bill and needed the cash. £60 for a 60G. Phil put a tenner down as a deposit and rang me. I sent a telegram to my parents, who were on holiday, telling them that I was going to sell the piano which was supposed to be mine but which I could not play. Back came the reply: "Over our dead bodies." It looked as if I would have to sell the motor-bike and go back to my push-bike for transport. Still, if Brian could cycle from Hounslow to Denham, I certainly could.

· I went to see Dr Miles Bickerton, who owned the airfield, about hangarage; we agreed that it would cost £6 per month folded, £7 spread. At the weekend Phil (who had now made up with Wilbur) and I discussed the purchase of the Moth with him. In his opinion it was a very dodgy buy because of its weak undercarriage and lack of spares. On the strength of his advice we forfeited our deposit. A year or so later the Moth was sold by R.K. Dundas for £1,300 and is now in the Canadian de Havilland Museum and worth a fortune. Whether Wilbur's advice was good or whether he just wanted to keep us flying the club machines nobody will ever know.

Next we went to Cosford to look at Tigers being disposed of by the RAF. One very large hangar contained row upon row of fuselages, and another, wings. In each locker there was a very brief summary of the aircraft's engine and airframe hours. Quite apart from the bewildering choice, there was the snag that if one was purchased it had to be removed within seven days of completion of the sale. We had no idea of how to move it or whether Nightscale's Aero Services would do a C. of A. or what it would cost, so that idea went out of the window.

We then learned that if we formed a group and joined the PFA we could get a Kemsley Trust loan and petrol tax rebate on the hours flown, so this is what we did. Peter Heywood would act as our CFI to keep the Club happy, and Phil and two other members beside myself would be the Group. Each week we would hold a meeting at the White Hart in Chalfont St. Peter to discuss the setting up and running of the Group. The only thing that ever seemed to get resolved was whose turn it was to get in the next round of drinks. When we had ensured a good year's takings for the landlord of the pub we joined the PFA. Just before Christmas 1954, we saw an advert for a Tiger based at Rochester, operated by Shorts. It had a new C. of A., had been re-covered and had a low-time engine, all for £225. We all took a day off and went to Rochester in one of the Group member's cars. We told Shorts we would buy it and asked the PFA for a Kemsley loan and the purchase was completed.

My job was to go and see "Bick," as he was affectionately called, to get the hangarage sorted out. At first he wanted £12 per month, but when I reminded him of the price we had agreed a few months ago when the

Gipsy Moth was on the cards he reduced it to £7 per month. Despite his eccentricities I always respected him as a man of honour.

Although the purchase was made in early January, bad weather prevented it being picked up until February 1st. Vernon (who was still a student pilot and member of the Group) and I decided to go and bring the Tiger back to Denham. Vernon was authorised to do a solo return leg and I flew the East Bucks' Taylorcraft to Rochester. Despite the wonderful clear weather we had to fly into a fairly brisk headwind. When we arrived we had to wait for a pilot from Shorts. If we did not crack on we would run out of daylight and I still had to be checked out. After three circuits the pilot felt that I was safe enough to take the Tiger away. By this time it was something like 15.45, and we had work out our route back and get airborne ASAP if were to reach Denham in daylight.

It was agreed that I would taxi out and take off ahead of Vernon. Taxying the two machines in a freshening tailwind took more valuable time. Vernon was having even more trouble keeping the Taylorcraft going in a straight line than me. At the far end of the airfield, with checks completed, we took off – or at least I did. Vernon had ground-looped again and unbeknown to me had wisely called it a day. By the time I realised he was not with me I was almost over the Lee Valley reservoirs and I considered I had passed my point of no return – I would have to press on. I raced across the northernmost fringe of London until I spotted my firm. The lights were already on in the labs and I had to turn slightly to the north-west to avoid Northolt. It was well into twilight when I reached the Colne Valley and turned south for Denham. I was now in the after-glow which ends the day and I still had to fly a couple more miles and land. By that time it was fairly dark. I was going to do a quick circuit and land, but on my final approach a large cloud blotted out the remaining afterglow, and suddenly it was pitch-dark. I was now faced with a night landing on my first solo on a new type. Enthusiasm had got the better of my judgement but I was committed to land. The first attempt produced an almighty bounce and I went round again at low level in order not to lose the field. My second go was all right – I was down. As I taxied up towards the club I went into a large pothole and was stuck. Jan Ferguson, who had just become an instructor, cycled over to me and guided me into the Blister hangar. I was down all in one piece, and an older and a much wiser pilot than had taken off earlier in the day. The group's comments are still not printable.

We still flew the club aircraft from time to time, but being private owners was proving expensive. The flying rate we had set ourselves, plus a monthly sub to cover the repayments and something in the kitty for maintenance, meant that the Tiger was more expensive to fly than the club machines if you did not take the petrol rebate into account. By the time we had paid the first repayment we had only enough money to pay the last month's petrol bill. It was obvious that we would not be able to pay the next instalment. Phil came up with an idea which at first sight seemed like madness in the extreme: reduce the flying rate to £1-7s per hour and pay all bills promptly. On the face of it the Tiger would be repossessed and we would still be paying off our debts long after it had gone, so why not fly it and have fun? By not flying the club aeroplanes we put in more time on the Tiger, got a larger petrol tax rebate and were in a position to pay the next instalment.

Regrettably Eddie resigned from the Club, which further weakened our ties with it as we no longer flew the Club machines. Inevitably there was a falling out and we joined the East Bucks Flying Club on the north side of the airfield. Our social life was now centred on the Clubhouse instead of the Hawk's Ridge restaurant.

It was about this time that Phil announced that at some time he would like to be an instructor and we should do some aerobatics. The club instructors were not keen to teach us as they would lose their flying payment, so we decided to teach ourselves. We had a copy of 1732a which was a manual produced by the Central Flying School for instructors, plus the owners' manual which gave the various speeds to carry out the manoeuvres successfully.

We would practise by using a fire poker as the stick and the armchair as the cockpit. For a loop or stall turn we reduced to an imaginary one-third throttle, pushed the poker forward to start the dive and, when we called out the correct airspeed, pulled the poker back between our legs and walked up the wall as far as we could, pushed our head back into the armchair and closed the throttle. Having gone through the drill a few times it was agreed that we should have a go on the first good day.

The following Saturday the weather was perfect. We got the Tiger out, gave it an extra-special walk-round and off we went. We would climb to 5,000 feet just east of Princes Risborough, where there was a prominent railway line which we could use as a reference, should we become disorientated. Before attempting any aeros we each did a spin and recovery, just to make sure we could get out of any trouble we got into. The first manoeuvre following a clearing turn was a stall turn. Phil did the first to the left and I did one to the right. After another clearing turn Phil did a loop, then I did one. We then did another couple of loops each before trying a slow roll. Phil went first again but, once inverted, could not complete the roll, and pulled out by pulling the stick back. We had lost quite a lot of height and climbed back to 5,000 feet before I had a go. My attempt was, if anything, not as good as his; I got the Tiger onto its back but could roll no further, and I pulled the stick back to get back to level flight, having lost about a thousand feet. We decided to call it a day and went back to Denham.

We got a cup of tea and sat outside the Club, discussing our efforts. In front of us sat two young men ostensibly watching the aerodrome movements. Later we learned that they had been listening to us and decided they would have a go for themselves. While we chatted the two of them got on board the Club's Tiger and off they went. Sometime later they came back and the passenger got out of the front cockpit with his face covered in blood. The pilot had decided he would demonstrate a loop to his friend. He dived the machine very hard and pulled the stick back sharply. The passenger was not strapped in as tightly as he should have been; he slid forward and, as the stick came back, his head was pushed forwards and downwards and the locking lever on the compass, which was unlocked, skewered one side of his nostril, which accounted for all the blood.

The following week there was a notice on the notice-board to the effect that the Tiger should not be spun. We went off to try our luck at the slow roll, without success, and on our return saw the Club Tiger stall over the airfield and spin to the left. The spin stopped, but the Tiger immediately went into a vicious spin to the right, turning much faster than it had done to the left. By the time it had recovered it was only about 500 feet above the airfield. The two crew got out looking very off-colour and got a right-royal blast from the CFI. It was the same two who had tried their hands at doing a loop the previous weekend. Apparently their original attempt had been so violent that the rigging had been strained, hence the different spinning characteristics left and right.

The club had the use of a Moth Major, G-ADHE, and Phil and I got checked out in it. It was not as good as the Tiger and sank quickly in the round-out due to the unstaggered wings, so that you had to be quick with your check to avoid a bounce. It also had another characteristic; at 1,950 rpm it would develop rough running and sometimes stop. One Sunday morning I went up in the Moth Major with one of Phil's friends. The cloud base was only a few hundred feet and tight circuits were about as much as we could do. On one of the downwind legs, he inadvertently put the throttle onto the magic 1,950 rpm, whereupon the engine began to run rough and stopped. Over the wind in the wires I could hear Paddy calling on every Saint he could lay his tongue to. While he was making his appeal to the Saints he closed the throttle. The prop was windmilling and immediately burst back into life. Over the Gosports came Paddy's voice extolling the promptness of the Saints to his supplications.

John Cosmelli had bought the Hirtenberg, G-AGAK, and once checked out I would fly it when the Tiger was not available; it was a big folding-wing open-cockpit parasol aeroplane with a 7-hour endurance.

TOP: HRH The Duke of Edinburgh arriving at Cranwell on the 28th March 1953 in Devon VP961 for the Coronation Year Passing Out Parade.
BOTTOM: The Duke inspects the Flying Wing Parade. Harvard FS752 (coded AH) is identifiable in the background.
Photos: by kind permission of the Air Officer Commanding and Commandant, Royal Air Force College Cranwell.

Two views of the South Bank helicopter landing site during the mid-1950s before it officially became known as Battersea Heliport.
TOP: Whirlwind XA871 at the top of the steps.
BOTTOM: John Crewdson's Agusta-Bell 47J-1 G-AODI.
Photos: John Havers.

TOP: The Saunders Roe Princess flying boat, seen moored at Cowes on the 20th August 1953.
BOTTOM: Don Chubb runs up the Heath Parasol G-AFZE at Redhill on the 23rd August 1952.
Photos: John Havers.

Some of the weird and wonderful contraptions dreamed up by Lt. Cdr. John Sproule and displayed beneath a Dragonfly at 1950s naval air displays.
TOP LEFT: The Flying Bedstead (Mk. 2, naval version).
Photo: Charles E. Brown via Richard Riding.
TOP RIGHT: Witch on a Broomstick. Photo: Peter Amos.
BOTTOM LEFT: Magic Carpet. Photo: Peter Amos.
BOTTOM RIGHT: Antique Flying Bicycle. Photo: Peter Amos.

TOP: Whirlwind 3 XG588 off Lee-on-Solent, demonstrating the lifting net developed by Lt. Cdr. John Sproule. Incidentally, he ditched in this very machine, along with Lt. Simpson, on the night of the 2nd December 1957.
Photo: by kind permission of the Ministry of Defence – © British Crown Copyright/MOD.
BOTTOM: Lt. Cdr. John Sproule (5th from L.) at Negombo, Ceylon in 1956 along with his team and Dragonfly 551. Photo: via Sandy Sproule.

TOP: A DH Sea Venom is towed along the beach at Littlehampton after a wheels-up forced landing on the 30th January 1955. Photo: John Sproule via Sandy Sproule.

BOTTOM: Tiger Moth G-ANUH was the mount of Roy Mills at Denham in the fifties. Photo: Roy Mills.

With full-span ailerons it was heavy in the roll. It originally had a tailskid but this had been replaced by a castoring tailwheel. It seemed that whenever I flew it the tailwheel would become detached and I would spend time walking round the airfield following the skid marks until I found where the tailwheel had come off, while keeping a sharp lookout for landing aeroplanes and getting out of their way. We did, however, do one or two very pleasant cross-countries in the company of Phil and his wife in the Tiger. These came to an end when 'GAK was written off on a cross-country when the weather deteriorated, and it spun into Butser Hill while attempting do a 180 out of the weather.

In 1956 Margaret and I went to the Jersey Rally, escorted by an RAF Pembroke from Farborough. The official reason for the Pembroke's trip was to encourage recruiting on the island, but they acted as escort for the long sea crossing from Eastleigh. Only thirty aircraft took part and it was a wonderful weekend with a return delayed by bad weather. The following year we went the Rally of the Swiss Watch at Bienne and experienced the rigours of French bureaucracy. The following year the group moved to Elstree. Margaret I got married and went to the Jersey Air Rally again, as part of our honeymoon. Again it was the long sea crossing from Eastleigh, with an RAF Anson as escort. The navigator of the escort aeroplane had worked out that with the headwind we had we might well need to borrow their dinghy to finish the trip. As we neared Jersey, one of the crew opened the fuselage door and showed us the dinghy. On board the escort machine the crew were running a sweepstake on whether we would make it and, if we did, how much fuel would remain. In the face of the wind I opted to go low and slow, thereby saving fuel and getting under the full force of the wind.

With that expanse of water there was no way that you would not get your feet wet in the event of the engine stopping for any reason. Who won the bets is probably still classified but there can't be many newly-weds that have started their honeymoon with an RAF escort and a large fraternity of fellow aviators around.

This was our last trip abroad in the Tiger. Phil had got his instructor's rating and was anxious to instruct with a Club; another had got his Commercial and was no longer interested, and another was in financial difficulties and needed the money. The Tiger was sold and a few weeks later was written off in similar circumstances to the Tiger it had replaced. Apart from not having enough money to be a private owner, I liked the camaraderie of Group flying, so with part of my profit from the sale of the Tiger and a loan from my father we bought a "Maggie" 'KKR and accepted the inevitable: we fitted an 11-channel ECHO radio. We went to Dinard as a proving flight and had to admit that, used when necessary, it was a useful piece of kit. We purchased a pair of long-range tanks from

Rex Nicholls of the Experimental Flying Group and took his advice on taping up the outboard flaps.

In 1959 Margaret and I flew up to Oslo using a portable homing radio. Margaret read the Morse IDs and turned the loop aerial to get the null and tell me the course to steer. We went through northern Europe and saw the Arnhem Bridge off to our right. We spent the night in Bremen and the following day went to Skovende, outside Copenhagen, for a couple of days; then it was off to Oslo via Malmo for lunch. The day after we arrived was midsummer's day, and we went for a night cruise on Oslo fjord and saw the numerous bank-side parties and fires. Unfortunately the weather went sour and we had to content ourselves with a bus ride to Lillehammer rather than flying up to Bergen.

Both the Norwegian and German people were most courteous and helpful. Our return was via Kastrup, where we joined the big boys and had to have the airport fire crew assist us off the main runway because of the strong surface wind. Lunch was taken in the SAS staff restaurant and then it was on to Bremen again, where we were stuck for a couple of days because of weather. When we came to leave, we started to work out our flight plan in the restaurant and were asked to move into the corridor, as some of the Lufthansa passengers waiting for a flight were becoming unnerved at seeing two flying-suited people poring over maps. The rest of the return trip was uneventful.

The fifties were drawing to a close. Well-equipped American aeroplanes were coming into the country and gradually non-radio aeroplanes were not welcome at a lot of airfields. The control office where you booked in was now a tower with someone acting as a controller. "See and be seen" gave way to curt announcements of your position round the circuit and authorisations to land or take off. A new generation of private pilots were appearing. Out were going the flying suits and helmets, in were coming lounge suits and flight cases. The hours required to get a licence were going up, along with the hourly flying rates. This was the end of the postwar era and the beginning of the swinging sixties.

Tempus fugit!

CHAPTER 14
MEMORIES ARE MADE OF THIS
(with apologies to the late Dean Martin)

by

Noel Collier

[NOTES ON THE AUTHOR: Noel was born in 1930 at Sidmouth, East Devon, and has lived there all his life. Like many ambitious teenagers he served three years with the Air Training Corps before being called up for National Service with the RAF during 1949-1951.

On discharge he then served for 22 years with the Royal Observer Corps and was awarded the coveted Spitfire Badge for examinations and the ROC Long Service Medal.

He has been a member of Air-Britain since 1950, contributing regularly to their publications over the years, and he won the Air Writers' Trophy in 1960.

After obtaining his PPL in 1964 he became a founder member of the Dunkeswell Flying Club. – Ed.]

It seems like only yesterday when at the tender age of six my parents coaxed me on to the promenade at Sidmouth in Devon, which is still my home town, to witness the flypast around the South Coast of the Short S.23 Empire flying boat "Caledonia," pride of Imperial Airways, and registered G-ADHM. It was being shown off to the great British public in late 1936 prior to undertaking long-range trials with extra tankage for experimental transatlantic flights; the image of this advanced design of the time is still imprinted in my memory.

What really triggered my love of aircraft started during the war years when copies of the now legendary *"Aeroplane Spotter"* became my most treasured possession, passed on by my now brother-in-law who taught aircraft recognition in the Royal Artillery gunnery classes. These famous silhouettes helped one to identify all manner of different aircraft during the second World War.

And so to peacetime. Private flying was very sparse in Devon at first, but one fine Saturday afternoon, while cycling near the old Exeter by-pass, the sight of a BA Swallow landing in an adjacent field caught my eye. This turned out to be a Cirrus-engined Swallow, G-AFHC, flown by one Bertram Arden. The field, now the headquarters of South West Water, contained of a hangar full of gems, including Swallow G-AFGE (with a Pobjoy engine), BK897 (which was dismantled), Tiger Moth BB724 (which was previously G-ACDA of the early de Havilland School of Flying) and the infamous Surrey Flying Service AL.1 G-AALP. Also in the background was the remains of Swallow G-AEAU, previously flown by the Bristol & Wessex Aeroplane Club at Whitchurch and now broken up for spares. Upon further enquiries we were invited to contribute our hard-earned pocket money for a 20-minute flip in G-AFHC; this was so exciting that my colleague and I went back for more. Next time it was G-AFGC, flown, as far as I can remember, by an ex-Coastal Command pilot called Day. His past WW II association with the sea soon came to light when a steep descent was made off Peak Hill at Sidmouth to beat up a boatload of trippers just putting out to sea off the York Steps; zero feet, mind you, and then around the parish church tower a couple of times – what would the CAA say nowadays at such flying?

It transpired that Bertram Arden and Company also had an Auster V G-AJHJ and a modified Taylorcraft Plus C G-AFTN, in both of which I flew. In the latter we performed some cloud-dancing at 5,000 ft or more which was delightful; she is now preserved in the transport section of the Snibston Discovery Park at Coalville, Leicester along with other Austers, I understand.

Arden's Field, as it was called locally, was used extensively by Bertram Arden and his close friends during the early postwar years. An air taxi service was advertised using Auster 5 G-AJHJ, but such commercial endeavours were disapproved of by the management of Exeter Airport and soon ceased. Bertram continued flying on an *ad hoc* basis into the 1950s. *[Some further details are given elsewhere in this book. – Ed.]*

Memories of ATC camps at Locking and Aston Down stand out so well. "Anybody for night-flying at 2300 hours?" came a voice at the billet door; "can just take three, draw straws, be at flying control at 2400 hours."

So green, us 'sprogs' – what a laugh the regulars had on us; so keen we were almost fist-fighting between ourselves. Flying control looked very cold and deserted at midnight, I can assure you. We'd been well and truly 'had'!

The next day the Station Flight Boston ALA67, while landing, took the top deck off a double-decker bus on the A371 road which runs adjacent to Weston-super-Mare, killing one passenger on the top deck. Very sad indeed.

Camp at 20 MU Aston Down was something else: hangars full of Tempests, Lancasters, Austers, Lincolns and – what stands out in my mind – Mustangs FB120, HB839, HB890, KM132 and KM783. They were parked well away from the rest of the aircraft and I often wondered what became of these. Many Tempests were devoid of their flying control surfaces and a large number of Austers went to civilian operators from here, including a batch to the Belgian Air Force (VT976 to 997). Lincolns and Lancasters appeared to be a mix, on overhaul for limited future use or scrap. With hindsight more should have been preserved for posterity.

I was one of the lucky ones chosen to go on an air test in a Lancaster B.7, NX785, which included feathering both port and starboard propellers in turn and a touch-and-go landing at Kemble amidst lines of more Lancasters each side of the runway. Once airborne again I took up the bomb aimer's position in the prone position: boy, what a view! Whereupon a Spitfire formated below us over the Bristol Channel, the image of which still shines in my memory.

The Ferry Pool provided a full day's flying in Anson C.19 VL335 picking up and depositing flying crew at Lyneham, Luton, Waterbeach, Biggin Hill and Wroughton. A break for lunch in the Percival canteen at Luton provided the time to log some of the early production Prentices including the demonstrators G-AKLF & G-AKLG, plus the experimental VN684 with twin fins and rudders.

1950 saw the 'cold war' preparations in earnest and common over Devon skies were the B-47 and the B-36 of the Strategic Air Command, the latter with their familiar and unmistakable sound. No less than a formation of 18 of these monsters was seen at sunset over the North Devon coastline setting course across the Atlantic one evening. The B-47s practised air-to-air refuelling with the KC-97s night and day. These were the halcyon days for spotting, with variety almost unlimited.

My 20 years in the Royal Observer Corps was very rewarding; our Post above ground was W.4 on Peak Hill, which had unlimited views out to Portland and Start Point. Many exercises were laid on during the summer evenings for the ROC which often included Sabres from Chivenor and Lancasters from the School of Maritime Reconnaissance at St. Mawgan.

"Exercise Ardent" held in the early fifties stands out well in my memory as it involved all of the United Kingdom. Most of the activity was in the eastern counties but I do recall logging the first Canberras recorded by the ROC and a Dutch Navy Harpoon en route to Culdrose, our Post being highly commended for being the only one in 10 Group to correctly identify this rare bird. Those of us in the Royal Observer Corps during the fifties will never forget the comradeship and enjoyment we experienced, especially at the Annual Camps at Waterbeach and Stradishall which were a must for many of us.

I shall never forget creeping into No. 56 Squadron's hangar at Waterbeach one lunch hour to log and photograph four Swift Mk. 1s – all with teething troubles – undergoing an engine change. Nearer home Chivenor opened its doors annually to the Royal Observer Corps and I experienced flights in a Tiger Moth, Argosy, Beverley, Hastings, Comet C.2 and Whirlwind, to name a few. Resident Sabres, Hunters and

Vampires were just common everyday 'grind' as far as we were concerned.

January 1952 will always be remembered by most of us in the UK for the infamous "Torry Canyon" going across the narrow straits of the Isles of Scilly and becoming wrecked on the rocks. On the 10th January in appalling weather we saw over Sidmouth Dragonflies VX597 and VZ963 en route from Lee-on-Solent clawing their way westward to Culdrose to help with the disaster. Later that same month on the fine morning of the 25th I logged the first local sighting of two of 849 Squadron's new Skyraider AD-4Ws or AEW.1s, as the Navy designated them, WT944 and WT946. Skyraiders became a great favourite of mine and I recorded 46 of the 50 supplied to the Royal Navy over the period before they were retired in 1960.

Wellingtons, Mosquitos and Sunderlands still plodded the skies in those far-off days, whilst Exeter carried on with Spitfires and the Beaufighter TT.10s for many years, the latter being replaced by Mosquito TT.35s. The Navy was still managing with a few Firebrands, and the odd Monitor TT was logged, also a Sturgeon on rare occasions, whilst Westlands struggled to perfect the Wyvern in Somerset and Devon skies. VZ739, the one and only Wyvern T.3, forced-landed successfully with turbine blade failure on the marshes at nearby Seaton on the 3rd November 1950; Sqn. Ldr. D.A.S. Colvin survived the crash.

A typical day's spotting in South Devon in 1952 also included Ansons, Wellingtons from the Air Navigation Schools at Thorney Island and Hullavington, Attackers and Fireflies from St. Merryn, with the odd Barracuda, Messenger PH-NDR, Chrislea Ace on air-test out of Exeter where they were built, Brigands, SA-16 Albatross, Oxfords, Meteors, Lincolns, Valettas, Varsities, the odd Short Sperrin, Ambassador and the Apollo on air tests. We were very fortunate in the Lyme Bay region that this was a test area for Boscombe Down and many other aircraft came such as the Avro Ashton.

Not so prevalent in those days were airliner movements, for we had no Amber 25 or Upper Red 8 at this time. Fortunately we occasionally saw the DC-6Bs of Swissair and the TWA Constellations on the Shannon – Paris route; that is the NW–SE track. Much smaller brethren on a daily basis were the Jersey Airlines Rapides (and later, Herons), on the Exeter – Channel Islands route. One big surprise was a Hillson Praga HB-UED which passed over the garden on the 14th March 1953 en route to Roborough from Hatfield – quite a *coup* at the time. The majestic Princess flying-boat G-ALUN was seen following the coastline on the 11th May, returning at contrail height – would you believe? – an hour later. Netherlands Mk. 4 Fireflies on the 22nd July made a rare appearance en route to Culdrose. Sycamores WT925 and WT959, previously G-ALTA and G-ALTB respectively, flew past on the 9th October.

Glorious spotting excursions to nearby Merryfield on our motorcycles was often the order of the day. Merryfield was home to 208 AFS with Vampires, while Westlands also used the base, which contained a large hangar always full of new Wyverns. From the open doors on the 15th October we logged about fourteen of them, all seemingly awaiting delivery to the Royal Navy after mods, whilst the Welkin NF.2 prototype stood forlorn and wingless outside for many months.

Back in Sidmouth 845 Sqn appeared on the 26th March 1954 with three of their new ex-USN Sikorsky S.55s (WV200, WV205 and WV219) en route to Culdrose, whilst Bristol Freighter 31 UB722, No. 186 off the line, flew over on the 19th May a week before delivery to the Burmese Air Force.

The 14th August 1954 was a day to remember; parked out at Exeter I discovered the Dragonfly G-AJOV with large placards lashed on to the sides of the pods which said *"The Evening News."* I had seen this helicopter at low level around the coast and I mentioned my interest to Capt. John Crewdson, busy on a preflight check, noting that the operator was Autair and the fact that the helicopter had wooden blades etc. Imagine my surprise when he asked me what I was doing that afternoon and would I like a ride? Wouldn't I just!

"Just sign the blood chit and pay the return landing fee and we are off."

My first helicopter ride: straight down the river Exe at zero feet, the guys digging for sandworms near the estuary didn't even look up as we passed majestically over their heads. Around the coastline low-level to Sandy Bay and then back westwards along to the Great Western line which runs along the coast from Exeter down to Dawlish and Teignmouth. Hey now! We are making a low pass, we can't go through the railway tunnel. Hey! John is going between the famous rock – the 'Parson and the Clerk' – and the cliffs following a train which has just emerged from the tunnel. Then we land on a sandbank off Teignmouth much to the interest and amusement of some of the holidaymakers; then off again. There's a boat load of trippers which John spots and we make a pass at them, and then the skipper at the tiller enters into it and steers towards us and we make another pass, and all too soon we are down as far as Dartmouth and the Royal Naval Academy. Such a beautiful scene and there in the mouth of the estuary were some basking sharks to be observed. Then low-level right back up to the river Exe and to the inevitable traffic jam on the Exeter bypass which was on John's itinerary. We didn't have an M5 motorway in those days and it became part of the annual holiday to be stuck in this traffic jam as you headed westward for

Torbay and Cornwall, so we had to circle these beleaguered motorists before landing back at Exeter to pay the landing fee. All told, my helicopter baptism lasted 90 minutes, which cost the *"Evening News"* a dizzy pound a minute! Finally back at Exeter, I thanked John Crewdson before he departed for his base at Gatwick.

The coming of the jet age for commercial aviation saw me board a Pan Am Boeing 707 N708PA at Heathrow for the USA in September 1959; no tunnel to the central area in those days, just a few austere huts and buildings on the northern side. BOAC was obviously first across the pond with their Comet 4 and both aircraft were standing amongst loads of propliners: this certainly portrayed what the future would hold. We flew out via Santa Maria in the Azores, as Gander was fogged; a refuelling stop was essential in those early models which struggled against the prevailing westerly winds. Onwards from La Guardia to Buffalo in no less than N7429, a Capital Airlines Viscount – talk about home from home! Spotting across the pond was always interesting but though it was mainly a family visit I did log plenty of Stratocruisers, Constellations, DC-4s, DC-6s and DC-7s and even a civilian-operated Martin Marauder executive. I had a flight from Bell Aircraft in a Bell 47 Ranger over the Niagara Falls and an internal flight in American Airlines DC-6 N90739. I returned to England in Boeing 707 N709PA; both of those early 707s do not exist any more as they were destroyed in accidents.

To end my *spiel*, here are some extracts picked out from the log which may be of interest: on 23rd June 1954 we logged no less than 23 B-47s which seemed to head towards Berry Head and then turn to the east, and then on the 21st October I witnessed what I believe was the first Hunter to do a supersonic dive in this area. (This caused quite a bit of comment in the local paper and I even had a solicitor's clerk coming to my door to confirm that such an occurrence had happened, as one of the locals had complained.) On the 14th April 1957 I logged the Convair 340 G-ANVP, Napier's test-bed for the Eland engine. Believe it or not, on the 22nd January 1958 and again on the 24th, Sputnik 2 was visible; in fact it didn't appear again over the UK after that time. The 23rd May brought five Dutch Avengers, while on the 25th May DH.86 G-ACZP came up from St. Mary's to Exeter. On the 19th July Peter Twiss came over in the Fulmar G-AIBE to Culdrose, presumably for their Air Day. Prestwick Pioneer XL664 went to Roborough on the 22nd July and the 9th September saw Sycamore G-AMWH advertising "Shell" on the side.

I have continued my spotting activities up to this day, but a new field of activity opened for me in February 1964 when I decided to commit myself to a flying course at Exeter Aero Club to learn to fly the Auster J1/N Alpha – but that's another story.

CHAPTER 15

AS IF IT WERE YESTERDAY

by

Neil Jensen

[NOTES ON THE AUTHOR: Neil's flying experiences during the fifties are described here. It was not until the late sixties that he regained his PPL, on 600 Squadron Flying Group's Chipmunk, G-APPK. In partnership with Brian Stevens, he founded Sportair Flying Club in 1970 and offered the full PPL course for £200 on the Fournier RF-5 and single-seat RF-4. Prior to the 1973/4 fuel crisis the club grew to be one of the busiest at Biggin Hill and one of the very few to encourage aerobatics, formation flying and air racing. Inevitably this brought about involvement with the Tiger Club at Redhill where in due course he was able to base his beloved Bücker Jungmann, G-BECW. When displaying this aircraft he would brief the commentator that the Jungmann, whilst carrying authentic Swiss military markings, was of German design (1934) but was actually built in Spain (in 1951, as a CASA 1.131) and was being flown by an Anglo-Scot with a very Danish surname.

Over the years he also had the pleasure of owning the Mk.1 Percival Proctor, G-AIWA, which carried its RAF markings, R7524. He had reason to regret selling this lovely aeroplane as soon afterwards it was to meet its end when the next owner parked it in a tree at La Ferte Alais. He found that the Percival Gull Six G-AERD, which replaced the Proctor, had very serious handling problems. These were only resolved when the fabric was stripped from the wings following what could have easily been a calamitous take-off accident at the 1984 PFA Rally at Cranfield. After repair it was 15 mph faster.

Other historic aircraft that passed through his hands were the Miles M.17 Monarch G-AFLW, which he bought when Christies auctioned off the Strathallan Collection in 1981, and the pretty little high-winged Monocoupe 90A, G-AFEL, whose five-cylinder radial engine had a rather strange beat plus the unnerving habit of misfiring every so often.

He remains a member of the Tiger Club, having joined in 1969, and succeeded Lewis Benjamin ('Benjy') as Chairman. He was deeply involved in persuading members to fund the rescue of the Club in 1990 and in establishing it at Headcorn when it became necessary to move from Redhill. – Ed.]

Many is the time that I have tried to recollect why I chose to fly. I had joined the Naval Section of the Combined Cadet Force at school, yet something made me switch to the RAF Section. Was it that I had a cousin doing his National Service in the RAF? He spent much of his two years sitting in a field somewhere in East Anglia waiting for the radio to come to life with a call from a pilot asking for a "fix." A quick swing of the aerial to get the strongest signal, check the reciprocal to ensure that it was slightly weaker, then telephone the controlling unit with the bearing. They would then plot the intersection with two other bearings and pass the "fix" to the pilot with an indication of what class of "fix" it was. Not my idea of a lot of fun.

No, it probably goes back to 1944 when my father sent the rest of the family to stay with friends in Norfolk whilst the "Doodlebugs" were at their worst. At that time we lived between Biggin Hill and Kenley and had a barrage balloon in the next field but on the wrong side of the house. I can clearly remember as a seven-year-old having tea just after arriving at the Norfolk cottage and asking why the tractors were making such a noise. The "tractors" were P.47 Thunderbolts and P.51 Mustangs flying from East Wretham as part of The Mighty Eighth. Soon afterwards I was befriended by a USAF Sergeant who was no doubt badly missing his own family back in Kentucky. He took me all over the station, sat me in P.47s and P.51s, had engines started for me and then sent me home with a pair of cannon shells. Live or not, they certainly came out of the live ammunition store. When my father next arrived up there he dropped them down the well; I wonder if they are still there. Could that friendship with Sergeant Mankowitz have started a love of the air?

The Primary Glider that the school RAF Section endeavoured to bungee-launch for short hops on the playing fields did not do much to foster things but visits to the Royal Aircraft Establishment at Farnborough and the Aircraft and Armament Experimental Unit at Boscombe Down probably helped. At the former we were treated to a fascinating address by the Director who at that time was Dr Arnold Hall, later to become Sir Arnold Hall, managing director of Hawker Siddeley Aircraft. I can clearly remember the RAE's vertical wind tunnel for checking the spinning characteristics of extremely accurate scale models, which included the Javelin.

My first flying experience occurred in 1953 when an AOP Auster visited the school. The flight was very brief and I recall the horror during the landing approach of wondering how on earth the Army pilot intended to set this noisy contraption down on the tiny bit of grass surrounded by so many trees, yet still avoid the first XI cricket "square."

The CO of the school RAF Section was Dr Bryan Thwaites, also later knighted, whose connections with Oxford enabled him to arrange for a small number of us to spend a week with Oxford University Air Squadron which was then at Kidlington. I flew 10 hours on Chipmunks during April

1954. We were not allowed to solo as we were civilians but did a dummy solo with Sqn. Ldr. Hart, CO of OUAS, sitting in the back doing and saying nothing. I still have his verdict: "Jensen made very satisfactory progress whilst flying with OUAS and could have soloed easily had this been possible. He appears to have plenty of natural aptitude." I expect he wrote that of everyone.

Training continued with the school CCF and through this it became possible to attend the RAF's Aircrew Selection Centre, which was then at Hornchurch; this resulted in the offer of a Flying Scholarship to this seventeen-year-old. The Wiltshire School of Flying at Thruxton converted eagerness into genuine enthusiasm for the air during August 1954, using the venerable DH.82A Tiger Moth. Initially my instructor was Sqn. Ldr. Bowry, who was serving on the Rotary Wing Flight at Boscombe Down. More than once he would fly over in one of the unit's helicopters, hop out, don a leather helmet with Gosport tube and settle into the front seat of the Tiger. I went solo in G-ANNP on the second day of instruction after three hours dual. Now I knew I really wanted to fly.

John Heaton became my instructor and it is him I must thank for any sound flying habits that have stayed with me. What a sublime August it was. Fine weather plus the delight of gaining confidence in this new element. One day whilst pottering around solo I saw an extraordinary silver arrow pass beneath the Tiger. The next day we read in the papers of the maiden flight of the P.1, later to become the Lightning.

John Heaton and I flew to Sandown in the Isle of Wight for the dual landing away cross-country. We had just commenced the return leg to Thruxton when his voice through the Gosport tube invited me to lose some height, then search amongst the trees along that part of the coast of the island. John told me that there was a nudist camp located there, but the residents must have been rather coy about prowling Tiger Moths as there was little to see. The qualifying solo cross-country, on the 14th, took me to Portsmouth (one of many fine grass airfields long since gone!) and Shoreham. I refuelled at the latter and asked someone to swing the propeller for me.

"Aren't you going to chock the aircraft?" he asked.

"We don't normally bother at Thruxton," I replied.

I am now aghast at such a cavalier and dangerous attitude, especially when one remembers that the Tiger has no brakes. I am pleased to say that in later years I have learnt a far more responsible attitude towards swinging propellers with the Tiger Club.

The two years of National Service was to most adolescent males the fast track to becoming grown men. Having by now no doubt in my mind that I wished to become neither soldier nor sailor, the RAF sent me a 4/-postal order representing one day's pay for an Aircraftsman Second Class and instructed me to report to RAF Hornchurch again. With the Flying Scholarship and PPL under my belt, the selection process simply required another medical. Onwards to RAF Cardington for kitting up and to await the formal results from Hornchurch whilst having one's eyes and ears opened to the crudities of life as a raw AC2 by Corporal Jennings who had charge over all aspiring aircrew. The few of us who received the good news that we had been selected for pilot or navigator training then had the pleasing task of handing back our coarse airmen's shirts, which were replaced with smooth, cotton officer-style ones.

Next to the Initial Training School at RAF Kirton-in-Lindsey on the top of a bleak Lincolnshire wold where Officer Cadets were transformed into Acting Pilot Officers. The National Servicemen amongst us were still paid as AC2s and at the weekly pay parade we called out the last three digits of our RAF number, marched forward and were handed our pay to the nearest pound, in my case £1! My RAF number was 2773000 which presented me with a problem. Should I call out "0, 0, 0" or "Triple 0" or "Zero, Zero, Zero"?

The only times we got near to an aircraft at Kirton was when some of us were bundled into an Anson for a short local flight and when we mounted guard duty at night in one of the hangars. It was hard to see how the latter advanced our training as we were armed with rifles without bolts and the only aircraft were gliders, upon whose taut fabric wings the resident pigeons would direct their droppings from the trusses in the hangar roof. They certainly ensured that one did not sleep whilst doing one's stint patrolling around the hangar.

Other recollections of those twelve weeks at Kirton are of the weekly visit to "The First & Last," the pub in the village adopted by our course, where we mixed quantities of bitter with cheese and raw onion sandwiches. A delightful Welshman on our course, by name Roger Rhys-Evans, (where else could he have hailed from?) had fractured a rib playing rugby and his chest was bound into a solid plaster cast. I can remember the sympathy we felt for him after we all returned one evening from "The First & Last." His agony from the swelling effects of large quantities of beer was too dreadful to behold.

Generally we were extremely fit from drilling, PT and the various sporting activities, although much time was also spent in the classroom or simply "bulling" one's kit and the barrack block upon which weekly inspections were made. There were also the leadership exercises during which the nominated team leader had to devise a way of getting his colleagues across such obstacles as a water-filled ditch with hopelessly inadequate poles and ropes whilst the instructors tossed thunderflashes into the water to liven things up.

Then at last we were on our way to our first flying station which in my case was No.6 Flying Training School at RAF Ternhill. My friends Clive Elton and Anthony Preston have already told of their experiences in *"More Tails of the Fifties"* so I shall confine myself to just a few instances that come to mind from my time on No. 123 Course at Ternhill and later on the same course at No. 5 Flying Training School, RAF Oakington.

It was the custom on training stations, unbeknown to us newcomers, for the senior course to put the incoming new course through some outlandish or demoralising procedures. I recall doing PT at an incredibly early hour and having to write a report of our first impressions of Ternhill for our supposed new instructors, actually the then senior course. I should have become suspicious when I noticed a colleague's paper with "B***s" writ large across it. When our turn came to welcome a new course it happened that they had already started their flying training elsewhere and were therefore unlikely to be hoodwinked. As it turned out we were able to upstage their know-it-all attitude after they had been there a short time by organising a night escape and evasion exercise in which all courses were to participate. Mike Dyson, our course leader, conducted a briefing with us all crowded into the Mess ante-room including some of our instructors and even the CO, Gp. Cpt. Carter, there to lend credence. Each course was to find its way undetected across open country to a rendezvous some ten miles distant where coaches would be waiting to bring everyone back. Two or three courses were despatched ahead of the unsuspecting new course but they simply slipped round to the rear of the Mess and waited silently in the dark for the new course to depart. The rendezvous was genuine but the coaches were not. I can still remember hearing in the early hours the plaintive voice of one of those who had covered 20 miles in the dark calling to Mike Dyson outside his room: "Mr Dyson, you may be an officer but you are certainly no gentleman."

Plt. Off. Troughton was my instructor on the Provost and he sent me solo (Exercise No.13) after 6½ hours on the 13th February 1956 at approximately 1300 hours. This took place at the satellite training airfield of RAF High Ercall near Shrewsbury on packed snow. Luck must have been on my side because, having made an unremarkable first solo flight, Plt. Off. Troughton walked back to where I had parked, took a long look at one of the undercarriage legs, then indicated that I should shut down the engine. It transpired that one tyre had just punctured and was in the process of deflating. When eventually we returned to the crew-room at Ternhill the ritual cutting off of my tie took place where it was hung in the order in which we had soloed. Mine was one of the early ones at Ternhill but I gained pole position later at Oakington on the T.11 Vampire.

The Provost was a delight to fly and was probably an ideal initial trainer as it required no previous experience yet did virtually all that the Harvard had done. I suspect that the powers-that-be, after deciding in favour of the Jet Provost for all-through jet training, had reason to regret the lack of a piston-engined tail-dragger that demanded a subtle combination of hand/eye coordination with judgement of speed and height. Just as with the Tiger Moth during those war years, if one could not three-point the Provost in a crosswind without drift, one was not going to waste the tax payers' money by getting as far as instrument flying before one's shortcomings became evident.

Mention of the Jet Provost reminds me of a cross-country to RAF Hullavington where there was an experimental flight of the Mk.1 variety with its unnecessarily long tricycle-undercarriage legs. Having lunched in the Mess, I inspected one closely but felt no regrets that my mount was the earlier Alvis Leonides-powered version.

Shropshire was a beautiful part of the world from which to fly, with the Welsh mountains to the west and the landmark of the Wrekin to the south. However, if the wind was from anywhere between north and south-east we were made very aware of it by the industrial 'clag' it brought with it. The Met. Officer at Ternhill was a rather short, bald man whom we called Cu-Nim Jim. He had been there some time and really knew his local weather, with the result that if Cu-Nim Jim told us at briefing that a warm front was approaching from the west and that the Ternhill cloudbase would be down to, say, 1,000 ft at noon with visibility of 3 nm, that would indeed be the case. Rarely was he even half an hour out in his forecasts.

During the latter stages of my nine months at Ternhill I was happily engaged in some solo exercise when a Vampire approached and proceeded to do a complete 360° turn around me, making me feel as though I was stationary. How jealous I felt; it was indeed time to be progressing to the next stage.

A new sound greeted one on arrival at RAF Oakington, the distinctive scream from the centrifugal compressor blades of the Goblin engine in the Vampire. My instructor was Flt. Sgt. Smith who had survived carrier landings in the Fleet Air Arm, was demobilized after the war, but then decided to re-enlist with the RAF; however his timing was bad and he was not granted a commission. All his FAA friends, he said, were either now of senior rank or dead. I must say I was never enamoured with the idea of trying to put an aircraft down on a heaving deck and rely upon picking up the wire with my tail-hook to prevent me from toppling off the sharp end.

Smithy was a brilliant instructor and we got on famously. The first familiarisation flight was a shock to the senses. For a start one could not really hear the engine which was completely smooth. Acceleration from release of brakes seemed phenomenal, the rate of climb exhilarating and, wow, the 'g' loading in that first turn! Everything seemed to happen so much faster than in the Provost yet I was off solo in the T.11 in six hours. Shortly after came the first FB.5 solo flight. The single-seater which we flew thereafter for all solo exercises has a totally different cockpit and, apart from spending time in it with the Pilot's Notes, the only preparation one received was with one's instructor beside the cockpit and two airmen draped over the tail-booms to raise the nose.

Smithy said: "Right, that's the landing attitude. Off you go!"

Handling was not dissimilar to the T.11 and one soon settled down at 10,000 ft getting to know the aircraft. "My God, the fire warning light has come on." Try to remember the drill. Climbing turn to look for smoke. None! Now I notice that the light has gone out. Keep turning. It has come on again. Now off again. Well, you have probably guessed what was happening. The fire warning lamp incorporates a red filter over the bulb, which was positioned in a prominent position just to the right of the gun-sight mounting. As the aircraft turned, the sunlight was falling intermittently on the instrument panel and the filter reflected this back as though the lamp was dimly alight. Having calmed down, I enjoyed the rest of the 40-minute flight and carried out a respectable first landing in the FB.5.

The single-seater was a joy to fly. The cockpit, when once one was installed, was roomy but sitting centrally with one's head within the bubble canopy gave one a fabulous all-round view. The wings seemed way back and the nose fell away out of view beyond the bullet-proof screen. What a contrast it must have offered to an earlier generation of Fighter Command pilots who grew up on a view, at least when on the ground, that was blocked by RR Merlin or Griffon or even Napier Sabre. The control column had the macho "spade" grip, ideal for using two hands on when pulling as hard as one could during a tail-chase when one was fighting the "greying out" of a constant 7g. How well I remember my vision diminishing into greyness with just the small patch of sight remaining focussed upon the formation leader 200 yards ahead in a steep turn as I strove to stay on his tail. Pull any harder and all sight is lost. Relax a fraction, yes, he is still there. Try to "get a bead" on him? No way! It was all I could do to keep him in sight and wait for the wing-waggle signal to rejoin. More often than not one would lose the leader, he being one of our instructors and therefore somewhat more cunning than us, and soon after one would hear, "Dagger! Dagger! Dagger!" to indicate that one was metaphorically riddled with holes from his bullets, he now sitting infuriatingly upon one's own tail. On other occasions a tail-chase might result in one losing the whole formation. It never ceased to amaze me that one moment the sky could be full of aircraft and the next there was not a dot to be seen, even on a gin-clear day. One had read that about dog-fights with the Luftwaffe and not really believed it.

One particular tail-chase remains very clear in my memory. It was a day of towering, brilliant white cumulus clouds and the instructor leading the formation took us on a glorious medley of swoops and turns around this majestic scenery. On rejoining formation he led us back to Oakington which at the time was right under an enormous Cu-Nim. To have enjoyed the dazzling sunlight and grandeur we had just left and then run in and 'break' in the black monsoon conditions below made me feel very privileged.

We students were constantly reminded that there were two things to be avoided in the Vampire FB.5. Negative 'g' could cause unwanted fuel to swill around in the engine compartment with the possibility of it catching fire and, despite the twin booms and rudders, the small amount of vertical surface meant that recovery from a spin was more a case of luck than judgement. There were some who could not resist the temptation to try spinning the FB.5 and almost invariably they had cause to regret their action, especially as the single-seater was not equipped with an ejection seat. Climbing out cannot have been easy whilst the aircraft and pilot were being subjected to the various accelerations inherent in a spin.

All dual instruction continued in the T.11 and a very special memory is of a flight with Smithy just after midnight on a gloriously clear June night with unlimited visibility. We hurried through whatever exercise we were carrying out and headed down to the bright lights of London. In those days controlled airspace stopped, as I recollect, at 11,500 ft. We were up above 20,000 ft. Quite apart from the metropolis itself with the black snake of the Thames winding through it and the colourful lights of the West End, even Piccadilly Circus being discernible, we could see every town in the South East including the half-moons of coastal towns with the corresponding French coastal towns beyond. Paris was just a glow on the horizon. We proceeded to aerobat with this glorious plateau of lights moving around us as though we ourselves were stationary. A truly unforgettable experience, and the more so when we learned on our return to the crew-room that we were not the only T.11 performing aerobatics over the centre of London that night!

Unless we were carrying out a formation exercise, we would always be on the lookout for other aircraft that we could 'bounce.' The USAF T.33s invariably seemed easy meat but a Meteor presented a problem low down whereas one could expect to get the better of him at high altitude. One day on a high-level cross-country two Hunters came up on either side of me, then, after a wave, opened up and left me standing. How I yearned to fly that most beautiful of aircraft, a wish never to be fulfilled as Duncan Sandys decided that the days of manned aircraft were limited and one way of cutting back on the strength of Fighter Command was to disband the Auxiliary squadrons. On completion of my National Service I had hoped to fly Meteors from Biggin Hill and I believed that in due course the Auxiliary squadrons would replace the ageing Meteor with my dream machine, the Hunter.

Escape and evasion exercises were part of our training, even if the one I described at Ternhill was designed solely as a means of putting down a rather bumptious new course. The intention was that we should have some idea of what it might be like to exist and then escape from behind enemy lines. Our instructors, local police, farmers or anyone would constitute the "enemy." One such exercise was planned for all courses then at Oakington and details were posted well in advance. These showed that we would be dropped after dark in pairs somewhere inside the large Thetford military training area. We would have to find shelter for ourselves until 9.00 am the next morning at which time cards bearing the name of all students would be placed at 20 or so different map references scattered throughout the training area. We were to collect as many cards as possible bearing our own name before making our way to the official rendezvous at the end of the exercise. Throughout this time the "enemy" would be searching for us so we had to make use of all natural cover. Our course saw this as a good test of our initiative and we agreed amongst ourselves that, irrespective of where each pair was dropped, we would make our way to a specific map reference during the hours of darkness whilst it was much easier to evade the enemy. When the cards were put out each pair would then collect all the cards for our course and take the rest of the day to reach our unofficial rendezvous where we would distribute the cards before progressing, again in our pairs, to the official rendezvous.

Not surprisingly, the "enemy" smelt a rat when all the cards for 123 Course disappeared simultaneously from the various map references soon after 9.00 am. The interrogation to which we were subjected individually was harsh and uncompromising and was overseen by the CO, Gp. Cpt. Kirk. As far as I was concerned, we had obviously been rumbled but I felt that the manner in which the exercise had been planned, plus the prior notice that was given, created a perfect invitation for us to use our own initiative. As a punishment we were dropped back in the Thetford training area and told to make our own way back to Oakington. The last laugh remained with us though, as the father of Bill Votier who was on our course ran a bus company in nearby Norwich. Bill made his way to the nearest telephone and asked his father to send a coach as quickly as possible. The coach managed to pick up most of the course and get back to Oakington ahead of the C.O. and our instructors.

Towards the end of our training some of us were chosen to compete for the aerobatic trophy. This was to be judged in the air by another squadron commander sitting in the right-hand seat. Smithy and I worked out a sequence for me that included a full upward 360° vertical roll, an "Upward Charlie" as we used to call it, followed by a stall turn. The T.11 had a slightly larger fin and rudder than the FB.5 but the stall turn, coming as it did after the vertical roll, was still a rather optimistic manoeuvre. Smithy would sit beside me saying: "It's not going to work." Often it did not and we would flick out and have to recover from the ensuing spin before trying again. On one occasion I had been practising on my own in a T.11 and had again spectacularly flicked out of my attempt at the stall turn. I must have been slow to close the throttle because, back in the crew-room enjoying a coffee, another student, by name John Dibben, came in having just landed, and reported having seen a most unusual contrail corkscrewing vertically upwards.

Incidentally, John had a somewhat unusual nickname. Being the shortest in stature on 123 Course, whenever we went on parade he found himself in the middle of the rank. Came the day that, whilst we were standing to attention, the drill sergeant found reason to inform us that the middle rank was crooked. What he actually said was: "There's a dog-leg in the middle of this rank." From then on John became known as "Dog-leg Dibben."

As far as the aerobatic trophy was concerned, I had to fly on a day when there was no horizon and duly flicked out when attempting the stall turn. So annoyed was I with myself that I tacked another Upward Charlie and stall turn onto the end of my sequence but, even though that worked, Sqn. Ldr. Nicholls was unimpressed.

The course ahead of ours had a bad time with several fatal accidents. We had none and the incidents that did occur all seemed to involve my good friend Chris Baker. He certainly flew with great enthusiasm but also managed to be in the wrong aircraft at the wrong time. Two Provosts were written off as a result of incidents whilst Chris was with an instructor. Two Vampires were also destroyed, both in fairly spectacular fashion. His solo incident involved failure of the rear bearing in the Goblin of an FB.5, causing a flame-out. Being Chris, it had to happen on a low-level cross-country so that he had none of the height one might normally expect with which to glide to one of the many airfields that were available in those days. He went through a couple of hedges and over a ditch. Later he said that he had no recollection of taking his feet off the rudder pedals and placing them against the instrument panel. This was how he came to a halt and, since everything beneath the panel had by then disappeared as he careered across the East Anglian countryside, he departed the aircraft by ducking under the panel and claims he did not stop running until he ran into a hedge.

The end of our course brought both sadness and elation. For me there would be no more flying as my two years National Service had but three months to run with no prospect of a posting that would enable me to get my feet off the ground. The elation though was shared with Smithy as two of his students, Nigel Morgan and I, had between us gained the Flying Trophy and the Cup of Honour.

The nearest I came to an aircraft during the months waiting to be demobbed was when I sailed in a dinghy on Lough Erne in Northern Ireland. I had been posted to RAF Castle Archdale, once a very grand country estate bordering the lough. It had been a Sunderland station during the war but by the time I arrived the only Sunderlands were at the bottom of the lough. For some reason it remained an RAF station, even though there was a far larger number of army personnel stationed there as a consequence of the IRA, who were getting mildly active in the late fifties. I still have one of their manifestos that I removed from a telegraph pole. There were only six regular RAF Officers there and my role was to enable them to get some leave. This meant that I performed all kinds of duties including Assistant Station Adjutant, Motor Transport Officer and Mess Secretary. I also found time to sail on the beautiful waters of Lough Erne with its rather quirky winds. Maybe that was why a number of Sunderlands had come to grief there.

Flying in the fifties did not cease altogether for me since, despite having gained my RAF wings, the University of London Air Squadron saw fit to enrol me, the reason given being that I could help to keep the aircraft utilization up in periods of bad weather. The aircraft in question was the Chipmunk but, though I had flown the "Chippie" four years earlier at Kidlington, it was a slight shock to the system after the Vampire. Firstly, the engine threatened to stop at the top of a loop whereas I had been accustomed to half-rolling at the top of a loop in the Vampire and pulling into another loop to form a vertical figure eight. Also the "Chippie" would float on landing if one approached too fast. The Vampire had those 'barn door' flaps with which to slow down, plus airbrakes if necessary. In those days ULAS flew from RAF Biggin Hill with its very nostalgic Officers' Mess, whilst the squadron headquarters were across the road from Imperial College, where I was now endeavouring to get back to some serious study after the two very enjoyable years in the RAF. For me, training evenings at ULAS HQ were spent sitting in the bar and in the process earning enough to cover my bar bill. I did not even have any travel costs.

After this my flying came to an abrupt halt until the late sixties when I bumped into Brian Stevens whom I had known at Kirton-in-Lindsey before he had gone to Canada for his flying training. In due course we started Sportair Flying Club, opening our doors for business on the inauspicious day of May Day 1970. The 1973 fuel crisis brought an end to my involvement with Sportair though the club has continued in a different form since. My own interests turned back to earlier flying times with the acquisition of one of the Spanish-built Bücker Jungmanns which was my pride and joy for 20 years. During this time I also became involved with other classic aircraft, though each of them, like the Jungmann, were from the prewar era. I have also had tremendous fun flying Tiger Moths and Stampes with the Tiger Club and got to know some great characters there. But all that is another story.

CHAPTER 16
THE CAITHNESS SAGA
A COMBINED REPORT ON THE TIGER CLUB'S VISIT
TO SCOTLAND IN 1963
with contributions by
Lewis Benjamin, James Gilbert, Nick Pocock and Neil Williams

[Apart from Nick Pocock's contribution, written specially for this book, this chapter was first published in "The Tiger Club – A Tribute, Vol. I, 1957-1966" by Lewis Benjamin, to whom my thanks go for allowing me to reproduce it here. – Ed.]

LEWIS BENJAMIN'S INTRODUCTION
The Caithness Saga, as I write *[in 1988]*, occurred some twenty-five years ago. It has, over the ensuing years, become something of a legend. As if the occasion hadn't been memorable enough in itself, it was also recorded for posterity by members with a gift of literacy and who, in the best tradition of the Japanese theatre, were able to see the same events but through different eyes. I won't say such an adventure couldn't happen again, but with bureaucracy working the way it does these days with its stranglehold on anything that flies, the odds are against it.

I had written:

"CAITHNESS: Redhill to Marseilles is a long trip to give an air display, but it's no further than the north of Scotland, yet that's just where we went recently. Caithness, as this jaunt will long be known, was quite an adventure. It all started when some farmers from up there saw one of our displays, met Bill Chesson, and firmly requested us to visit them, all expenses paid.

We left, all eight aircraft, immediately after the display at Sywell on Whit Monday, to fly to Yeadon, refuel, and on to Middleton St. George, our overnight stop. A man-made mist by courtesy of ICI was sweeping across Middleton as we arrived in two formations, first the Turbs and then the biplanes, Tigers 'NMZ and 'RAZ in company with 'ROZ the Stampe. Beneath us the runway lights of this RAF master diversion station led us in a steady stream landing that left the runway controller nervously playing with his Aldis lamp, obviously unaccustomed to such rapid circuits after the resident Lightnings.

Wing Commander Flying was John Severne, and the following morning we asked permission to snatch a quick practice and at the same time entertain our hosts for their hospitality. I think the sight of Lolita on the wing of 'RAZ waving to the station personnel as she flew over the married quarters and station HQ won't be forgotten for many a long day.

Like the ten green bottles, we were already down one; James Baring had gone into Tollerton with a burst oil-lead, down but not out. Newcastle and half way, and the seven were suddenly reduced to four. James Gilbert couldn't start his Turb, Arthur Humphreys, also Turb-mounted, stayed with him, as did Don and Tessa Lovell in the Ambassadeur. Perth and four of us. The three biplanes led by Neil Williams flew across the Highlands in the beautiful evening sunshine, alternately slope-soaring, then hugging the base of the cu-nim that lay across the tops of the peaks, in an endeavour to conserve fuel on this, the longest hop direct to Castletown. Above us like a mother hen was Bill in the Musketeer.

Inverness had closed, and our diversion, if necessary, was on one of the two disused airfields that lay on the long plain beyond. The promising wind proved fickle, became a steady headwind, a nor'easterly that was to stay with us and to bring some trying weather. We chose Fearn and went down. No sooner were we down than a friendly farmer arrived and offered us transport and fuel; they even found a funnel and a chamois! Refuelling over, the three of us (Nick Pocock was in the Stampe) flew off into the evening to leave behind some fifty fascinated and friendly people, all of whom had come out to welcome us.

Castletown proved to be a fine-surfaced disused airfield right on the coast, in clear view of the Orkneys and edged by the bluest sea outside of the Med. The local hospitality was red-carpet. Not since Cobham's day had a bevy of light aircraft visited this corner of the country; everyone knew about us, everyone bothered and lent a hand to entertain and befriend us.

Two displays had been planned, both in the evening, on the Wednesday and Thursday. Since it didn't get dark till midnight (how much further north can you get?) the seven o'clock start was in plenty of time. On the Wednesday afternoon, to everyone's delight, the three Turbs in close formation flew in low over the airfield, followed by the Ambassadeur. Full strength. The day was fine, brilliant sunshine boosted the air of excitement. A food marquee, complete with two field kitchens and Calor gas, provided hot food from 2 – 9 each day, and the kindly folk who looked after it were forever forcing hot soup and coffee on the crews and helpers.

A pilots' briefing tent was already established. Hugh Neil, from Stirling, had driven up through the night just to be on hand to help, and help he did by taking over all refuelling and maintenance, as happy to be of assistance as we were to see him. Hugh, a good friend of "Bish's," had been a chief engineer during the war – I think at Perth – so Tigers were right up his street. (What most didn't know was that Hugh was on duty the *whole* time, camping out by his aircraft. He was later made an Honorary Member for that remarkable service to us all).

From fine weather to total clamp – just like that. Twenty minutes before seven a vast fog bank swept swiftly in from the sea. The airfield lay under a pall of damp cloud, the base of which hung around the 100-foot mark. The locals shook their heads sadly as we postponed the start for an hour. To no avail. The show was cancelled until the following night. The same thing happened the next night too, only this time it waited until seven to visit us. We had co-opted a Cessna 210 for the fly past and no sooner was he off than he was in it, up through and was gone, back to Perth and clear air.

It was a tremendous disappointment. 600 miles to show our paces and then this. A "one aircraft up at a time" display was improvised, and for an hour and a half we cavorted beneath the fluctuating base with occasional loss of shape as someone skirted too near the cloud.

The strangest sight, I was told, was when Lolita stood on the wing and occasionally disappeared into the cloud as I strove to stay in touch with the ground, and Nick's slow rolls just above the deck delighted his audience, but it was all below a hundred feet and very spectacular.

Although only scheduled for the two evening performances, considerable pressure was brought to bear for us to remain until Saturday and put on a show in the afternoon. The overwhelming hospitality clinched this, and all but one, 'RAZ, elected to stay on. Business commitments on the following Monday necessitated my return. As I write this some days later there are still two aircraft somewhere up there!

The return from Caithness was as full of adventure as the journey up – more so. The trouble was twofold, mainly weather and some mechanical. Perhaps one day someone will write more fully on this trip, of the characters we met, of the characters that went. For instance, James Baring made a sudden forced landing beside an outback loch. Neil reported: "He seemed to be on fire – the smoke in fact oil streaming out behind him." Neil somehow got down beside him in the special Tiger and then mounted James aboard, the fuselage cover acting like a sort of windscreen, and careered off.

Thus was James transported to Inverness. He later borrowed Horace Henderson's car (Horace was the prime mover in getting us up to Caithness) – drove 700 miles non-stop to London to appear in court, probably to appear on another of his parking charges, won his case, and then immediately returned complete with spare part for his Turb.

Must ask James to write up the account of his twenty-five-mile early morning tramp to Horace's for breakfast, and his attempted conversion by two earnest evangelists (wickedly sent up to his bedroom by Neil) whilst James was trying to sleep off the effects of his walk and the drink of the previous night. One of the shaken women was later to have stammered, after being turned out in no uncertain manner: 'He is never likely to see the Light.'"

It was a great adventure, regretted by none and enjoyed by all. James Gilbert later wrote a long and absolutely delightful account which because of its length I was only able to publish but a snippet at a time: Here is, without question, the choicest snippet.

JAMES GILBERT'S STORY
"I borrow a diesel-engined Land Rover and drive through the high-hedged, dewy country lanes to the airfield. No one else is about, and except for the skylarks and curlews the landscape is altogether deserted. I untie my Turbulent, start it up, and take off towards John O'Groats, the northernmost point of the mainland of Britain. Then I turn out to sea, towards the misty shapes of the Orkney Islands. Orkney itself, bigger than the others, is wreathed in Harr, covered by a thick, curving mist generated as that moist sea air flows slowly over its shores.

It was my ambition to land there; no one from the Tiger Club ever has before, so remote and strange are these islands. I turn back to Stroma. A little island clear of fog, shining in the sunshine. At one end is a lighthouse, huge and white; I circle it at a low altitude, than drop down over the sea for a low run alongside its beacon tower. Beside it is a monstrous foghorn like a giant's saxophone, and I aim my tiny Turbulent right at it, as if I intended flying down that vast black throat. Just as I pull up over the top, some wit who has been watching me sounds it off, in a monstrous cow-like moo, deafening even above the noise of my engine, a roar that almost frightens me out of my seat and into the sea.

If I cannot land on Orkney, perhaps I can on Stroma. True, it has no aerodrome, or indeed anything else much, and true it would be an illegal and foolhardy thing to do, but there is one field of short, sheep cropped island turf that looks smooth and level and just about long enough. I have always made it a rule never to land in any strange field I have not walked over first to inspect, but is not today a good day for breaking rules? I drag the field twice from a low altitude, then set up my approach.

Low and fairly slow; it looks plenty long, so no need to slow right up as for a really short landing. Touch down in a perfect three-pointer, and run on, slightly uphill, towards the end of the field. Run on and on, unaccountably she will not slow down, uphill though it is. Brakes on a Turbulent are differential only, for steering while taxying, but you can obtain some braking action with them by pumping the rudder pedals from side to side. I pump, with increasing terror, as the end of the field looms up ahead. With fifty yards to go it is bitter, certain knowledge that I am not going to stop before reaching that solid stake and wire sheep fence. At the last minute I turn the careening beast sharp right towards rough ground and a ditch; she leaps and bounds, the tail coming up, and the whole aeroplane dives with a deafening crash nose-first into the ditch. There is a rending, splintering sound as the propeller disintegrates, then absolute, stark silence. I am hanging face-down in my straps in the wreck of my aeroplane as it sits, tail in the air, nose in the ground. I undo my straps and clamber down over the wing. I sit, near to tears, on the edge of the ditch.

I am an idiot. A three-hundred-hour idiot. I will be drummed out of the Tiger Club. My friends will never speak to me again. It will take a month to get the wreck off this lonely island and back to the shop to rebuild. I will be prosecuted for every flying offence in the book. I will be penniless for years trying to pay for fines and repairs. I have done something so stupid I can hardly believe it. There cannot be more than one boat a week to this forsaken islet; I will not even be able to leave the scene of my crime for days.

The curlews call, and the waves lap against the nearby rocks. Somewhere a sheep is baaing; "baa," it says, "idiot, baa." Mechanically, I take hold of the tail of my Turbulent and pull her out of the shallow ditch. Strange, there doesn't seem to be much wrong with the airframe. On closer inspection, miraculously, there doesn't seem to be anything wrong with the airframe. But the propeller must be smashed into a million pieces. But there's only four inches snapped cleanly off the end of the tiny blade. Still, what use is any prop with four inches missing off one blade, Unless, of course . . . and a mad idea begins to form in my mind. Today I must have really gone crazy. Suppose you sawed four inches off the *other* blade, and could get it to balance?

Normally, these VW engines turn at about 3,000 rpm in this installation. But I own a VW *car*, and I know the engine in that turns at 4,000 rpm for long periods, cruising flat-out, with no damage. At 4,000 rpm I would be getting more horses out of the engine, perhaps enough to offset the inefficiency of the cut-down propeller. Enough to take off from here? For the first time since my recent abrupt arrival I take a good look at where I am. For a start, I was trying to land with a 5 kt tailwind. And this field has a deceptive double curvature, so that the lip over which I touched down was not the lip at the end of the field, but a false one halfway down!

I was trying to land *downwind*, and using only half the available run!

Over the dewy turf, on a tractor, comes one of the island's inhabitants and addresses me in a Pictish, Gaelic, Orkney accent that is next to impossible to comprehend. Could he, I ask him, find me a hacksaw anywhere on the island? He thinks the lighthouse people have one and drives off to ask. There is a little village of crofts in the centre of the island. It is a medieval village; there are no roads or gardens, each croft being surrounded by a rolling sea of green turf, criss-crossed by tracks where the inhabitants of Stroma have been in the habit of walking to work, or to each others' houses.

Till he returns I burn with impatience. The hacksaw comes, and with it I bite off the other tip. What's left is a sad runt of a propeller, but when I start up the engine it runs smoothly and sweetly. I swear there is less vibration than ever before. Full-power revs are not excessive, and taxying up and down the field seems to reveal no lack of acceleration, so far as you ever experience acceleration in a Turbulent. So I strap up, and back up to the topmost corner of the field, and taxy at full throttle down the field. Yes, I think she would have flown there. Once more, and then the real attempt. At first it seems doomed to failure, not to say disaster, then the tail lifts, and we slowly, slowly, gather speed; at the far end of the field, yellow with fright, half stalled, we get airborne. Soon we are properly flying, at a decent speed and altitude, very chastened, back towards the mainland . . ."

LEWIS BENJAMIN CONTINUES
James Gilbert's journey back to base at Redhill – he flew the entire way with the sawn off propeller – was a long, tedious and occasionally hairy trip. And he wasn't the only one who couldn't hurry. I couldn't, yet I needed to. I had recently opened my Colindale shop, and since it was a one-man business, there was no one else to open it on the Monday; Lolita and I set off in Tiger 'RAZ on the same journey and at an indicated 65 kt. We had to transport the Standing-on-Wing (SOW) rig in position on top of the aircraft, and such was the extra drag, coupled with the fine pitch prop fitted, it was the only speed available to us. Five more legs and a further eight hours flying were to follow before we got back to Redhill.

The following portion of the Saga was actually published some three years later in the *"Rag"* under the heading: "Let me off this time and I'll never do it again." It was the first of a series of "I was there" events presented in the belief that it's good for the soul to confess and that others may learn from the lesson. To be honest I don't think it works, for Michael Jones in the same issue had written a stern warning about careless swinging of propellers *sans* chocks etc. He'd also like a pound for every incident since.

"We couldn't stay on. After the two abortive attempts on the Thursday and Friday to put on a show, we had to resist the entreaties of our friends and hosts to join them for a third try. It wasn't easy, but we had to be back in London on the Monday.

Farewells, and we turned Tiger 'RAZ into wind at Castletown and hurried back to Thurso and the little harbour to dip our wings in salute and then to head towards Inverness. Above us around 1,500 feet a solid layer of cloud hung darkly. After a while we left the comfort of the solitary Thurso road and climbed steadily to the plateau between the twin peaks of the Caithness range. We slipped through skirting the cloud and sank thankfully down to the coast. Across Dornoch Firth bucking the wind at a cheerful 200 feet to speed across the lowlands towards the airport at Inverness. Cloud base 1,000 feet.

Tea, refuel and a word with the Controller. He phoned Aberdeen. To make Perth direct was out. The rest of Scotland lay beneath a mantle of fog. Only the east coast was clear. Aberdeen weather was down to two miles and a cloud base of 800 feet. We consulted the map and reckoned that, provided we followed the Moray coast and only moved inland beyond Elgin, we'd miss the high ground. It was worth a try anyway. We could always return. It was dank and chilly, Aberdeen was on our way, and anyway it might not be as bad as forecast.

Up past Lossiemouth with the vis. dropping as we left the coast to edge inland. No longer the clean definition of cloud and land. Instinctively I wiped my hand across the lenses of my goggles and followed the lonely Aberdeen road. A lorry driver waved. His wipers were busy, the road glistened. I hadn't realised I was so low. The misty drizzle had suddenly reduced our little world to that road and the hills which rose steeply either side of us. The map clearly showed the valley and the big plain beyond it. Too late to turn back and with it the stark knowledge that we either scraped through or we were going to have to climb up through, with the certainty of 8/8th cover beneath us. Vis. had nearly gone. The rain beat on my face. I glued my attention to that road and then, suddenly, we were through. Now the road led us to the railway – the very railway which actually crossed the edge of the runway. All I had to do now was to stay with it. Every sense said: "You were lucky, don't push it, get down, make a precautionary, the weather is worsening!" But the roar of the engine, the sureness of our position, and with it the knowledge that the airport wasn't nine minutes away weakened my senses.

Just a little further – decide then. And then it was too late. Imperceptibly the rain, the cloud and the fog become one. Impossible now to lob in anywhere. All that was visible was a hazy railway track 80 feet below. Nothing else showed, not even the fields either side, just the wet blinding fog. The marshalling yards – and no more than a mile to go – HT cables, a heave back into the mire and push down the other side. Blindly searching for the runway. A chimney passed. Too late to worry. A huge white numeral; that's all we saw, not even the edges of the runway – just one figure and in a flash we were down the runway.

They were a nice crowd at Aberdeen. No fuss. "Didn't see you," they said; "let's get your Tiger in a hangar!" I wish now, and I wished it then, I had stayed in Inverness."

NEIL WILLIAMS' STORY

"The display had been a good one and the natives more than friendly. Aeroplanes and pilots had been refuelled, and with some reluctance we prepared to leave for our long flight south. We needed two days for this, as we were at Castletown Aerodrome in Caithness – almost as far north as you can go on the mainland of Britain. Benjy had already left on the previous day, as he was only able to achieve 65 kt in 'RAZ with the rig in position. James Gilbert was wondering whether to saw off any more propeller or add wood screws to the other blade in an attempt to stop the engine from shaking itself out of the airframe, while Nick Pocock's Stampe refused point-blank to start at all – so James Baring and I decided to leave in formation. We took off, gave the locals a farewell beat-up, and set course across some of the most barren country in Scotland.

Peat bogs, marsh and heather were the order of the day; for mile after mile nothing moved on the ground, no vehicle (no roads), no trains (no railway) – not even a sheep. The sheer desolation was indescribable, and instinctively James and I closed up into a tight formation. I was flying the "Canon," and it was going beautifully; I felt that James was a braver man than I in flying a Turbulent over such country (incidentally, Norman's own machine loaned to James for the trip).

These thoughts were interrupted by the realisation that James had dropped back a few yards, but was still flying steadily on course. As I watched, he slowed even more, until eventually he was several hundred yards behind. Feeling slightly irritated that he should break formation over such poor terrain, I rolled into a 360° turn to let him catch up. He flew straight past without even a glance at me as I levelled out alongside. "Miserable blighter," I thought, when suddenly I realised he was in trouble. The next second, my heart nearly stopped altogether, as a great trail of white smoke erupted from his engine. "You're on fire," I shouted, realising in the same instant that he could not hear me.

The ground was completely unsuitable for any sort of landing, but the map showed that the coast was only a few miles ahead. James was obviously trying to reach this area but surely he would never make it? The smoke became thicker and trailed forty feet behind the aeroplane, when we suddenly crossed a low hill and there below us was a clear, calm loch. But more important, alongside the loch was a beautiful field, big enough to land a Turbulent. James shut the throttle and spiralled left, while I followed him down, carefully keeping out of his way. The picture is still imprinted on my mind – the loch, the hills covered with heather, a tiny dark blue aeroplane with a white smoke trail and a beautiful green field. James straightened low over the water, his reflection almost touching him, the smoke still persistent. As I got lower, I saw that the field was very rough – apart from a narrow strip in the centre.

Suddenly I realised that what I thought was smoke was in fact oil. The Turbulent's windscreen was black with oil and I feared that the landing was rapidly becoming impossible. But with falling oil pressure there is no choice, and with relief and admiration I saw the skid bite into the turf just inside the field. What a sight I saw as I overshot – cowlings, wings and windscreen were glistening black with oil, but James sat there unconcerned and waved.

Now it was my turn! I brought the Tiger in as slowly as I dared, low over the water, and as the grass appeared behind my wing, cut the throttle. The "Canon" bounced, touched down again and lurched to a halt. The silence could almost be felt when I switched off, for there was no sign of life apart from a few sheep who stared at us dully.

We took off the Turb's cowlings, cleaned off the oil and started up. Immediately a jet of black oil squirted into the air, and we quickly switched off. We found that we needed a new oil pipe; it was fractured and impossible to repair. Darkness was a couple of hours away, but I didn't want to leave James alone in that wilderness. Looking at the map, we found that we were exactly on track; the other pilots en route to Inverness should have spotted us, but we had to console ourselves with pointed remarks about their navigation. We saw nothing and needed a two-seater aeroplane to get James back to civilization.

As I cursed the fact that I was flying a single-seat Tiger, a crazy thought struck me. This was a special Tiger, stripped, light and with a powerful engine: powerful enough to lift both of us (one in the slip-stream) over the hills which surrounded the loch? It was worth a try. We picketed and covered the Turb and removed the luggage which occupied the space normally taken by a standard Tiger's front cockpit. James found that by standing on the pickets and holding on to the centre section struts, his head was level with the top wing. He was game to try it. We paced the field and found that the level strip was fifty yards with a good overrun. We started the engine and James climbed in. He packed himself in with all the baggage and, last of all, took on board the wooden cockpit cover which he wedged in over his knees as a sort of windscreen. James pronounced all systems "go," and I prepared to take off. Even the sheep were taking an interest by this time.

We taxied downwind towards the loch and turned into wind. The idiot sheep stared blankly as James pulled down his goggles and nodded. The wind was about 15 knots as I opened the throttle. The tail rose slowly and the flock of sheep got nearer. At 25 knots I started pulling and with a final bounce we were airborne! The sheep did a very creditable bomb burst beneath us as we slowly gathered climbing speed. James hung on grimly, with beard and moustaches fluttering, and his flying jacket billowing out behind him. Surely his ancestors must have sailed in long ships – he looked the picture of a Viking, thirsting for the spoils of war!

Meanwhile the Tiger circles, climbing slowly. What an aeroplane! But now I was becoming concerned, because I was using full throttle and the slipstream and cold would be weakening James. But at last we cleared the hills and could throttle back slightly. Every now and then James half-turned and nodded, signifying that he was OK, and soon Inverness appeared before us. The Tiger handled almost normally, in spite of its unusual burden, and as we taxied clear of the runway, James was grinning; he seemed to have quite enjoyed the experience! Not so Don Lovell, who had almost given us up. The expression on this face when we arrived made it all very worthwhile!"

NICK POCOCK'S STORY *[written in 1998 specially for this book. – Ed.]*
"I was honoured to be invited to add my own story of the Caithness trip to those of Lewis "Benjy" Benjamin, Neil Williams, and James Gilbert. To assist my memory I dug out an earlier article I had written, log book entries and aerobatic notes, plus a search for my photographs taken during the trip.

My journey started on Monday June 3rd 1963, leaving Redhill with Tony Mabelis as a passenger, for Sywell. I was flying the Stampe SV.4C G-ASHS which I had ferried from Lognes, France, on February 28th 1963, when the Tiger Club first bought it as F-BCFN. At Sywell I switched ships, picking up Stampe SV.4B G-AROZ (ex-F-BDGQ, named by Norman Jones in memory of the late Leon Biancotto).

On departing from Sywell I flew a rolling 360, keeping in position in a strong wind, although my notes fail to explain why I flew the manoeuvre. Whether for practice, show, or just because 360 degrees were "there"?

We then flew to Leeds, and then on to Middleton St. George, where Wing Commander John Severne, O.C. Flying Wing (today Sir John Severne, AVM, KCVO, OBE, AFC, DL) welcomed us, showed us around the English Electric Lightnings, and arranged overnight accommodation for us and our aeroplanes.

It was interesting to remember that in 1957 I had been posted to Middleton St. George for a few months during my National Service, straight from trade training as a Junior Technician Instrument Fitter, working in the calibration shop, and on Meteor NF.11s. During that time I did not fly, so I now got a completely different view of the airfield – from a pilot's perspective.

The next day, June 4th, I flew an aerobatic display at Middleton St. George before leaving, which included a Lomcevak from 800 feet, with a recovery at 200 feet. Neil Williams, with whom it was customary to exchange critiques in our efforts to improve our skills, said that it looked low. (Looking back, it would seem that I was probably lucky to have survived until I eventually drifted out of exhibition aerobatics in 1968.)

We flew on to Newcastle, and from there headed for Perth. Benjy was leading the formation of biplanes as we approached the mountainous area of southern Scotland. He had instructed me in formation flying, so when he climbed his Tiger Moth up into the clouds I followed faithfully in the Stampe, clinging to his murky wingtip, while Neil stayed on the other wing. We had no radios. Eventually we broke out on top of the clouds, and then flew over some spectacular mountain scenery.

From Perth, we set course for Thurso, but landed on a disused airfield at Fearn to top up the Super Tiger's tank. A local farmer provided some petrol from a can, and we took off for the last leg of our flight to Thurso.

On reaching our destination on the north-eastern tip of Scotland, we found that all the fields around the farmhouse where we had been invited to stay were full of grazing cows. Neville Browning, whose farm in Essex I had been in the habit of visiting, had his cows trained to disperse at the sound of an aircraft, but these Scottish cows had apparently never even seen an aircraft before (and neither had most of the farmers!), so they continued grazing. I finally set the Stampe down in a corner of a field which Benjy had picked out. I then tried to keep the inquisitive cows at bay, and clear a path for the other aircraft, by taxying in circles, accompanied by noisy bursts of engine power. Eventually we got the aircraft parked. Farmer Horace Henderson, our kind host, did not seem to appreciate my humour when I apologized for chasing the cows by saying: "I hope it did not curdle the milk." He indicated another field, without any cows, which he had intended us to use.

We stayed the night in the farmhouse; Mrs Henderson made us cocoa in the kitchen before going to bed. Being single, I had immediately fallen in love with her daughter, Elaine. Although Elaine was very kind, however, the feeling was not mutual. (This was just as well, as six months later I was to meet a lovely American girl, to be followed by thirty-six years of marriage, two children, and a grandaughter, whose mother, our daughter, has more hours flying as a flight attendant than I have piloting!)

The following morning, after a walk down to the quayside and lighthouse at Thurso, we flew the aircraft over to the disused airfield at Castletown, where we donned our metaphorical barnstormers' hats, and gave joyrides to local people. I took Elaine up for some relatively gentle aerobatics in Tiger Moth G-ARAZ and, later, Colin Campbell for an aerobatic ride.

On June 6th we gave more joyrides, and I flew aerobatics with a passenger in Tiger Moth G-ARAZ. This was the scheduled Air Show Day that Benjy has previously described. My aerobatic display in the Stampe was strictly limited by a 250-foot ceiling, with a quarter-mile visibility in drizzle. Lining up with the runway I dived down to about fifteen feet at one hundred knots, pulled up into a climbing half-roll, and flew inverted at about one hundred and fifty feet. I had to use the direct view of the ground below as my only reference, as the "Scotch Mist" on the windshield obscured visibility ahead. I then half-rolled back to normal flight and descended back to fifteen feet above the runway. This was followed by another pass in knife-edge flight.

Included in my written notes was a comment made by a local ex-second-World-War bomber pilot named Robert, who had been brightening the dreary day by consuming generous quantities of relaxing beverages: "Stupid bastard! But you knew what you were doing alright."

I did not like to think that I was "showing off," although I had hoped that Elaine would be watching. I used to ask myself if I would enjoy flying aerobatics over a desert island, where nobody was watching? I might even enjoy it more.

From my records it would seem that we did not fly on June 7th, so it was probably on that day that we were shown to a small shed, in which was a homebuilt gyrocopter powered by a motorcycle engine. The builder explained that he had not yet flown it. It just so happened that Neil Williams was attending the Empire Test Pilots' School at Farnborough at that time, and was always ready to fly anything with (or without!) wings, except the early Rollason Condor. I pointed out that the rotor blades seemed to have been mounted upside down, with the camber on the underside, which did not look right.

This did not deter Neil from offering, or accepting the offer, to fly the machine. After dragging it out of the shed into a green field full of bleating sheep, the owner started the engine. Neil climbed aboard, opened the throttle, and started a run across the field, while reaching up with one hand in an attempt to spin the rotor blades. Bouncing over the uneven ground on small unsprung wheels, Neil, with characteristic determination, pressed on regardless, while startled sheep scattered in all directions. The machine never left the ground. Later, Neil claimed that we did not tell him about the inverted rotor blades.

The Tiger Club group did not include a parachutist, but a fellow from County Durham had volunteered to jump in the display. He had found a couple of friendly, pretty waitresses, and invited me to join them for a foursome. Clearly a case of two birds in the hand being worth one in the bush? Nevertheless, I could think only of Elaine. These girls were the "evangelists" which, as Benjy described, we talked into "ministering" to another somewhat hung-over member of our group.

On Saturday June 8th the weather improved enough for another air display. I started with a Lomcevak and followed with inverted turns and a rolling circuit, during which at that time I liked to reverse the direction of roll alternately, as I had seen Rod Jocelyn do in Budapest the previous year. Then a Cuban Eight "off-the-deck," followed by knife-edge flight, and ending with a vertical climb, push-over and pull-out.

Later that day I flew the Stampe to Evanton, but returned to Thurso again due to the sea fog which had rolled in.

The next day, when it was time to leave for the homeward trip, the Stampe's Gipsy Major 10 Mk. 1 refused to start. Neither the time-honoured procedure of banging the impulse coupling with a tie-down stake or other suitable "graunching iron," nor the efforts of a passing Automobile Association road patrolman, nor our show promoter, Bill Chesson, a used-car salesman, who could normally get anything to run, could get even a kick out of the normally reliable Gipsy. Since four of us needed to get back to London, and the real world of earning a living, our gracious host, Horace Henderson, kindly saved the day by loaning us his little car. We drove for twenty-four hours, passing through some tantalizingly beautiful scenery, where I would have prefered to linger. Our parachutist friend left us at County Durham, while James Baring and, I believe, Australian Dave Allen and I continued to London to conclude a wonderful experience.

Since I was unable to contact my old friends, whose names I used, I hope they will excuse me, and will enjoy this light-hearted reminiscence."

[Thank you, Nick, for rounding out the story of this enterprising trip all those years ago. – Ed.]

CHAPTER 17

AROUND FILTON AND OTHER PLACES –
AGAIN
by
Edwin Shackleton

[Edwin Shackleton continues his story with his various experiences in the late fifties and throughout the sixties which eventually led to his inclusion in the "Guinness Book of Records" as "most experienced passenger." – Ed.]

I continue my account, as related in *"Tails of the Fifties,"* taking interest in all aspects of aviation and flying in more different aircraft against a background of working in the industry.

The most important feature to me and the employees at Filton was the formation of British Aircraft Corporation, bringing together the teams of Vickers, English Electric, Hunting and ourselves in February 1960. We were soon to learn that the Hunting 107 short-range jet design would be adopted for the BAC 1-11 project. Filton would produce the fin and rear fuselage but, more significantly, our laboratory would be responsible for a large share of the main structural test programme. Indeed a fuselage fatigue test in a water tank grew to a full-scale wing/fuselage test with the signing of the American Airlines order in July 1963. Our role, along with that of the Hurn Stress Office, was to provide us with our busiest and happiest time at Filton.

The helicopter industry was also being amalgamated and Westlands took over the helicopter interests of Bristol, Fairey and Saunders Roe in 1959/60. I recall a visit to Eastleigh to the Saunders Roe (ex-Cierva) hangar in February 1960 where the P.531 (forerunner of the Scout and Wasp) was developed. The prototype Hiller XROE-1 Rotocycle, G-46-1, was also then under evaluation there, as was one of the two Currie Wots built by Viv Bellamy, G-APWT, that had been fitted with a Rover gas turbine engine.

Bristol Airport was expanding slowly, having moved from Whitchurch to Lulsgate, and Dan-Air made their debut there in March 1960 with a public static showing of an Ambassador, Dakota and Dove. I took the opportunity to make my first flight in a Dove for the noble sum of five shillings (my 21st type!).

The Shackleton Sales Weekends were a good opportunity to see the newer American lighter civil types – kept out of the UK until 1958 by import restrictions. At the May 1960 event at Kidlington, I flew with Joe Tysko in the new Cessna 210 with that odd undercarriage retraction system. We also had first sights of the Tipsy Nipper, Jodel 140, Aeromere Falco, Piper Aztec and Cessna 150, 175, 180 and 310.

Later in the year at an Army Air Corps show at Middle Wallop was the most unforgettable sight of the M.L. Utility inflatable wing observation aircraft actually flying, maybe its only public appearance. It never made it as a front line aircraft! On the 5th September 1960 Godfrey Auty flew the Fairey Delta 2 WG774 into Filton on its last flight before conversion to the BAC 221 with longer fuselage and scaled Concorde wing. What a way for a world speed-record holder (1,132 mph flown by Peter Twiss) to be lost. But it *did* play a valuable part in Concorde development.

The 1961 Shackleton Sales Weekend was held at Coventry airport and this time I was able to fly in a Beech Queen Air 65, G-ARFF, when Shorts were the Beech agents. The next month we had an Air-Britain (Bristol Branch) visit to St. Athan where, somehow, we had contrived permission to see the preserved Junkers Ju.87D and Defiant – which were even pushed out of the hangar for photography. Afterwards, at Cardiff airport, our little coachload took turns to fly in the Club's Auster Autocrat.

A significant date at Filton was 23rd June 1961 when the Bristol Bulldog G-ABBB made its first flight for 27 years. Much of the restoration work was "unofficial" and George Kington, senior foreman in Structural Research, was responsible for the manufacture of parts for the gas starter system. We then did a test set-up using kerosene and pilot Willy Williamson came along to see a test run. One of my section, Ken Dodd, then produced drawings for the clearance report! On the 27th June the prototype Carvair G-ANYK landed at Filton (only 6 days after its first flight) and I sneaked in my seven-year-old son Michael to see it – and we nearly got stranded aboard when the steps were being moved away.

Airways-watching over Filton was made interesting with sightings of B-52s and C-133 Cargomasters. The first Canadair CL-44 was seen on the 1st July 1961 but most exciting was the spotting of the YC-97 Stratofreighter (turboprop-engined) on its limited transatlantic operations.

On an earlier theme, Bovingdon was the scene of an open day on the 11th March 1962 to see the B-17G Fortresses that were used in the film "The War Lover." It was the first time I had seen the use of broom handles for guns and paint to represent battle damage!

Sywell was the location for the 1962 Shackleton Sales Weekend. I managed to fix a deal with Steels Aviation to fly in their Cessna 172 from Staverton to Sywell on a day trip along with my Air-Britain friends, Pete Elliott and Ray Appleby. An added bonus were flights at Sywell in a Beech Travel Air and Brantly B-2. On the way to Sywell we spotted a biplane on the 'disused' airfield at Chipping Warden. Our identification of it as a Stearman was confirmed next day on a car journey stop: it was

G-AROY, imported by John Jordan – and I flew in it with John from Badminton over 21 years later. I missed the first flight of the Bristol 188 from Filton (to Boscombe Down) on the 14th April due to the Sywell second visit.

A family holiday to North Wales towing a hired caravan behind our Ford Prefect was phased to coincide with the World's First Commercial Hovercraft Service. This used the bizarre Vickers VA.3 between Rhyl and Wallasey. Irene, Michael, Julie and I enjoyed the 'skim' over the Dee estuary water and sand on that first day's operation. The controversial subject at that time was whether the hovercraft was an aircraft or a ship – but it was finally classified as a hovercraft! Earlier in the week, we had called at Shell Beach conveniently adjacent to Llanbedr, and had had the unusual view of a Jindivik take-off.

On the 18th August, it was announced that three Lockheed U-2s were due to arrive at Upper Heyford the next day for air-sampling tests. Publicity was deemed necessary after the Gary Powers U-2 'shooting down over Russia' incident. Nice timing gave me a chance to get some good landing photos. Farnborough Air Show '62 was to be a rear-jet special with maiden appearances of the VC.10, Trident and DH.125. I went to the Battle of Britain show at Abingdon, and chose a joyriding flight in a Heron rather than the Dragon G-ADDI – such a mistake – but the sight of a line-up of ten Argosies on the perimeter track was well remembered.

We made a special visit to Heathrow on the 8th February 1963 to see the first arrival in the UK of a Tupolev Tu.114, so impressive as it crossed the Staines Road. My diary records the first flight of the second Bristol 188 at 1621 hours on the 29th April with further flights on the 8th, 9th, 15th, 16th and 17th May.

That summer, I paid the first of six consecutive visits to the Paris Air Show, taking the four-day break with Reg Bloomfield and Dave Molyneux and flying by Air France Caravelle to Paris (Orly). We met up with Bristol friends and Pete Davies persuaded us to go to the Eiffel Tower to see something special. This turned out to be P-47D Thunderbolt 44-20371 which had just been handed over to the Musée de l'Air. Coincidentally there was another P-47 (N5087V) in the Air Show flying programme which then belonged to Republic but now resides at the USAF Museum at Dayton as N347D. We had planned to return home by BEA Vanguard but heard that there was an air traffic controllers' strike. BEA would not offer a refund, only a ferry alternative which I refused. We went to the British Embassy, who did not know of the strike, and borrowed enough money to buy tickets for the British United Silver Arrow Service – train to Le Touquet, Viscount to Gatwick then train to Victoria.

One of the new types at Paris was the Cessna 336 'push-pull' Skymaster N1707Z. The local Cessna agents brought it to Filton for Godfrey Auty to evaluate it. I latched on that it would be positioning back to Lulsgate and flew the 7-minute flight back, rather to Godfrey Auty's surprise. A couple of weeks later, calling at Heathrow, I was amazed to see a Douglas C-74 Globemaster 1 (HP-379, "Heracles"). In trying to get near, I entered a customs area and was reprimanded severely by a customs officer who, in a change of heart, then found the superintendent in charge so I could take some close photos!

Publicity surrounded the record-breaking flight of a B-58A Hustler from Tokyo to London on the 16th October 1963 (8,028 miles in 8 hr 35 min, averaging 938 mph). It landed afterwards at Greenham Common, thus negating, so I thought, any chance of my seeing it. I rang the USAF base next day, explaining that we were working on our own supersonic aircraft (in fact the first metal had recently been cut for the first SST test specimens) and asking whether we could see the B-58. A call back gave permission for *that* afternoon as the B-58 was departing next day. Quick phone calls, permissions for half-day leaves, and seven of us were Greenham Common-bound! The USAF made us welcome, allowed us to photograph the B-58 in the hangar, even opening the doors for more light, and gave access to the cockpit (no photos there). I think we were the only UK civilians to go there!

On a family trip back from my parents in Ipswich on the 27th April I logged the Champion Challenger crop sprayer N9873Y at Boxted, Maule Bee Dee G-ASPH at Stapleford and a USAF Cessna U-3B ("Blue Canoe," 06048), at Booker – all quite unique in the UK. May Day saw the first flight of the BAC 221. The next day I went on a charter trip by British Eagle Britannia 312 G-AOVF to the Hanover Air Show. Well-remembered was the terrible noise from the hovering wing-tip-swivelling jets of the VJ-101C and also the first sight of the Hamburger Hansa. A particularly good 'spot' on finals, seen well away, was the twin engines and trousered undercarriage of a KZ-IV which is now in the Billund Museum. The first KZ-IV flies with the KZ collection at Stauning.

On the 11th July 1964, the US Carrier "Essex" was open to the public at Portsmouth with a complement of Tracker, Tracer, Sea King and a UA-1E Skyraider. I asked where their C-1A Trader was and was told it was at RAF Thorney Island. We found it there but parked well around the perimeter track, but we managed to get near enough for photos!

A family holiday in Falmouth was a good opportunity to see the newly-operating BEA Sikorsky S-61N at St. Just where a temporary polythene hangar was erected pending completion of the Penzance heliport. Michael and I had a 'stay on board' return flight to St. Mary's on this new helicopter type.

With the forming of the British Aircraft Corporation, Filton acquired a Hunting President, the civil version of the Pembroke of which only four were built. This was used largely on the Toulouse run but I managed a local flight in August 1964. Farnborough '64 was a Shorts/Beagle show with the introduction of the Belfast, the turboprop Skyvan and also the Beagle 206 prototypes (X & Y) and Beagle 242. About this time, we also saw our first Beech King Air (N790K) which remains in production 34 years later.

Reward for work on the BAC 1-11 came in January 1965 in the form of a proving flight in G-ASJI, the fourth of a batch bought by British United. We flew a 40-minute leg from Gatwick to Le Bourget but were not allowed to disembark before our return flight.

Sir Winston Churchill died in January 1965 and we visited Heathrow and Northolt to see the visiting aircraft on the day of his funeral. At Heathrow, a worthwhile line-up included the US Presidential VC-137A 86971, French Caravelle, Belgian Air Force DC-6A and an Il-18. The Greek Royal Gulfstream 1 had disappeared into a BEA hangar. Northolt had an 'army' comprising F-27 (Prince Bernhardt), SO-30P Bretagne, Convair 440, C-119 Packet, Pembroke, Valetta and Dakota. A well-timed return to Heathrow gave us a chance to see King Baudouin of Belgium, General de Gaulle and Eisenhower (the latter shaking hands with his motor cycle escort) as they departed.

A BEA Trident was our transport to Orly in June for the 1965 Paris Air Show. We met up with Brian Lavers in his Mini for a tour of the local airfields. Highlight was a visit to Creil where IGN had their photo survey fleet of B-17G Fortresses and the high-aspect-ratio Hurel Dubois HD-34s. In September, a show at Blackbushe included a turbine-engined Autocrat and this was also the only time I have seen the Robinson Redwing flown on display.

An unusual sighting on the 11th May 1966 was the sole Handley Page Hermes 2 VX234 (ex G-AGUB) which descended over Filton for tests over the Bristol Channel.

The Biggin Hill Air Fair saw the first appearance of the Aero Commander 100 and 200, purely as demonstrators. The replica aircraft for "Those Magnificent Men and their Flying Machines" were beginning to appear and cause excitement.

In June, a family holiday in Guernsey included flights from and to Southampton in British United (ex-Air France) Viscounts. June 30th was a special day with a trip from Filton to Leavesden in the Bristol Siddeley Dove G-AJGT, primarily to see the Mitsubishi Mu-2 demonstrator. I waited in the top of the control tower and the Mu-2 did a nice low-level flypast. Then I had a flight, my first in a Japanese aircraft, which included a refuelling call at Hatfield (with a first sight of a Twin Otter on a military demonstration) – and the pilot of the Mu-2 was Captain Honda!

In August, Air Porter were due to demonstrate the Pilatus Turbo Porter at White Waltham. We saw Ladi Marmol fly HB-FCK in from Southend but learned that the local management would not allow local flying. Hurried re-arrangement followed and Ladi offered a flight for me, Michael and Julie (aged 11 and 9) to Booker. One of the potential customers said he would drive my Prefect with Irene to meet us at Booker. We had to fly a dog-leg to Woodley and back to Booker and as we did a STOL landing the Prefect also arrived.

Farnborough '66 was not one of the outstanding shows but a visiting helicopter was causing recognition problems on technicians' day (Monday). It was the first Bell Jet Ranger to appear in Europe – quite unexpected – and I traced it to Blackbushe. At the end of the week, I had fixed a flight in the company Hunting President to Wisley, scrounged a lift part-way in a director's car, then hitched to Blackbushe – and *there* was the Jet Ranger, N8590F, and also an Italian military Agusta Bell 204B (MM 80355). It was my lucky day as I flew in both types. Joe Mashman, a pioneer Bell pilot, was captain of the Jet Ranger. From Blackbushe I hitch-hiked to Odiham from where I flew back to Filton in the President.

Back home, I took the family over the Severn Bridge, open to the public for the first time. Irene and I had watched the official opening by the Queen on the previous day, the 8th September 1966.

In November, a friend in Filton Flight Operations arranged flights for me in MacAlpine's Queen Air 80 and an East African Super VC.10 5H-MMT. The latter was on a crew-training flight from Wisley and there were about eight in the forward cabin. I went back through the freight compartment into the main cabin which was very quiet but so weird with no one else around! I didn't stay.

Peter March fixed me a flight in early January 1967 in an RAF Chipmunk from South Cerney. This was a farewell flypast of the Primary Flying Squadron before transfer to Church Fenton. At the end of the month, I saw the recently completed Walrus at Yeovilton, a type that I had seen regularly at Martlesham early in WW II.

I had my first executive jet flight in the Bristol Siddeley HS.125 G-ATPB on a short trip to Chester, primarily to take a company director for an RAeS lecture in March, but Flight Operations sneaked in a few friends!

The 1967 Paris Air Show paraded an F-111A, Fokker F-28, AH-1G Hueycobra and Aero Spacelines Mini Guppy – a nice new selection. My highlight was to fly on the scheduled Breguet 763 from Bristol Lulsgate to Orly. This type was brought into service primarily to deliver Olympus 593 engines for Concorde in the lower deck with passenger space in the top deck. The 93-minute flight gave time for full meal service in the noisy cabin. Descent was a pleasant quieter contrast. Return home was by the Skyways Coach Air service, coach to Beauvais, HS.748 to Lympne and coach to Victoria. It was an interesting but rather too extended experience.

Early 1968 visitors to Filton were 3 Islanders (in one day) and a Portugese Nord 2501 Noratlas 6417. Another trip with Peter March was to Henlow to have a view of the Spitfires and Hurricanes massed for the *"Battle of Britain"* film. As we approached, an Alouette 2 took off and Peter was keen to photograph it. It landed, disgorged some cameramen and a couple more boarded. I gesticulated to the pilot and, next thing, I was aboard, airborne and looking down on the fighter line-up. We landed, disembarked and the Alouette G-AWEE departed; I never knew why it was there. Later it collided over Eire with one of the Blue Max SE.5A replicas in August 1970.

Next month, in May 1968, we had a family holiday in Switzerland travelling there by train, ferry and train. It was great to see the Pilatus P2, P3, Porter and *Twin* Porter flying and especially the low-level flying through the valleys of Vampires and Venoms. Climax was the return journey by Balair Convair 990 from Basle/Mulhouse to Gatwick in just 62 minutes.

At the USAF display at Upper Heyford, Brian Stainer mentioned that an Islander was to carry out deck landings on HMS "Hermes" and that he was turning down his own opportunity to visit. I offered to go on his behalf and give him my film – which he accepted. Quick arrangements and I was at Portland just three days later to board one of two Wessex 1s for the flight to HMS "Hermes" in Lyme Bay. The Wessex were soon there, rotors folded and lowered below deck, clear for the Islander. Colin Newnes from Britten Norman, an ex-navy pilot, did an approach, then a touch-and-go, before landing. Engines off, a push back and then a first demonstration flight, then the captain climbed aboard G-AVUB and I took a back seat. HMS "Hermes" was steaming into a steady breeze and we were quickly airborne from the 700 ft deck, taking quite a short circuit. With the wheels on deck, brakes were applied and after a v-e-r-y long moment of apprehension, we stopped OK! What an experience, sadly never repeated in any other aircraft.

The Royal Air Force 50th birthday was celebrated at Abingdon that August. At the press preview, I had my first experience of sitting on the door sill of a Whirlwind 10, having an aerial photo tour of the assembled static aircraft ranging from Camel, Hurricane, Spitfire, Defiant and Beaufighter to V-bombers, VC.10 and Belfast.

My 1968 diary tells me of a very diverse year with the arrival of the first F.4K Phantoms for the Royal Navy at Yeovilton on the 29th April and a wide-ranging display at Filton (Boxkite, Sea Vixen, first BEA 1-11, Super Mystère etc). At Lyneham, we saw eleven aircraft piloted by ladies fly in and park in front of a 99 Squadron Britannia (well, they were the British Women's 99 Club!). Farnborough introduced us to the Japanese YS-11 (748 look-alike) and the Sud 330 before they had names. At Bovingdon, we were able to see the German element of the *"Battle of Britain"* aircraft with Spanish versions of the Heinkel 111 and Bf.109 (CASA 2-111 & Ha.1112) plus an interesting two-seat Hispano Ha.1110 which has since gone into hiding in Texas. An interesting contrast was a visit to Ken Woolley to see his Foster Wickner Warferry DR613 (Wicko G-AFJB).

A New Year visit was by Royal Navy Sea Devon from Yeovilton to Culdrose. The press day showed how four Wessex had been involved in an all-environment camouflage exercise using water-soluble paint so that rapidly-deployed helicopters could be quickly changed from, for example, a Middle East to a Norway background. This was the start of a now well-established process also in fixed-wing aircraft – and of course we were able to see the camouflage effects in air-to-air/ground views against different backgrounds.

The Shuttleworth Trust continued their good work and at a mid-May '69 show, the Grainger Archaeopteryx was watched in awe.

Another Paris Air Show was enjoyed and I travelled this time from Heathrow to Orly by Air France Boeing 727 Srs. 200. Air France were the first airline to operate the Series 200 outside the USA and I flew in F-BOJA, the first of a batch of ten. At Le Bourget, I flew in a demonstrator Twin Otter. Return flight was in a Japan Air Lines DC-8 on its way to Tokyo via Anchorage. The Heathrow leg, only 46 minutes, still gave time for a full meal in super comfort and decor.

The Army Air Corps held a press day prior to their weekend airshow and all of the press who wished were taken on a positioning flight to Old Sarum. I flew in Beaver XV270. One of those 'flyers' was John Edwards of Airfix and as a result XV270 was the subject of the Airfix 1:72 kit. The return flight to Middle Wallop was to be a rehearsal for the weekend's mass flypast and I managed to contrive a flight in a Scout helicopter – no one else was interested.

To those of us in Filton, the most significant events of the decade were the successful maiden flights of the Concorde prototypes (001 from Toulouse on the 2nd March '69 and 002 from Filton on the 9th April '69). Sir George Edwards used to make 'pep talk' visits to Filton but we always had the feeling that the Government were ready to kill it. Only the French kept the project going, but its success was only made possible by the UK-designed intake ramp control system which slowed down the supersonic air to make it acceptable for the Olympus engines.

The Concorde fleet has flown more supersonic hours than all of the world's air force jets. Of that we should be very proud.

*   *   *

Incidentally, I am still taking every opportunity to add to my formidable list (still accepted by the *"Guinness Book of Records"*); at the time of writing (January 1999) I have managed a grand total of 657 different types of aircraft, of all the varieties you can think of, from microlights through balloons and helicopters up to large airliners.

CHAPTER 18
TRIALS AND TRIBULATIONS
OF AN ARMY PILOT
by
Col. (retd.) John Moss, MC, MRAeS

HOW IT STARTED
I was about 6 when I first flew. My father had been an infantryman and also an RFC observer in the Kaiser's war and therefore had several aviating friends. All I remember about that first flight was that it was in a blue Puss Moth. After that I saved up my pocket money and flew occasionally with a well-known first war pilot called Major Bonikson, who eked out a living with a Gipsy Moth based near Leamington Spa. I also flew whenever Alan Cobham's circus came to town; in fact this nearly put an end to my flying career, and everything else for that matter; what happened was as follows.

I had saved up ten shillings (equivalent to about £20 now). This princely sum allowed me to be aerobatted in an Avro 504K. In order to make a profit Cobham's employees realised that speed of turn-round was of prime importance. As a consequence the pilot took off without my being strapped in. The loop was all right as centrifugal force kept me in my seat, but the next in the sequence was a half-loop followed by a half-roll in which gravity came into play. Luckily I was holding onto the straps like grim death and so survived to tell this tale.

By then the war was approaching and I was at a public school which had an excellent Officer Training Corps and, to cut a long story short, by the end of 1944 I was commissioned into the Royal Artillery and then posted to India where, having been trained in jungle warfare, I awaited my posting to Burma. However this never came to pass as the atomic bomb ended the war.

I then spent a few pleasant months with rifle and shotgun in the Indian forests; not that I shot much, but I did learn to survive in the jungle and actually enjoyed it. I also went on an intelligence course, a small part of which was devoted to air matters; amongst other things this entailed being flown in a Tiger Moth which I was expected to navigate. Needless to say, I got hopelessly lost, but fortunately the Indian pilot knew his way home. However this renewed my old interest in flying.

Shortly after this event and towards the end of 1945, a notice appeared in orders to say that volunteers were needed for training as Air Observation Post Pilots in the UK. This seemed almost too good to be true, so I applied and was recommended by my Indian CO. I trotted off to see the MO, who examined me, then waved his hands in the air and pronounced me "fit enough to fly two aeroplanes."

A month or so later found me winging my way to Delhi in a Dakota with a brother officer who had also been selected for flying training. I was suffering from prickly heat at the time; it was bliss to sit in the relatively cool aircraft.

When we got to Karachi we were transferred to a York, the transport development of the Lancaster. We found to our amazement that we were to escort a dozen nursing sisters to the UK. This did not seem to be a particularly arduous duty, but actually was more than we expected.

The range of the York was short, which turned out to be to my advantage as I had to spend most of the journey in the Elsan being violently airsick, much to the amusement of the nurses, to whom I had boasted that I was returning to the UK to learn to fly! As far as I can remember our route was Karachi, Habbanyiah (Iraq), Cairo (night stop) and Castel Benito (Libya). Believe it or not we spent two weeks at this last-named and benighted airfield waiting for an engine replacement for the York.

My companion had the sense to scrounge a lift on a passing aircraft which had stopped to refuel, leaving me to escort the nurses home. Eventually we staggered on across Europe until we got to Paris, where another emergency was declared, so we spent 24 hours there. By then we had exhausted all our money, so we traipsed round Paris in a crocodile, like a well-behaved bunch of schoolgirls. Eventually we fetched up at Lyneham about 16 days late.

LEARNING TO FLY

The Royal Artillery had learned from bitter experience that not all gunner officers were experts in directing artillery fire from the ground, let alone from an aeroplane, so our course of some eleven or twelve potential pilots assembled initially at the School of Artillery at Larkhill near Salisbury, where we fired off a vast quantity of 25-pounder (that is, field gun) ammunition, of which there was an abundance at that time. Eventually we became quite proficient at this art and, incidentally, at using the military wireless sets (radios) which were temperamental and unreliable. Apart from one very low-level flight in an Auster we did no flying during this part of the course. After some six weeks at Larkhill we were packed off to No. 22 Elementary Flying Training School at Marshall's of Cambridge. I never fully understood how this worked; all the flying and ground instructors were Royal Air Force personnel but the rest of the staff were civilian. The Station Commander was a RAF Wing Commander.

I see from my No. 1 log book that I first flew in a DH.82A (Tiger Moth) on July 11th 1946. I did not go solo until August 6th after some 11 hours and 30 minutes instruction. My excuse was that the weather was pretty poor for high summer.

I do not claim to have enjoyed this period. A number of potential pilots were "Returned to Unit." This threat always hung over all of us until the course was finished. However, I really did enjoy my first solo; my sense of relief was almost overwhelming when, in the course of a check ride with the Flight Commander, I managed to do a couple of reasonable landings. The Flight Commander then climbed out and told me to do one on my own. I remember singing with joy and relief as I flew round the circuit. I only wish I could claim that I did an immaculate landing, but it must have been adequate as I was allowed to complete the course.

For some reason that I never discovered, we then started to alternate our flying training between DH.82As and Auster 5s. Although the cockpit layout was different, the Auster having side-by-side seating whilst the DH.82A was fore-and-aft, the aircraft handled much the same. However one could aerobat the DH.82A but not the Auster; maybe that was the reason. This reminds me of an episode which occurred to a friend of mine (one "Nobby" Clarke) who was on the course following ours (there were usually two courses on at the same time). Nobby was an experienced Officer from the Airborne Artillery, who had made several operational jumps. On his first air experience flight in a DH.82A at Cambridge, he discovered that his allotted instructor was a keen, young, inexperienced Sergeant Pilot. This NCO proceeded to do his utmost to impress Nobby by carrying out a hair-raising aerobatic sequence. Having eventually regained straight and level flight, he felt a tap on his shoulder and, looking round, saw that Nobby was standing up, having undone his straps but with his speaking tube still connected. Nobby then told him in no uncertain terms that he intended to jump if this blankety-blank nonsense did not stop. It did! (I should have explained that we always wore parachutes in the DH.82As.)

My only real black occurred shortly after I had accumulated about an hour's flying. The Station Commander decided that it was time for his monthly hour of aviating. Accordingly I was detailed to taxi a DH from the hangar to the Control Tower and hand it over to the Great Man. All went well until I arrived at the Tower, where I was to keep the engine running, then hand it over. It had been impressed on me that it was of utmost importance to keep the engine ticking over fairly fast or it would oil up. This I did until the Wing Commander hoved in sight, when I hopped out and threw up a quivering salute. As I did so, the aircraft, relieved of my weight, started to trundle off empty, pursued by the WingCo complete with parachute. Fortunately he caught it or this account would be a good deal shorter.

The only other event which stuck in my mind was during night-flying. One of our Indian Students was doing his first night circuit. The Tower noted he was low on finals, but having no radio contact could do little about it. Suddenly its engine stopped but the Tower could still see his lights stationary above the ground. The fire engine tore off to investigate and found the aircraft resting well above the ground, supported by a belt of trees, but with no sign of the pilot. It eventually transpired that he had climbed down to the ground, hitched a lift in a passing car and retired to the Mess for a stiff drink.

Personally, I enjoyed night-flying; for some reason I found landing easier than in daytime.

I can still remember my first solo cross-country and the sense of achievement when I actually arrived at the right airfield (Cliffe Pipard) and also managed to get back to Cambridge.

As far as I was concerned, one of the best parts of the course was the shooting. A friend of mine who was also on the course used to shoot rabbits with me on the airfield. By that time I had acquired a motorbike and we puttered around the airfield at night, shooting rabbits caught in its light. One of us would drive the bike and the other would shoot over the driver's shoulder. We shot a number of rabbits that way and also went duck-shooting at last light on some common land which was partially flooded, yielding a few birds. Eventually the day arrived when the course, or what was left of it, was deemed ready to move on to the final stage; I cannot remember our starting strength, I estimate it was about fifteen, but only eight were left at the end of the EFTS stage.

The next stage was the 43 Operational Training Unit, Andover. This was much more relaxed; to start with the instructors were Gunner officers who had learned their Air Observation Post trade in combat, although the OTU was under RAF control. I was extremely lucky with my instructors, who were always patient and good-humoured. I will not go into the details of the course: suffice to say that by the time we had completed it we were fairly competent pilots, capable of landing and taking off from small bumpy fields in most weather conditions and, of even greater importance, capable of adjusting artillery fire from low level.

This might be an appropriate time to explain how this was done. Generally an Air OP pilot would be allotted to an Artillery Regiment, which ensured good liaison. Of course there were many and various means of carrying out a shoot, but let us imagine that we had air parity, that is, the opposition's fighter aircraft and our own were about equal numerically but no more; therefore it was vital that the Auster was only visible to hostile eyes for as short a time as possible. In order to achieve this the pilot would establish communications with the artillery by means of a rather temperamental wireless set, which required "netting in" to the correct frequency whilst the pilot flew at about 50 feet. He would probably have been given the location and grid reference of the target. He must now zoom up to an altitude from which he could locate it on his map. Having done this he would then dive down to the comparative safety of low-level flight amongst the trees and valleys, from whence he would give the gunners their orders for engagement. When they were ready to fire he would be told and also given the time of flight of the shell, which might be as long as 30 seconds. The pilot would give the order to fire, still remaining at low level. The guns would then report "shot," meaning that the shell was on its way, but the pilot would wait a few seconds before climbing up to an altitude from which he could observe the fall of shot. This process would proceed until he was satisfied that he had the target bracketed with shell-fire. We would then order the guns to engage in earnest.

If this sounds difficult and complicated, then I can assure you it was, and required considerable training to reach the necessary degree of competence, which was the aim of the OTU course. Fortunately the Artillery ranges are quite near Andover and, as I said before, there was almost unlimited ammunition available at that time.

It goes without saying that the course syllabus included a much broader programme than correcting artillery fire. We had to learn to cope with small short Advanced Landing Grounds (ALGs), bad weather and generally living in the field with a light and somewhat fragile aircraft.

The weather at the end of 1946 was abominable with snow and frost so we were all sent home, but eventually the course came to an end on January 14th 1947. Nowadays there is a formal Wings Parade at this point, but as far as I can remember we trooped into the Mess, where we were rather casually presented with our wings, followed by a few pints of beer.

I must have had some leave then, as there is a gap in my log book, but I was then posted back to Andover, to 657 Air OP Squadron RAF, so I knew many of the pilots, most of whom had seen war service and were well decorated, including the CO, Major Harry Simms DFC.

An Air OP Squadron was a typical British compromise, but one that worked extraordinarily well. The operational pilots were all gunner officers, although the adjutant was an RAF pilot. The technicians and engineer officer were also RAF, whilst the signallers and drivers were gunners. 652 Squadron was unique in that it had two Flights, one having Auster Mk. 4s, 5s and 6s whilst the other had Sikorsky Hoverfly 2 helicopters. This was, of course, by way of a trial, all three services being interested in the potential of the helicopter. I managed to scrounge a trip in a Hoverfly in August '47, during which I was allowed to try and fly it, but without much success.

I seem to have been fairly busy at that time, clocking in about twenty hours a month on exercises, shoots, photographic sorties and cross-countries, not forgetting aerobatics in the Tiger. However I had one unfortunate incident in July: I was instructed to fly up to Felixstowe, accompanying another Auster. We were to give a demonstration to some army cadets on two succeeding days. At the end of the demonstration, a Verey pistol was to be fired from our aircraft. On the first day, I flew as second pilot, and fired the pistol from its mounting through a hole in the floor. On the second day I was left on my own and followed the same drill, but when I fired the Verey there was a loud bang and the pistol shot up into the cockpit, which filled with green smoke. I could not see the instruments, let alone the ground, but luckily my guardian angel was with me that day as the smoke cleared and, although there was still a fire in the cockpit, I could see a large field beneath me, towards which I headed. In my haste to put the aircraft down, I collapsed the under-carriage, which was perhaps fortunate as I only ran a few yards. I opened the door, got my feet on the ground but, as in a nightmare, I could not move. I was still strapped in! Having resolved that problem, I ran a few yards to observe the shambles. The fire was still burning, but not too strongly. I had time to reflect that I was heading for two unpleasant inquiries, from both the RAF, which owned the Auster, and from the Army, which owned the No. 22 Wireless Set. I realised that I might be able to rescue the 22 set, which would reduce the legalities. This I did, just as the fire wagon drove up and dowsed the fire. I did not not need to be an aeronautical genius to realise that this Auster was unlikely to fly again!

By this time my ground crew had arrived and asked what had happened. I explained that I had fired the Verey pistol through a hole in the floor, to be told that this particular aircraft had no hole, although it did have the mounting. Next day an Auster took me back to Andover where I was interviewed by my CO, Major Harry Simms. Fortunately for me he was very understanding and, as standardisation was all the rage at the time, he gave me a check ride and I was allowed to continue with the squadron. However the situation was not helped by the *"Daily Mirror"* which carried a headline: "PILOT FIRES, PLANE FALLS IN FLAMES." The next day was Sunday, so I went to church to say "thank you."

A few months later I was posted to Germany; I never did discover whether the posting was the result of the prang, but I do not think it was.

GERMANY IN 1947-8

I arrived in Germany in September 1947 on posting to 652 Air OP Squadron, stationed at Lüneburg, not far from the border with West Germany. It was commanded by Major Colin Kennedy who had been on the course before me at Andover. Fortunately he was a keen game shot which helped.

Initially I was posted to a Flight, carrying out much the same training as I had done in the UK, but after a bit the CO decided he needed an MT (Motor Transport Officer). As I had done this job in India, I got lumbered with it again. This did not stop my flying, it just made it more difficult; I still managed about 7 hours a month.

Not many officers had cars in those days, but my father found me a 1936 Morris which he shipped over on the ferry. I remember going to fetch it on a filthy day in February, map-reading off a half-million map in the dark. Gradually the car lights got dimmer and dimmer until they eventually went out altogether, and so did the engine. However being MTO had its advantages, as I got a long tow back to Lüneburg next morning and soon had the old Morris sorted out.

We all kept our hands in at night-flying, which was treated seriously, using the minimum amount of light on the ground. Two lines of flares were considered a luxury, usually a single line was sufficient. Jeep headlights were also utilised, having the advantage that they could be switched on and off quickly, whereas the flares had to be lit individually.

Navigation at night was a major problem, usually relying on dead-reckoning, but in all honesty it was rarely practised at that time.

In order to hone our short-landing techniques, there was a practice strip on the airfield. This had some quite high trees at one end. The object of the exercise was to waffle down over them using engine, with the airspeed just above the stall, then just before touchdown to give a burst of engine and hence, hopefully, execute a short landing.

After I had been at Lüneburg a few months, the powers-that-be decided we should move to Celle, a rather larger RAF airfield further west. Like Lüneburg it was an ex-Luftwaffe field with an excellent Mess, with good facilities: the Germans did not stint themselves.

I had some home leave due to me at that time and so escaped the actual move, but on my return was not best pleased to learn that I had been made Station Welfare Officer (the MTO job had fizzled out). Actually the job turned out to be quite interesting and did not interfere with the flying. I met quite a few RAF and WRAF officers, and also did some gliding in liberated German gliders. I got my old Morris completely repainted by a German garage for the cost of some 200 cigarettes!

At that time, everything was very relaxed. Our flying training was in the hands of our Flight Commander and exercises with troops on the ground were rare occurrences: a very different state of affairs from a few years later when the Cold War reared its ugly head. By April '48 I had accumulated nearly 400 hours, which the gunner authorities considered sufficient, so I was recalled to Woolwich whilst my fate was being considered. By this time I had been granted a regular commission, but had never served seriously in a Royal Artillery Regiment. This was to be rectified: I was posted to a Field Regiment in Hong Kong.

MALAYA 1948-50

Once more into a crowded troop-ship, though I must admit that the officers were not badly off – in fact I found myself in a cabin with one male and one female officer. I found out later that this occurred because the Womens' Royal Army Corps had just embraced 'proper' army ranks, but the ship's staff had not caught up with the times. The situation was rectified before bedtime! The voyage out was fairly leisurely; we dressed for dinner where we were joined by a few officers' wives and some WRAC officers. We went ashore at Aden and Suez but, after about three weeks at sea, I was instructed to report to the Officer Commanding Troops, who told me that an Emergency had been declared in Malaya (now Malaysia) and my posting had been changed to 26 Field Regiment stationed in that country. As I had never been very keen on the idea of soldiering on a small island like Hong Hong this suited me, partly because I had a small arsenal of rifles, shot guns and fishing rods with me which would be useful in Malaya but not in Hong Kong. Furthermore there was also an Air OP unit in Malaya.

We soon landed in Singapore, where I was instructed to report to Headquarters, Royal Artillery. This I did and was directed to an office in which an irascible staff officer operated. When I arrived, he was clearly in a hurry to get away. I explained to him that I was an expert pilot, and would be much better employed in Air OP.

He said: "Don't you know there is a war on? Anyway, it's about time you did some proper soldiering!"

He then grabbed his golf clubs and departed in a bad temper.

That evening I caught a narrow-gauge steam train to Tampin where the Regiment was stationed. I reported to the OC Train who was horrified to see that I was unarmed. However I soon rectified that by digging out my heavy game rifle and loading it, but nothing happened during the journey. I was met at Tampin by a driver and vehicle who took me to Regimental Headquarters. I found the camp almost deserted, being manned by the Quartermaster and a few troops. The QM painted a gloomy picture of the situation in the countryside, explaining that one never knew who was about to shoot you or give you a grenade instead of an egg. However he issued me with a revolver, webbing, jungle-green uniform and a Sten gun and sent me off to war in a Jeep with a driver, in the hope that I would find the Regiment. Fortunately we did and I reported to the Adjutant, who promply sent me on patrol with a sergeant who knew vaguely what was going on. This all sounds like a fairly improbable line-shoot, but I swear it is true. The fact was that at that time everyone was feeling their way, though eventually the Regiment made a name for itself as jungle soldiers who, in many cases, out-infantried the infantry! However this saga is supposed to be about flying, so I will skip most of the "jungle bashing" and concentrate on what aviating I was able to scrounge in Malaya, such as it was.

Luckily, 656 Air OP Squadron was commanded by a friend of mine, Major Alistair Noble. The squadron had been through the Burma campaign where it had done a magnificent job, and was still doing one in Malaya. Of course the personnel had changed, a two-and-a-half- or three-year posting being normal. The Squadron was based just north of Kuala Lumpur on Noble Field, a short grass strip only suitable for light aircraft.

However, back to the jungle; after a few months charging rather aimlessly around Malaya, the Gunner Troop which I commanded was moved to Bahau. My remit was to cooperate with the police, to eliminate the Communist Terrorists and to keep law and order in a expanse of jungle about the size of Warwickshire: not a bad job for a 24-year-old Subaltern!

I soon realised how invaluable aerial reconnaissance would be to me and to my police partner, Capt. Bob Smith, who incidentally had been a Gunner Officer during the war.

I had already been checked out by one of the squadron pilots, Captain (later Lieutenant Colonel) John Chanter, who kept a fatherly eye on me during all my flying with the Squadron. I had also acquired a car, a small drophead Standard, in which I used to wander around unescorted, never, fortunately, encountering any trouble in two-and-a-half years. Among other things, this car enabled me to drive to Noble Field to keep in flying practice and hence to carry out aerial reconnaissances for our own anti-terrorist operations.

Unlike the squadron pilots, I knew our own patch quite well. The Terrorists lived in well-sited jungle huts, which were virtually undetect-able from above the jungle canopy, but if one had some idea of where to look it was possible to peer obliquely and see underneath the trees. Thus I found several hideouts, though only one proved to be occupied. Having got a good fix on the camp from the air, we went back the next day on foot. We found it without much trouble, but the CTs (Communist Terrorists) must have been alerted by the aircraft's engine noise on the day before, because they melted into the jungle on our approach. However we did collect some useful documents and equipment.

Navigating over the jungle was not easy. However it was usually possible to follow a road until one reached a point not too far from the objective, after which it was necessary to rely on dead-reckoning.

When patrolling in the jungle on foot, we found that food was always a problem. Everything had to be carried, including the heavy wireless sets (designed for vehicle use), weapons, clothes and material to make crude shelters (it rained a great deal in the forests). If a patrol picked up a hot trail, it would frequently run out of food, and would then request an RAF air-drop, which was quite a performance. In the first place, it was necessary to find, or even make, a clearing. This had to marked with a smudge-fire and the area made secure. At that time, 1949, it took about a day to set up the air-drop, by which time the CTs would be many miles away.

I did a bit of thinking about this to see whether Austers could be used instead of Dakotas and came up with the following idea: two Austers would be required for the drop, each with a "dispatcher" (an Auster could carry about 200 lb of supplies as well as the two crew). The patrol on the ground would send the map reference of the dropping area, which would be in virgin jungle. Two smudge-fires would be lit, one at each end of the DZ, and the foot patrol lined up between them. The Austers would time their overhead arrival shortly after the fires were lit and then line up on their smoke. The supplies and stores, having been previously wrapped in paper and sacking, would be free-dropped at low level through the jungle canopy. Although the odd package got caught up in the foliage, about 95% of them dropped to the ground, where they were marked and collected by the patrol. Even beer bottles were dropped this way and arrived intact.

I never really found out how my flying was authorised, either by my unit or by the Air OP Squadron; I suspect it was not, but I assumed that someone thought I might be useful as a reserve if needed. At any rate, I was allowed to continue flying, even spending one leave doing a refresher course at RAF Sembawang on Singapore Island and at Kluang, an Air OP base about 50 miles north of Singapore. During this most enjoyable course, my mentor was again my good friend John Chanter.

Rereading this, I realise it gives the impression that I had not much to do in my real job of chasing CTs, so I want to put the record straight. For nearly two years I was in and out of the jungle, covering hundreds of miles on foot and having a number of successes as well as my share of blank patrols. *[John is too modest: he was Mentioned in Dispatches and also awarded a Military Cross in Malaya. – Ed.]*

At that time, in spite of the communists, Malaya was a beautiful and more or less unspoilt country. There were numerous hospitable planters around who, although living in fear of their lives and those of their families, extended their hospitality to us whenever the situation allowed. I also got some shooting, including a rogue elephant which was leading a herd intent on destroying a newly-planted rubber plantation. I also shot duck and pigeons.

In 1949 and by coincidence, Alastair Noble (the Air OP Squadron Commander) and I both inherited small legacies at about the same time, so as we both had leave due, we decided to do a Far East tour, taking in Singapore, Hong Kong, Formosa (Taiwan) and Siam (Thailand). By chance we also had a day in China, which was then in the midst of a civil war! It was a wonderful trip, I only wish it had been longer.

·   It was a bit of an anti-climax returning to Bahau, and to the routine patrolling, but for me this did not last long for my Battery Commander, who had now also moved up to Bahau, decided that I should take over an administrative job. This I hated, though it did have its moments. It certainly curtailed, but did not eliminate, my flying with the Air OP. I see from my log book that I even flew the Battery Commander on a reconnaissance trip in December '49.

In 1950, much to my relief, I returned to proper soldiering, but did not fly much. At that time the CTs realised that the railways, running up and down the country, were often the only means of transporting rubber, oil and other produce to the outside world. They also discovered that a train could be derailed simply by unscrewing the plates which held the lines in place and pulling the track from its alignment just before the train arrived. Consequently we were detailed to patrol the railway line to deter the CTs. This was a deadly boring job, but it did have its moments.

An Auster would occasionly be ordered to patrol the line and to cooperate with us. On one occasion a rather exuberant pilot cut his low-flying a bit too fine and flew through the telephone wires alongside the track. Instead of a bloody accident all that occurred was a flash as the smoke of ages was suddenly removed from the copper, which curled in bright spirals from the poles. The Auster flew off rejoicing and unscathed.

Another strange event occurred a bit later. Again I was on patrol on the railway. It was a filthy evening with rain and low cloud when I thought I heard an Auster-like noise. Apart from thinking "better him than me," I dismissed it from my mind. However a few days later, I heard that an Auster carrying a Brigadier had gone missing. An infantry patrol went in search but found nothing.

I heard later that a Malay clairvoyant had sent a message to the police to say that she had "seen" the crash and described where it was and how to get there. A patrol was sent and found that, for the most part, the instructions were valid and could be followed, but there came a point when everything went wrong.

Several years later a patrol stumbled on the remains of an Auster. There were a few scraps of uniform too, and also part of a medal ribbon which was identified as belonging to the Brigadier. I offer no solution, but it is a fact that the wreck was found at a point not far from where the clairvoyant's instructions went wrong.

My last job in Malaya had little to do with aviation or patrolling; it involved keeping the railway running in spite of the CTs' increased efforts. This was achieved by running armed Scout Cars on the tracks in front of the train. I did not get much flying at that time but I did get quite a few locomotive hours!

And so home on another troopship, in time for Christmas 1950.

BACK TO 652 SQUADRON, DETMOLD, GERMANY

When I arrived at Liverpool, I was delighted to find my father and sister waiting for me; somehow my father had pulled rank and came aboard the trooper – we were driving home an hour later!

After a pleasant leave, I was pleased to hear that I was to be posted back to 652 Squadron, now stationed at the pleasant town of Detmold about 50 miles west of Hanover. The advantage of Detmold was that the airfield belonged to the Squadron, though we shared the mess with 10th Field Regiment, Royal Artillery. I was lucky as I had a number of old friends in both units.

The Squadron still had three flights of Austers, all Mark 6s, plus a Tiger Moth and a Mark 5 which unlike the 6 was fitted with dual controls.

I soon discovered that soldiering in Germany was no longer the carefree business of 1946. The Cold War was taken very seriously and we spent a significant proportion of our time on long exercises working alongside our allotted Division Brigade or Gunner Regiment. We also spent more time directing artillery fire on the ranges.

I had not been at Detmold long when I was surprised and delighted to hear that I was to do an attachment to a United States Field Artillery Battalion which was stationed in the South of Germany. I went by train, travelling all night. I arrived, looking and feeling very bedraggled, to be ushered into the CO's Office, where I was given a warm welcome, being put under the care of Lieutenant Victor Simpson, who turned out to be a very good friend with whom I remained in contact for some 20 years.

We have not led the United States Forces in many technical fields, but Air OP was one of them. Before the United States entered the war, they had watched our development carefully and then adapted it to their own requirements. This they did by having two observation aircraft, plus crews and ground personnel, on the strength of each field artillery battalion. This had its advantages and disadvantages, but as far as I was concerned they were all advantages, as I was allotted an L-5 (the US equivalent to the Auster). This was to be for my exclusive use during my detachment. Victor Simpson gave me half-an-hour's dual, then sent me off solo for nearly two hours. We were operating off a tarmac strip, which

174

was a new experience for me. When I came back from this sortie, there was a stiff wind across it, resulting in a humiliating ground-loop. However the L-5 was a sturdy aircraft and came to no harm.

It was interesting to note differences in the flying techniques adopted by the Americans and ourselves. We believed that survival in conditions of air inferiority or parity required us to fly at ultra-low level on operations if we were to survive. The US Army, however, took the view that they would have air superiority and could fly much higher. Later on, US Army Aviation rediscovered "nap of the earth flying," of which it is now a great exponent.

Correction of artillery fire also differed. As I have explained, our Air OP pilots controlled the fire, whereas the Americans always carried a Gunner Observer for that purpose. I do not propose to argue the pros and cons of the two systems: suffice to say that US Army Aviation is now a most efficient and dedicated force.

After a very interesting and enjoyable fortnight, during which I was given some dual in a twin-engined L-17, my detachment ended, but I was flattered when my CO arrived in an Auster to take me home. Actually this was a good excuse for him to renew his friendship with the CO of the Field Artillery Battalion; they had not met each other for some time.

It was a bit of an anti-climax returning to the humdrum life at Detmold, especially as I was greeted with the news that our Annual Inspection was due shortly; this was dreaded by one and all. Flying virtually ceased whilst we practised various intricate drill manoeuvres, which had been laid down by the Royal Air Force (remember the Squadron was an RAF unit).

On Day One of the inspection we were inspected by a Senior RAF Officer (Air Vice Marshal). The RAF personnel paraded in the front rank carrying rifles with blue-blancoed slings. The soldiers stood behind with Sten guns with khaki slings. The next day a senior army officer took the parade, but the slings had to be reblancoed so that the soldiers could carry the rifles! We marched and counter-marched in extended lines to the accompaniment of a military band. I do not know what it achieved, except that it was a relief when it was over!

Having got over the bull, it might be an idea to describe a set-piece exercise. These became increasingly more demanding and drawn-out as the tempo of the Cold War quickened. I will skip over the early exercises, because initially we had not established the drills for deployment, and indeed we had to discover these by trial and error; fortunately the errors did not result in anything too dramatic though we did have the odd accident.

Coinciding with the quickening tempo of the Cold War, there was a change of COs. The new CO realised that the Squadron, being the only

Air OP unit in the British Army of the Rhine, would be hard-pressed and would need to establish drills for deployment and for operations in Germany. The Royal Artillery had long since evolved such drills, but ours varied from Flight to Flight within the Squadron, so the CO sat down and wrote what was to be our "Bible," which for better or worse was to be followed precisely.

I will explain, using the new drill book, how a Flight of four Austers was to be deployed and operated.

Usually, before an exercise was mounted, an Orders Group would be called by the Divisional Commander to whom the Flight was allotted. An area then would be designated for assembly. In those days, the fifties, we controlled the whole of the British Zone and could use any farmland for an exercise. The first step would be to send one or two Jeeps with radios and trailers to a rendezvous in or near the Assembly area. An Auster crew would then aim to arrive overhead in that area in time to carry out a reconnaissance, hence finding a suitable field to serve as an Advanced Landing Ground (ALG). Having found one the Auster pilot would then write a message to the ground crew in the Jeep, giving the map reference of the field and also drawing a sketch map of it – no easy undertaking when flying at about 50 feet! This message was then put in a coloured sleeve and dropped to the Jeep crew. The Auster would then potter off to look around the area, thus allowing sufficient time for the Jeep crew to check out the field. This was done by driving the vehicle up and down it. If it was 300 yards long and if the vehicle's springs were intact, the field was acceptable; incidentally, one of the essential requirements was a nearby wood in which the aircraft could hide from prying Soviet eyes.

All being well, the Auster would return to Detmold to call up the rest of the Flight which would take off at intervals. Aircraft would approach the field at low level in order to carry out a concealed approach. This entailed flying over the field at about 50 feet and then completing a very extended circuit from which a landing was made. Directly the Auster had rolled to a stop, it was marshalled to its hide in the trees and there camouflaged with a net. After about 30 minutes the whole Flight would have arrived, followed by the ground vehicles. During an exercise several ALGs would be occupied in a similar manner; we really became adept at reducing to a minimum the time for which the aircraft were exposed.

Of course, once the exercise had started, we would have opposing troops, who were usually, but not always, British. It was quite normal to have two Flights from the Squadron on opposite sides.

Occasionally the exercise would end up on the artillery ranges, in which case live ammunition would be used, and we could practise our skills (or otherwise) in directing artillery fire. However, generally speaking, the aim was to test the abilities of the units to manoeuvre in an effective manner.

Inevitably, on these major exercises which might last for weeks, we would be used by staff officers and COs for reconnaissance and for liaison; this was no bad thing as one got to know the "brass hats" who, with one or two exceptions, were generally considerate and understanding.

I see that I have omitted some very important parts of the Air OP equation, the personnel who made up our unit. I have mentioned the pilots, the adjutant and the engineer officer, but not the soldiers and airmen. To go back to the pilots: at that time about 70% of them had seen wartime service in the Artillery and were now regulars, while a few were on short service commissions or were National Servicemen who had extended their service for a year in order to fly. Almost without exception they were a splendid bunch of individuals on whom one could rely in any circumstances. The senior NCOs were also an excellent crowd, but it was the National Servicemen and junior regulars who always surprised me. We asked them to use their initiative far beyond that expected in a normal unit. For instance a section in a Flight consisted of one Captain or Lieutenant (pilot), one driver/signaller, one driver, one RAF airframe technician and one RAF engine technician. On an exercise (or for that matter in war) these might operate for weeks at a time without supervision, except for the pilot whose technical knowledge was usually sketchy. Not only did these four men keep the aircraft and the vehicles in good order, they also fetched rations and stores. As if that was not enough, one of them was expected to operate as the rear observer, sitting in the rear seat of the Auster watching for enemy aircraft. In my five years in Air OP I was only let down once, and that was really my fault.

I was on an exercise, and was flying without my rear observer, who was in the Jeep. I found what I thought was a suitable field, wrote a message and drew a sketch map, dropping these to the ground party which was waiting at the rendezvous. I then pottered off for a while to give them time to check the field. When I returned to it the white 'T' was out, indicating that all was well, so I set myself up for the usual concealed approach. The landing was more or less uneventful, except for the scream of brakes! I realised too late that the field was much too short. I got out and paced its length which was 200 yards (i.e. 100 yards too short). It also had a highish hedge on the upwind end. I had two choices: send for help, which would mean stripping the aircraft and bringing it out on a three-tonner, or lightening it of any unnecessary kit such as the radio (which weighed about 25 lb) and my own sleeping bag etc. (which accounted for about another 60 lb) and then having a go at taking off. I decided on the latter, so we lopped off some of the hedge, lowering it a bit. I climbed in, started up, taxied to the downwind end and ran the engine up to full with the two men holding on to the tail like grim death. On my signal they let go, and I shot forward towards the hedge. I left the flaps up, but pulled them down about 40 yards from the hedge, which I cleared by a foot or two. I returned rather shamefaced to the old ALG which fortunately was still occupied by the Flight. I cannot remember what excuse I offered, but we carried on with the exercise and all was well.

It was about this time that I learned of an old RFC and RAF technique for picking up messages (I think it was used on the North-West Frontier in the 30s). It was not difficult, but it was necessary to carry a crew member, usually the Rear Observer.

The troops on the ground who had written the message had to acquire two fairly long posts, then make holes for them in the ground so that they would stand up like the two verticals of a rugger goal, about 6 yards apart. A piece of stout cord was then knotted together to form a loop about 8 yards long. The message was put in a bag and tied to one strand of the loop. Two vees were then cut in the top of the poles, the loop was fitted into these vees and the poles placed in position so that the top of the loop was taut whilst the bottom part, containing the message, hung several feet below it. The aircraft doing the pick-up flew with the doors removed, the Rear Observer being provided with a sort of fishing line terminating in a large wire hook.

Having found the message party on the ground, all that was required was a very low level pass, flaps down, so that the loop, with the message tied to it, could be hooked and hauled inboard. After a bit of practice, it was quite simple, and had some advantages over our very temperamental radios.

I had another rather embarrassing experience about that time. By then I was a Flight Commander and could therefore authorise my own flights. I decided I needed some more practice at forced landings. The recognised method was to fly over a piece of unfamiliar ground, cut the throttle, select a field and make an approach to it. When all looked satisfactory, power was applied at about 50 feet AGL followed by a climb back to one's original altitude. I followed this drill but found that the only possible field had standing corn in it; however, as I did not intend to land, I continued my approach with full flap. As I got near the ground I realised that the ground sloped upwards rather steeply, so I applied full throttle, but unfortunately the Auster's rate of climb was less than the gradient. Inevitably the long stalks of corn reached up and caught my undercarriage, stopping the aircraft in a few yards; unfortunately it also turned over. Having heard of pilots injuring themselves by undoing the straps in a similar situation, I switched off mags and fuel, opened the door and then braced myself before undoing the straps, and got out undamaged. After a short wait the policeman from the nearby village arrived on a bicycle and eventually arranged for a car to pick me up and take me back to Detmold.

As I have explained previously, the Auster belonged to the Royal Air Force, and their Airships were not enthusiastic about paying for replacements for the stupid soldiery. Accordingly, a few days later, my CO escorted me to the RAF Headquarters, where an Air Vice Marshal gave me a rocket and told me to do better next time! After that the rules for forced landings were changed: full flap was not to be applied except in a real forced landing.

After that debacle life returned to normal. Some of the pilots, including myself, were members of the Royal Artillery Aero Club, which had several aircraft, including a Miles Messenger. These were all based in the UK at Christchurch. Somehow we persuaded the Club to base this Messenger at Detmold, where it could be used by any Gunner who was a Club member. My old CO, Harry Simms, flew it out to Detmold, accompanied by his wife. I flew it several times; it provided a means of flying long-suffering wives and girl-friends around the local countryside, which included many beauty spots, Schlosses and lakes. Unfortunately the aircraft's oleos were not reliable and it became a bit of a hangar queen.

There was also some excellent gliding available at an RAF Club at Scharfholdendorf, near Hameln. There was a collection of prewar German gliders there including the *ab initio* "Broomstick." This was a bit hairy to fly, but great fun. The pilot was strapped to a seat at the front of an open framework on which the wings and tail were mounted. There was a stick, pedals and a means of releasing the tow-rope, but no instruments of any sort. It was not too difficult for a trained pilot, but a complete novice must have had problems! The accepted criteria were as follows: if your eyes were not watering and the flying wires were humming, your speed was about right. If your eyes were watering and the wires were humming strongly, you were going too fast, and the wings might detach themselves. If the wires weren't humming and your eyes weren't watering, you were just about to stall!

Two more stories and then I must leave Germany. Once more, I was on an exercise, and was carrying out an reconnaissance in an area I knew quite well. I was looking for a suitable field for an ALG and recognised one that I had used before; unfortunately it had cattle in it. One of our rules was that one never landed in a field occupied by animals, so I bumbled off to look elsewhere. After about 20 minutes I had found nothing suitable, but was becoming increasingly aware that I must land shortly as I was in dire straits!

The only possible field was the one that I have already mentioned, but this would mean breaking two rules, firstly by landing near animals, and secondly, by landing without a ground party being present. However needs must when the devil drives so I made an approach and landed. The cattle never even looked up. I stopped the engine and jumped out and dropped my slacks just in time. To my supreme embarrassment one of the heifers then moved sideways to reveal a flaxen-haired German milkmaid milking away. I do not know who was more embarrassed!

Towards the end of my tour in Germany, I was detailed to fly an aircraft from Detmold to Rearsby, the Auster factory near Leicester. Normally this would have been a pleasant trip, with refuelling stops at Eindhoven, Coxyde and Manston, but unfortunately on this occasion there was a strong headwind, which meant I was crawling along at about 45 knots.

Another problem when flying across international borders was that our tactical HF wireless sets were quite useless for air traffic purposes. Naturally we always telephoned in advance before flying to an airfield, but this did not help when things went wrong, though I can only remember one embarrassing incident caused by this communication drawback. In this case, I was told to pick up a Brigadier at Kosted, about 60 miles from Detmold, then fly him down to an American Air Force base at Stuttgart. I found this enormous airfield without any trouble, but huge Flying Fortresses were droning around. I was expecting a green from the Tower but no one took any notice of me. I tried the wireless but with no response, so I decided to stand off until I could see a clear gap and then make a dirty dart at the runway. All went smoothly: I had not finished my landing roll when a "Follow Me" Jeep appeared with an armed military policeman sitting in the back. On closing down, I was told that I was under arrest for making an unauthorised landing. Fortunately the Brigadier then stepped in, explaining that he was a General (Brigadiers are Generals in the United States forces). After this was assimilated, all was sweetness and light.

I then discovered that the reason for the visit was that the Brigadier was to negotiate for a new Mercedes at the factory at Stuttgart, and I could come along too. We then spent a fascinating hour or two in the Mercedes Museum, which was of particular interest to me as I had a 1935 drophead Merc at that time.

Apparently a satisfactory deal was struck. The next morning we were refuelled and sent off in style for home. The Americans proved to be very good hosts once our problems had been sorted.

Whilst on the subject of communications, I am reminded of the difficulties of radio procedures. The RAF and Army used completely different systems. This did not bother us as we only communicated with

TOP: John Cosmelli's Hirtenberg HS.9A G-AGAK was based at Denham during the fifties.
BOTTOM: H.J. Warwick's Moth Major G-ADHE, also based at Denham.
Photos: Roy Mills.

Two of the BA Swallows at Bertram Arden's private field near Exeter in the early fifties.
TOP: The Pobjoy-engined G-AFGE.
BOTTOM: The Cirrus-engined G-AFHC.
Photos: Noel Collier.

TOP: Bertram Arden's aggressive-looking Auster V G-AJHJ.
BOTTOM: The *"Evening News"* S.51 helicopter seen at Exeter on the 14th
August 1954.
Photos: Noel Collier.

MEMORIES OF THE CAITHNESS SAGA.
TOP: Stampe G-AROZ would not start and was attended by the AA's Highland Patrol.
BOTTOM: Neil Williams in the homebuilt gyrocopter, which remained earthbound for very good reasons.
Photos: Nick Pocock.

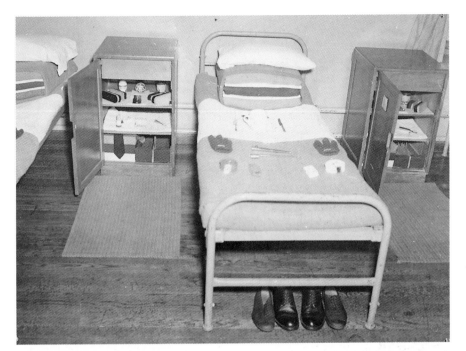

TOP: A nostalgic photo for all those who did their National Service in the RAF. Neil Jensen's kit is laid out for inspection at Kirton-in-Lindsey. Photo: Neil Jensen.
BOTTOM: Hunting President G-ARCN was operated by BAC from Filton during the sixties. Photo: Ted Ashman via Edwin Shackleton.

TOP: Edwin Shackleton, together with his trusty Leica camera, was at a wintry South Cerney for the final Chipmunk flypast on the 10th January 1967; the aircraft is WD390.
Photo: via Edwin Shackleton.
BOTTOM: Col. John Moss flew aerobatics in this Tiger Moth, T6107, at Detmold in the early fifties. Photo: Col. John Moss.

the Army, but in 1954 we acquired a Chipmunk instead of the non-radio Tiger; this was for practising aerobatics, but it was also useful for visiting RAF airfields, because we could then talk to them on the radio. However this meant some rapid thinking over procedures. I found it difficult to re-adjust my brain when I switched on this new-fangled VHF set. It would be boring to go into details, so I will just leave the subject except to say that, a few years later, the situation was further exacerbated when each army aircraft carried two sets, to talk to the Army and the Air Force, using different procedures on each set! As I said earlier life became increasingly hectic as the Cold War increased in tempo; we spent more time on exercises and became very well acquainted with the British Zone of Germany. However we still managed to enjoy ourselves with shooting, fishing, gliding and skiing, but all good things come to an end.

By November 1954 I had accumulated about 1,200 flying hours, having spent four years on my second tour in Germany. However I was brought to earth with a bump when the posting authorities announced that I was to return to the UK on a posting to a Royal Artillery Selection Regiment. I will not bore the reader with detals of this dreary job, but it was our task to place newly-drafted National Servicemen into the right slots. However there were compensations. The unit was at Oswestry on the Welsh borders, where not only was there good fishing and shooting but there was an Auxiliary Air Force Air OP Squadron not far away, commanded by an old friend of mine who graciously allowed me to keep my hand in with his Austers which, although in great demand at weekends, were little used during the week, so life could have been much worse. I also met my future wife there, whilst my father and stepmother lived in mid-Wales about 50 miles away. However this job did not last long. Whilst I was in Germany I had passed an exam for entry to the Royal Military College of Science at Shrivenham, so I will skip the next two-and-a-half years, which was the duration of the Technical Staff Course. During that time, I did manage to do a little flying with the Royal Artillery Aero Club and also at Middle Wallop.

I emerged from the course with the military equivalent to a BSc, but it was with great relief that we shook the dust of the RMCS from our shoes. To my delight I was to be posted to the Light Aircraft School at Middle Wallop.

By that time, 1957, our family had increased by two sons. Whilst we were at Shrivenham we had existed in a rather cramped flat, but now I had reached the lofty rank of Major and so was entitled to a decent quarter; we were fortunate to find a pleasant house on the banks of the River Avon, near Stockbridge, which suited us very well.

My new job was my idea of bliss; I was to be the Trials Officer and would be responsible to the then War Office (now Ministry of Defence) for testing new equipment for the Austers and Skeeter helicopters of the newly formed Army Air Corps, to which I had been allowed to transfer.

My command was not imposing, consisting of one Auster 9 and one Skeeter 12. I had a Captain (a pilot) to help me and three excellent Royal Electrical and Mechanical Engineers to do the real work. However the reader may have detected a small fly in the ointment: I had not been trained on helicopters! The reader will also know that piloting a light fixed-wing is not an 'open sesame' to driving a helicopter.

At that time the fledgling Army Air Corps (formed by amalgamating the Air OP and the Glider Pilot Regiment) was busily equipping itself with Saunders Roe Skeeters and Auster 9s. The latter presented no problem, but Skeeter training did. Clearly I could not do my job without being converted to helicopters, but all the conversion courses were full; however there was a loophole. The 'training machine' had realised that Majors and Lieutenant Colonels commanding AAC units and also filling associated staff jobs would need to have some knowledge of helicopters. Therefore short familiarisation courses were organised. These consisted of some 15 hours of dual instruction with a little solo. During 1959 I completed several of these courses until I had sufficient hours to qualify as a helicopter pilot. However I see from my final report that after about 90 hours I was deemed to be rather heavy-handed, possibly due to the erratic nature of my instruction; I would not disagree!

We were now ready to get on with the trials; this proved to be an absorbing task.

Generally speaking, I decided which trials were required but sometimes the War Office directed them. It would be tedious to detail them, so I will just mention a few of the more interesting ones. I see from my log book that my first trial was involved with radio and the second with homing, two aspects of army aviation which had been neglected in the past.

Remembering that the Cold War was at its zenith, radiological and nuclear subjects were major problems; consequently we cooperated with Porton Down in order to establish how helicopters could assist in detecting areas of nuclear contamination.

As one of the prime tasks of an Army pilot was observation, I spent many hours testing various stabilising devices for binoculars. Some of these worked remarkably well, improving artillery observation to a significant degree. We pioneered ultra-low flying by using a tape recorder, which instructed the pilot what course to follow, giving courses, speeds and timing, and also describing the features in the countryside below. This allowed the pilot to concentrate on the task in hand rather than on the map (no GPS in those days).

There was a certain amount of risk in some of these trials, in fact we had three incidents in about three days (and nights). At that time I was lucky to have the assistance of a pilot who was awaiting a permanent posting. We were both involved in trialling some Schermuly flares, which were supposed to illuminate the ground in the event of a night forced-landing. As far as I can remember, his first attempt was successful, but on the second, nothing happened. I was on the ground in a vehicle, and to my dismay heard the noise of the helicopter fade away. We rushed around the airfield in the dark, looking for what we feared might be a badly bent helicopter. We did find it eventually and were relieved to find that both pilot and helicopter were unhurt. The flare had failed to go off but somehow the pilot had managed to land successfully (many years later he was promoted to Brigadier!).

A day or two later, he and I were practising ultra-low flying when we managed to fly through several low-tension electric cables. Remarkably neither of us nor the Skeeter were damaged, but we landed immediately to make sure all was well. We were thereupon set on by an infuriated villager who had lost her electricity.

The third incident was caused when by chance I flew over the house of my ex-CO from Oswestry days, who was now farming in Wiltshire. I thought it would be civil to drop him a 'good luck' message, which I did. Unfortunately he did not retrieve the message but got onto the Air Traffic Control at a local RAF airfield, complaining about low-flying helicopters (he had no idea it was me). There was all the making of a first-class row when I returned to Wallop, but fortunately he then rang Wallop, withdrawing his complaint. In fact he had later found and read the message, so all was well.

Shortly after this I was told that I was to accompany Brigadier Weston, the Director, Army Aviation, together with two other officers, both friends of mine, on a visit to the Canadian Air OP and to the United States Army Aviation Center at Fort Rucker. The Canadian visit was very interesting, but I best remember it because we were taken duck shooting! We then moved on to Fort Rucker, which was most impressive. It was vast compared with Middle Wallop and much more advanced. The HU-1 (Huey) helicopter was undergoing trials, together with a range of other excellent helicopters and fixed-wing aircraft. Trials were going on to establish the efficacy of wire-guided missiles fired from helicopters against armoured fighting vehicles, with very encouraging results.

After a few days the Brigadier and the other two officers left for the UK, but I was allowed to stay behind to improve my knowledge of American Army Aviation developments.

A year or two before this visit, a friend of mine from 652 Squadron days, and one of the few early helicopter pilots, had been posted to Fort

Rucker as the British Liaison officer. He and his wife very kindly invited me to stay with them for my extra two weeks, which I found quite absorbing. It was truly amazing how far the US Army had progressed since 1951 when I last had contact with it. I was allowed to fly a number of their aircraft, dual of course, and much enjoyed my stay there.

And so back to the UK, where I was shortly due for some leave. My wife Janet and I decided to go to Guernsey, so flew over commercially. Whilst we were there, we made friends with the CFI of the Jersey Flying Club. After checking me out in the Club Auster, we decided to visit the other islands by air. This was great fun until we decided to visit Alderney. We had of course cleared it through Air Traffic, but having arrived overhead and asked permission to land, I was questioned as to whether I had landed there before (by civil standards the field was quite short). I replied in the negative, whereupon I was told I could not land. I asked politely how one achieved a first landing! However, I then explained that I was a practising army pilot, used to short strips, so eventually I was allowed to land. In the end we enjoyed our trip to Alderney!

One of the last trials that we carried out in the fifties concerned the use of Infra-Red Night Goggles. These had been developed for night-driving and were 'active,' which meant that they would only operate when a source of "Black Light" was available. A Skeeter was equipped with the necessary electronics and goggles. A suitable dark night was chosen and we had the whole airfield to ourselves, though the Fire Section were standing by.

As far as I remember we both had a try at flying with goggles and both decided that it was impossible to judge height and distance, so that was the end of that, at least for many years. Now, of course, Night Vision Goggles have improved out of all recognition and are a necessary adjunct for helicopter night-flying.

So that about brings me to the end of the fifties, which was a most interesting decade for me. I count myself very lucky to have been a founder member of the Army Air Corps, and to still be involved with it, albeit somewhat tenuously. Also I am still flying, though only a microlight!

CHAPTER 19

REMEMBER, REMEMBER!

by

Chris Dearden

And it was the fifth of November, as it happened. Not that there's too much significance in that, except it provided the lame excuse for a flight in the Chelsea College Tiger, 'MNN.

Really this is a story of stupidity. Crass stupidity. My very own stupidity, compounded by incompetence. The story of my life, maybe! "Ah! yes, I remember it well."

In 1955 things were pretty quiet at Redhill aerodrome. During the week there were people at least going through the motions of working at Tiltman Langley and sundry other ramshackle outfits there. On a Saturday, though, it was Ghostville.

On this particular Saturday the luminaries of the Tiltman Langley Sports and Social Club were beavering away in a field near East Grinstead, setting up for their annual firework party.

"I know!" Ian had said to me on the Friday, "we could fly over in the Tiger tomorrow afternoon and bomb them with toilet rolls."

I vetoed the toilet rolls idea, firstly because I couldn't see the point, secondly because chucking things out of aeroplanes can be just a little bit illegal (in peacetime, at any rate) and thirdly because as pilot in charge muggins would have got the hammer if anyone had decided to complain. But I agreed to the jolly jape of stooging over to have a look and said I didn't see any harm in his making air-to-ground rude gestures if he really felt he must, though I wasn't going any lower than 800 feet over the site.

So the immediate step was to go along and see Chiefie (now late and much-lamented) at the College to ask if I could have the Tiger.

"There's just one thing," he said. "Tomorrow being Saturday, we shan't be here and the place'll be all locked up." Then he gave me a knowing nod and added: "But come with me. I'll show you . . ."

Lying on the ground beside the hangar was a short piece of apparently useless iron bar. Chiefie picked it up and instructed: "When the doors are shut you can stuff this in the gap between them . . . about there, and lever it this way, at the same time as you give the bottom of the door a sharp kick . . . about there. Then you can slide it open. And don't forget to close up again when you've done." His bluff, Yorkshire manner gave him an air of great authority.

I thanked him and promised to obey.

Poor security? Nonsense! Without the classified information as to exactly where and how hard to kick the door you'd have been on a loser trying to gain entry. Now, that's security!

Fuel was a minor problem at Redhill in those days. There wasn't any. And I knew that 'MNN's fuel state was far too low for peace of mind, even on a local hop. But fear not, gentle reader! Some time previously I'd acquired a (10 gallon, I think) metal drum and had it filled with aviation spirit against just such a situation as this. Now was the time to fish it out from under its plastic cover behind the garden shed and put it to good use. Added to what little was already in the Tiger's tank it'd give us a comfortable hour's trip with contingency allowance, based on an average consumption of seven gallons per hour.

A Morgan three-wheeler was not the ideal transport for the drum but, keen young idiot that I was, a way was found to match the will. Somewhere along the line I must have picked up Ian. I can't quite recall. Time has drawn a kindly curtain over that detail!

So there – eventually – we were, a right pair of prunes on Redhill aerodrome in the early afternoon of November 5th, 1955. Chiefie's method of opening the hangar worked like a charm and we trundled the unsuspecting Tiger out. What followed would not have disgraced Laurel and Hardy. Suffice to say we did at last get most of the juice into 'MNN . . . Start-up, warm-up, run-up, routine checks, Ian pulled the chocks away and climbed aboard. We were as ready as we were ever likely to be!

The generally accepted rule at Redhill was that one took off and landed according to the windsock on the southern boundary. Anything else apart, the signals square had long since fallen into disuse and reverted to nature.

As a brief diversion from the story, I remember only one occasion when the square was used, and that was in 1947. During the 'circuits and landings' part of my training my regular instructor had handed me over for a session with the Chief – not my favourite person, nor I his, I fancy. Anyway, after I'd done about five reasonably good landings he came on the Gosport speaking tube.

"Where do you think the wind is this evening?" He spoke with an ominously sarcastic drawl.

"Well, er," I floundered in the mire of such an apparently banal question, "right on the nose . . . er, westerly."

The CFI went ballistic and said he didn't give a stuff where I thought the wind was (having just asked me). Hadn't I bothered to look at the signals square? (About which I hadn't yet been told.) Hadn't I seen the landing-T? Didn't I know what it was for? Which way was it indicating? That was what mattered, not my opinion. I'd better pull my socks up!

And so forth. (Some of those ex-RAF instructors still weren't quite reconciled to the idea of dealing with bloody civilians.)

Well, really! I thought (but didn't say), you might have mentioned it sooner, Treasure-Pops, and not let me keep on landing the wrong way. It smelt of a put-up job and from then on I treated the signals square with contempt. I just flew to the southern windsock.

On that afternoon in 1955 it hung against its mast like a disenchanted carrot, just now and then suggesting that north-to-south might be worth a try as a take-off direction.

So up and away! There was no problem in finding the bonfire site. We'd previously told the Head Luminary of our intention to visit and he'd given us some useful landmarks as pointers. And there were the worker ants, scurrying about all over the field; the seniors building the ramps and frames for the set-piece fireworks, the juniors heaving wood onto the pyre.

I flew a few circles and did the obligatory wing-waggling bit while they down there did the obligatory handkerchief-waving bit and Ian did his optional gesturing bit. When we'd all become thoroughly bored by this pantomime – which was pretty soon – we stooged off to marvel at the glories of the winter landscape around the Surrey/Sussex border.

Can there be such an animal as the pilot who, at one time or another, hasn't let the passenger have a turn at the controls? Ian had flown with me often enough before so this had become routine. It was while we were heading back to the 'drome that he asked: "Is it all right if I try a dummy approach this time?"

Hell-fire! "If you like," I said blandly. "But as soon as I give you the word, open up and climb away." (Any qualified instructors wishing to go ballistic may start NOW. It gets worse!)

At the time I felt rather smug, sitting there uttering words of wisdom as if I knew what they meant . . ."Turn onto the cross-wind leg now . . . Close the throttle. Ease the speed down to sixty-five, and . . . trim." Putter-putter-putter. "Turn onto final about now . . ." Putter-putter. "Line up and watch the ground well ahead."

We were a stack too high for any possibility of a landing off this one, but that had been my guiding intention in the name of preservation. "Open throttle and climb away," I called at what I guessed to be the right moment.

Ian responded magnificently but the motor didn't. It protested in a sequence of alarming pops and bangs. The airspeed began to withdraw its support in sympathy.

"I have control," I bellowed, rather too loudly, into the Gosport ("I have control" – what a laugh!).

Clearly it was the time for a quick decision – a craft in which I do not excel. From the height we were at, a 'straight ahead' landing was not an option. Even if I'd shed it in a spectacular sideslip we couldn't have avoided an angry confrontation with the up-wind hedge. Think again, Whittington, and sharp about it! Do something, if it's only resign.

It dawned on me that the engine hadn't quit completely. It was still delivering some power in fits and starts. Not enough to keep us in the air, but some. Fine, thought I. Here's the answer. The height can be traded off against a gentle, three-hundred-and-sixty-degree, power-assisted gliding turn round the perimeter, bringing us nicely back for a north-to-south landing with room to spare. A brilliant idea – except it didn't work.

Just as we were over the southern boundary, and starting to curve round the eastern end of the 'drome, things dramatically deteriorated. The 'fits' became longer than the 'starts.' 'MNN began going down like a lift heading for the basement. There was nothing else but to do a smart 'left hand down' and aim for an east-west landing.

But in my state of anxiety, now bordering on paralysis, I did exactly what every 'sprog' pilot is drilled not to do; I held the nose up on the turn instead of letting it go down as I should and could quite safely have done. Sheer ineptitude! No excuses! I loused it but good!

'MNN pitched forward and literally fell out of the sky then, with a sickening lurch, put her port wing down decisively. An incipient spin! In those micro-seconds the thought made its brief journey across my tiny mind that had we been just a few feet higher the spin would undoubtedly have developed and we'd have gone in sharp end first. Such events can be terminal! As it was, the wing struck the ground and the rest sort of spiralled down after it.

When all the shaking, rattling and rolling had subsided she just sat there, ticking over as sweet as a nut. Here the astute reader will put yet another black mark against my name. And rightly so! I hadn't even had the gumption to cut the switches when I realised I'd lost control.

I left Ian 'minding the shop' while I got out to see what damage had been done. He gave me a reproachful look as if to say: "Even I could have done better than that." Maybe I took it as a further reproach that his normally slightly ruddy complexion had turned a rather attractive shade of pale. Certainly I was sweating like the proverbial.

What now? About a six-inch length of the port aileron hinge gap was blocked solid with turf and mud. I raked this out with my fingers and then sacrificed a handkerchief and a deal of spit to wipe the area clean for inspection. Oh, joy! It hadn't even marked the paintwork. No apparent damage whatever. And even the undercarriage was still in good shape.

As soon as we'd taxied in I switched off, Ian got out with remarkable alacrity, put the chocks at the wheels and swung the prop again. I ran the motor up to full power, throttled it back, ran it up again, held it there, idled it, ran it up again. It never missed a single beat. In view of this I briefly considered giving it another go in the air, but then decided I'd just been stupid enough for one day. So, in a state of mystification, and now being persons of a nervous disposition, we put the old girl to bed.

First thing on the Monday morning I reported to Chiefie that I'd had a wee spot of engine trouble, resulting in a heavyish landing and just a little bit sideways. I gave him the details. He laughed like a drain. He would!

Later he told me that he'd checked the thing over and the only fault he'd found was some water in the fuel filter. We looked at each other and shrugged – just one of those things. Though I had a feeling the wise old bird suspected something.

To my lasting shame I never confessed that I knew jolly well how the water had got in there. Lamely on the credit side, though, I made certain that I did the next flight in 'MNN – I made it alone, just in case there was any lingering trouble. No one else should get crunched because of my crass stupidity.

As for the famous flight, the 'Remark' in my log is simply 'Engine failed during overshoot. Landed OK inside field.' Maybe it was all that needed saying.

But beyond that, remember: do not store fuel in a tin can behind the garden shed. Remember: do NOT tip it straight into an aeroplane without even the elementary precaution of putting it through a wash-leather filter. Remember, remember? It was a lesson I shall never forget!

And I did enjoy the firework party that 5th November. I felt quite lucky to be alive.

*   *   *

So there'd be another day and eventually fuel would become available again at Redhill. I didn't realise in '55 that there was an interesting, and apparently practical alternative solution to the refuelling problem. It was only in the very early sixties that it was made clear to me what I should have done!

An acquaintance of mine was flying his Turbulent from Staverton back to Redhill. As he approached Guildford he came out of his habitual daydream and noticed that the fuel gauge (that bit of wire poking up through the cowling) was reading 'Not very much.' No hope of making Redhill – or anywhere useful for that matter. Big problem!

As every keen young pilot knows, running out of fuel in the air through sheer misjudgement and lack of attention is a cardinal sin, punishable by something unspeakably horrid, making suicide seem a happier way out. The Min. of Civ. Av. was not open to lame excuses like: "Sorry, I didn't notice those little green Martians drilling that hole in the tank and letting all the fuel out. And then there was that plague of locusts, and what with having to fly around that sudden, tropical storm and one thing and another . . . well, you know how it is." No, they don't! An excuse needed to be astoundingly better than that if it were to be accepted.

And did Matey take the easy option of simply jumping over the side without a parachute? Did he hell! He lobbed his Turb down on the swathe of grass along the southern side of the Hog's Back, walked to the nearest roadside phone box and rang the AA . . . "I've run out of fuel on the Hog's Back."

After (presumably) the formalities of membership number, exact location and so forth he was advised to go and wait by his vehicle. Help would be sent.

Imagine the scene. The Patrolman duly arrives with the can of petrol. Pity the poor lad . . . "Right, sir! Is this your veh– . . .? AARRGH! It's an aeroplane!?"

"I know it is," Matey replies. "I never said it wasn't. I just said I'd run out of fuel."

The said petrol is then tipped in, the elastic rewound and away goes our hero home to Redhill. As easy as that!

But I wonder what happened to the Patrolman when he'd returned to his depot and reported what he'd just done. I hope they were kind to him and suggested that perhaps he'd been overworking, that he was suffering hallucinations, that it was time he took a nice long holiday – like retiring.

This story first came to me through a mutual acquaintance and when I next saw Matey himself I asked him if it were true.

"Yes," he muttered as blandly, as if refuelling an aeroplane on the Hog's Back were the most common event in the world, not really worth talking about. Or was his reticence merely a fog to obscure a fiction? Had it been anyone else I might well have opted for the fiction idea, but his story was so in keeping with his naturally cavalier style that it rang true.

Now why didn't I think of simply phoning the AA when 'MNN needed fuel in '55? That's a thing I can't remember! I guess I just lacked the imagination to take the tide at its flood, to capture the spirit. As it was, I acted like a prize prune and posed a greater hazard to life and limb than did someone landing a Turbulent on the Hog's Back. Who shall cast the first stone?

Yet whatever the judgement, whatever the rights or wrongs of it, it's hard to deny that those bright and carefree years were richly laden with happy lunatics – of whom I'd like to think I was one.

CHAPTER 20
TEACHING AND TESTING
by
Ambrose Barber

[NOTES ON THE AUTHOR: Ambrose Barber learned to fly as a young National Serviceman in the early fifties. In his contribution to "More Tails of the Fifties" he described how he and his contemporaries gained their 'wings' on Harvards and then converted onto early jets. After leaving the RAF he flew as a part-time instructor at Fair Oaks before finally going supersonic in 1957 while acting as a Hunter flight test observer with Hawkers. He subsequently had various managerial appointments with the company, was elected a Fellow of the Royal Aeronautical Society in 1984 and retired from BAe as a Divisional Director, Military Aircraft. A member of the Tiger Club's early display teams, he still enjoys 'three-pointing' with his friends in the Southdowns Auster Group. – Ed.].

"Once you have tasted flight you will walk the earth with your eyes pointed skyward."
(Attributed to Leonardo da Vinci, 1452-1519)

It is the 4th November 1998 and I have just landed the old Auster back on its farm strip on the Sussex-Hampshire border. It has been one of those perfect autumn flying days. Taking advantage of the superb visibility, I've enjoyed nearly three hours in the air. Now, as I trudge up to retrieve the orange windsock from its vantage point by the airstrip, I look across to the South Downs four miles away. The sunset is stunning, with Butser Hill silhouetted against great swathes of crimson sky. Higher still, a glorious pattern of altocumulus clouds, bathed in shining gold, drifts in gently from the west. Arrested by the beauty of the fading sky, I'm overtaken by a sense of good fortune. What a pleasure it is to be able to just potter about in uncontrolled airspace, visiting friendly strips and meeting like-minded people! Pausing reflectively, my mind travels back to my earliest encounters with aircraft, in the days when Austers were *new*!

The first time I got up close to an aeroplane was thanks to my alert mother. In May 1940 a Swordfish had force-landed on the sands at Selsey Bill after one of the biplane's bracing wires had parted and, as a short-trousered little schoolboy, I was on the scene before the village policeman! When, years later, I glided unobtrusively into a deserted Surrey field with a dead engine, I can't think why the appearance of excited little boys popping up from nowhere took me by surprise – obviously the club still thrives! Anyway, the Swordfish was the subject of a splendid seaside race between the incoming tide and the Royal Navy finding and fitting a replacement flying wire. I can vividly recall the Navy winning by a satisfyingly small margin! Later on there had been the indescribable thrill of being conducted in and out of wartime aircraft resident at RAF Halton while my father, a bemedalled 'retread' from the '14-'18 War, was serving there in 1943-44. On the second occasion I was allowed up into the cockpit of a Halifax while WAAF trainees were being taught to run up its four Merlins. This was heady stuff indeed for a thirteen-year-old, never mind the WAAFs! Already captivated by the works of W.E. Johns and stimulated by the aeronautical variety of the busy wartime skies, this experience was to sow the seeds of an intractable addiction.

Reinforcement, if any were needed, was provided two years later when I left the ground for the first time as a member of 523 Flight, Aldenham School's ATC contingent. An Anson and Dominie at RAF Henlow were followed by rides in a Tiger Moth from Panshanger and another Dominie from Bovingdon. Elstree aerodrome was an easy walking distance from the school and there, amongst other types, smart new cream-coloured Austers could be viewed from a respectful distance.

The first airfield I got to know from the 'inside' was Redhill in 1950. I was to see much more of it later as a member of the Tiger Club, but at the time I was a hopeful young student of aeronautical engineering. Redhill's grass was still reinforced in places with metal mesh tracking which had supported wartime fighters there. The single row of hangars housed No. 15 Reserve Flying School at the north end, then British Air Transport (the airfield operator), the flying school/club aircraft, our Chelsea College hangar (now at Shoreham) and then the Surrey Gliding Club (before moving to Lasham), to be followed by F.G. Miles arriving from Woodley. At the end of the row, next to the wartime control tower, was Tiltman Langley Laboratories.

Our chief engineer, J.R. Burnett, and several of his staff were Licensed Engineers so, in addition to the parts of aircraft used for instructional purposes, our hangar contained some machines which were, from time to time, actually flyable. One student, a young ex-RAF pilot called Brian Gates, kept his Gipsy Moth G-ABJJ with us. Other flying machines were, at various times, Hawk Trainer G-AJDR, the Redwing biplane G-ABNX and the pretty little Chilton DW.1 single seater G-AFSV, which we prepared for air races. While at Redhill, I had passenger flights in the Club's Austers, G-AJED with fellow student P. Britton, and G-AHCK with the Club Instructor, Alan Sproxton.

When my studies were concluded for the time being, call-up was next on the agenda. Being destined for the aircraft industry, my natural choice was to spend the next two years in the Royal Air Force, and with it was the chance to be assessed for flying training. Just as I was due to leave Redhill we got the College's Tiger Moth airworthy, and it was my turn to go up with Gates who had promised to let me try handling the flying controls. Imagine my frustration when, during final checks before take-off, she wouldn't quite 'clear' one of her magnetos – my chance to practise ahead of the game was gone!

I first got to steer an Auster towards the end of my national service. In March 1954 I had already held a private pilot's licence for six months on the strength of my Service training, but had yet to 'exercise its privileges.' Now home on leave, I rode my Douglas twin the ten miles over to the Fair Oaks Aero Club. The airfield (already referred to as "Fairoaks" on 1940s flying maps) was all grass in those days. It had been very active in providing elementary training for potential RAF pilots and, at the height of WW II, it used Smiths Lawn in Windsor Park as a satellite field. Afterwards it had continued to host No. 18 Reserve Flying School but now, with the Korean war safely over, RAF VR flying had been curtailed as an economy measure and their silver Tiger Moths and Chipmunks were gone. I recall being greeted by the sight of a handful of club Tiger Moths and a couple of Austers in addition to several privately-owned types. There was also a single Tiger Moth, one of several belonging to the London Transport Flying Club.

Beside the old control tower was a little wooden building where Jack Holland was 'major-domo' both as Club Secretary and Company Secretary of Universal Flying Services, the airfield operator – itself a subsidiary of the Blackburn and General Aircraft Company of Brough in distant Yorkshire. Jack smiled: "Yes, the Club aircraft may be hired by members," and "Yes, here is a membership application form." This was just completed when in walks a stocky figure of authority with a pink weather-beaten face.

"Ah!" says Jack, "here's the CFI, Wing Commander Arthur."

He greeted me, and after a few penetrating questions about my Service flying we walked outside and he set about introducing me to Auster Autocrat G-AJDV. Although it was a long time ago, I distinctly recall how totally unprepared I was for the shortness of the take-off run, finding myself climbing away at what felt like a suicidally slow airspeed after the Vampires I was currently flying. This sense of insecurity was enhanced by the unaccustomed absence of an RAF parachute! Despite this, I must have managed to give an impression of being more at home than I felt because I see from my log book that after 35 minutes I was sent off on my own.

I returned from leave to RAF Merryfield where my Vampire course was coming to an end. No. 208 Advanced Flying School had been set up there in 1951 to train day fighter pilots onto jets and there we had found ourselves part of a bachelor camaraderie totally absorbed in that flying. Training along with regular aircrew, some from piston-engined squadrons, the regime was demanding and not without incident, but we had the adventure of our young lives as I endeavoured to relate last year in "National Service Pilot." To gain one's wings at Her Majesty's expense and then be given a single-seat jet fighter to fly is the stuff of schoolboys' dreams, and even now it causes me to smile! Of course, temptation lurked for that extra sensation. Not content with having a similar casualty rate to ours, someone from our neighbouring Weston Zoyland AFS was seen to fly a Meteor fighter under the Clifton suspension bridge. Seven of their pilots were airborne at the time. We heard that after exhaustive interrogation only five were eventually eliminated and I believe the guilty hero was never nailed. Perhaps, after all these years, he could describe the adventure for the rest of us! When this escapade was emulated three years later with an Auxiliary Squadron Vampire, the little fighter could be identified by its tragic wreckage.

At Merryfield my room-mate, Jock, had already departed for Scotland and like Algy, my other national serviceman chum from Harvard days, I was posted to 11 Group. Having accepted us with insufficient time remaining to join a squadron, Fighter Command would give us desks to fly, with what real flying we could scrounge. In this respect, our fortunes varied quite a lot. Jock found himself with a Chipmunk at his disposal while Algy had access to a variety of types including a Meteor. My nearest airfields were St. Mawgan and St. Eval, both Coastal Command! St. Mawgan having provided the right-hand seat in two Lancasters, I then tried my luck with St. Eval. In addition to their fleet of Shackletons, their HQ flight had a Mosquito! With this in view, they obligingly commenced my twin conversion on their Oxford, but my luck ran out when they rumbled my national service status – oh well! Many years later, I felt greatly compensated by a delightful ride from Hatfield to Lee-on-Solent beside George Ellis in DH/BAe Chester's late-lamented Mossie, G-ASKH.

At that time, the RAF was giving every encouragement to its national service flying graduates to extend their commissions and the prospect beckoned of leaving my admin desk as adjutant of a small Radar Station to rejoin longer-serving contemporaries destined for one of the Second TAF fighter squadrons. Against this, the aircraft industry, for which I'd trained previously, was itself recruiting and I felt, amongst other things, that if this was still to be my ultimate destination then the train should not leave without me! A choice had to be made soon.

When I was next home on leave I visited the flying club again. By the time I met him, Wing Commander Cyril Arthur AFC had become a long-term fixture at Fair Oaks. His flying went back to the 1914-1918 war and he was reputed to have pioneered some early air routes through the Far East in the twenties. He had become the CO of the wartime RAF Elementary Flying Training School at Fair Oaks, staying on to run the club as well as No. 18 RFS while it lasted. We flew together again, this time in one of the club's Tiger Moths. It was delightful to be reunited with my *ab initio* trainer and this time we were spinning and aerobatting happily over the North Downs above the Hog's Back. Afterwards he asked me whether I planned to stay in the Air Force, the question much on my mind as the end of my two years' service approached. Like an enthusiastic 'gentleman' amongst the 'players' I'd had to grapple with the dilemma of whether to turn professional. I confessed to the WingCo why I was instead seriously contemplating my flying future as a dedicated amateur, half expecting his scorn. Instead, he nodded in affable acknowledgement, declaring "an old head" to be "on young shoulders." I like to think the seasoned old aviator helped me come to a difficult personal decision and a month or so later I handed in my kit and proceeded on terminal leave.

My first civilian job was in the drawing office of the RFD Company at Godalming, as a draughtsman working on air-sea rescue equipment. Inevitably, I missed the flying and with it the crew room chatter. Those who enjoy 'opening the hangar doors' will know exactly what I mean. Nearly twelve months later, I had managed little more than five hours' flying on a draughtsman's pay, so in desperation I mustered enough of the latter to complete the flying instructors' course at Fair Oaks in the summer of 1955.

The training was carried out on the club's Tiger Moths. My fellow student was Robin Brodie-James and our tutor was Ron Cobbett, an ex-RAF instructor and the CFI's deputy. Robin and Ron were good characters to work with, which made for a congenial course. Eventually, both left the club to fly as commercial pilots. We trained to cover the PPL syllabus of instruction plus the Tiger's limited repertoire of aerobatics. It was less than three years since I'd done my own basic training and both the exercises and their accompanying patter were still helpfully familiar. Since the Tiger is flown solo from the rear cockpit, it followed that as a would-be instructor one trained in the front cockpit. When neither of us were flying with Ron, Robin and I flew together doing 'mutual' in which we took it in turns to sit in the front cockpit, while the other played the part of the 'pupil' and occasionally assisted as the prompter!

At the end of the course, WingCo Arthur tested us for our Assistant Instructors' Ratings. My only glitch was the execution of my slow rolls.

Determined not to drop the nose when rolling out, I anticipated the need for top rudder so early that my bootful completely countered the ailerons' roll (none too powerful on a Tiger anyway) and I hung upside down sorting out my crossed controls while the WingCo lost all the change out of the top pocket of his flying suit! Nevertheless, Robin and I both got our 'tickets' and for the rest of the season picked up such crumbs of instructing as the Club could spare, grateful for the chance to try out our newly-acquired skills.

A regular visitor to Fair Oaks then was Norman Jones, soon to found the Tiger Club. At that time he was buying up surplus RAF Tiger Moths 'as lying' at RAF Cosford for, I seem to recall, £50 a time. Two of these had been checked over at Cosford by Webster, our club's chief engineer, and given Permits to Fly. Robin and I ferried back one each and they subsequently gave good service at Fair Oaks as G-AODR and G-AODS.

The following spring Vickers Armstrong (Aircraft) Ltd launched a heavily-subsidised flying perk for employees working at Brooklands and Wisley. When the first Vickers course started in April 1956 I had four *ab initio* pupils to take through to their Private Pilots' Licences. There was a steady supply of candidates from the same source. Occasionally, there was an Auster conversion to handle but mostly we flew the faithful Tiger. It was a tremendous scheme for the lucky Vickers people and for us too. Even as a part-timer I was flying up to 28 hours in a good month that summer. Of course, as any instructor who has taught a batch of pupils starting together knows, they all get to the spinning stage together, they all tend to bash the circuit together and so on. I would finish a weekend hoarse but quite uncomplaining! It is very satisfying to sense when pupils finally click with the knack of three-pointing a Tiger. Sitting there in front, I would raise my arms out of the cockpit into their full view as the moment of touchdown approached so that they could see that I knew they could do it on their own, even if they didn't themselves!

The standard short cross-country for our PPL pupils used Lasham and Dunsfold as turning points. The longer one was Fair Oaks–Hamble airfield–Portsmouth airport–Shoreham airport–Fair Oaks. The wartime control tower at Fair Oaks was now unmanned and we had no radios, these aerodromes being visited by visual reference to the accepted authority of their signal squares. We taught people to read maps and to keep a lookout the while. To this extent, I suppose our open-cockpit flying was unchanged from club flying in the thirties. The next year Fair Oaks Aero Club would get two civilianised Chipmunks, called "Klondyke Kate" and "Diamond Lil" on account of their greater hourly flying cost, but it would be about 1960 before the club got its first nosewheel aircraft, an American Tripacer.

In the summer of 1956 I was due for the renewal check for my instructor's rating. To ensure that all went well I practised my slow rolls and made sure the WingCo fastened up the pockets on his flying suit before take-off! He was not without a sense of humour. On another occasion, he and I wanted to fly on a day when the airfield was deserted due to a very strong southerly wind. He ordered a Tiger to be brought out and instructed a couple of his mechanics to hang on to our wingtips throughout start-up and until our take-off run was safely under way. In due course, they were to be ready to grab us again during our extremely short landing run. After an exhilarating local flight we came in over the hangars in the steepest approach of my life and, landing beside the mechanics with negligible ground speed, it worked. I suppose that was how they'd done it in the Royal Flying Corps!

I think the most exciting part of the PPL syllabus was the final exercise, done dual only, to demonstrate engine restarting in flight. Tiger Moths are not equipped with engine starters. Their propellers are swung either by hand or, if you've enough height, by the aerodynamic energy generated at near the maximum speed attainable diving with the engine stopped. By commencing at 4,000 feet, one could, if it ever failed, still exercise the option at 2,000 feet to convert the demo into a forced landing for real!

Having expounded the theory to one's pupil, we throttle back at 4,000 feet over open country and switch the fuel and mags off. The prop keeps windmilling and we hold the nose up to reduce airspeed. As we approach the stall, the prop finally stops and glares reproachfully at us. There is an eerie silence.

With optimum gliding speed I say: "Check possible causes of engine failure."

"Fuel on, switches on!"

"Now move the throttle to one third open and ease the stick forward into a vertical dive."

When we get to what feels like the vertical, the prop obligingly moves, only to stop again defiantly as it comes up against the engine's compression. I prattle on above the increasing noise of the wind in the rigging, comforting both of us by trying to sound very laid back.

"We need to push the stick that bit further forward still, so that we're just over the vertical to get those last few extra knots. Look out sideways and check the horizon. That's more like it!"

The prop gives a perceptible little movement before disappearing once more into its blurred rotating disc and, *yes,* the soundtrack is restored!

"Making sure that the engine doesn't overspeed, we now ease out of the dive."

It worked every time but I always felt a secret sense of relief nevertheless!

The only startling moment I had instructing was when one pupil, a handsome six-footer, froze on the controls in his first-ever spin. Thus stimulated, my adrenalin rapidly overtook his and after a moment of strenuous silence all was well again, but it left me to reflect on how it went wrong for him. Despite Lieutenant Wilfred Parke RN discovering how to recover from a spin back in 1912, inadvertent low altitude "Parke's dives" still regularly claim their victims. The standard instruction aimed to breed neither panic nor complacency and therein, I suppose, should lie the instructor's perceptive skill. My own initiation had been without the hype of prior briefing. Having demonstrated the Tiger's stall, my genial RAF Grading School instructor, Mr Bailey, simply invited me to follow him through as he applied the rudder. Chatting normally the while, he asked me, as the Lincolnshire fields rotated below, what I thought the aircraft was doing. "Is this a spin?" I enquired equally calmly, and so it was. It was left to the Prentice and Vampire to teach me some of spinning's sharper lessons.

Instructing at Fair Oaks turned out to be just a fulfilling interlude as, in the autumn of 1956, my pursuit of the real and earnest led me to join Hawker Aircraft Ltd, whose design organisation had advertised for a flight test technician at Dunsfold aerodrome. On starting work at Dunsfold I let my instructing taper off but remained a Fair Oaks member until after joining the Tiger Club in 1964. Looking back, I had gained much from the teaching experience, finding that I enjoyed the process and for a few months I did some teaching at ground level as well. I also learned not to judge people by first impressions – probably the star out of my 20 pupils had seemed the least prepossessing until we had broken the ice. Above all, there was all that flying which I could not otherwise have contemplated.

Many, and better qualified than I, have described at length the virtues, history and limitations of the little Tiger Moth. What is more elusive to explain is the loyalty so many of us still seem to harbour for her. Certainly, as an inexperienced young instructor, I relied heavily on her viceless predictability and the dependable willingness of her anti-quated engine but why, 40 years on, do I remain faithful to her? More responsive and flightier young mounts there are with which to ride the skies but, I suppose, we have our reasons – nostalgia and, I suspect, some secret bond forged that very first time we flew alone. Since then, hardly a year has gone by that one of her sisterhood hasn't wheedled her way into my log book – so often it is the warrior queen herself, "ACDC."

Being a woman she will outlast me but for now, at each re-acquaintance, I am in the presence of an old flame from the past.

Strapped in, there is a *frisson* of anticipation as, like two geriatrics stepping uncertainly onto the dance floor, we taxy out in our slow ungainly way, weaving towards the threshold of another consummation. Here we can trust each other still, as we did then, that first time.

"All clear! Stick back and throttle open hold,
With tail up high we steer the grassy way.
The seasoned mistress knows my touch of old –
Reluctance gone, we gently climb away.

Here sights and sounds are as they ever were,
The little Moth still sings her old refrain;
As though by magic it is Lincolnshire
And, suddenly, we're twenty-one again!"

*　　*　　*

In 1956 Hawker's design team was still based at Canbury Park Road, Kingston upon Thames, and it was there that I was called for interview with Bob Marsh. During this, I learned more of what the Dunsfold job would entail. Bob headed up the design projects and it was the role of his Project Office to be the conceptual 'sharp end' of Hawker's leadership in fighter design. From time to time projects gave birth to prototypes and his department had a small section at Dunsfold to brief the test pilots and monitor the results. The Hawker P.1067 was undergoing continuous development as the single-seat Hunter and the first P.1101 two-seater would soon be joined by a second prototype. His technical office at Dunsfold was run by Fred Sutton, for whom I would work and, yes, the new two-seaters might provide occasional opportunities for a flight test observer.

The interview seemed to be going quite promisingly when in walked the commanding figure of Sidney Camm, Hawker's revered chief designer; we rose to our feet. Sir Sidney then asked various questions which he addressed through Marsh, starting with "Where's he been?" and followed by "What's he flown?".

Bob looked at me while I reeled off seven types, some of which I thought should go down quite well until, prompted by Camm's unimpressed snort, I realised that none of them had been designed by the great man himself!

After a bit more discussion, he turned to me and said: "How much d'you want?", for which bluntness I was totally unprepared. Sparing my further embarrassment, he followed it with: "I know, as much as you can get!"

Although Camm had been Hawker's chief designer for 30 years and would continue as Technical Director for 10 more, he still liked to feel he'd picked all the members of his team. With Camm's inspired designs,

Hawkers had followed on from Sopwiths with a succession of highly successful military biplanes and monoplanes, reaching the zenith in piston-engined fighters with his Tempest and Sea Fury. Now 63 and far from easing off, he had taken Hawker Aircraft into the jet age with the Seahawk and Hunter. Even so, in my youthful way, I didn't yet fully appreciate what a privilege it would be to work in such a team.

At Dunsfold, Fred Sutton's flight test section occupied the ground floor of the wartime control tower, with the test pilots immediately above us and the controllers aloft in their glasshouse. Test flying at Dunsfold was divided into 'production' and 'experimental.' While the bulk of flying was to clear production Hunter Mk. 4s and early Mk. 6s for delivery, we were concerned with flight development which entailed testing of a more exploratory nature. Upstairs, Neville Duke, as chief test pilot, led this experimental testing assisted by his deputy, Bill Bedford. Both had a wartime flying background but now, with Duke's test flying curtailed by back injury, Hugh Merewether, a younger pilot recruited from Duke's No. 615 Auxiliary squadron in 1954, was increasingly pulling his weight. Shortly, Bill would succeed Neville and, eventually Hugh himself and then Duncan Simpson (at this time on Frank Bullen's team of production test pilots) would, in turn, take over as CTP.

From my desk I could (and did!) look out over Dunsfold airfield. The Hunters stood on the concrete apron outside with the main runway beyond. One of my earliest 'memorable movements' was the high-speed arrival over the Tower of the bright scarlet prototype two-seater, which then taxied in, having put up the speed record from London to Rome and then back again. Out climbed Bill Bedford followed by Frank Murphy (former chief production test pilot) with his shock of prematurely white hair.

Our office was the focal point for technical liaison between the design specialists at Kingston, Bill Turner's engineering teams under Alan Wigginton and Bert Hayward in the 'experimental hangar' and, of course, Bill and Hugh upstairs. In those days we could record measurements made in flight in three ways: in the cockpit with pencil, stopwatch and roller knee-pad, by a modified 35mm ciné-camera photographing instruments specially mounted in the gunbay, or using a light-sealed little box with pinpoint lights deflected by calibrated transducers onto photosensitive paper rolls rotating against a timebase. Both the rolls of camera film and the paper traces required painstaking and laborious work to read and reduce the indicated results into true values which could be reliably plotted. From time to time instrumentation failure frustrated our quest for precision and tests had to be repeated. Each morning Fred would have to sign our Daily Report to Sir Sidney and Bob Marsh, confessing the progress of the previous day's flying by each of the

Hunters engaged on experimental work, a process which contributed to keeping everybody on their toes!

With the arrival of the second prototype, the flight development work to clear the Hunter two-seater for the RAF was under way in earnest and throughout 1957 there was, from time to time, both need and opportunity for a flight observer. I did not have to wait long for my turn. While January 22nd may have been a routine day for Bill Bedford in his new job as CTP, for me it was anything but! Both two-seaters had shown a tendency to shockwave-induced rudder vibration or 'buzz' during transonic dives. The newer prototype, XJ627, had been instrumented with a paper trace recorder so that the onset and frequency of this intermittent characteristic might be caught and analysed. Bill came down for our technical briefing with Fred and the format of the flight was agreed.

The friendly Harold Duffield has checked me out with flying suit, Mae West, one of the new-style bone-dome helmets and oxygen mask. So equipped, we strap ourselves in – one set of straps for the parachute, another for the ejector seat, leg restraint straps around the ankles and test-pad strapped to the knee. The cockpit is far from cramped but no space is wasted. Sitting on Bill's right, I listen as he briefs me on the ejection procedure. The hood is closed and our ground-crew friends unclip the steps. When all is clear, Bill presses the starter and the checks begin. I had previously made myself reasonably familiar with the cockpit but while we taxy out with the oxygen 'dolls-eyes' blinking as we breathe, I find myself taking in my immediate surroundings afresh, sensing their peculiar combination of sights, sounds and smells. We make our way to the east end of the airfield and, vital actions done, line up for take-off. XJ627 has the more powerful Avon 200 series engine and when the brakes are released we accelerate down the runway like I have never experienced before!

After unstick, Bill holds the Hunter down momentarily to build up speed and then up comes the nose and we just keep on climbing, going through 10, 20 and then 30 thousand feet in what seems like no time at all. At well over 40,000 feet we prepare for our first dive. Below, there is plenty of broken cloud but not enough to frustrate the exercise. After a final tug on our shoulder straps Bill wings over steeply and stands the aircraft on its nose in a full-throttle dive with the recorder running. Far below I can see a patch of open countryside through a hole in the clouds. I watch the Mach meter, waiting for the rudder vibration. It does not come. With no more fuss than a perceptible quiver of the needle our Mach No. is through 1.0 and sliding over 1.05. As we descend rapidly the Mach No. begins to drop away through the critical range and there is still no buzz. As we ease out of the dive the recorder is switched off with almost a feeling of anti-climax and then we're on our way up again.

Climbing back up to altitude on each occasion we repeated the exercise several times, no doubt distributing sonic booms liberally off the South Coast in the process! Sometimes we did manage to record traces of the elusive 'buzz' which, when it occurred, was only too apparent through the rudder pedals. There were then other tasks to be done to complete the morning's work and my log records that in the course of low altitude testing we reached a level speed of 600 knots. This was quite fast for those days, being within 35 knots of Duke's world speed record of 727 mph but, with the benefit of its area-ruled hood fairing and 10,000 lb thrust engine, this variant was no slouch. In trying out the steering on the way home, I did some rolls which, with powered ailerons, were a delight to perform – less tricky than a Tiger and much less effort than the manual Vampire. It was altogether a pretty impressive aeroplane. After landing there was a lot to reflect on and back in the office we listened to the cockpit voice recorder – yes, it was all there!

In those days the conquest of the 'sound barrier' had caught the public imagination and Neville Duke had become something of a household name. To emerge from Neville's shadow must have been challenging, particularly for someone with Bill's competitive nature. But during his ensuing eleven years as Hawker's CTP the P.1127 'jump-jet' would catch the same public's imagination and, with it, Bill would come to enjoy a comparable reputation. His natural resilience and determination were quickly appreciated in the wake of the misguided 1957 Defence White Paper which cancelled 100 Hunters destined for the RAF. Assisted by David Lockspeiser, his efforts were a decisive factor in a comparative number being bought by the Swiss Air Force and a larger number still by the Indian Air Force.

By contrast, Hugh Merewether projected a somewhat different personality. No less enthusiastic and dedicated, he was a tall and meticulous aeronautics graduate who would join in with us in poring over the test results we'd plotted. Both, as you would expect, needed to be skilled fast-jet aviators and possessed of that highly-controlled imagination which we ordinary mortals would call courage . . . In our eyes Bill and Hugh complemented each other well.

Being the 'new boy,' I had been the last member of the flight test section to get a two-seater ride but as further opportunities arose, only Fred and I, having the stronger stomachs, were the ones to be taken up repeatedly! Having said this, not all the flights requiring a second pair of hands and knee-pad were of an acrobatic nature. During several flights with Hugh, we carefully recorded the indicated heights and airspeeds flying with, or past, a calibrated Venom from Boscombe Down to ascertain pitot position errors. On other occasions we flew a series of precisely stabilised levels to measure performance at specified altitudes. After careful treatment at desk-level all this information would find its way into the Hunter T.Mk. 7 Pilots' Notes publication. More exciting was our pre-arranged arrival at RNAS Ford in an 18 knot crosswind when Hugh had to ascertain that the aircraft was still adequately controllable when the tail parachute was streamed on touchdown. Skillfully accomplished with a degree of heavy breathing, this tolerance would also be recorded and factored for future operational reference by others.

Not only performance but every other aspect requiring flight proving or development testing came through our office. The Hunter was a beautiful design; structurally robust and pilot-friendly, it was destined to become a classic. But before it was optimised for the RAF, let alone the other twenty air forces which were to take delivery, the effect of every change and innovation had to be explored and verified. Faced with this welcome technical variety, we had to be aeronautical jacks-of-all-trades and, for deeper knowledge, we relied heavily on our specialist counterparts at Kingston. A number of these design colleagues got two-seater rides as a mutually useful experience and one, H.E.J. Rochefort, the middle-aged Head of Research, returned on a number of occasions to experience at first hand the effect of trial modifications to eliminate rudder-buzz in high Mach No. dives. Success was eventually ours, but my log book records that it was still being experienced while we were diving with one of the unsuccessful 'fixes' in June 1957, by which time repetition had been found to crack a bracket in the rudder linkage.

In those pre-computer-prediction days it was called experimental testing with good reason as, after initial slide-rule calculations, much of our work was optimised by honest trial and error. Sometimes one had to see the funny side of it. The larger cockpit of the two-seater made greater demands on the cabin pressure, temperature distribution and demisting. The plan was to improve the system's performance by the addition of extractor louvres mounted externally behind the cockpit canopy, and a test flight was devised to measure this. After a prolonged 'cold soak' at altitude we came plummeting down in a max. rate descent to 1,000 feet. Hugh then hammered across the Sussex landscape at 585 knots while my job, despite the vibration, was to jot down regular readings of cockpit temperatures at head, hands and feet level. On landing back after all this, we opened the hood only to find that sometime during our flight the much vaunted louvres had been sucked off without trace!

In September, Hawkers had an embarrassing surprise at the SBAC show when, in full view of the afternoon's audience, one of the prototype two-seaters shed its cockpit canopy onto Farnborough's main runway. After anxious investigations back at Dunsfold and a minor alteration to the hood-locking mechanism, a degree of uncertainty remained. As an expediency, it was decided to check that the safe clearance between the 'lock' and 'unlock' modes was maintained at various combinations of speed and applied 'g' in case unpredicted structural flexing could incline the canopy to come off again. For this I was provided with some thick feeler-gauges, made up for the purpose. These I had to offer up to the safety gap at each condition, noting down the measurements on my knee pad. Separately, we were due to test the two-seater for gun-firing fumes, it having a different installation from the single-seater. This involved making a gas concentration recording while we emptied the magazine in a long continuous burst at low altitude, using solid non-explosive practice rounds.

We flew down to Selsey Bill and there, just off the coast, Bill hauled us round in the required series of uncomfortable manoeuvres at 1,500 feet over the grey sea below. At times my arms felt like lead and, with my eyes repeatedly focussed inside the cockpit, after a bit my stomach didn't feel too good either! But I see from the roller-pad sheet still in my possession that I managed to note down, in figures of increasing shakiness, that the safety gap actually increased between unstick and 600 knots by just over 0.1 inch, such was the tremendous aerodynamic suction flexing the cockpit canopy at high airspeed.

Finally, we moved on to the gunfiring. I had done this on previous occasions at 475 and 600 knots and this was a repeat at 600 knots. We hurtled down over the sea in a very shallow dive and at 1,000 feet Bill pressed the firing button. There was the familiar rattle of high frequency reports and accompanying vibration, only this time, curiously, there was a split-second delay before the last 30 mm round made itself heard.

With the seascape ahead unfolding pretty rapidly, I think we pulled out at about 300 feet and then, to restore my stomach's composure, Bill let me fly XJ615 home to Dunsfold. After he'd landed, we discovered a hole smashed through the nose radome and the ricochet from the sea resting just under our feet below the cockpit floor. It was the nearest I ever got to being shot down! Years later, when we were both running separate departments at Kingston, Bill still kept the battered round on his desk as a treasured memento of this freak marksmanship!

I made three more test flights that autumn and then, at the end of 1957, the first production Mk. 7 two-seaters were beginning to come off the line for acceptance trials by the RAF. It had been a memorable year but now, with the new-found responsibility of a happily expectant father-to-be, I left experimental test flying to those with a more controlled imagination! The phlegmatic Fred Sutton went on a bit longer. Looking back, we had both taken part in these adventures as part of our job, without the incentive of any flying pay, just for the privilege it undoubtedly was.

On the lighter side of aviating, I had discovered that just north of Dunsfold aerodrome lay Rydinghurst where the farmer, an ex-Fleet Air Arm pilot, had a little airstrip. I soon made John Wright's acquaintance, enjoying a flight with him in his Cub G-AFSZ and landing there in a Fair Oaks Tiger with Trevor Wooderson, one of my old Vickers pupils. This taste of farm flying led me to join Jack Miller's Wellcross Grange syndicate at Slinfold where, over a period of five years, I was able to fly Austers G-AHHU and 'MKU and Tiger Moth G-ANDE. It was a period when my personal flying was supported by the participation of many Hawker colleagues, particularly from Kingston, as willing passengers and crew.

In 1958 the members of Hawker's project office moved back to the site of Sopwith's WW I factory on the Richmond Road, Kingston and their attention was beginning to turn to a vectored thrust fighter concept. To meet this ground-breaking testing (literally at times!) our select little technical office would become strengthened and known as the Flight Development Department. But for the time being, Dunsfold had continuation testing to do on the newest Hunters which were now enhanced with wing leading-edge extensions. I found myself allocated the aircraft being used to assess handling characteristics with this mod such as manoeuvrability rates, stick force per 'g,' onset of buffet and so on. This included exhaustive spinning programmes, first on the single-seat Hunter and then on the two-seater. They covered both erect and inverted spin characteristics and recovery actions, which I monitored from the safety of the instrumented telemetry cabin! Here, in R/T contact with Bill and Hugh, it was fascinating to watch the roll and yaw needles depart in opposite directions when the spin was inverted.

Hugh got so intrigued with his study of inverted spinning that he extended it to the Hawker Tomtit, an elderly open-cockpit biplane once belonging to Neville Duke and in 1958 still kept at Dunsfold. In this he practised inverted spins to his heart's content and eventually demonstrated this demanding and uncomfortable manoeuvre at, I think, a Royal Aeronautical Society garden party later that year. My initial amusement at Hugh's masochism was given a sharp jolt one morning when he breezed into the office saying he would much like to explore the effect on the inverted spin of moving the Tomtit's C. of G. Ideally, what he really needed was some man-sized ballast strapped into the front cockpit. Everybody looked at me, quietly creasing themselves.

"Parachutes?" I enquired guardedly.

"Of course!"

For some reason which I can't recall, the intercom system in G-AFTA was incomplete to the extent that Hugh could talk to me but I could only reply with sign language. It was a fascinating sortie. If you are not in current practice on inverted spinning, and I certainly never had been, then it demands clear headed concentration under the influence of negative 'g' to stay fully attuned to the correct and necessary recovery actions. A mixture of pride and professional curiosity, but mostly I suspect the former (!) induced me to give Hugh, sitting behind me, the thumbs-up each time for yet another one!

In addition to the Tomtit, Dunsfold still stabled the Hawker Hart G-ABMR and our Hurricane G-AMAU, as well as two executive people-carriers in the form of Anson G-AHXK and Rapide G-AHGC. The latter was in use by Hawker Siddeley Aviation as late as 1965 when Bill and I were making liaison visits to RAE Bedford. On occasions, Bill could be highly supportive of those he was in a position to help. It was typical of him that on hearing, after taking off from Bedford, that I wanted more multi-time towards a twin rating, he climbed out of the single-seat cockpit in the nose and, coming aft, ushered me forward through the pilot's doorway to complete the flight and land at Dunsfold while he remained sitting back in the cabin. Bill generously, if rashly, sat in the cabin again throughout our next trip up to Bedford. It gave an interesting interpretation to the term 'dual,' which time I duly logged on the way to my rating.

It was during these visits to RAE Bedford that I first got to know a young Flight Lieutenant on Aero Flight who was being let loose there on a couple of early examples of our P.1127: his name was John Farley. Many years later, I was sitting at my desk at Kingston when the telephone buzzed and John was put through from Dunsfold. We'd both moved on in the intervening years and he was now our Deputy Chief Test Pilot and I was then the Commercial Manager.

"Ambrose, there's a spare place going in the Harrier demonstrator for three flights tomorrow. Duncan's coming with us in the Hawk, but you'll need to be down here early, mate!"

I needed no second bidding.

Above the Downs the altocu has turned from gold to pink. The wind-sock's down, the hangar's closed, it's time to get a drink!

CHAPTER 21

SOME THINGS YOU JUST HAVE TO DO FOR YOURSELF

by

John Farley

[NOTES ON THE AUTHOR: John Farley was a Royal Aircraft Establishment Farnborough engineering apprentice from 1950 – 1955. While still an apprentice, but determined to become a test pilot, he approached the Commandant of the Empire Test Pilots School. Group Captain Sammy Wroath explained that while his engineering background was fine, he would have to learn to fly first. So he applied to the RAF for pilot training at the end of his apprenticeship.

Following one tour on Hunters and a part tour as a QFI at Cranwell, he got his place on the course at ETPS in 1963. He was then posted to the RAE Aerodynamics Research Flight at Bedford, from where he started flying the P.1127 prototype at Dunsfold in 1964. Three years later he joined Hawker Siddeley Aviation as a test pilot at Dunsfold, retiring as CTP in 1983.

He has flown over 80 types and was the first Western test pilot the Russians invited to fly the MIG-29. – Ed.]

On the day I was writing this during December 1998 the Prime Minister, Tony Blair, announced on TV that he had called a halt to the current wave of RAF attacks on Iraq and that all the aircrew involved had returned safely.

Some forty years earlier Duncan Sandys, then Minister of Defence, had announced to the House of Commons that in future RAF manned aircraft were to be replaced by missiles.

When Duncan Sandys published his Defence White Paper on the 4th April 1957, I was a student on No. 110 Vampire course at 8 FTS Swinderby and working towards getting my wings in three months' time. Sandys' paper caused rather more concern among the instructors than it did among the students. As students we had more pressing things to worry about, like passing the course in the first place, rather than considering an RAF that did not fly aeroplanes. Of course there would be aeroplanes and we were determined to fly them. So we pressed on.

It was a hard school in those days, resulting in only seven of the 37 short-service officer cadet pilots who had joined the RAF with me actually being awarded their wings. After the No. 110 Vampire course pass-out parade we got our first clue that the post-Sandys RAF was not sure what to do with us. Expecting a few days off before going straight on to the next stage of training, either a fighter or bomber operational conversion unit (OCU), instead we found ourselves sent home on extended leave.

A month later, still on leave, we got posting notices to 7 FTS Valley which, it appeared, was to be used as a holding unit for problematic new pilots like us. Fortunately, like Swinderby, Valley had Vampire 5s, 9s and T.11s, and with reduced numbers of new students there were aircraft available that we knew. We were to fly these to maintain our very newfound skills.

Unlike Swinderby, none of us was killed at Valley although I don't know why not. At this stage, with only about 100 hours solo to our names, flying together in two-seat T.11s provided a potentially lethal temptation to see just how high or fast they would go. There were other stupidities, like one sortie with Barrie Tonkinson (Barrie later tested Harriers for HSA) where, from a position of some advantage at 40,000 ft, he and I observed a Valley instructor leading a pair of students – as opposed to real pilots like us you understand – as they popped up through the cloud tops at 15,000 ft. To a pair of fighter pilots-in-waiting they were just asking to be attacked.

The dive, plus the manoeuvre we subsequently carried out, probably achieved the aim of startling the formation, but it also overstressed our aircraft, broke the engine's rear bearing and left the poor DH Goblin with no alternative but to shake and quit. Being above total cloud cover, over the Welsh mountains, and with limited standby instruments and no means of navigation in a gliding jet might have bothered an experienced crew. But we just got some steers towards base, established ourselves in the overhead, spiralled down, broke cloud on the downwind leg, kept our speed up on the runway, cleared neatly on to the taxiway and got out to await a lift. Clearly there was a Being of greater ability than Duncan Sandys looking after the future of RAF pilots. Not surprising when you think about it.

After a short wait the Wing Commander Flying drove up in his Land Rover. He asked us what the trouble was and we said: "The engine, Sir."

He did not say a word, got a broom out of the back and pushed the handle into the air intake. When he found the engine would not turn he remarked: "Well done, chaps," and, without more ado – or conversation – gave us a lift back to the offices. On a point of detail, the "well done, chaps" was later retracted after the instructor we had bounced returned in quite an unpleasant frame of mind.

But I digress: the point of this story is not to discuss Vampire trips but Hunter flying. Flying of the sort that you will remember was to be no more if DS had his way. However, despite the best endeavours of the politicians, and five months after getting our wings, some of us from

Swinderby joined others on No. 36 course Hunter OCU at Chivenor. We flew the Mk. 4 Hunter – there were no two-seaters in those days – and after the Vampire it seemed like a spaceship to us. With hindsight it was akin to passing your driving test and then being given a Formula 1 racing car to drive. Three months later six of us were told we had passed the OCU.

Then things *really* went wrong and so the story can start.

It was now nine months since the White Paper and the RAF had decided to give priority of posting to its permanent commission (PC) fighter pilots, at the expense of the short-service men on eight- or twelve-year engagements. There were two PC chaps among the six who had passed our No. 36 Hunter course, so off they went to Hunter squadrons, while the remaining four of us were posted to a ground job.

I cannot begin to describe just what a blow that ground posting was to us. For two years we had struggled, against seemingly impossible odds, to satisfy our instructors, only to be grounded by a politician. We had studied, we had marched, and we had flown. We had done everything asked of us. That even included walking through a village knocking on doors and getting permission to enter peoples' gardens in order to pick up pieces of wrecked Vampire after one of us was killed on a solo sortie. We did not deserve a ground tour. We had been good enough and determined enough for anything the RAF asked of us. We deserved to fly.

Our posting was to the Royal Radar Establishment (RRE) research centre at Malvern. At that time RAF Fighter Command, to whom we now belonged, was struggling with the problem of how to defend the UK against air attack from bombers that had a supersonic dash capability, using slower sub-sonic Hunters. One idea was to fly a Hunter towards an incoming bomber but offset by a few miles to the side of its radar track, then, while the bomber was still many miles away, turn in towards its track and so get a shot at it as it momentarily crossed in front.

For such a manoeuvre to succeed the fighter had to be displaced to the side by just the right amount and turn in at just the right moment along a very precise curved path for the target to pass by within range of the fighter's guns, say between 100 yards and 500 yards. Furthermore, the interception pattern depended on the bomber's speed and altitude.

In order to see if this idea was practical, a trials unit was set up at Malvern where, among its many facilities, RRE had an experimental ground-controlled interception (GCI) station called Z Block. In one room was the fighter controller with his radar display and lots of transparent sheets – called overlays – on which were drawn various combinations of bomber and fighter tracks for different speed and height cases. In another room was a technician able to "fly" a simulated bomber blip across the controller's screen.

When the controller saw an incoming "raid" he had to alert what he thought was the best-positioned UK fighter base so that a fighter, "flown" from that location by another technician in another room, could be scrambled. When the fighter blip appeared on his radar the controller had to choose the best overlay, slap it on his screen and talk the blip along the path given on the overlay.

When the interception was a success that was fine, but when it failed the RRE boffins running the trial needed to know why. Had the controller chosen the wrong overlay? Had he scrambled the fighter too soon – or too late? Had he issued the wrong instructions to the fighter? Perhaps the fighter pilot had not "flown" accurately enough? Did the bomber pilot stick to his brief?

These matters were left to an observer to judge. After watching a few interceptions it was easy to spot what had gone wrong and any junior NCO could have done the task. The trouble was that Fighter Command had none of those to spare, but it *did* have plenty of new Pilot Officers without a job – like Ken Cooper, Maurice Harvey, Mac McLaughlan and me.

RRE had no RAF officers' mess so we lived in a local hotel – the Horny Old Arms (today replaced by a block of flats called Hornyold Court!). Because the trial had a high priority we worked shifts, involving weekends, evenings and nights, which meant we often had time off during the day and in the middle of the week. As a result the opportunities for revisiting girls that we knew, who lived near our former RAF stations all over the UK, were exceptional. But none of this apparent luxury lifestyle, with no secondary station duties, no parades, in fact none of the disadvantages of service life, was the slightest compensation for us not flying. Not the slightest.

Then one day Mac McLaughlan had to go to Barnstaple Magistrates court in order to sort out a little matter involving his Austin Healey 2000 sports car that had happened when we had been at Chivenor. After his court business was done Mac paid a visit to our old instructors. There he found the station had 84 Hunters, very few new students and much staff continuation training going on. He left in no doubt that all the flying one could wish for awaited anybody posted to Chivenor.

When Mac got back to the Horny Old Arms we talked long into the night about how such a posting might be arranged. But in our hearts we knew that nobody at Malvern was going to help. Our local boss there was an RAF Squadron Leader engineer who went glassy-eyed at the sight of a radar scanner and seemed delighted to be away from aeroplanes. Clearly serious perverts didn't even bother with sex.

I can't remember who first mooted the idea that our salvation lay in the offices of Fighter Command Headquarters at Bentley Priory. But the more we considered this the more certain we all became. It was time to plan.

We needed to nose around Headquarters but, having no invitation, what would be the best time? On proper RAF stations Wednesday afternoons were traditionally taken up with sport – another perversion so far as real aviators were concerned – and so the number of people minding the shop was greatly reduced. Wednesday afternoon *had* to maximise our chances.

The next Wednesday Mac and I set off for Bentley Priory in his Austin Healey. As we drove I don't think either of us had a clear idea of what we were looking for when we got there, but we knew we would recognise it when we found it.

What we found was an office that contained two Flight Lieutenants. One was responsible for posting day-fighter pilots while the other dealt with night-fighters. From there on it was all downhill. While the day-fighter guy was busy getting an early lunch before playing sport (ha!) we listened sympathetically to the night-fighter man explaining about his awful ground job and how he had to spend his hours filling in these terrible posting forms when he really should have been flying.

When he left for lunch we bade him farewell in the car park. As his car disappeared round the corner it took only a moment to pop back to the empty office, put our four names on the appropriate day-fighter paper-work and leave a deserted building. Mac enjoyed his drive back to Malvern, while I sat as a passenger dreaming of the day when I could swop my old converted Ford 5 cwt van for a proper bird-puller.

The following week our boss at Malvern came to see us in the room we used for our tea-breaks when the controllers changed over. He was very cross. He would never understand the RAF. We had been posted. Just as he had he got us trained and doing a useful job. Posted. It was ridiculous. We pulled long faces, and muttered: "Oh! no – not really sir?", then added how much we loved working for him on such an important job, to say nothing of living in the Horny Old Arms. The 1957 batch of students at RADA could have done no better . . .

Ten days later we were airborne at Chivenor. Three weeks after that the Wing Commander flying stood up at the end of Met. Briefing, read out our four names and said: "Together in the Station Commander's Office at nine o'clock and don't take your caps off."

What followed was just like a scene from a "B" movie. We stood in line, at attention, with our hats on, while the Station Commander continued to work head-down with the papers on his desk. He gave no indication that he knew we were in the room. Eventually, after what seemed an age, he raised his head, looked us up and down and, reading from a piece of paper slowly spoke our names.

We stood in silence – going sixpence, half-a-crown, and dustbin lid – while he stared at us.

"Well, is that *you*?"

We each just managed a "Yes, Sir."

He intoned that he had reason to believe we had interfered with Her Majesty's posting process and finished by barking: "Have you got anything to say for yourselves?"

"No, Sir," came out four times, followed by more silence and more staring at us.

Finally he spoke again.

"Well, I have. It's the best thing I've heard of since the war; would you like to go to Hunter Squadrons?"

We all owe that man. Mac thinks his name was Pleasance. Terrible how one forgets – I really must confirm it with the Public Records Office at Kew one day. I don't think such a story could happen today. It happened for us because the Group Captain behind that desk was a WWII commander, a man who understood that what matters above all to a fighting service is the motivation of its troops. And we were motivated. Perhaps he even felt he would have done the same thing as us if he had been in our position.

The rest as they say is history. Mac eventually finished up training British Airways 747 Captains; Maurice went on to become the one star in charge of the whole RAF Air Traffic Control system. Ken did his time on Hunters and was last seen in Holyhead with his collection of old MGs and young Welsh dolly birds. While I got a day job testing Harriers.

CHAPTER 22

LEAVING THE LANDING LIGHT ON

compiled and edited by

Peter Campbell

[This chapter is compiled from three main sources: (a) my personal records from the fifties, (b) "British Civil Aviation News" (BCAN), published by Air-Britain (Historians) Ltd, (c) contributions received from various other sources. I gratefully acknowledge the permission given in each case to reproduce the material. – Ed.]

Yes, the title is hardly original! But it seems appropriate for introducing a chapter about that most basic of flying activities, operating from private landing fields, which are often associated with the owner's home.

Before the second World War there were plenty of these fields, and now at the end of the century there is no shortage of private strips up and down the country, for a variety of very good reasons. But back in the early fifties private and business flying in the UK was really only just getting on its feet again after the strictures of the war. There were not that many private strips in use, and I am unaware of very much ever being published about them previously. I have therefore tried to collate what information I have been able to find into this general overview of the scene. In addition I have included a few venues where aircraft were to be found in long-term storage, together with some disused airfields which were 'appropriated' for private or business flying. The list will obviously not be complete, of course, and as you read this you will probably say: "Aha! He hasn't mentioned such-and-such a venue." If so, then you have the pleasure of being one-up on the rest of us!

BEDFORDSHIRE

In 1957 Mr N.A. Rogers kept his Alpine G-AOGV at Castle Mill, three miles east of Bedford.

Mr K. Spencer-Thomas kept his Gemini G-AKHP at Honeydon, three miles west of St. Neots; this, one of few surviving Geminis today, was not used very often, and the first time I caught up with it was at the 1958 W.S. Shackleton Weekend at Kidlington, when the owner flew in with his dog as P2.

A venue in the county which has a long aviation heritage is Woburn Abbey, now used annually for the DH Moth Club Weekend. Two events of note took place there in 1959, although flying from the Abbey's beautiful grounds had begun a long time before. As Air-Britain's *"British Civil Aviation News"* (BCAN) stated early in that year:

"Of fascinating potential is a National Rally to be staged at Woburn Park, Bucks, by the Duke of Bedford on May 2nd. This beautiful location once housed the various aeroplanes owned by the Duke's late grandmother – a remarkable lady, who learned to fly at the age of 68, and was an enthusiastic private owner until March 2nd, 1937. On that day she took off from Woburn on a local flight in her Moth Major G-ACUR – and was never seen again."

John Bagley duly reported on the Rally in a later issue of BCAN.

"That redoubtable peer, the Duke of Bedford, has now added an airstrip to the other amenities of the ancestral home at Woburn Abbey, which already boasts a herd of bison, a traction engine and a remarkable collection of fruit machines. On May 2nd a large proportion of the country's light aircraft arrived to grace the opening of the strip and to inspect the rest of the ducal domain. Some of the arrivals were a little hair-raising, due to the rather short strip being about eighty degrees out of wind, but the only casualty was the Yorkshire Club Rapide G-AHGD which tipped up on its nose when a loose engine cowling panel jammed one wheel.

Altogether, the Editorial census (aided by a report from D.J. Goldsmith) recorded 103 visiting aircraft, plus the Blériot XI, Pup N5180 and Brisfit D8096 from the Shuttleworth Collection. It is a long time since we saw more than 100 genuine visiting aircraft at any event – indeed, this may be a record – and there were a number of more than usual interest, to southern enthusiasts, at least. Particularly interesting were the two Tipsy Belfairs G-AOXO and 'PIE, excellently finished at Sherburn many years after their genesis at Belgium. G-APIE, indeed, carries the Avions Fairey inspection record, showing that work ceased at Gosselies in March 1948, immediately before final covering of the structure. Another rarity from the same district was the Globe Swift G-AHWH (last seen by the author at Derby twelve years ago, on 21.6.47!). Of eleven Tiger Moths, G-ANOD from Southport Sands, the elegant scarlet Taxi Tiger G-AHVU, and G-APRA from Norman Jones' stable were particularly notable. The latter, named "The Sue Burges," is specially modified for dropping parachutists, who are provided with a hole in the starboard wing to inspect the scenery before dropping onto it. From this vehicle, Mr Nepean Bishop deposited Mr Mike Reilly in the trees behind the Head Cowman's cottage.

Among the veteran visitors, eight Hornet Moths must surely be a postwar record at any event: they were G-ADKK, 'DNB, 'DND, 'DOT, 'DSK, 'EET, 'HBL and 'MZO. (The fact that G-ADKK actually flies may surprise those who know it only as a shape in the back of the hangar at Denham.) Other veterans included Comper Swift G-ABUS, Leopard Moth G-AIYS, Aeronca G-AEVS and Cygnet G-AFVR, while modern light aircraft were represented by Linnet G-APNS, Prentice G-AONB, Turbulents G-AJCP, 'PBZ, 'PIZ and 'PKZ, Turbi G-AOTK, Jackaroos G-ANZT, 'OIR, 'PAJ and 'PAO, Chipmunks G-AOTM, 'OPZ and 'OZV, and the Tipsy Nipper OO-NIF.

Among 30 assorted Austers, Short's rebuilt Alpha G-AOXR and H.B. Showell's Aiglet Trainer G-AOFS were unusual, and the long-awaited Auster 5 G-APJX from Croydon deserves mention. Of nine Geminis, G-AKDD was wearing a really spectacular American-style colour-scheme in red, white and black."

Incidentally, I have recorded the complete list of aircraft attending this event in the new 1999 edition of my book *"The Fifties Revisited."*

"For the second event on the new Woburn Abbey airstrip, the Duke of Bedford played host to the "First International Helicopter Rally" on Sunday May 10th. Rather to our surprise, a number of interesting machines turned up, and a good time was had by all (except the bison, no doubt). The highlight of the flying display was the little NHI Kolibrie G-APRZ of European Helicopters Ltd, making its first public appearance in this country. It is painted brilliant orange overall, with small black letters on its diminutive fin. For normal crop-spraying purposes it wears an enormous swept-back boom, fed by tanks under the cabin.

A second novelty to most British enthusiasts was provided by the Army Air Corps, who included one of their two Turboméca-powered Alouettes. This was XN133 (c/n 1186) which was flown to England last September as F-WIPH. It is still finished in the dark blue colour scheme favoured by the French Navy who are the principal users of the type. This tea-kettle was accompanied by Skeeter 12s XL736, XL738, XL808 and XM814, Whirlwinds XJ765 and XK970, and Auster 6 VF514, all in standard Army Air Corps markings. One of the Skeeters and a Whirlwind cooperated with two scout cars in the destruction of an enemy "tank": an event in which the Army's pyrotechnical abilities were convincingly demonstrated.

More civilised demonstrations were given by Fison-Airwork's Hiller 360 crop-sprayers G-APKY and G-APOF, Bristow Helicopters' new Widgeon G-APTE and Westland's demonstration Widgeon G-ANLW which up-lifted a bubble-car. Joyrides were available in B.E.A.'s S.55 G-ANFH "Sir Ector," and a solitary Tiger Moth G-AOBH got into the event somehow. (Another fixed-wing machine to be seen was the Rapide G-AHGD, left over from the previous weekend, which was apparently being dismantled for transport by road back home.)

However, in many ways the most significant aircraft present was an anonymous framework of blue-anodised dural tubes in the static park, with a two-bladed wooden rotor above and a McCulloch flat-four engine behind. This proved to be Mr John Howell's Bensen Gyrocopter; had he been able to find a piece of chalk, it would have carried its letters G-APSY and thus saved the questions asked by innumerable spotters! This has been built in a garage in Queen's Gate in central London, but has not yet flown: it was not complete and there were no pistons in the cylinders! It is expected to be flown about the end of July, probably at Snetterton Heath airfield in Norfolk. About three more Gyrocopters are nearly complete and are due to appear on the register soon."

BERKSHIRE

The Gemini G-AKFY of Flightways used a strip at Lambourn, near Hungerford, in connection with local racehorse stables, e.g. on the 2nd July 1956.

BUCKINGHAMSHIRE

Builders K. McAlpine Ltd maintained a strip at Westfield Farm, between Henley and Marlow; in 1959 their Piaggio P.166 G-APSJ was based there.

CAMBRIDGESHIRE

Newmarket Racecourse was sometimes used: on October 30th 1957 five aircraft turned up for the "Cambridgeshire" race: Rapides G-AKNY and 'LBA, Gemini G-AKFY, Dove G-ANAN and Auster 5 G-APAH.

In 1960 Farmair's Super Cubs G-APLY, 'PPI and 'PVR, together with their Alpha G-APOA, were at Sutton Bridge, north of Wisbech.

CHESHIRE

In 1960 the Cheshire Flying Club started at the wartime airfield of Calveley, six miles east of Crewe, with Auster 5 G-AOFJ.

CORNWALL

In 1955 Tiger Moth G-ANOS was kept in a field near Bodmin.

The St. Mawes Motor Engineering Co Ltd purchased a new Cessna 310 in 1959, G-APTK, which was based on a strip locally.

Perranporth was also active in the late fifties, mainly as the home of the Cornish Gliding Club; they operated a number of gliders including Olympia G-APXC, and used the Tiger Moth G-ANFW for aero-towing.

CUMBERLAND

Cumberland Aviation Services, who operated out of Silloth, were forced by its closure to move at the end of 1960 to the disused airfield at Crosby-upon-Eden, 3½ miles NE of Carlisle (still very much in use today). Their fleet at the time included Autocrat G-AGVI, Aiglet Trainer G-AMTE, Workmaster G-APMJ, Rapide G-AIUL and Grunau Baby glider SE-SFW.

DEVON

Not strictly speaking within the remit of this review, but fascinating throughout the fifties nevertheless, was RAF Chivenor in North Devon. In 1952 the Wrafton Flying Club operated Autocrat G-AJEA, Auster 5

G-AJXC and Rapide G-AKNY, and a daily service to Lundy Island was maintained.

During 1957, M.L. Looker of Devonair operated the Auster G-AJXC, which was still servicing Lundy, and the Hawk Trainer G-AKAT; this was not used very much but I remember seeing it flying on April 28th whilst I was on a geological field trip in the area.

By 1958 Auster 5 G-AIKE was also present, and during a personal visit on the 21st July 1959 I noticed that Alan Turley's Hawk Trainer G-AIUE was also based there. The Aerovan OO-ERY was also present, skulking at the back of the hangar. On another visit two years later I also had to resist efforts to sell me the Aerovan, the plans for which (to restore a regular service to Lundy, amongst other things) had fallen through. *[The demise of this aircraft was told in "Tails of the Fifties." – Ed.]*

Another area surrounded by considerable mystery was near Exeter, where for many years Bertram Arden kept a collection, mainly of prewar aircraft, at a barn on his farm just off the Exeter bypass, which legend – or, more accurately, Bernard Martin – has it, was protected by trouser-eating pigs! (It is fair to say that this expression has now entered enthusiasts' folk-lore!) Noel Collier kept enthusiasts in touch through the pages of BCAN, and the details that follow are from his reports.

In 1952 the collection included the Surrey AL.1 G-AALP, Swallows G-AFGC, 'FGE, 'FHC and the remains of 'EAU. Other aircraft owned by him were Auster 5 G-AJHJ, Taylorcraft Plus C-2 G-AFTN and Tiger Moth BB724 (ex-G-ACDA); these were kept at nearby Haldon Moor. I remember visiting the site in the sixties and finding very little to indicate that it had ever been an aerodrome, although it had been used by the Teignmouth Aero Club prewar.

By 1956, the Taylorcraft G-AFTN had been taken to RNAS Yeovilton for C. of A., and Swallow G-AFGE had moved on to Rochester. In 1958 the Auster and Tiger Moth were still in a barn on Haldon Moor, along with an old Exeter Corporation bus. Back at the farm were the wings of Swallow G-AFGD, still wearing their RAF colours and the impressment serial BK897, and the fuselage was thought to be somewhere around also. The same aircraft were reported at the farm and Haldon Moor in 1959, and by 1960 G-AFTN had returned to the farm.

The former US Navy base at Dunkeswell came into use in 1959 by the Taunton Vale Gliding Club, using Slingsby Cadets (including VM649). The Messenger 4A G-ALAI, "Sky Hook," was used for aero-tows.

The disused airfield at Predannack was used on the 8th July 1957 by Taylorcraft Plus D G-AHLJ.

ESSEX

The disused airfield at Great Dunmow was used by the Great Easton Flying Group, operating Autocrat G-AGVG.

During March 1958 the former USAAF base at Boxted was taken over by Airspray (Colchester) Ltd. It appeared to be primarily a repair base for Tiger Moths, such as G-ANOF, 'NRX, 'NLE and 'HWC. In 1960 identifiable components of Jackaroo G-APHZ and Tiger Moths G-ANRX, 'NOF and 'HWC were to be seen.

Blunt's Farm *[no exact location known – Ed.]* was also used during 1960 for spraying work by Crop Culture (Aerial).

For several years Clacton airstrip was used for joyrides for holidaymakers at Butlin's camp using Auster 5s G-AJVT, G-AKWS and G-AMSZ.

In 1959 the Bonanzas G-APTY and N9866F were based at Wormingford, near Colchester, and the Travel Air G-APUB (owned by Woods of Colchester Ltd) was a frequent user.

In 1960 Fyfield Hall was home to Autocrat G-AIBX, while the Messenger 4A G-AKZX was based at Stanford Rivers, three miles SE of Ongar.

Proctor 4 G-AOAR used a private strip near Colchester (which was neither Boxted nor Wormingford).

GLOUCESTERSHIRE

Lydney was home throughout the fifties and much of the sixties to Argus G-AJSN, owned by the Hon. B.L. Bathurst. Geoffrey Jones recalls that the strip was just west of the town and to the north of the A48. It was about 550 yards long and was aligned approximately 050/230.

English Bicknor (which is still operational today) was another active strip throughout the fifties, with Mr H. Knight's Autocrat G-AIRB based there.

Blakeney was built in 1960 to accommodate Mr G.S. Salariya's Alpha G-APTR.

HAMPSHIRE

In 1960 Warners, who owned several holiday camps on Hayling Island, used Cessna 172 G-ARAV for pleasure flights.

The disused airfield at Ibsley was used by Autocrat G-AJAC on the 30th August 1957.

HUNTINGDONSHIRE

RAF Westwood, near Peterborough, was home to Autocrat G-AHAV throughout the fifties; Messenger 2A G-AJFC and Super Cub G-APZJ of Derek Crouch Ltd divided their time between this strip and one at Eye in Suffolk.

Apethorpe had been a strip since before the war and was owned by the Tomkins family; occupants at various times included a Gloster Gamecock (G-ADIN), two Tiger Moths (G-AHME and 'HRC) and a Messenger G-AKIR. I am indebted to Charles Tomkins for the information and photos he provided for *"Tails of the Fifties."*

ISLE OF WIGHT

The old aerodrome at Ryde was hardly used, but I noted the Autocrat G-AGYM there on the 3rd September 1953.

KENT

Gravesend, prewar home of the famous Percival marque, was more or less deserted by the fifties. However Charles Oman recalls flying Tiger Moth G-ALIX into the airfield from Panshanger in August 1953. He recalls that there were a few Magisters in one hangar, which were believed to be owned by a company in bankruptcy.

He has also reminded me of the rather gruesome place that Gravesend earned in aviation history in October 1949, when an Autocrat hired from Elstree, G-AGXT, had been used by the murderer Donald Hume to get rid of his victim, Stanley Setty. The torso of the victim had been wrapped in brown paper at Gravesend, loaded into the Auster, and dumped in the Thames Estuary; however it floated ashore later and was discovered by Scotland Yard.

F.G. Miles' Gemini G-AKEL used Gravesend on the 14th June 1956; were there any movements after that time, I wonder?

In 1960 Alphas G-AHCM and 'OXR were giving joyrides from the old aerodrome at Mussel Marshes on the Isle of Sheppey; I noted 'OXR over Leysdown on the 30th August.

LANCASHIRE

In 1958 Lord Derby's Apache G-APCL used a strip at the ancestral home at Knowsley Park.

Southport Sands were used throughout the decade by S/Ldr. Giroux and his Fox Moths for pleasure-flying (also see "Tails of the Fifties"). G-ACCB fell into the sea on 25th September 1956. G-ACEJ continued for some years, going to either Thruxton or Eastleigh for C. of A. renewal, and Tiger Moth G-ANOD was used in 1959. In 1960 Giro Aviation's operations were supplemented by Autocar G-AMZV and Jackaroo G-APAL.

By courtesy of Lewis Benjamin, I have pleasure in reproducing an article which first appeared in the Tiger Club's magazine, the "Tiger Rag"; this was written by Jack Newbury, who flew from Southport in 1956.

"I think that one of flying's more pleasant experiences is to sit in the open cockpit of a light aeroplane, on a Summer's day, in shirt-sleeves, doing circuits and bumps. To get paid for it adds to the pleasure.

This is just how I spent my Summer holidays some years ago. Through an advert in "Flight" I met S/Ldr Giroux MBE, who ran a small company at Southport which owned two Fox Moths. He was a veteran of the first World War and flew one aircraft himself. The other was flown by miscellaneous chaps like myself, who had a few hours to spare and needed the money.

The Squadron Leader was a wonderful character. He no longer flies but still lives at Southport. He kept his aircraft in the municipal bus garage. Every day he would arrive at the garage with his little dog. He used to talk about the dog and the aeroplanes in almost the same breath, and in the same terms. "I think 'EJ would like a little more oil this morning, and see if Graham will take some water!" When satisfied that yesterday's technical snags had been cleared, he would tuck his travelling rug and a few spare parts on the baggage rack of the aircraft, put the dog on the seat in the cabin and proceed, with a mechanic on the wing, past the buses and down to the beach. He usually took 'CB (G-ACCB), which he always felt was rather sloppy, and therefore a little more tricky to handle. I would follow in 'EJ (G-ACEJ).

At the entrance to the beach there was a ramp which used to accumulate seaweed. You had to taxi quickly over this to avoid the main wheels sinking in. If that had happened of course the aircraft would have turned on its back. Somehow it never did, although the tail left the ground on several occasions. Part of the vast beach was licensed as an aerodrome. You simply picked a path for take-off clear of weed and pools on the driest sand you could see. I never met any holiday-makers on the beach on those summer mornings, although the horses drawing the shrimp carts from Morecambe Bay often used to plod along at the water's edge.

After take-off you set course inland for the centre of Southport, sometimes climbing as high as 500 ft! From there you flew to the coach park or the railway station, depending upon where the greatest number of trippers could be seen arriving. You then proceeded to make a series of shallow dives pointing the way to the main beach aerodrome. On some days we did the dives in formation, always with S/Ldr Giroux in the lead, always with the ball of the turn and slip indicator hard over to one side as he instinctively edged away from the other aircraft!

On arrival we went to the booking hut, cleared out the debris from the last high tide and opened for business. Small lads acted as linesmen, guarding the roped-off boundary of the sand aerodrome. They worked for a few shillings a day, plus the occasional aeroplane ride. I always arranged with them to let the rope droop to the ground at the far end of the "runway" in case the aeroplane failed to lift off. More than once I was glad of this unofficial runway extension.

On the fence we erected a long sign advertising the flights and the aeroplanes. The message ran: "Built by the firm that built the Comet." The local wits suggested that "Built by the fathers of the men who built the Comet" would be more appropriate, since the Fox Moth dated from the 1930s.

The Squadron Leader knew his market. He wasn't allowed to tout for business; but he would stand in front of the hut in his leather coat and talk about flying to likely groups of four – the capacity of the cabin. It was one such group – they turned out to be all-in-wrestlers from an act on the pier – who gave me the fright of my life. They so overloaded my aircraft that not only did I go through the rope but, by the time we got to the Ainsdale Hotel a few miles further down the coast, we were still no higher than the second floor windows. I'm sure that I bent the throttle trying to get that little extra power from the tired old engine.

There were short trips and a long cross-country across the river estuary and around Blackpool Tower. Once we had got a booking for Blackpool the remainder of the load went there too, regardless of what they paid. However, one US serviceman with blonde girl friend booked the long flight (8 minutes) and said they wanted the cabin to themselves. Now, although the cockpit was outside, there was a small window in front of the pilot, so that he could pass messages to the passengers and keep an eye on them. I looked forward to an entertaining quarter of an hour. As soon as we were airborne, however, a hat was promptly stuffed in the window and I spent the rest of the flight busily adjusting the trim.

The pre-flight briefing was meticulous. On a typical occasion it went like this: "Now the wind is coming from the north so you are taking off towards the Big Dipper. If you can't get the height, arrange to cross it where it curves downwards. Don't fly over the Winter Gardens until the open-air band concert finishes. If your engine fails aim between the white pillars of the pier, the others have still got their bracing struts. Get round the circuit quickly, there will be a queue today because the cold wind will stop them settling on the beach."

As the tide came up the aerodrome got smaller and smaller, so you were eventually landing on a narrow strip with dunes on one side and the sea on the other. In these conditions there always seemed to be a cross wind and it wasn't unusual to end the landing by running into the sea. The aircraft was then pulled unceremoniously backwards onto dry land; the passengers got out, and you taxied back for the next lot hoping that by then they hadn't lost their nerve. At low tide the sands at Southport go out some mile and a half. People drive their cars as far as they can and then have a picnic or simply doze off in deck chairs. From the air you could see the rising tide creeping round the slightly raised patches of dry sand where the cars were parked. Every day someone got cut off and the local amphibious vehicle (DUKW) owner would circle around them haggling over the price of a tow. It was a very one-sided bargain with the water rising steadily by the minute.

The customers were delightful. For most it was their first flight. One chap gave me 2/6 as he climbed into the cabin and asked me to do a loop to "frighten the missus"; he didn't know that she had previously climbed in on the other side and had implored me to make it a nice, smooth ride. I compromised on a rather steep turn, which was about all that the Fox Moth could do anyway, and they both seemed satisfied. There was a spring-operated air speed indicator on one wing strut, visible from the cabin. Age had weakened the spring so that it read about 25 mph faster than the authorised ASI in the cockpit. Only the smallest and brightest lads seemed to have doubts about the 100 mph we achieved on the circuit. One chap complained that the total flying time was only 2 minutes 37 seconds; but, as the Squadron Leader explained, "4 miles for 5/- in a taxi of the air wasn't bad." Still, we gave him another ride for nothing.

One year, when I got back to London, I read in the papers that 'CB ("the sloppy one") had fallen into the sea with a heavy load aboard (I immediately thought about my all-in wrestlers). They all escaped with cuts and bruises. But with only one aircraft left the Squadron Leader didn't need any help the next season. So ended a very happy encounter with one of the characters of the aviation world."

LEICESTERSHIRE

In 1958 Mr N.S. Granger's Autocrat G-AIBH was based in Upton, 4 miles NW of Hinckley.

Braybrooke, near Market Harborough, was home in 1959 to Alpine G-APFW and Apache EI-AKI, both operated by Alcock and Priestley Ltd.

On the 16th April 1955 there was a private rally held in the grounds of Bosworth Hall, Husbands Bosworth, at which the following aircraft were noted: Auster 5 LX-REX, Autocrats G-AIGV & 'JRN, Hornet Moths G-ADKC, 'DKM and 'ESE, Kitten G-AMJP, Messenger 2A G-AKKN, Proctor 1 G-AIEX, Sokol PH-NEM and S.51 G-ANZL.

Dragon Rapides (such as G-ALBC) used a strip at Melton Mowbray in the mid-fifties, probably in connection with racing meetings; the Lockheed 12 G-AGTL also used it at least once.

LINCOLNSHIRE

In the early fifties, the Auster 5 G-ALYG was kept at Stroxton Lodge four miles south of Grantham. The owner, Mr V.G. Manton, had modified the airframe and fitted a Gipsy Major engine (the first Mk. 5D?), but could not get a C. of A. However in 1951 it was flying on a permit for test purposes. It is thought that it was later taken to Bardney, near Lincoln, where the local PFA Group operated Taylorcraft Plus D G-AIRE. It is said that Hawk Major G-ADWT was thought to be based there too. Interestingly, the airframe of G-ALYG has been at Henstridge for a number of years, awaiting an eventual rebuild as a Mk. 5.

Mr C. Gregory's Taylorcraft Plus D G-AHGZ was based for most of the decade at a private strip at South Rauceby between Grantham and Sleaford.

LONDON

From about 1952 onwards there was a helicopter site at the South Bank; the landing site was on what had previously been the base of the dome which had been such a highlight of the previous year's Festival of Britain Exhibition. Of course we now know it as Battersea Heliport.

Regular visitors included naval Whirlwinds (such as WV221), BEA's Sycamores (such as G-AMWH), the Dragonfly G-AJOV used for a while by the *"Evening News,"* and the *"Evening Standard's"* Dragonfly G-ANAL (later re-registered G-ANZL for reasons of taste!). Incidentally, I was privileged to win a free flight in the latter during 1954.

On 24th August 1955 the Dragonfly G-AOAJ suffered a minor mishap there. The day was so hot that there must have been insufficient lift for take-off, for it left the ground, became partly uncontrollable and suffered minor damage when it came down on some nearby railings.

Charles Oman recalls that in December 1955 he flew with Capt. John Crewdson of Helicopter Services in the Agusta-Bell 47G G-AODI from Willesden Rubbish Tip to Gatwick! The company was investigating the possibility of using Willesden as a helicopter landing area, with the intention that newsreel films could be quickly conveyed from there to the BBC TV studios at Shepherd's Bush.

MIDDLESEX

Arthur Ord-Hume used to keep his Luton Minor G-AFIR in a field behind his house in Evelyn Drive, Hatch End. *[For wonderful reads chronicling both his aircraft building & flying and a social history of several decades, do read his books* "On Home-Made Wings" *and* "Flight on Frail Wings." *– Ed.]*

NORFOLK

In 1956 The Norfolk and Norwich Aero Club stored four Tiger Moths, G-ANFL, 'M, 'N & 'O, at the disused airfield at Rackheath. These were moved to Panshanger during 1957 for conversion. At that time the Fakenham Flying Group was formed, flying Tiger Moth G-ANCS from a field at Docking owned by Mr T.F. Ringer, owner of Autocar G-AJYO (see *"Tails of the Fifties"*); the Group moved to Little Snoring after a short while, and Messenger 2A G-AJFH was also based there; in 1959 they again relocated, this time to Foulsham.

North Denes, near Great Yarmouth, was also used for joyriding; in 1957 and 1958 Auster 5s G-AKOT & 'KPI of Anglian Air Charter were fulfilling this role, and also present in August 1957 were Messengers G-AGPX and 'KKC and Auster 5 G-AKXR.

On 19th March 1959 Fison-Airwork Ltd organised a display of agricultural aviation at Bexwell, near Downham Market. Demonstrations of spraying were given by Hiller 360s G-APNR and 'POF, EP.9 G-AOFU, Super Cub G-APPI, Chipmunk G-APOS and Tiger Moths G-AIZF and 'OXX. Other aircraft present were Autocrat G-AIRC, Alpha G-AJEB, Tiger Moth G-ANNI, Dragon Rapide G-AHLF, W/S S.55 G-APKC and Hiller 360 G-ANOB.

During the late fifties, light aviation flourished at a number of local aerodromes such as Fakenham, Swanton Morley, Foulsham, Little Snoring, Seething, Felthorpe and Tibenham, local boat-business owner Jimmy Hoseason keeping his Autocrat G-AHHM at Felthorpe (again, see *"Tails of the Fifties"*).

In 1960 Airspray's Tiger Moth G-APFS was based for a while at the disused airfield at Langham, near Wells (still in use today), and Farmair's Super Cubs were using a strip at Stoke Ferry, near Downham Market.

Another nearby base also used in 1960 for spraying, this time by Crop Culture (Aerial) Ltd, was the disused bomber airfield of Bexley.

NORTHANTS

Messenger G-AHZT used a strip at Daventry on the 12th August 1956.

OXFORDSHIRE

In 1959-60 Sugarswell Farm, near Shenington, was home to Tiger Moth G-APKE (used for towing by the Coventry Gliding Club), and the strip was also used by Crop Culture's Tiger Moths, such as G-AHNC and 'NCT.

In 1960 Tripacer G-AORO was based at Steeple Ashton.

The wartime airfield of Windrush, near Witney, was home in the fifties to the Autocrat G-AIPW, although I remember that I was never able to locate the airfield! However I did eventually get there in 1998, as the result of an invitation by Roger Bailey to attend a special memorial to an event that had taken place during the second World War.

It appears that a newly-qualified pilot, Sgt. Bruce Hancock, who was based at Windrush, had told his colleagues in the local pub that if the opportunity arose he would be prepared to ram a German aeroplane. On about the 12th August 1940, he proved himself to be not just a line-shooter. He was piloting an Anson when he spotted a Heinkel 111 bombing Windrush village in mistake for Brize Norton; he deliberately rammed the bomber from beneath, causing both aircraft to crash and losing his life in the process. On the 23rd August 1998, Diana Barnato-Walker unveiled a plaque on the airfield to commemorate this act of courage.

SCOTLAND

In 1957 a complete Klemm L.25, G-AAUP, was discovered in a garden shed belonging to a Mr Grant in Dumfries; it was apparently in good condition although it had not flown since before the war.

In 1960 Tiger Moth G-ANPC was based at the Scottish Gliding Union's site at Portmoak (still operational today).

The Turbi G-APBO used to operate out of Rutherglen, near Strathaven.

W.G. Gordon's Tiger Moth G-AHUV was based at Blair Atholl in Perthshire from about 1960 onwards; after a spell at Perth it is still there today!

SOMERSET

A strip at Crewkerne belonging to the North Perrott Estate Company was home first to Autocar G-AOHZ and, later, to Gemini G-AJTG, which was flown down from Fair Oaks on 27th January 1959.

Weston-super-Mare (where Bristol Freighters were produced) was also used in the late fifties for pleasure-flying in the Messenger G-AKBM.

STAFFORDSHIRE

Tatenhill, a wartime airfield, was reopened in 1958 and became home to Ind Coope's Dove G-APCZ.

SUFFOLK

Hornet Moth G-ADNE appears to have been based on a strip at Herringfleet, north-west of Lowestoft, sometime in 1955; it was flown to Shoreham and back on the 16th September.

SURREY

Early in 1958 Mr Robert Jones, owner of Stiles Farm (sometimes referred to as Stilemans), Munstead Heath, Godalming, was forbidden by Hambledon Rural District Council to maintain a private airstrip in the grounds of his estate. In fact several aircraft were based there round about that time; he had Gemini G-AJWF, which was later exchanged for Cessna 310 G-APNJ (now at Northbrook College, Shoreham Airport), and his daughter had Hawk Trainer G-AKKR.

Ranmore Common, Dorking, was the home of L.G. Atherton's Cub Coupé G-AFSZ for several years in the mid-fifties, and was later used by Norman Jones in Super Cub G-ARAM.

Another well-known strip, owned for many years by John Wright, was Rydinghurst Farm, Cranleigh, to which the Cub G-AFSZ had moved; it was also home to Auster 5 G-APHU and, later, Gemini G-AJZO.

Seale Farm at Tongham, just off the Hog's Back, has also housed aircraft since the fifties.

In 1958 there began a series of Helicopter Garden Parties at Ripley which continued throughout the decade and into the sixties. As I lived only a few miles away, each year on the appropriate Saturday afternoon I would take up a strategic position just outside the grounds with telescope at the ready. Denis Fox reported (in Air-Britain's BCAN) on the 1958 one as follows:

"Through the kindness of Mr and Mrs Charles Hughesdon, their delightful garden at Dunsborough Park, Surrey, was the venue of the RAeS helicopter party on June 11th.

Of the thirteen machines which arrived, it was the Brantly B.2 G-APSF which attracted most attention. Its outstanding characteristic is its diminutive size, and it was quite dwarfed by the adjacent Skeeters. With a disposable load of only 635 lb (largely absorbed by two occupants and 31 gallons of fuel, etc.) it is clearly no weight-lifter – but a very fascinating personal runabout, by any standards.

Strangely, the only Service participation was that of the Army, in the shape of a tightly-knit quartet of Skeeters – XL735, XM553, XM554 and XM560 – led by no less than a Brigadier in his "one star" Skeeter.

From the MOA came W/S S.51 XF260 (WA/H/106), W/S S.55 XD186 (WA.29) and Bristol 171 XL826 (13474). While the Sycamore and Whirlwind were in yellow rescue colours, the Dragonfly compromised with a dayglo front and camouflaged rear!

The Westland stable produced Widgeon G-ANLW, W/S S.55 G-APDY and Skeeeter 8 G-APOI, and BEAC – seizing the opportunity to earn some honest pennies – trotted-out W/S S.55 G-ANFH and Bristol 171 G-AMWH in a joyriding role. In their new scarlet colours they attracted such attention that even the Director of a most eminent research establishment was seen proffering several honest pennies for a whizz round the stately home! *[N.B. I have lists (more or less complete) of visiting helicopters for all the garden parties. – Ed.]*

SUSSEX

Wellcross Grange, near Horsham, now known as Slinfold, was active from the early fifties; Messenger G-ALBE was based there, then Auster 5 G-ANIR, and then after its demise in April 1958 Autocrat G-AHHU.

Another famous Sussex strip is that at Bognor Regis belonging to LEC Refrigeration Ltd, which in the early fifties was home to Messenger G-AJVC and Autocar G-AJYO. The Company later acquired the Gemini G-ALMU, a Dove G-ALEC (which crashed in a Cardiff street on its delivery flight on May 6th 1959) and an Anson G-AHIB.

From 1960 onwards the motor racing meetings at Goodwood Motor Circuit (the former satellite airfield for Tangmere) attracted many light and business aircraft, especially on Easter Mondays, and indeed these provided an ideal opportunity, when weather permitted, for owners and operators to attend the first 'proper' light aircraft meeting of the season. In 1960 no less than 106 aircraft were present including 26 assorted de Havilland types, 25 Austers & 16 Miles types!

WALES

One of the earliest postwar operators from disused aerodromes was Billy Butlin. The new holiday camps were proving attractive to a public unused to being able to go on holiday freely, and several Butlins camps had an extra attraction to offer in the form of pleasure flights. The venues used were Pwllheli (Broom Hall), Skegness (Ingoldmells) and Filey (Speeton), and the aircraft were also used for communications between camps and Head Office in London. The Butlin fleet was at its greatest in 1948, and included the Martlet G-AAYX which was used to give aerobatic displays. But by July 1950 all the aircraft had been disposed of.

Nevertheless reports show that in 1950 Broomhall was still in use, with flights being given in Autocrat G-AFWN. Other aircraft present at that time included Sparrowhawk G-ADNL, Gemini G-AKHB, Dragon Rapide G-AKUB, and the wrecks of Autocrat G-AIGY (crashed 1/8/50) and Percival Q.6 G-AFIX (crashed 6/5/49). Later on, in 1958, Vivian Bellamy had the concession for pleasure flying at Pwllheli, and his DH.86 G-ACZP also landed there on one occasion (see *"More Tails of the Fifties"*). In 1959, one of the two hangars was being used for growing turkeys, while the other was labelled "Dragon Airways" and from it Alpha G-AGYT was supplying joyrides to another generation of holidaymakers. Even as late as 1974 I can recall a Gemini and a Cessna being present.

In 1955 Auster 5 G-ANIL was kept in a field near Aber. The strip at the test range at Aberporth was also in use at this time; Ferranti's Autocar G-AOBV used it during May 1956, and Flight Lt. H.B. Iles' Miles M.18 was based there in 1959. Firefly WJ151, normally based at Llanbedr, made a round trip to Shoreham from here on the 30th August 1957 and another the next day from Llanbedr.

Cardiff (Pengham Moors) was officially closed in 1953, but several years on it was still being used by the Cardiff Aero Club with Autocrat G-AHSW and Tiger Moth G-ANEV; the Tipsy G-AISA was also based there. A report says that they were "operating under considerable difficulties as the runways were also being used by sundry 'L' drivers and motor-cyclists."

By 1958, although the hangars had been dismantled and shipped off to Gatwick, there will still four local residents: Autocrat G-AHSW, Tipsy G-AISA and Tiger Moths G-ANEV and 'NFP.

Even in early 1960 there were still aircraft there, although not in flying condition; the Ministry of Aviation's fire-fighting school had the use of the wreckage of the LEC Dove G-ALEC and two Comet fuselages, G-ALYU and an uncompleted Mk. 2 marked up as DH106/45.

Pengham Moors was finally closed for good on 31st March 1960.

In 1959 the Chipmunk G-APPK operated from a private strip near Bridgend.

In 1960 the flying comedian Stan Stennett (who over the years has owned several aircraft, including a Bonanza) made local news when an engine failure over Port Talbot in his Cessna 170 G-APVS meant that he had to glide for 14 miles to the ex-RAF airfield at Llandow, where he cleared the final hedge by some ten feet!

A site at Heldre hills was used over a number of years by the Montgomeryshire Group, first with Tipsy G-AFVN and later with Turbi G-APFA.

WILTSHIRE
The Avon Flying Group (employees of the Avon Rubber Company, probably) operated Tiger Moth G-ANRM from Melksham.

A strip at Beckhampton, Avebury, was used on more than one occasion (e.g. by Rapide G-AKNY on the 2nd July 1956 and Gemini G-AKFY on the 8th August 1957), probably in connection with local racehorse stables.

Baydon Manor, near Marlborough, was the home from 1956 of Mr H.O. Stibberd's Auster 5 G-ANIE, which was in a silver and blue colour scheme.

In 1959 Mr T.M. Keegan based his Consul G-AJXE at Keevil, and four Pioneers were there on detachment from Andover; two noted by myself on the 23rd July were XL557 and XL558. In 1960 Mr Keegan also kept his Prentice G-AOMK locally at his home at Ashton House.

In 1960 Air-Britain's BCAN reported of an event at Marlborough College as follows:

"The latest addition to the list of private airstrips is Marlborough College, where the playing-fields have seen a number of recent movements. Norman Jones brought in the Turbulent G-APNZ on June 17th, followed by S/Ldr. Francis in G-APVZ on the 20th, and S/Ldr. Hayter in Alpha G-AJAE from Christchurch two days later. The College CCF Centenary Parade on June 28th attracted Mr Jones and S/Ldr. Hayter again in the Jodel D.117 G-APOZ and Auster 5D G-AGLK, while two CCF cadets flew-past in Tiger Moth G-ALSH and Jackaroo G-AOIX. A more spectacular flypast was provided by S/Ldr. Slater with most of D Squadron, Boscombe Down, including three Harvards, FT375, KF183 and KF314 as well as a Canberra, three Meteors, a Valetta and a Hastings!"

Lewis Benjamin tells me that these visits were connected with S/Ldr. Francis's official responsibilities for recruiting for the RAF.

YORKSHIRE
From 28th April 1957 Crosland Moor airstrip was used by the Halifax Gliding Club, using Kirby Kite BGA 291 (ex-G-ALNI). Residents in 1958 were Dove G-AKYS and Gemini G-AMME.

Netherthorpe was used by United Steel's Apache G-APMY.

Arras Farm, Sancton (near Market Weighton) was home in 1959 to Mr N.B. Stephenson's Wicko G-AFJB.

CHAPTER 23

SHOESTRING SAGAS

by

Lt. Cdr. J. S. Sproule RN

(with a postscript by Roy Nerou)

[This chapter is a melding of two articles originally published during 1968 in "Pilot" magazine, and I am grateful for permission to reproduce them here. Again I also appreciate Sandy Sproule's invaluable assistance. – Ed.]

I first saw an Aeronca ultralight aircraft while I was holding up a glider wingtip for John Nielan at the Fairey's Garden Party at Hayes in – it must have been – the summer of 1935. We were demonstrating the prototype Slingsby Falcon III sailplane, and as the little pot-bellied, wire-braced aeroplane wallowed past on its stubby undercarriage with two-cylinder engine clattering away, I thought: "What an ugly little contraption – who on earth would want to own one of those?" Little did I know that ten years later I would be the proud owner of an Aeronca, and – after a twelve-year interval – yet another one! And, incidentally, form a great admiration and affection for what I came to consider to be one of the most efficient and best ultralight two-seater aeroplanes ever built.

The Aeronca C.3 which I saw at Hayes in 1935 was being demon-strated by the Aeronautical Corporation of Great Britain, the resounding title of a small organisation which had acquired the licence from the Aeronautical Corporation of America in Cincinnati. The entrepreneur behind the project was one "Bones" Brady of the Aircraft Exchange and Mart, who organised production in a small factory at Peterborough. Here they were to build the light aeroplane for the masses, selling at £395 flyaway. The future seemed bright, for was it not well-known that aviation was the coming thing?

A number of Aeronca C.3s, i.e. American-built Aeroncas, were imported prior to the building of about twenty English versions, before the Aeronautical Corporation of Great Britain inevitably went bust. A great pity as it was a brave venture. The English-built Aeronca was designated the Aeronca 100, as it differed in minor detail from the American model to meet UK C. of A. regulations. The English versions of the aircraft were powered by the same two-cylinder Aeronca-designed engine as the original, but licence-built by the JAP Company as the J99 model rated at 36 bhp, as opposed to the 42 bhp of the American article. The JAP 99 was modified to UK standards by the addition of dual ignition, and if handled properly was a very good engine.

In early 1936, shortly after the Aeronca came onto the British scene, the really epic ultralight flight of all time was made by Flying Officer David Llewellyn, who flew solo from Lympne to Johannesburg in an Aeronca C.3 in twenty-three days at a cost of £26. The story of his flight makes stirring reading, including such feats as the crossing of the Mediterranean from Palermo to Gabes on instruments and a forced landing in a tropical storm in Northern Rhodesia at an altitude of 6,000 ft. In order to take off again, Llewellyn had to substitute a spare set of high-compression pistons, during the fitting of which – all alone in the middle of the uninhabited bush – a vital gudgeon pin circlip pinged off somewhere into the long grass, necessitating a five-hour square search on hands and knees!

Most of the Peterborough-built Aeroncas found owners and quite a number of them were operated by the clubs between 1936 and 1939, notably at Hanworth and Lympne. They provided really cheap flying which was usually about 25 shillings per hour for dual and £1 per hour for solo. One school advertised an all-in price of £14 for the 'A' licence, the PPL of the time.

So, when the opportunity came for me to fly an Aeronca in 1938, I had begun to be aware that this funny-looking little aeroplane was not such a joke as it had first appeared.

The Aeronca C.3 which I first flew at Barton-in-the-Clay – where I had got my 'A' licence under the subsidised Civil Guard Scheme – was called "GLADYS," being registered G-ADYS. A justifiably nervous instructor screwed up his courage sufficiently to crouch beside me in the cabin on a quick circuit, and for a quid an hour I was off. I enjoyed the aeroplane from the start. To me, weaned since the age of thirteen on gliders – and in 1938 built like a whippet – 40 hp was a surfeit of power; flying in a two-place cabin ship, albeit only two-cylindered and wire-braced to boot, was big stuff indeed. I could, moreover, get hold of G-ADYS whenever I liked as all the other chaps at Barton showed a marked preference for the more powerful Moths and Avians.

The war came and went, and one day in 1946 a very droll and enterprising gliding friend of mine called Steve Stevens rang me up and announced that he had bought an aeroplane and would I like to go halves with him? When he said it was an Aeronca I immediately said yes, how much, where is it, in that order. It appeared that the Aeronca was located at Woodley and that Steve had paid all of £250 for it. This seemed a pretty reasonable figure when divided by two and it only remained for us to organise the assistance of two other gliding chums, with their glider trailers, for us to be examining our prize on home ground at Brighton.

G-AEWV was a genuine Peterborough Aeronca 100 with JAP J99 engine, and an expired C. of A. The machine appeared to be in good condition, though it was manifest that it had been in store since the beginning of the war. While all was generally well, to make a really good job of things there was quite a bit to do. For some months after the first flush of enthusiasm G-AEWV stood untouched, as for one reason and another both Steve and I were otherwise occupied. So when I found myself appointed to HMS "Siskin" at RNAS Gosport, having elected to stay on in the Fleet Air Arm with a permanent commission, the obvious thing was to get the Aeronca to this famous old airfield where there were aeronautical facilities of long standing. At this stage, Steve very kindly let me have his share in the aircraft as he had transferred his attentions to yachts. So G-AEWV became my sole property and I was a private owner at last – a thing I had dreamed about since my school days. Sole ownership not unnaturally added great impetus to the task of making G-AEWV fly again and no sooner was the machine at Gosport than I found myself one Sunday afternoon progressively tearing all the fabric off the Aeronca's fuselage and wings, fully aware that with each rip I was putting the first flight further and further away!

For the more completely I examined G-AEWV the more I came to the conclusion that a really good strip-off and start-again was desirable if a really first-class restoration was to be made. So everything had to be laid bare and thus began many happy spare-time hours of dismantling, cleaning and painting and generally buffing-up, so that when all went together again, G-AEWV would be really as good as new. Nice grey paint was applied to all the fuselage tube structure after checking for rust, and clean new fabric which, when doped, rang to the touch. Well do I remember the long summer evenings of solitary toil at the far end of the small tin hangar to the west of the old Gosport airfield. What fun it was to see G-AEWV gradually getting more and more like the real thing – with the priceless satisfaction of doing it with one's own two hands! And what a privilege it was to be doing it at Gosport where, if you stretched your imagination a little on a still evening, you could hear the hiss of Smith-Barry's Le Rhône rotaries being blipped – and smell castor oil!

After about ten months of spare-time work, the Aeronca's fuselage was completely finished, the engine re-installed and run, and wings and empennage covered and ready for assembly. At this stage, in the winter of 1946, with the problems of the C. of A. and the ARB looming up – and I must confess an impatience to get flying – I committed G-AEWV to Portsmouth Aviation for final assembly. One memorable day, therefore, after coughing up the inevitable extension to the original quotation, my Aeronca 100 stood ready for me to fly away at Portsmouth Airport, complete with C. of A. A big moment indeed, and the aeroplane looked a picture! How cunningly designed for the maximum performance for minimum power! Short undercarriage legs with as little in the wind as possible – and streamline-section wheels. Thin 36 ft-span wooden spar wings with Clark Y aerofoil and high aspect ratio. Well-formed steel tube fabric-covered fuselage – with the largest possible slow-revving propeller at the nose. A funny-looking little aircraft in truth, with Blériot-like cabane and RAF wires, but beauty is in the eye of the beholder as a warthog is a gazelle to its mother!

So, in spite of the squat and pot-bellied looks and the prehistoric wire bracing, the 36 hp Aeronca added up to efficiency, and the designer, J. A. Roché, knew exactly what he was doing long ago in the 1930s. G-AEWV handled beautifully and was the nearest thing to a miniature Fieseler Storch when flown solo. In a breeze at Gosport I could be airborne off the hangar apron the short way – and with two up and full fuel the take off was not much more than that of a Tiger Moth, with cruising at 70 mph. Not bad from two cylinders burning 2½ gallons per hour! Of course the aeroplane was slow and a cross-country could get very tedious into a headwind. But all in all the little aircraft was a really practical two-seater flying machine and if you picked your days and flew fairly low into headwinds, you could at least kid yourself you were covering the ground.

I flew G-AEWV continuously as personal transport for over two years and went quite far afield on various jaunts and holidays, crossing the Channel via Lympne to Gris Nez on several occasions. To extend the range and to take care of headwinds, I soon found it necessary to make an overload tank. This consisted of two sawn-off jerry-cans welded together and pressurised by an old Rolls Royce Silver Ghost hand pump to make the petrol go uphill. Pilot and passenger sat on this robust container, which carried an extra eight gallons of juice – and incidentally raised the seat level six inches and improved the view considerably. The fuel was fed through a plastic tube into the main tank via a small piece of quarter-inch pipe brazed into the main tank filler cap, the only other visible evidence of this removable and highly unauthorised mod being the half-inch hole in the windscreen! With the overload fuel plus the full main, one could stay in the air for about six hours and it was very nice to have such autonomy on a long trip. My most amusing expedition was to the La Baule rally with an exceedingly brave and trusting friend who shall always remember for suggesting, at the end of the frolics, that we head for home the short way via Jersey – and back to England direct to Eastleigh. It had certainly not occurred to me to return to the homeland across nearly eighty miles of water on Messrs JAP's two cylinders, but the francs were getting low and, the suggestion having been made, the trip was on.

We had a very enjoyable few days in Jersey and one morning set off for Albion, two-up with luggage and loot in the form of various bottles from La Baule, and full tanks – including the illicit extra eight gallons.

Take-off in these circumstances on our 36 hp used a good deal of the St. Peter airport runway, but G-AEWV eventually came to terms with Sir Isaac Newton and we began the long climb to 3,000 ft, the height at which we had decided to cruise. We darted, very figuratively speaking, across the water to the mainland and after a careful line-up between two good landmarks on the Cherbourg peninsular at cruising height, we set the compass and aimed ourselves for England across the foam. It was a milky day with no horizon, but the artificial article I had fitted, salvaged from a heap of scrapped ones at Gosport, performed nobly and, after an hour of sitting poised in space with not a single ship in sight, St. Catherine's Point loomed up right on the button. A splendid feeling of achievement pervaded the Aeronca's cabin, and I would not have swapped G-AEWV for Lindbergh's "Spirit of St Louis." The fact that our engine had run properly for the hour's crossing of the open sea was not a very remarkable thing in itself, but nevertheless the memory of the trip remains clearly etched, after all this time.

I sold my quite perfect G-AEWV for £250 in the spring of 1949 owing to an imagined financial crisis. I have been regretting it ever since. I had flown nearly 200 hours in her with 100% serviceability throughout and not a spit out of the JAP J99. After a few weeks I had the usual feelings of remorse and regret, particularly when I heard that the new owner – a farmer – had attempted to take off through, rather than over, one of his hedges.

In due course I progressed to a Chilton rebuild and then to an excellent Piper Cub Coupé which I bought, believe it or not, for £200 with six months' C. of A. At this stage I went seafaring in the Mediterranean and this, and the onset of matrimony, put a temporary end to private aeronautical activities for a while.

But to revert to the Chilton: in June 1948, I became the owner and restorer of this most unique little aircraft, having found it in a very 'as is' and dismantled condition in the old Chilton hangar-cum-barn at Savernake, near Marlborough. I bought the machine from A.R. Ward who, with the late Hon A.W.H. Dalrymple, had designed the Chilton DW/1 while they were students at the de Havilland Technical School at Hatfield. I paid the princely sum of £50 over a gin and tonic, and I bore my prize away in a truck packed with stolen hay into which we stuffed the fuselage and wings for safe transit. The truck broke down in the middle of Andover at the stroke of midnight, but that is another story.

My interest in Chilton ownership sprang from a flight I had made in one at Portsmouth in 1939. Dalrymple had telephoned me to say that he would arrive in the demonstrator at the Portsmouth Flying Club at 3.30 one afternoon and he duly arrived and I had my flight. And it was a big event for me as I did not have a lot of aeroplane experience at the time. I was most impressed when, on my enquiry as to where he had arrived from, Dalrymple mentioned an airfield in Scotland! The Chilton had flown to Portsmouth non-stop using the optional overload tank and Dalrymple seemed to think that such a long flight in his very small aeroplane was hardly worth mentioning!

The restoration of G-AFGI took place in the woodworking shop at RNAS Gosport where I was Lt. Cdr. Flying at the time, and therefore fairly well fixed for such privileges.

Such a restoration, working single-handed to the standards I set myself, was quite a big job owing to the sad condition of the machine, and it took almost every available hour of spare time for fifteen months. G-AFGI must have been neglected for about seven years after Group Captain Pedley's forced landing at Hatfield, and at Savernake a colony of healthy and very regular rats had inhabited the leading edges of the wings, while industrious insects had consumed all the soft furnishings, i.e. the hammock-type seat, safety belts etc. So everything had to be stripped and cleaned to the bone and the secret places opened up for inspection and making good. Fortunately the casein gluing of the very lightly-built structure was perfectly satisfactory, but just to make sure that the rats had not nibbled away anything vital in periods of famine, I opened up the ply skin of the wings at intervals along the spars top and bottom, so that the webs etc. could be looked at on both sides throughout their length. In addition to this, all metal fittings were removed for repainting and the bolts cleaned and retreated before putting back in place with a dressing of yellow chromate. Cadmium plating turns into white powder on the best of bolts if left in wood long enough – so out they all had to come.

All a considerable labour but splendid fun to do on such a miniature and elegantly-designed little aeroplane. And there is a great kick to be had in cleaning up a dilapidated-looking article and making it look as good or better than new; particularly when the initial outlay has been small! The 32 bhp water-cooled Carden Ford engine was obviously in need of a complete strip and overhaul, so I conveyed it in the boot of my car to the workshop of my friend Sam Youles in Waterloo Street in Hove. There I took the engine quite apart to its nuts and bolts and I handed these in several oily buckets to my old chum Dave Walden, Sam's mechanic, with the instruction to "please, put all this together again as well as possible."

One of the things I discovered on the engine strip, by the way, which explains Group Captain Pedley's clouds of steam prior to his forced landing, was that the key in the water pump drive shaft had sheared. Perhaps someone had forgotten to drain the water some freezing cold winter and turned the propeller.

Dave Walden was a motor mechanic from way back and I could not have placed the engine in better hands. What he did not know about the internal combustion engine was not worth knowing and he was incapable of doing anything other than the best possible work. He had, moreover, an intimate knowledge of the engineering resources of the Brighton district, i.e. where to get the best rebore and the best crankshaft regrind and so on. All good motor car stuff, you must note, but this, if carried out to Dave's standards, was fit for aeroplanes.

When the major engine overhaul was finished Dave was very happy with £10 for his spare-time work, and I think that, all-in, the engine expenses came to a total of £25 or so. The engine ran beautifully when it was installed, and I did over 100 hours behind it with justified confidence, as it never missed a beat.

A feature I remember with nostalgia about the Carden Ford Chilton was the very quiet and motor-car-like tickover – you could hardly hear it. The noise at the 100 mph cruise speed was like a small buzz-saw, but again this was pleasing to the ear, as it was producing satisfactory results and only using 1.8 gallons of fuel per hour! Regarding the Carden Ford engine as a prime mover, I can only say that, in spite of its weight, I found it perfectly adequate in the clean and lightly air-framed Chilton. Take-off and climb were not to be sniffed at and in my experience the water cooling system was no more bother than if it had been in a car. And it is interesting to note that in 1937 a new Carden Ford engine with twin ignition and completely converted ready to install cost £85. And how splendid to be able to go down to the village and buy spares for a few shillings over the local Ford dealer's counter!

The Chilton's propellers were all designed by Dalrymple and Ward and beautifully made in the workshops at Chilton Foliat by one Fred Luscombe. Obviously some experiment had taken place in this field as, when I bought the aeroplane, Ward had thrown in a selection of the diminutive propellers for me to try out – rather like being given a sheaf of arrows! After testing them all I settled on one with scimitar-like blades which seemed to work best on all counts.

I flew G-AFGI at Gosport for the first time on the 4th September 1949 and I was very quickly at home in it. I can only sum up the aeroplane as being sensitive but quite stable and viceless. In other words, a miniature Spitfire. After a while one learnt to let the machine ride the bumps with only the smallest control movements and it really was the nearest approach to the dream of flying with very small personal wings. The large split flap made approach and landing very easy indeed and once the machine was on the ground it was down. I am sure my friend Ranald Porteous of Beagle, the greatest living expert on Chiltons, will bear me out on all this, i.e. that the type had delightful and easy flying characteristics. And Ranald Porteous, who was and is no lightweight, was in the habit of performing all known aerobatics in the Chiltons. Proof indeed by his continued and happy presence among us, that Dalrymple and Ward had done their stressing sums correctly!

In the winter of 1949 I put G-AFGI back in the workshop again and set about designing and fitting a sliding cockpit canopy. I found that an Olympia sailplane perspex hood moulding turned back to front was readily available and an ideal shape, so I organised Wokingham Plastics Limited to make me one with various doubling pieces in the right places! I mounted the hood on three dural rails and arranged a bungee and cable in the rear fuselage to spring-load the hood rearwards. The hood was pulled forward and shut against the new windscreen by a small ratchet winding handle on the right of the cockpit. This gave a backlash-free system with an infinite variety of opening positions. A simple means for jettisoning was also incorporated.

The hood mod was a great improvement to the Chilton in all respects as one did not have to dress up and you could sit about 2 in higher. And it made G-AFGI look even more like a small Spitfire. Getting the improvement legally permitted or the Permit to Fly was at that time another matter, however, as this took far longer than the actual work and needed much more tenacity of purpose! From the ARB's starting point of "We won't come and look at it, and remove it forthwith" to eventually getting the mod passed as airworthy by the late A.R. Weyl, acting as consultant to the PFA, took a long time. In all fairness to everyone, I understand that things are much better these days, but after a whole winter's careful work with only one's personal safety at stake in the long run, the general palaver was a pest at the time. "Remove it forthwith" indeed! Not likely!

As I said earlier on, I flew G-AFGI for about 100 hours and I eventually bought a very nice Piper Cub Coupé, G-AFSZ, early in 1951 and sold the Chilton to Hugh Kendall. Hugh was an old gliding chum of mine, but he painted my nice blue and silver G-AFGI what I thought was a rather odd mauve colour. But his most important innovations were the general gingering up of the engine and some very crafty work on propellers. With these activities and various small cleaning up mods, he made the machine cruise at 130 mph flat out – an incredible speed for an engine nominally rated at 32 bhp. As no Carden Ford Chilton had ever done this sort of speed before, Hugh's next most obvious task was to look around for some unsuspecting handicappers. I was therefore delighted to see him romp home first in the South Coast Air Race in the September of 1951 at Shoreham. What a boost the bookies could have given to the Sproule Aeronautical Sport and Pastime Fund had I put my shirt on G-AFGI, as the odds on the Chilton winning were very long indeed!

I have always regretted selling G-AFGI, as I have always done with the various aircraft I have rebuilt in my time. There is no better and more rewarding pastime than buying them cheap and tatty, making them good and flying them. But selling your children, so to speak, is always painful and the recollection of parting with the Chilton is now much more so as this thoroughbred little English aeroplane of prewar days is now almost extinct. The Chilton Monoplane, designed in 1937 by Dalrymple and Ward while young students, was indeed a light aeroplane classic. No doubt the de Havilland training had a great deal to do with it – and the fact that Dalrymple and Ward were both practising pilots. Even today, given the same design requirements, I doubt very much whether anyone could offer any better solutions to the various problems; the machine was simple and cheap to build and there was not an unnecessary stick of wood anywhere. And it was strong and looked and flew right. What a pity the drawings have been lost, as with the RF-4-type cowled Volkswagen engine installation, and various minor modifications such as the sliding hood, I am sure that a latter-day Chilton would still be outstanding.

And so the years in the Navy rolled by, and when I found myself commuting to London from Sussex each day, having been appointed to a Ministry job, a very strong urge to have an outlet from the frustrations of bumf-pushing began to make itself manifest. A near-neighbour was the now famous and quite unique Wing Commander Ken Wallis, who mentioned to me one day that he was building a Bensen gyrocopter. After I had seen him fly his machine across Shoreham Airport, I was fired with sufficient enthusiasm to start to build one myself. The construction of my gyrocopter in the front room of our old house in the middle of Shoreham by Sea is quite another story, but it will suffice to say that it ended with an almighty bump at Tangmere which effectively eradicated my enthusiasm for gyrocopters – at any rate that particular one! Shortly after this brush with the force of gravity, I happened to see an advertisement in *"Flight"* for an Aeronca. As I had managed to sell the somewhat bent gyrocopter, my aeronautical sport and pastime fund was in a state of liquidity, so one day not long afterwards, my brother-in-law and I found ourselves driving out of the main gate of RAF Little Rissington with Aeronca G-AEFT perched on an adapted boat-trailer. I confess that as we loaded the aircraft, after an interval of twelve years since I had had anything to do with Aeroncas, I had a distinct feeling of "Here we go again: what have I let myself in for this time?" However, back we went to Shoreham, the wings were stored in the roof of a friend's workshop and the fuselage ensconced in my garage, with the car banished to the open air. There my car was to stay for the next two years as this was how long it took to refurbish G-AEFT to proper flying condition.

G-AEFT, built in 1936, was a C.3 crossed with a Peterborough 100 model at an early stage in its career. From the log-book it had lived in the open air for a long time and had once been blown away in a gale. It had also been ditched in the sea off Folkestone and, incredible to relate, a Wing Commander friend of mine with whom I dealt in the Ministry of Defence actually recalled seeing it do so as a small boy, while playing with his bucket and spade on the beach! The latest episode in G-AEFT's chequered career, after postwar rehabilitation, was a forced landing in an orchard at night, the pilot having run out of fuel.

So the poor old Aeronca had suffered a broken wing and a stove-in nose and had, after a passage through Stapleford Tawney, found its way to a shed behind the Officers' Mess at RAF Little Rissington. The machine had been bought by a syndicate of young pilots and a certain amount of repair work had been carried out before the inevitable happened and the syndicate was dispersed through postings elsewhere. At this point I had appeared on the scene, and at first sight quite a lot appeared to have been done and the job of rebuild did not look too formidable.

Upon close inspection at home however, I found that I would have a great deal to do to make G-AEFT a good aeroplane again. Once again all the fabric came off, once again I began to scrape off paint and, to cut a long story short, this time had a really big job on my hands. The fuselage and tail surfaces took a whole year to refurbish, during which time I managed to find a brand new JAP J99 engine for an expenditure of £40. It is truly remarkable what you can find if you begin to rootle about for things and – come to think of it – this is half the fun.

The wings of G-AEFT were quite a task, as I had to begin again and make two new spars for the broken wing. The spruce was obtained from Slingsby's in Yorkshire, and the following summer was spent remaking many ribs and reassembling and cleaning and refitting all the multitude of fiddling little fittings in the piano-wire-braced structure. The fabric work was a big job in the confines of a smallish garage and this time I was on my own – no experts from Gosport were on hand to do the work for me. With a 36 ft wing span one gets quite nifty at sewing fabric to ribs, and doping such a big area develops the muscles. I was not entirely alone in all the above activity, however, as soon after I had installed 'FT in my garage, there was a knock on my front door and three young boys rather timidly indicated that they were in the ATC and "could they look at the aeroplane?" How they had got to know is a mystery, but news travels fast where old aeroplanes are concerned. The upshot was that for the whole two years of restoration, every weekend had three pairs of keen young hands to scrape and clean, hold things up and sweep up the shavings. We had the greatest fun and for me, one of the nicest things to come out of the rebuild of my second Aeronca is that she launched two of the boys on aeronautical careers. For the middle boy got past a Halton selection board with flying colours by being able to expound on how he worked on an old aeroplane at the weekends, and John, the eldest, did likewise with a similar Naval inquisition. He is now a Lieutenant RN and instructing on Wessex anti-submarine helicopters at Portland. Both swear that being able to talk about the Aeronca at their interviews did the trick, and they have kept in touch with me ever since.

In the fullness of time all the pieces of 'FT were complete and ready for assembly, so a truck was borrowed to transport the wings and I towed the fuselage behind my car to the old blister hangar at Shoreham. There young John and I erected the machine and the day came when we put on the last dab of silver dope and the machine was finished.

The aeroplane, which we had rigged by eye from first principles, flew hands-off from the word go and it was strange to feel so immediately at home in the type after such a long interval since flying G-AEWV. The Permit to Fly went through with no difficulty at all, and for the rest of that summer of 1963 I was a private owner again. In the spring of 1964, however, local hangarage difficulties at Shoreham made life very difficult and I received an offer for the machine which, at the time, I found hard to refuse. So Aeronca No. 2 passed into new hands and I am delighted to say that it is still going strong at RN Air Station Yeovilton, where it is operated by a syndicate of young Observers, none of whom was born when she was first built! My last Aeronca is thus in excellent company among the Phantoms and Buccaneers of my old Service – and long may she continue. Please note that she is far older than the Navy's last Swordfish, and is in regular syndicate use.

Needless to say, I now regret ever parting with such a priceless example of a fast dying breed – a classic ultralight aeroplane in the truest sense. For it is simply not necessary to have large lumps of power to have fun in small aeroplanes – in fact the less power the better! The funny-looking wire-braced JAP-engined two-seater of 1935 was a well-designed and docile little aeroplane which provided safe flying at shoestring cost. I am convinced that there is still scope for a simple and cheap 40 hp two-seater to meet a similar specification, and no doubt with a modern approach a better aircraft would be achieved. But the designer would have to be very talented indeed to match the Aeronca ultralight in all its particulars.

*   *   *

POSTSCRIPT

by

Roy Nerou

[The above article was of course written over thirty years ago. Since then, the Aeronca G-AEWV had several owners and was based at Fairoaks for some time before being written off in 1964; it is rumoured that parts of it are being united with complementary parts of G-AETG to produce a further hybrid.

The Aeronca G-AEFT was once again rebuilt by Ron Eastman, this time for John Moss at Middle Wallop, and is currently active in the hands of Nick Chittenden.

The Chilton G-AFGI had several owners before coming into the hands of J.E. McDonald in the seventies; after being lovingly rebuilt yet again it is currently airworthy at White Waltham, flown by his daughter Kathy.

There are several more examples of original Chiltons being lovingly restored, and it is especially encouraging that at least five or six more brand-new ones are either being built or are already flying. But one might well ask how this has been possible if the original drawings were lost as John Sproule describes in his article?

The answer is a fascinating one, and I am indebted to both David Elliott (who is building two brand-new Chiltons) and Roy Nerou (who is rebuilding two original ones) for enlightening me. So as a postscript to this chapter I therefore include some major extracts from the information pack Roy Nerou sends out to prospective Chilton-builders. – Ed.]

"The Chilton was designed during 1935-36 at the de Havilland Technical School by students A.R. Ward, son of the Hon. Sir John Ward, and the Hon. A. H. Dalrymple, son of Lord Stair, under the supervision of Marcus Langley. By early 1936 Ward and Dalrymple were ready to start construction at the stately home of Ward's parents, Chilton Lodge, Chilton Foliat, hence the aircraft's name. The Chilton was first flown on the 16th of April 1937; this was carried out by a fellow student at de Havilland's, Ranald Porteous, who subsequently became Auster Aircraft's test pilot during the 1940s and 1950s. Although the aircraft flew faultlessly, the 30 hp Carden Ford engine overheated and the radiator and cowling required slight modification. After the prototype, G-AESZ, came G-AFGH, G-AFGI and G-AFSV (fitted with a 44 hp Train engine). All flying took place from High Trees on the edge of the Savernake forest near Marlborough, a private landing ground owned by the Earl of Cardigan. The Chiltons were too small for impressment and all four eventually spent the war in storage in the Earl's hangar at High Trees.

TOP: 1901 Air Op. Flight, 652 Air Op. Squadron at Detmold in 1953. Col. John Moss is holding the shield.
BOTTOM: Sometimes Austers got bent – but no one was hurt on this occasion. VF 573 hit trees avoiding an obstacle and crashed at Altenruthen, W. Germany, on the 18th August 1953.
Photos: via Col. John Moss.

TOP: Rotary flying at last! Skeeter Mk. 12, XM527, at Middle Wallop in the late fifties.
BOTTOM: Auster AOP.9 XN412, seen at Lympne in the late fifties en route to Germany.
Photos: Col. John Moss.

TOP: A line-up at Fair Oaks in 1955 includes the Universal Flying Services'
Tiger Moths G-AHRM, G-ANUD and G-ANOZ, Austers G-AHSO and
G-AIGU, and (probably) the GQ Parachute Company's Dragon Rapide
G-AJHP. Photo: Ambrose Barber.
BOTTOM: Ambrose Barber (in front cockpit) with Hugh Merewether in
Hawker's Tomtit G-AFTA, prior to doing some aerobatics.
Photo: via Ambrose Barber.

TOP: Ambrose Barber (centre) with close National Service pals Algy and Jock. Photo: via Ambrose Barber.
BOTTOM: Hunter T.7 XJ615 deploys its landing parachute at Dunsfold. Photo: Hawker Aircraft Co. (by courtesy of British Aerospace).

TOP: Lt. Cdr. John Sproule takes off from Gosport in his Aeronca 100 G-AEWV, sometime in the late forties. Photo: via Sandy Sproule.
BOTTOM: Lt. Cdr. John Sproule demonstrates the loading of his folding motorcycle into his Cub Coupé G-AFSZ. Photo: *"Motor Cycling"* via Sandy Sproule.

TOP: Lt. Cdr. John Sproule flies his canopied Chilton G-AFGI near Gosport, c.1950. Colour scheme is blue overall with silver fin and trim.
BOTTOM: Lt. Cdr. John Sproule, son Sandy (in cockpit) and John Dransfield work on Aeronca C.3 G-AEFT in the blister hangar at Shoreham, c.1963.
Photos: via Sandy Sproule.

Still in Chilton ownership G-AFSV was demonstrated throughout 1947-48 by Squadron Leader Ranald Porteous; in 1948 he took the 100 km Closed Circuit Speed record for its class.

In 1952 Group Captain E.L. Mole, who had obtained G-AFSV on loan from Mr Ward for racing, was instrumental with others in setting up the Ultra Light Aircraft Association (later to be renamed the Popular Flying Association). The Chilton was looked at as a promising aircraft for the postwar enthusiasts to build. There were originally two sets of drawings for the Chilton, the prototype set on which the stress calculations were based and a second set of working drawings that, as one of the employees remembers, were kept in a fitted wooden cabinet at the Chilton works. As the airworthiness requirements had changed somewhat since the Chilton was designed, the working drawings were loaned to the College of Aeronautical Engineering at Redhill as an exercise for the students to design an updated version. This was duly carried out and a modified version with high aspect-ratio wings was to be built by the students using a 50 hp Zundapp engine. For reasons not known it was not proceeded with. Unfortunately the drawings were not returned. Enquiries made on my behalf at the College some twenty years ago regarding the drawings were unsuccessful, as they had no knowledge of the drawings' existence.

During 1965 Mr Ward was approached by the late Chris de Vere with a view to building a Chilton. The original drawings still in Mr Ward's possession had by this time become faded to such an extent that it was impossible to produce a legible print. Mr Ward therefore engaged a firm to redraw them; however after this had been done it was found that there were too many drawings missing from the set to make construction viable, so no further action was taken.

Having been an admirer of the Chilton for as long as I can remember, I had over the years approached the various Chilton owners with a view to acquiring one of the surviving machines, but without success. During 1974 I contacted Mr Ward to ask about the possibility of building a Chilton. Mr Ward advised me of the problem of the missing drawings, but kindly offered to let me have prints from those drawings that existed. On checking through the drawings I found that most of the fuselage and centre-section drawings were missing, although the centre-section spars and airfoil sections were there, as well as the forward fuselage and basic fuselage elevation. This was encouraging as these were the key drawings, around which the missing detail could be added. There were no assembly drawings apart from the general arrangement drawings for the major component parts. It is unlikely that there ever were, as I was told by one of the original builders that this sort of detail was kept in the form of dimensioned sketches in a book available to the small team of builders, though the book does not appear to have survived.

At that time Wing Commander John McDonald had just commenced the rebuild of G-AFGI. John kindly consented to my request to closely examine the internals of his machine to gauge the extent of the missing drawings. After carrying out a comprehensive survey and photographing the aircraft in detail, it was obvious that a lot of work was required to complete the drawings to an acceptable standard of detail.

However in June 1978 I finally realised my ambition to own a Chilton monoplane when I exchanged my Comper Swift G-ABUS for the then Mikron II-powered G-AFSV. As it was my intention to restore 'FSV to her original configuration I commenced what transpired to be a very lengthy restoration, though the search for Train engines in France, moving house and the acquisition of several other vintage aircraft over the years has not helped. As I carried out 'FSV's restoration I took the opportunity to make drawings of the components and assemblies that I knew to be missing from the set. This further delayed my progress but I felt it a worthwhile exercise should I or any other Chilton owner need this information in the future. At this stage I intended the drawings purely for my own reference, so I did not stand on ceremony too much regarding finer points of draughting.

During 1980 I was contacted by Don Giffin from Canada who subsequently obtained permission to build a Chilton from Mr Ward. With the typical drive and enthusiasm of our North American friends he commenced construction, using the incomplete set of drawings with myself supplying him with the missing details hastily drawn on a piecemeal basis.

In 1984 I decided to restore the mortal remains of the prototype G-AESZ that I had acquired some years before. Because of the extensive nature of 'ESZ's rebuild it was obvious that a comprehensive set of drawings would assist its rebuild, especially as it was my intention to contract out most of the work due to my commitment to 'FSV. Mr Ward kindly gave me the remaining components from the fifth uncompleted Chilton to assist with the re-drawing. Sadly, not long afterwards, Mr Ward died. This of course could have meant the end of the Chilton, however Mr Ward's wife, Mrs. Constance Ward, a charming American lady, has very kindly consented to further examples of this beautiful little aircraft being built."

[It's good to know that examples of these wonderful little aeroplanes, built to an historic, efficient and timeless design, should be able to continue doing what they are best at for a long time to come. – Ed.]

CHAPTER 24
". . . ITEM WILLY FOX"
by
Peter Amos

Blackbushe in the fifties was a far cry from the strangely silent place it is today, all but hidden behind large hedges alongside the A30. In fact, when I recently went looking for it on the way home from a visit to Reading I nearly missed it – I was still looking for the 'old place' as I last remembered it! Gone now were the Bellman hangars, which once held the maintenance facilities for Silver City, Eagle, Airwork and the large 'new' hangar built for the United States Navy, and gone were the Nissen huts which did service as the terminal building – I just did not recognise the place.

In the far-off heady days of the late forties and fifties, Blackbushe still had a north-south runway which actually crossed the A30 (although it was rarely if ever used), and the FIDO installation was still *in situ*. It was also very busy with charter companies coming and going, and with maintenance being undertaken on airliners such as the Handley Page Hermes, Douglas Dakota and DC-6 in the two hangars on the south side of the A30, with Vikings and Lockheed Lodestars and the like in Airwork's hangar 'up the Yateley end' in a slight depression in the ground. Then the U.S. Navy moved in from West Malling and built a very large hangar over on Yateley Common and this was probably the last straw as far as the 'anti-aircraft' locals were concerned.

Then owned by the Ministry of Civil Aviation, Blackbushe aerodrome was the one furthest west (apart from Woodley which we took in occasionally) on the Sunday cycling tours which David Freeman and I undertook during the late forties and early fifties from Redhill, where we both lived in those days. These tours also took in Farnborough en route and Heathrow, Northolt, Langley and Hanworth Park on the way home. We were usually quite 'knackered' at the end of these marathon excursions (which from memory ran to something like 148 miles round trip!) but grimy, hungry and happy.

Blackbushe was also a very friendly place by comparison with other MCA-owned airfields; in a grassy ditch alongside the A30, opposite the Nissen huts which served as the terminal buildings, we used to stop and eat our sandwiches at lunchtime, watch the aeroplanes and listen to the never-to-be-forgotten clarion call come over the Tannoy such as ". . . Item Willy Fox" (as they used to say in the old phonetic alphabet). This wartime leftover must have been used to alert the fire section and other interested bodies (including us) of the impending arrival of an aircraft, in this case one of Morton's Doves.

But before this, sometime in 1948 I was fortunate to witness one of the two Bristol Beaufighter Mk. Xs sitting outside Airwork's awaiting delivery to the Dominican Air Force, and it was also about this time that I saw four Spitfire Mk. IXs with Turkish Air Force markings also awaiting delivery. While I have no intention of boring readers with details of the vast numbers of visiting and resident aircraft which we saw at Blackbushe in the fifties I must regale you with just a few of the highlights which I still vividly recall.

One such occasion was on 11th June 1949 when, on one of my early visits to Blackbushe, I recorded the following (unfortunately very few of the types seen have survived, let alone the actual aircraft): DC-3s G-AIJD, G-AJAV, G-AJVY, G-AKJN, G-AKLL, G-ALFO (and two others we couldn't identify); G-ALEP Douglas C-54B; G-AJEE Auster Autocrat; G-AJLI & VP-RBM Airspeed Consuls; F-BESE HP Halifax; OO-XAS & OO-XAV Short Stirling Mk. Vs; G-AHJD Bristol Wayfarer; G-AICS Bristol Freighter; G-AJFS Vickers Viking; NC2966 Grumman Mallard; G-AJWF Miles Gemini; and G-AHNA, a red Proctor. It is strange to relate that, with the exception of G-AJFS (which survived to be WFU at Southend in April 1964) and G-AJEE (which survives in store to this day) all the other UK-registered aircraft had been sold abroad by the early fifties. What would we give for a Stirling or two now?

On the first public day of the SBAC Show at Farnborough, the Friday, David and I would also often take in Blackbushe in the morning, and after the Show we would also cycle up there again to see the visitors leave. On one such evening, probably in September 1949, we were to witness by far the most dramatic and frightening event of our young lives to that time. It was fascinating watching the multitude of weird and wonderful aircraft departing from Blackbushe, but as we watched what should have been just another RAF Lincoln taking off to return to base with, as we subsequently discovered, nine 'erks' on board who had been on a day out to the SBAC Show, we could not possibly have imagined the drama which was about to unfold before our very eyes.

At first all went well as the Lincoln commenced its take-off run from the east, but just as it was beginning to gather speed, disaster struck and, far from watching just another take-off, we were suddenly faced with the makings of a potentially major incident, as the aircraft suddenly swung violently through 90 degrees to port. It then recovered to carry on rolling straight ahead, and the pilot was faced with what seemed to us like an insurmountable situation: the control tower was by now directly in his path and he had too much speed to stop but too little to take off. The tower loomed ever closer and we stood rooted to the spot, powerless to do anything except wait for the inevitable disaster which must surely follow. What must have been going through the controllers' minds as they saw the heavy bomber coming towards them at full throttle? Suddenly, at what seemed to be the last possible moment, but still with nowhere near take-off speed, the pilot literally yanked the Lincoln into the air – but it was by no means flying! We could hear the whole airframe protesting at such treatment as the mighty beast hung there just on the stall, somehow still in the air. Every rivet in its mighty frame was protesting – the noise was indescribable.

We wondered what the pilot would do next; he had somehow got it off the ground and air traffic had survived, but now Eagle Aviation's hangar was in the line of its flight path to the south and again we waited, with bated breath. Actually, on reflection, I don't remember breathing at all since the port wheel had stopped the bomber dead in its tracks for that brief moment – we were too dumbstruck! By now the pilot must have thought he'd used up a considerable number of his nine lives but unbeknown to us he still had one ace left up his sleeve.

The aircraft was still shaking violently – I've seen some strange sights in all my later years in this aviation business but I have never seen an aeroplane shake like that one did. Still on the stall, with next to no forward speed, it crawled along and he began losing what little height he had gained – at an alarming rate. The pilot then played his trump card – he retracted the undercarriage! From that moment his fortunes began slowly, oh! so very slowly at first, to improve and, although the hangar loomed ever closer, the shaking diminished. How he cleared the roof of that hangar I will never know – I seem to recall that the margin seemed little more than that with which he had cleared the tower but he was now beginning to 'fly' the thing; the shaking had stopped and imperceptibly he began to gain height.

David and I looked at each other, hardly daring to believe our eyes – he had made it. We waited for him to come round, land and hang up his hat, but not a bit of it: Lincoln pilots were obviously made of much sterner stuff! Round he came all right, but for a flypast down the runway and a wing-waggle before departing northwards for Lincolnshire, home and doubtless what he considered to be a well-earned pint! Perhaps he always took off like that – who knows? In our opinion, though, he certainly deserved that pint.

Years later David joined the RAF to complete his National Service and after basic training was posted to Debden. Strange indeed is the world of coincidence, but along the way he heard tell of the Lincoln which had taken a load of 'erks' to Blackbushe for a day out at the SBAC Show at Farnborough. From one of the 'passengers' in what could only have been that very Lincoln came the same story of 'our frightening experience,' but from the other side. The 'erks' had also apparently thought that their last day had come, but they agreed that the pilot had done a tremendous job, for which he was, from memory, awarded the coveted 'Green Endorsement' to his ticket. This honour was given only to pilots who had displayed airmanship of the very highest order, and which in this case was obviously for so very narrowly averting what could so easily have been a major disaster.

On the 4th September 1957 we again arrived at Blackbushe, to be greeted with the sight of the customary rows and rows of interesting visiting aircraft from the RAF and most of the air forces of Europe, which had landed earlier to disgorge their VIP passengers to visit the SBAC Show. However on this occasion the weather was 'on the deck' and we were not expecting much further action when we heard the unmistakable noise of large piston engines passing overhead. Suddenly one of those inexplicable holes in the cloud mysteriously appeared right overhead and through it flew a totally unexpected but instantly recognisable aircraft – a Martin Mariner amphibian. Surprise was not the word: we were, in the modern vernacular, totally gobsmacked! This was the last type of aircraft that we could have thought would have been on the end of such a lovely noise, but at Blackbushe in those days we really should have expected anything! Unperturbed by the appalling weather conditions its intrepid crew then brought the huge amphibian in to a perfect landing and we were then even more amazed to find that it belonged to the Dutch Navy.

I luckily managed to get a few photographs of the Mariner, as it taxied round the perimeter track in front of us, to record this unique event for posterity, and although amphibians, mostly French and Dutch Navy Catalinas, were not all that uncommon at Blackbushe in those days, this one was rather special.

In the late fifties, Blackbushe was also home to such airlines as Independent Air Travel Ltd, which was run by an ex-RAF Pole, Captain Marion Kozubski. I recall that one day we saw one of his Vikings undergoing an engine change 'in the field,' on an old RAF dispersal alongside the A30 in fact, with bits strewn all over the tarmac; luckily it was a fine day! Many years later I met a pilot, who now lives in my home village, who had actually worked for this colourful character and the stories he tells of the exploits of this "independent" airline would fill a book.

Then there were the early 'fire warning' scares of the period. If you were flying an early jet fighter and a fire warning light came on there was no argument, you just pulled the face blind and left! Most of these warnings were later proved to have been spurious and one such occasion occurred on September 1st 1958. We were watching the flying display at Farnborough, and the six red-painted Seahawks of the Fleet Air Arm's aerobatic squadron had completed their turn and were on the downwind leg of the circuit to the north of the airfield preparatory for a landing when one of them began to drop out of the formation. Soon after this we heard a bang and was somewhat surprised to see a live ejection taking place before our very eyes! Lt. R.C. Dimmock RN had left the sinking ship following a fire warning and was making his way earthwards to safety: never mind where the Seahawk went! The Seahawk (s/n XE462 coded 'R 106') then proceeded to dive into the ground, followed by the inevitable plume of smoke, which we saw to our horror was rising up from the general direction of Blackbushe. Needless to say, as soon as the show was over we headed to Blackbushe, where our worst fears were soon to be confirmed. As we turned the corner to face Silver City's hangar, the still-smoking remains of the Seahawk, which had crashed some 50 yards from the hangar, could be plainly seen. The occupants of the hangar and the Hermes on which they had been working had had a very narrow escape. "Everybody out" to save one life, unnecessarily as it subsequently turned out – the fire warning was later confirmed to have been spurious – had very nearly caused a major catastrophe.

So many serviceable aircraft were being abandoned due to this cause that soon 'questions were being asked in the House,' and action to remedy this wanton waste of otherwise perfectly good aircraft was given some priority thereafter.

There is so much more I could say about the goings-on at Blackbushe in the fifties, and I cherish my memories of the Blackbushe of yesterday: the strangly silent place of today, now hardly visible behind the large hedge alongside the A30 with its neat rows of little tin aeroplanes, could just as easily be on the moon!

However, before I leave this place of so many happy memories, "draw up a bollard" and I'll tell you a tale from the last days of the RAF at Blackbushe. The father of my first girl-friend (at least I thought she was, even if she didn't!) had been in the RAF during the war and had served out his time at Blackbushe. He told me that, sometime after the war had ended, one of the last resident squadrons there had been equipped with the Mk. III transport version of the dreaded Vickers Warwick. These aircraft were hated by all and sundry and not least of all by the Canadian tour-expired ex-bomber crews who had been detailed to fly them on transport duties. These gallant airmen had already had more than enough of the war; they were thankful to have survived thus far and only wanted to go home, in one piece and that piece preferably, still alive. They had had enough of flying in general, and flying in the Warwick in particular was, in their opinion, too much to take!

So it came to pass that they devised a simple system for avoiding the death with which they thought they would be dicing if they took these unreliable monstrosities off the ground. Arriving at the end of the runway in use in their supposedly 'serviceable' aircraft (a rare enough event apparently at the best of times!), and preparatory to opening up for take-off they would complete their pre-take-off checks with the engines run at full throttle to test the mag drop. Then, if they kept full power on until the cylinder-head temperatures went "off the clock" for just long enough and then chopped the throttle, the engines would apparently seize up solid. "Sorry, Sir, can't take off today – engine trouble!" Nobody could complain – after all, they *had* tried. When the last Warwick had been 'fixed' in this manner the RAF gave up the unequal struggle: the war was over anyway and everybody went home rejoicing!

My writing hand grows weary – I am getting old – my memories do not fade but I still have so much to do . . .

POSTSCRIPT

I did a little research which shows that there were two squadrons equipped with Warwick IIIs at Blackbushe in 1945-46, No. 167 and No. 301. No. 301 arrived in May 1945 and in July began operating regular services to Norway, Italy and Greece, until they left in January 1946. The squadron mentioned earlier could only have been No. 167, who received Warwick IIIs in November 1944 and began flying regular services to various Allied air bases in Europe and West Africa. The Squadron record says that in July 1945 the Warwicks were taken out of service for technical problems to be solved and that the crews in the meantime flew Dakotas from Croydon with No. 147 Squadron until the Warwicks resumed operating in September 1945.

No. 167 Squadron kept their Warwicks until February 1946 and I would hazard a guess that, from eyewitness reports, the technical problems were solved immediately after the Canadian crews were sent home!

CHAPTER 25

DE HAVILLAND AERONAUTICAL TECHNICAL SCHOOL: 1951-1955
by John de Uphaugh

At the age of seventeen I had never thought of doing anything else in life other than messing about with aeroplanes. So I joined the de Havilland Aeronautical Technical School as an apprentice on the 3rd September 1951. For some reason which escapes me, I gained a scholarship and thus my financially-pressed father avoided the fees which companies charged those apprenticed to them in those far-off days. Instead, *they* paid *me*. All of twenty-eight shillings a week, just enough to live on at the company's hostel at Sherrards House near Welwyn.

My first shock was to find that our first year was to be spent in the school workshops at Astwick Manor, outside the airfield boundary and without an aircraft in sight, in order to learn basic engineering skills. All very sensible and logical, but cutting a perfectly square hole in a chunk of steel and filing another to fit perfectly within it wasn't quite the stuff of my youthful dreams. One of our early tasks was to make a wooden toolbox, essential since those working on the factory floor were expected to provide their own tools. I still have that box, and very useful it is too. Occasionally we got our hands on something a little more akin to aviation like building the tail structure of Lord Ventry's ill-fated airship *"Bournemouth."* And, joy of joy, one day John Derry got his hands on a North American Sabre and treated us to our first experience of window-rattling supersonic bangs.

Our weekly wages did not allow much of a social life and certainly precluded visits to that seemingly distant and mysterious place called London. So we all busied ourselves at weekends repairing clapped-out motorcycles and hanging around Panshanger Aerodrome pushing and fuelling Tiger Moths, Hornet Moths, Chipmunks, Austers and other assorted aircraft, including an Aeronca which operated from there. Occasionally we got a flight as a reward. My log book records the faithful Tiger G-ALIX on many occasions and the Canadian-built-prototype DHC.1 Chippie G-AKDN, by then put out to grass with the London Aeroplane Club. Sometimes one of the motor cycles responded to treatment and we headed for Dunstable for some affordable (just) gliding on elephantine Sedberghs.

But the good news was that our canteen was right beside the Propeller Company's premises on the opposite side of the airfield to the main works, and some of us managed to inveigle our way into hitching rides in the aircraft kept there for propeller development flying. It seemed to me that this involved complete freedom to go wherever the whim took the pilot, provided that the right number of hours were recorded in the right conditions. For some reason which now escapes me the usually draconian staff at the School thought this air experience a good thing and let me have the necessary time out. Usually the pilot was Dizzy de Villiers and the usual mount was Ambassador G-AKRD. His favourite tourist attraction seemed to be the Forth Bridge, but occasionally we persuaded him to cross the Channel to look at Calais for a change – really quite exciting in an era when foreign exchange controls and apprentice poverty meant that "abroad" was a strange and exciting place, even when viewed from 15,000 feet. De Villiers also introduced me to the joys of aerobatics in a Chipmunk, which for some reason was at the disposal of the Propeller Company pilots, and to propeller-turbine flight in the Miles (or should it be Handley Page [Reading]?) Marathon II, originally registered G-AHXU. By the time de Havillands got their hands on this twin-Mamba-powered aircraft and fitted it with reversible pitch propellers – the first British prop-jet to be so equipped – it had been transferred to the Ministry of Supply and carried Service markings and the serial VX231. Those new propellers seemed to have teething problems and I was on board for one take-off which had to be abandoned when things went into reverse as we were gathering speed down Hatfield's tarmac.

At that time the demonstrator Dove G-ALBM, its nose emblazoned with an impressive array of flags of all the nations who had bought Doves, was being used as a communications aircraft and I got quite a few hours in that delightful little aeroplane. One flight is vivid in my memory: on the 15th August 1952 I went with de Villiers to Avro's at Woodford. Whilst he went about whatever his business was, I wandered across the apron to see what I could see. A large hangar beckoned and I entered. There before me, white, shining and immense, stood the prototype Vulcan, looking like something out a science-fiction movie with her ant-like acolytes crawling all over her impressive and futuristic bulk. At that time the aircraft must have been very much on the secret or restricted list, but nobody bothered me as I spent a happy half-hour poking around. So much for security.

Rather like the story I was told later when working for Handley Page. There all new employees were security-cleared and signed the Official Secrets Act. All, that is, except the cleaners, who were judged too dumb to know what they were looking at. Especially those with a bad command of English and thick Central European accents.

After my year in the School workshops I elected for a number of reasons to transfer to de Havilland's factory at Christchurch, in Hampshire. This had once been the home of Airspeed, whose beautiful, Hagg-designed Ambassador was occupying much of the production facilities, along with Vampire Trainers and Sea Venoms, all under the watchful eye of Major Hereward de Havilland. Later the experimental shop was in charge of navalising the DH.110 to become the Sea Vixen. One my more interesting jobs was working on the design of production jigs for this aircraft.

The atmosphere at Christchurch epitomised everything which was memorable about fifties' aviation. Here was a grass airfield, divided on its long axis by a stand of tall trees, from which de Havilland tested Ambassadors and Vampires. At one end stood Tommy Marshall's Flying School, the Tigers and Austers of which happily shared the airfield, without radio, with the heavier metal. They were joined at weekends and on summer evenings by a gliding club. And on warm summer lunchtimes Ron Clear, then deputy to Chief Test Pilot George Errington, would enthral the workforce – sunning themselves in the grass amongst the abandoned fuselages of the Horsa gliders that Airspeed had concentrated on producing in the war – with energetic displays in the Comper Swift which he kept in the Ambassador flight shed. (It was of course Clear who got into trouble landing an Ambassador on an extreme aft CG test. The ensuing bounce stripped the engines from their mountings and turned the Ambassador temporarily into what must have been the world record heavyweight glider.)

Occasionally George Errington would compete by doing spectacular things on the grass with a vintage Bentley, similarly housed as a stablemate for the Ambassadors. He once succeeded in turning it over in a cloud of dust and debris. Errington, like the Propeller Company pilots, was equally kind to apprentices and I spent many happy hours in various Ambassadors. Two things impressed me about this elegant aeroplane. One was its stately progress: it was in no great hurry to go anywhere. The oft-told story is that BEA wrote into the specification that its speed should be such that a proper, leisurely lunch could be served between London and Paris. The other was the way the triple tail shook when the two Centaurus engines were being ground-run.

At last I got to grips with real aeroplanes. I learned how to "bash" metal and roll it into the complex shapes demanded to skin fuselages. I learned to "sozzle" control cables. In particular I learned how to hoodwink the rate-fixers who, as their name implies, decided the rate for the job in those days of "piece work." And I learned that there was good money to be made by working "ghosters," which meant that when there was a panic on to get an aircraft ready you worked straight through the night from 08.00 one morning to 08.00 the following morning. That earned you triple-time rates.

At Christchurch I not only got to work on real aeroplanes. I also, courtesy of de Havilland's enlightened subsidised flying scheme for employees and the cashflow from "ghosters," learnt to fly. That, of course, was with rotund Tommy Marshall's Club, where my patient instructors were one Jack Elphick and none other than John Pothecary, contributor to these happy "tails of the fifties." (It was at the launch of the previous book that I caught up with John and felt inspired to jot down these notes.)

Christchurch was a lovely place from which to fly, provided that you avoided the Ambassadors and looked out for the sea fogs which rolled in very quickly on summer evenings. It was impossible to get lost. To the north lay the New Forest. That was my home and my father ran it so I knew every tree. Besides, there were still the huge runways of the wartime bomber fields like Stoney Cross and Beaulieu, still with the odd semi-active Lancaster. And to the south and east were Hengistbury Head, the Solent and the Isle of Wight. Even the dumbest student could find his way home, though I confess that on my first cross-country to Thruxton with building cloud I got a little lost and flew through Boscombe Down's restricted airspace at 1,500 feet. Luckily said cloud prevented a positive identification, and I gather that Tommy Marshall had to swear blind to an irate controller that none of the Club's aircraft were away from the circuit. Most of my flying was in a Taylorcraft Plus D, G-AHUM (which I believe eventually finished its active life with its nose buried in a hedge at Thruxton), Tiger G-ADWO and later several of the Club's Autocrats, including G-AHAT and G-AJAC.

Happy days – all gone now that Christchurch is buried under a business park and housing estates. But I wonder, if you go there late at night, whether you can still hear the echo of a pair of Centauruses being run up by someone working a "ghoster"? It takes more than a developer to remove all traces of history . . .

CHAPTER 26

CALEDONIAN CHARIVARI
(OR PRESTWICK PIONEERS!)

by

Dugald Cameron

[NOTES ON THE AUTHOR: Professor Dugald Cameron, DA, FCSD, FRSA, was born in Glasgow in 1939. Following his education at the High School of Glasgow and the Glasgow School of Art, he followed a career at the latter which continues up to the present day, and he was made its Director (equivalent to Principal in England) in 1991.

He is a Companion of the Royal Aeronautical Society, and flew from 1969 as a private pilot with the West of Scotland Flying Club, his first solo being in Cessna 150 G-AVVL. He also had a Commission in the RAF VR(T) from 1973.

In 1977 he founded "Squadron Prints" with Alan Carlaw and, to date, around 700 different prints of aircraft, a few ships, plus other miscellaneous subjects have been produced for the UK, USA and international markets. He is an aviation artist and enthusiast, and shares these activities with his other loves of steam locomotives and railways in general. – Ed.]

Living just over the River Clyde on its north side at Yoker, aircraft approaching and taking-off from Renfrew – Glasgow's airport and the centre of Scotland domestic commercial aviation – would regularly pass overhead or thereabouts. My first recollections were of Daks and what I now recognise as Ju.52s of BEA, thus dating these sightings to 1947. Trips with my father over the Renfrew Ferry and then the short distance by tram to the Hillington Road end, near the threshold of the NE end of Renfrew's longer runway, provided better views and I recall the ubiquitous BEA Rapides used on the Scottish internal routes developed by the great pioneers Sword, Fresson and Gandar Dower not much more than 10 years previously. Then I had no books to inform me and Ian Allan's "ABC"s which inspired my railway enthusiasms were just being introduced to the aircraft spotter. Commercial traffic was sparse at Renfrew then and there was little else. The Scottish Flying Club, whose 1934 Clubhouse had become the airport terminal, had a very difficult time trying to restart after the war and faced an obstructive bureaucracy, so there was equally very little in the way of private flying, officialdom apparently believing that such private activity would interfere with the few scheduled services then in being – about sixteen a day – in the late 1940s.

602 (City of Glasgow) Squadron of the Auxiliary Air Force (Royal from 1957) had been the first auxiliary squadron to form on the 12th September 1925 and at Renfrew; they had transferred to Abbotsinch, the airfield they had established in 1933. It was subsequently taken over by the Navy in 1943 and was now HMS "Sanderling," a major naval aircraft storage, maintenance and repair facility and, from 1947, home to 1830 Squadron Royal Naval Volunteer Reserve, the Fleet Air Arm's weekend fliers, and 1969 Flight of 666 (AOP) Sqadron Royal Auxiliary Air Force. In these days Abbotsinch was not as accessible as Renfrew by public transport – a problem which the auxiliary squadrons faced.

Like most 'spotters' I had a bike. When we moved to deepest Lanarkshire, trains were required though we thought nothing of walking from Paisley (Gilmour Street Station) to Abbotsinch and then round its perimeter. These days, it wouldn't be allowed by our increasingly nanny state, parents would stand to be punished.

The PSP tracking of Abbotsinch's runways began to break up and flying ceased in the summer of 1949 whilst new runways were constructed. 602 Squadron with their Spitfire 21s and 22s went back to Renfrew along with some naval aircraft on maintenance. 1830 Squadron went over to Donibristle on the Firth of Forth. Thus there wasn't much to see – just cocooned Fireflies, Sea Mosquitoes, Sea Hornets.

From the late 1950s it became possible to fly transatlantic from Renfrew in Loftleidir's DC-4 TF-ISE, the famous "Gullfaxi," between Iceland and Prestwick, and Renfrew and Copenhagen. It was joined by TF-IST "Solfaxi" and in 1957 by Viscounts TF-ISN and TF-ISU.

One major event for naval aviation enthusiasts was the autumn exercise of September 1957 when the NATO fleet assembled in the Clyde estuary. Seen there were the first two US Super Carriers "Forrestal" and "Saratoga" along with "Essex" and the British "Ark Royal," "Eagle" and "Bulwark." This was my first sighting of A-3D Skywarriors, F-3H Demons, FJ-3 Furies and F-4D Skyrays, along with much to-ing and fro-ing of their HUP-2 helicopters. The carriers were accompanied by the US battleships "Iowa" and "Wisconsin" and many, many other naval vessels – an unforgettable and unrepeatable sight.

For a period too in the mid to late fifties Scottish Aviation Ltd extended their RCAF maintenance contract to Renfrew using the old hangars (of 1917 vintage) and the old terminal. Sabres, T-33s and CF-100s were overhauled there including the first of the former for the reformed Luftwaffe and for Greece and Turkey. This also brought RCAF Daks and Bristol Freighters to the airport.

Eventually, around 1952, the Scottish Flying Club were allowed to fly again from Renfrew and for a few years their Hawk Trainers (Magisters) could be seen operating from the grass area near the Fire Station –

G-AKKS, 'KKY, 'HKP, 'JHG and 'JRV – and for a while in 1952 Tiger Moth G-AKCI was stored awaiting sale.

The one regular 'international' event was the arrival and departure of Aer Lingus' DC-3s on the Glasgow-Dublin route. One fondly remembers the "St. Laurence O'Toole"! These were supplemented for a short period by Bristol Wayfarers and in the 1950s the first Fokker Friendships. Air Enterprises based a few Rapides and Consuls at Renfrew for *ad hoc* charters and Army co-operation work and also had a Proctor, G-AIHG.

It was about this time that my serious enthusiasms began to move from railways to aviation – or more accurately to be shared, as they still are. It was on a Sunday morning cycle trip with my father to Renfrew during the summer of 1950 that I first saw the Spitfires of 602 Squadron. They were different from the earlier, more usually depicted marks, for they had larger fins and bubble canopies – Mark 22s – though 602 had a mix of 21s and 22s right up to their re-equipment with jets in January 1951. Now just what colour were the spinners? They certainly fired my youthful imagination and I would spend many hours trying to draw them or my development of them, not knowing then that many years later, with Alan Carlaw as partner, we would create a small business, publishing aircraft and other profiles called "Squadron Prints." How I wish that I could have recorded this period properly as so much detailed information seems to have passed us by and been lost forever. Even my good old friend, Wilf White, doyen of Scottish aviation photographers, hadn't really started until a year or so later. I did, however, have my photograph taken in one of two Moth Minors that were at Renfrew around then, 'FOB and 'FRY. Sadly, both print and negative have disappeared. Auster V, G-AKPH, owned by Norman Ewing, became one of the few private aircraft around. It also used a strip at Newton Mearns, a 'posh' southern suburb of Glasgow.

January 1951, and at last 602 began re-equipping with jets. They had been the first of the auxiliaries with Spitfires, in May 1939, and had them longer than any other operational squadron, until December 1951. Now, the curious and distinctive twin-boomed Vampires whistled over Clyde-side accompanied by two Meteor 7s, with the Harvards continuing for a short while. Single-engined Vampires with twin-engined Meteors for jet conversion and instrument work presented an odd mixture; however, the two-seat Vampire T.11 was some years off and didn't appear with 602 until a few weeks before their disbandment. They weren't the first jets at Renfrew as USAF F-80 Shooting Stars appeared there in 1948 en route to Germany. During 602's mobilisation at Leuchars in 1951, the USAF shipped F-84 Thunderjets over and they were prepared and flown from Renfrew. I remember seeing them and, at first, wondering what they were.

In November 1951, RCAF Sabres had also been shipped to the Clyde and roaded to Renfrew along with the Royal Navy's first four AD-4W Skyraiders. A friendly military policeman helped me over the fence from Haining Road to sit in one of the F-86s! A few years later the reverse happened when F-51 Mustangs which had been based at Iceland were repatriated from the Clyde via Renfrew back to the USA. A number of US Army L-23 Twin Bonanzas arrived around the same time. Haining Road gave good viewing to the rear dispersal areas with their PSP surfaces and the other Bessoneau hanger which 602 had used until their return to Abbotsinch in 1954 when the new and stylish Terminal was built on their dispersal.

Trips to Renfrew became more frequent and good viewing of 602's dispersal was possible from the adjacent King George V playing field. The dispersal was built during the war by the Lockheed Corporation to prepare aircraft shipped over to the nearby King George V Dock. The proximity of the river and its anchorages in the Firth made both Renfrew – doubled in size during the war – and Abbotsinch particularly valuable as delivery and preparation centres for aircraft from and to the US, a role which continued until Abbotsinch closed in 1963 prior to it becoming Glasgow's new airport.

During 1951, Scottish Aviation's Dak conversions for BEA began to appear in the wake of pioneer "Pionair" G-ALYF. They became the "Pionair" class and were all named after the greats of British aviation. This caused me to wonder just who these people were and fired my interest in aviation history. Many years later, I came to the story of G-AGZD "RMA Percy Pilcher" and discovered that he had been an assistant lecturer at the University of Glasgow and during the summer of 1895 flew his 'Bat' glider from the banks of the Clyde at Cardross – Britain's first aeronaut. He might just have beaten the Wrights had he not been fatally injured in 1899. Thanks to Philip Jarrett, this 'other Icarus' story has been told and the recognition due to Pilcher is now beginning to be accorded.

For a few years in the early 1950s, we spent wonderful summer holidays with relations in Blackpool and, like many others, I experienced my first flight from Squires Gate, in a DH Rapide of Air Navigation and Trading Co – 'KSG, I think, or 'LXI; it cost 7/6 (37½p)! This would be in either July '51 or July '52. There was much of interest there including the Dragons 'CIT and 'DDI, the DH.86s 'CZP of the Lancashire Aircraft Corporation and the withdrawn 'DUF in a silver and maroon colour scheme, one of a variety of aircraft collected by A.N.T.'s Russell Whyham. At that time, there were also two LAC Halifaxes, 'IHV and 'KEC, and two of their many Yorks, 'HFE and 'GOA, all standing outside their main hangars.

Seeing my enthusiasm, I was befriended by some of the pleasure-flying pilots who began to let me have any spare seats. Thus I had my first taste of flying in a light aircraft, A.N.T.'s Auster IV 'LVV. My profile sketch of this aircraft was signed by the pilot: "C. L. Shipman, 22/7/52 at 8.15," a true progenitor of the 'Squadron Print.' Squires Gate in the fifties seemed to attract the unusual in aviation, particularly in A.N.T.'s hangar where all sorts of aircraft were piled one upon the other.

I began occasional visits to Blackpool on my own thereafter, or with Jimmy Manson, of whom more later. Easter 1955 saw Hunters coming off the Hawker production line including WW663, 4, and 5, the latter in pea-green undercoat. The previous year we made sorties to Southport where, at Birkdale Sands, Giro Aviation's two Fox Moths, 'CCB and 'CEJ, were spotted, along with Avian G-EBZM stored in the hangar roof. I didn't know then of those Fox Moths' Scottish connections with Midland & Scottish Air Ferries and Scottish Motor Traction respectively, 20 years previously. We also went to Ringway which seemed a long way from central Manchester. The excitement for me there was a KLM Convair 340 PH-CGF and, after a long wait, a SABENA DC-6, OO-SDB. Visits to Blackpool ceased with my step-grandmother's death in 1956; however these relatively few and short visits were fascinating aeronautically both then and in retrospect.

To return to Renfrew and the local scene, by great good fortune (one Saturday afternoon in early 1953) I met and struck up a friendship with a couple of young spotters up from Prestwick, Jimmy Manson and Tony Wills. Saturday afternoons at Renfrew were particularly bleak, the main interest then being the activities of 602 Squadron with their Vampires and Meteors. Viscounts had begun appearing on the Glasgow-London route, operated solely by BEA with their "Clansman" service being inaugurated in October 1953 by G-AMOC "RMA Richard Chancellor." During the long lulls in the action, Jimmy and Tony regaled me with the delights to be seen 30 miles down the road at Scotland's transatlantic airport, Prestwick.

I had been there once or twice, during 1951, I think, and seen my first Stratocruiser, G-ALSB "Champion" of BOAC, a DC-4M North Star of TCA and the second prototype Viscount, G-AMAV. I had not known then the wonders lurking within Scottish Aviation Ltd's hangars, including the remains of their Fokker F.22, G-AFZP (some of whose seats would grace the newly-forming spotters' club) or the last Liberators, none of which I was to see. Occasional visits to Prestwick, where I enjoyed Jimmy's mother's hospitality, led to a week's stay with him in the summer of 1953. Thus began for real my enthusiasm, even passion, for aircraft and aviation and like those dozen or so other young lads of the original membership and the many that have since followed, it was fostered, informed and illuminated in the newly-formed Prestwick Spotters' Club. Despite the many changes in Prestwick's fortunes, the Club, now the Prestwick Airport Aviation Group, still flourishes, 45 years later – long may it continue!

The founders of the Club in 1953 were David Reid (Davie), the – sadly, late – Douglas Ronald and Donald MacDonald with Wilf White from Glasgow. Along with this more 'mature' group were John Hope, Jimmy Manson, Tony Wills, Andy McClymont and Aird Crooks. It was Davie, however, who organised, enthused and inspired the group of lads who had been meeting casually in the airport's public enclosure and discovered their mutual interests. An arrangement with the café concessionaire soon allowed the Club some space at the rear and a temporary canvas partition was erected. This gave way eventually to a proper arrangement and a permanent Clubhouse looking out onto the airport, which served the Club until the new terminal was opened in 1964 when other accommodation, including at one time the original police HQ, was used. It says much for the airport authorities and for the Club's volunteer officials that relations have been good over the years.

I joined the Club proper as 'Associate Member No. 1,' as by now living in far-off Larkhall and using my season ticket on the railways, I could manage at first only every other Saturday, then every Saturday; this could be very frustrating since one missed so much. Prestwick was a remarkable place for spotters in the fifties, as its USAF base with the 67th Air Rescue Squadron and 1631st Air Base Group was used as a transit stop to and from Europe and the USA by all manner of types including of course the SB-29s and, later, SC-54s, SA-16s and H-19s of the based 67th Air Rescue Squadron, and many of the current fighter, bomber and transport types, including the based C-47, old 51057. I well remember my first B-50, 7151 "Caribbean Queen" in August 1953. Occasionally, a real rarity would appear, the YC-97J turboprop conversion 22693 in January 1956 taking 6 hours 4 mins for the flight from Newfoundland, and later the similarly powered YC-121F 38157 in May.

The Bristol Brabazon made one visit to Prestwick on the 28th August 1951 with a Chipmunk posed beside it for size comparison. A prototype Comet jetliner came on the 5th April that year.

The US Navy was also a regular visitor with various marks of Neptunes, the odd R4D-8 Super Dak, SNB-5, and their contributions to the Military Air Transport Service (MATS) R-5Ds, R-6Ds, the occasional R-7V and, at least on one occasion, a WV-1 conversion of the civil Constellation and occasional PB1-W, Flying Fortress, JD-1 Invader and UF-1 Albatross. The WV-2 conversion of the Super Connie became common later on. During 1955, however, there were a few visits from AJ-2P Savages and P4M-IQ Mercators, the latter from Port Lyautey in

Morocco. Occasional visitors to the Clyde estuary were US Navy carriers. In 1954, "USS Franklin D. Roosevelt" visited and its HUP-2 helicopter visited Prestwick as well as, very unusually, an SNJ Texan. Additionally, on the military front, were North Stars of the Royal Canadian Air Force and their Daks, Expeditors and C-119s, with an occasional Neptune and of course Ansons, Oxfords and many other Royal Air Force and Navy types, including, in the summer 1953, a Buckmaster RP237. Among the many 'stars' seen at Prestwick in the early fifties before my time as a spotter were two rather exotic B-26 Invaders being delivered to the French Air Force from Mexico, where they had been used by VIPs – ZO01 "El Fantasma" and ZO02 "El Indio." Black and white photographs did little justice, I suspect, to their colourful paint schemes.

Over at SAL, one of their most enduring contracts was maintaining RCAF European 1st Air Division Sabres, T-33s, CF-100s, Daks and Expeditors and eventually in the 1960s, CF-104s. Occasionally, on air-sea rescue duties there were RCAF Lancasters. In the mid fifties USAF Sabres were also repaired and overhauled. There was always a trans-atlantic feel about the airport, extending to the lingering aroma of cigars in the warren of huts and corridors which made up the old terminal and led to the Hotel, originally Orangefield House; this had once been visited by Robert Burns. Pending delivery of Gannets, SAL converted about 100 ex-US Navy Avengers for the Royal Navy from around 1953.

Prestwick, strategically sited on the great circle routes between Europe and North America, was a convenient fuel-stop for all kinds of traffic, from the airlines to the intrepid light aircraft, flyers coming from the USA 'round the houses,' via Reykjavik in Iceland. In many ways it was a great place to indulge a passion for aircraft since such a variety of both civil and military could be seen there. In those days, long before air-band radios, one took one's chance, the only warning being what the airport's duty-crew board had chalked upon it in the way of imminent arrivals.

It was Davie's task to be pestered into constantly checking this board for early warning of aircraft whilst we awaited his return in anticipation; too often it was just more C-118s. We couldn't realise then what rarities they would become or how a preserved C-54 or C-121 would bring out the crowds as they did in the summer of 1998, fifty years later. Fifty years prior to 1953, aviation had just been born.

With its own Clubhouse, which eventually boasted a converted RAF radio together with photographic facilities, the Club increased its numbers, though a degree of selectivity was practised. Among those joining during 1954 was David Huddleston from Glasgow. He boasted an enormous telescope and had the use of his father's BSA Bantam motorbike. David studied law at the University of Glasgow in the time he could spare from learning to fly with the University Air Squadron. He emigrated to Canada in 1961 and joined the Royal Bank of Canada and then the RCAF in quick order, subsequently amassing 1,500 hours on the Starfighter and commanding the 1st Air Division in Europe. He eventually retired in 1995 as the Commander of Canada's Air Command as a Lieutenant General – "no bad" as we say in Glasgow.

Prestwick was a natural airport due to a benign curiosity of its local weather. It had been recommended by Jimmy Jeffs of Croydon to William Sword when he was developing his Midland and Scottish Air Ferries around 1932-33 and his aircraft had used a field at Monkton as well as the beach at Prestwick during that period. History I am sure will wonder why the vision of men like Sword and then the great David MacIntyre wasn't better realised, though what they did do was to lay the foundation for both Scotland's air transport and designing and manufacture of aircraft.

Prestwick during the fifties had many particular, even special, attractions for the enthusiast. If the scheduled airline side was restricted principally to BOAC, TCA, PANAM, SAS and KLM, American Overseas Airlines operated for a short time in the late 1940s and very early 1950s, and it was more than compensated for by the presence of the USAF and their general use of the airport by a wide variety of transiting aircraft as well as occasional light twin aircraft on deliveries to Europe and Asia, often by Jack Ford of Fleetways, with deliveries to North and South America of new British aircraft. Doves were common during the 1950s, to be followed by the odd Heron and, much later on, by its worthy successor, the HS.125. Viscounts became sought after 'cops' including those of Trans Canada Airlines, Capital Airlines, Continental Airlines, and such a rarity in 1955 as CF-GXK of the Canadian Department of Transport, the three each of the Venezuelan Linea Aeropostal Venezolana and Cuban Compania Cubana de Aviacion. In 1958 a single example went to TACA of El Salvador (YS-09C) and in that year Northeast Airlines took delivery of Viscounts, with Britannias being delivered to Canadian Pacific Airlines whose DC-6Bs were occasional diversions. Executive deliveries to the USA included Viscounts for US Steel Corporation. Occasionally a DC-6 or DC-6B of Italian, Linee Aeree Italiane diverted in, e.g. I-LIKE, I-LADY, I-LUCK and I-LOVE. Caravelles for United Airlines also fuel-stopped at Prestwick on delivery.

Over the main runway however was the complex of hangars used by Scottish Aviation Ltd – SAL – and this gave a very different dimension to the airport. During the late 1940s and 1950s, aircraft design and manufacture, aircraft conversion and modification, was concerned particularly with the DC-3/C-47/Dakota, although Liberator work was undertaken up to 1952. SAL also operated their own airline, Scottish Airlines, though its development was seriously inhibited by the postwar

Labour Government's policies; they also operated airlines for the Greek and Luxembourg Governments.

The development of Prestwick as a world centre of aviation was the great dream and vision of David McIntyre along with the 14th Duke of Hamilton. They established it in 1935 for flying training and it was greatly expanded during the second world war when it became the UK terminal for the Atlantic Ferry organisation – this is a full story on its own, as are the political wrangles in which McIntyre ("The Groupie") was forced to engage when peace came in 1945 and the airport was taken over by the Ministry of Civil Aviation. We spotters knew little of this or the fragile financial state of SAL while they developed the STOL Prestwick Pioneer and its sister the Twin Pioneer or "Double Scotch." The Royal Air Force and the then recently established Royal Malayan Air Force had much to be grateful for in having such appropriate aircraft available to them during the Malayan emergency. It was a happy coincidence that, like McIntyre and Hamilton, the first commander of the RMAF, Sandy Johnstone, was a former CO during the Battle of Britain of 602, the City of Glasgow Squadron, who had also been employed at Prestwick with the RAFVR prior to the outbreak of war.

My weekly visits to Prestwick always included a trek round SAL, easily accomplished since security was almost non-existent – hardly necessary in any case – and access could be gained through or over the modest retaining wall at almost any point! The black hangars with their interconnecting passages usually held some interesting types under repair and maintenance, and of course from 1953 onwards the Pioneer and Twin Pioneer production lines. Entry to the hangars was easy though unnecessary as there were plenty of holes in the corrugated cladding. During 1947 SAL took an interest in representing the Bell Company and a few Bell 47 helicopters, G-AKFA, 'FB and 'CX were imported and flown by their chief test pilot, the legendary "Cap" (J. Noel Capper).

It was during my first real visit to Prestwick – or "The Drome" as it was called – that Jimmy Manson introduced me to the delights within SAL's hangars including the prototype Pioneer still with its civil registration G-AKBF, finished in silver with the "Groupie's" flame-orange trim; it would soon become XE512 for the RAF. Also lying with their wings folded were Walrus G-AJNO and Proctor G-AHMT both in Scottish Airlines, the markings of 'JNO being cream and orange, and 'HMT being silver with orange letters. Scottish Airlines' activities at this time were largely concerned with the trooping contracts from down south though at various times during this period Yorks G-AMUL, 'M and 'N could be seen along with Daks G-AGZG, G-AMJY and G-AMPP, the latter remaining with the company on the summer Prestwick–Isle of Man route until Dan Air took over the route at the end of the decade.

261

Scottish Airlines at that time also owned various Rapides and an Oxford G-AHDZ. In one of the hangars was another Walrus, G-AHFN, silver all over with black registration, owned by the whaling company Charles Mauritzen. Both of the Walruses remained, it seemed, for a few years before in 1955 'HFN was towed down the Pow Burn on its way to Wig Bay, but before reaching its intended destination it foundered.

1954 saw the opening of a new subsidiary runway, 21/03. It was inaugurated by "Woody" in his Rapide G-ALPK, carrying members of the Spotters' Club. Captain L.H. Wood was a distinguished pilot who had the pleasure-flying concession at the airport for a number of years during the 1950s. The first flight of the Twin Pioneer G-ANTP was a much-awaited event in June 1955.

Prestwick's peculiarly fine weather made it a major diversion centre and this would bring many unusual commercial aircraft to it, typically during November and December, with the apron parking space being augmented by the North Dispersal and the old disused secondary runway 26/08.

Scottish Aviation was a great enterprise created by the "Groupie" – David MacIntyre. Designing and developing aircraft for world markets wasn't then (and isn't now) for the fainthearted. Doing it on a shoestring as David MacIntyre had to do, and for the noble reasons and vision of creating a great centre of aviation on the Firth of Clyde to supplement and perhaps eventually replace Clyde Shipping and shipbuilders, is the most eloquent testimony to a great Scot. It was a tragedy that he was to be killed in one of his own aircraft, the Twin Pioneer G-AOEO, in 1957 during a sales tour to Libya. That there is still aircraft design and manufacturing going on at the now British Aerospace plant at Prestwick is, given recent events and the cessation of the Jetstream 41 programme, some consolation. That too is another story.

The 41's predecessor, SAL's development of Handley Page's original aircraft into a best-seller, Jetstream 31, owed much to the endeavours of various members of the Spotters' Club of the 1950s including former SAL apprentices John Hope, who was to be become quality manager, and Bob Watt, a senior sales and marketing executive. Much later on one of the sixties club members, Gordon McAdie, would follow in Bob's footsteps.

Back again to the mid and late 1950s. The aim of my first visit for serious spotting was to see a 'Connie,' and I can well remember BOAC's G-AHEK (I think) appearing low from the south that late Saturday afternoon to land on the main runway. It was to see these 'common' aircraft that I went to Prestwick and I can recall David Reid's irritation at my lack of interest in such 'stars' – then – as a C-119 Packet, rather than the more common C-82s, or a Grumman Mallard, N2992. Once I had made my pilgrimage to Heathrow in the summer of 1954 my appetite had begun to be satisfied and my particular interests moved to American light twins. From what is now known, transatlantic operations by the big piston-engined airlines was pretty dodgy at times due to weather and the marginal range of these aircraft. The piston engine was at the end of its possible development, yet the safety record was good. Sadly there were two bad accidents actually at Prestwick: KLM Constellation PH-TEN crashed on rising ground after a missed approach on the 20th October 1948 and BOAC Stratocruiser G-ALSA undershot on Christmas Eve 1954. PH-TEN was commanded by the Dutch pioneer pilot, Captain Parmentier.

Some of the deliveries of light twin aircraft were made to Europe, the Middle East and even Asia and Australia via Canada, Greenland, Iceland and Prestwick. One or two Aero Commander 520s had passed through in 1952-3 along with the odd Twin Bonanza. I well remember a dark blue and white B-50 model, VR-ABB, in late 1954 and one of three Aero Commander 520s for the South Korean Air Force, No. 501. The first rather stylish Cessna 310 to appear was the grey, red and cream HB-LBC in March 1955, to be followed by F-BHDV for Turbomeca. 1955 also saw the first Riley Twin Navion, red and cream HB-LBA, and Apache ZS-DME. One Cessna 310 which I saw during my three weeks at Prestwick in July 1955 was white with red, N2657, which appeared along with a luxury conversion of a Catalina, N5804N of the Monsanto Chemical Corporation, finished in white overall with green trim and called "The Pelican"; it boasted little launches under each wing. That time I also saw on a beautiful sunny Saturday afternoon the delivery of Capital Airlines' third Viscount N7404 – it looked superb in the polished silver with a white top and red and light blue trim. There were also a couple of C-46 Commando deliveries to Brazil. Unlike many of such aircraft which still had the remnants of their wartime liveries and markings, these two were polished silver all over with only their registration in black and the Brazilian flag.

The mid 1950s saw a great variety of American charter companies being used to supplement the Military Air Transport Service in conveying US military personnel and freight between Europe and the USA. DC-4s, most of which were former C-54s, predominated with Seaboard Western, Transocean with their red and yellow colour scheme and Overseas National being most common. Two DC-4s/C-54s stand out in the memory: N56005 of General Airways, which boasted a beautifully rendered rose on its silver-and-green-trimmed fin and one of Overseas National's with its pink overall scheme.

The late fifties at Prestwick saw the final fling of the big piston era in regular transatlantic service with the DC-7B of PANAM, then the DC-7Cs of PANAM, BOAC, SAS and KLM, along with the L-1049G and H Super

Constellations of TCA, KLM and Flying Tigers. The Britannia 312 turboprops of BOAC were belatedly introduced in 1958, the same year as their Comet 4s inaugurated transatlantic jet operations, just beating PANAM's Boeing 707-120s. The Comets made occasional diversions to Prestwick, my first being G-APDD in December 1958. In the late summer of 1959, President Eisenhower visited his flat at Culzean Castle not far from Prestwick; he used the new VC-137s, 86970 and 86972, with the press in TWA 707 N744TW. Around the same time C-133s began to visit the base, my first seen was 62002 on the 5th September.

Regular jet operations at Prestwick had to wait until 1960 and the extension of the main runway over (yes, *over*) the Ayr-Glasgow main road. Traffic had been stopped by lights for quite some time as the runway threshold had crept nearer the road over the years. These days such a procedure would not even be countenanced yet it has proved to have been perfectly safe.

The immediate postwar decade was in retrospect an interesting – even exciting – one as the final development of the piston era gave way to the big jets. It certainly provided a panoply of aircraft for the enthusiast against the remarkable and rapid development of commercial aviation culminating in the jet age. I look fondly back to the Prestwick Spotters' Club/Prestwick Airport Aviation Group. Friendships formed there over forty years ago have been the most rewarding and enduring, now shared with our wives. What a great pleasure it is for Nancy and myself to share a meal with John and Pat Hope as we review the past and see it afresh and more clearly against the background of our respective experiences.

Prestwick was a great place for the spotter, for on one site there was a major international civil airport, a significant aircraft design manu-facturing, modification and maintenance organisation and an American military base. Mind you, there were quiet times which made the camaraderie and exchange of news and information in the Clubhouse all that more enjoyable – though Davie Reid's patience and tolerance must have been stretched to the limit!

The big jets with their greatly increased capacity and longer range had less to do with Prestwick's decline in strategic terms. It was Government stupidity, encouraged by BOAC's self interest, which did most damage. The coming of the Jumbos at the end of the next decade added another dimension to the problem. This aircraft brought about the introduction of mass air travel and the decline of it as a civilised means of transport.

What will the new millennium mean for the spotter?

CHAPTER 27

THE YEAR OF THE JACKAROO

by

Ginger Bedggood

[NOTES ON THE AUTHOR: Ginger was born in Croydon in 1933. Having watched the Battle of Britain as a schoolboy he was determined to become a pilot and admits to playing truant from school to watch the aircraft. However this seems to have convinced the authorities of his ambition and in 1949 joined the RAF at the age of 15.

He completed three years as an Engineering Apprentice at RAF Halton to qualify as a Junior Technician, then working on such aircraft as Lincolns, Hastings, Canberras, Varsities and Meteors. He also flew the latter briefly after being trained as a pilot on Tiger Moths, Prentices and Harvards.

During 1956, when a design draughtsman on the Viscount at Weybridge, he yearned to be up, up and away again in the sky. So he then went to Thruxton to work on the Jackaroo, and also instructed in Tiger Moths.

In the late fifties he instructed at Elstree and flew crop-spraying Tigers on the Isle of Wight. Later he joined the Denham Flying Club, becoming Chief Flying Instructor.

His later experiences with smaller aircraft included flying Dragon Rapides from Beirut & Khartoum, a spell as demonstration pilot for Aer Macchi and C.F.I./Manager, Oxford Air Training School.

He then joined British Eagle Airlines flying Viscounts and BAC 1-11s, and after the company's collapse in 1968 went to Gregory's at Denham as Captain on their DH.125 Jet Dragon, also ferrying the type to the USA.

In 1970 he joined British Caledonian, flying Boeing 707s and then Boeing 747s world-wide. He retired in 1984 and returned again to Denham, instructing in a full-time capacity at a more leisurely pace for another thousand hours. Now he writes stories, draws, paints and makes models of aeroplanes. What follows is an excerpt from his proposed new autobiography. – Ed.]

I was buried in the summer of 1957: not dead in the earth, but supposedly alive and well, working as a draughtsman on the Vickers Viscount in the design office at Weybridge. I was bored by being earthbound and resolved to change my drawing board for wings and my pencil for a joystick. I wrote the phrase "A place in the sun" on my drawing board and dreamed . . . I also wrote to a flying school in the West

Country. As a result I travelled by train and bus to a rolling green wartime airfield and walked up to the prominent white control tower standing high on the western perimeter. In the office upstairs I met the Managing Director and John Heaton, the Chief Pilot. Outside the sun was just beginning to break through the overcast.

"We have an interesting project here at Thruxton," said the M.D., "making a four-seat cabin Tiger Moth."

"We had our problems en route," he said, "but they have now been solved." (Not entirely as I would soon discover.) He then explained that in order to finish the job and get production going they needed an aeronautical engineer, a draughtsman, and a flying instructor who could also undertake some production test-flying and military contract flying.

"I see you were a Halton apprentice; what trade were you?"

"Airframes," I replied.

"That's good. Have you got an instructor's rating?" asked John.

"No," I was forced to admit.

"No problem, you can take a course here," said the director.

"How soon can you join the team here at Thruxton and start drawing the Jackaroo?" was his next incredible offer.

The sun was shining brightly all the way back to the bus-stop and I had to keep reminding myself that I was no longer just dreaming over my drawing board but had actually been offered an opportunity embracing all these positions! Bliss on a summer's day. Little did I visualise the aerial excitement coming my way in an infectious atmosphere of "Live now, tomorrow may not come." I started on the 1st of July.

Life quickly became a colourful kaleidoscope of aeronautical events. Mechanics in the morning: I supervised dismantling the Tiger Moths earmarked for conversion to Jackaroos and started the production line in the Nissen huts adjacent to the big black hangar. In the afternoons, upstairs in the white control tower, my pencil portrayed the detail shape of the "Build it first, do the drawings later" Jackaroo. Then, in the evenings (which never came quickly enough), I flew the Tiger on my instructor's course and spoke and spat into the Gosport tube until I was too hoarse to even whisper.

That very first day of July was also the day I first took to the air to learn to teach in the Tiger. G-ACEZ was the aeroplane I flew, once the mount of test pilot Geoffrey Tyson, famous for his routine of picking up handkerchiefs with a hook on his wingtip. My tutor was John Heaton, once a wartime fighter pilot; he had flown Curtiss P-40 Kittyhawks in the Western Desert, which fact helped no doubt to account for the differences from such a course today. Different? I'll say it was; have you ever flown uphill at a tank? Or flown a circuit inside the aerodrome boundary, round the perimeter track at a height of three . . . yes, THREE, feet?

These delights were yet to come however, and whilst totally immersed in coping with the instructor's course, the first unwanted thrills arrived on the July 21st, the day of the line squall.

It was mid-afternoon when the hot still atmosphere of summer was interrupted by sporadic gusts of wind outside the black Nissen hut that served as the flight office and instructors' briefing room. Dirty and ill-lit, the windows long since sealed by the dust grime of years, cobwebs filled its every nook and cranny and even damped the swing of the one naked bulb hanging from a threadbare flex in the centre of the corrugated roof, now disturbed by the breeze through the open door.

The sharp crack of thunder following so quickly after the lightning flash signified the nearness of the storm.

"All the aeroplanes back to the hangar," came the cry from the CFI. Briefings forgotten, we rushed from the hut, eager to comply.

"Someone give me a swing," I shouted as I climbed into G-ACEZ, my favourite Tiger Moth, accompanied by the first spits of rain.

The sky to the west was now filled with towering black clouds, their edges outlined with bright orange as they obscured the sun and dimmed the brilliant daylight. All too frequently the base of this now unbroken street of cloud was joined to the ground below by a black column of heavy rain, this was a line-squall.

I quote:

"THE METEOROLOGICAL HANDBOOK FOR PILOTS
H.M.S.O. LONDON 1942
(price 3s 6d)
Under certain conditions of temperature and humidity the increase of wind at the cold front may be very marked. This squall is called a line-squall because it occurs simultaneously at many points along the line of the front. The cumulonimbus is always very large and is characterised by the very heavy rain or hail and thunder."

"Throttle set, contact." The Gipsy Major roared into life.

"Chocks away."

A burst of power was needed to push the tail around, the Tiger having no brakes. The sky burst, too, as the wind whipped up and the rain drove hard on the fabric wings to sound like a thousand drums, heralding in the line-squall.

With the wind from the west and the hangar to the east, downhill, disaster loomed. A stronger gust weather-cocked the Tiger half round into wind and I was forced to counter with a burst of throttle against the rudder once more to regain direction and point towards the hangar. Now to cross the tarmac runway. Without the drag of the tail-skid in the grass the speed increased still more, aided by the tailwind.

Now the Tiger veered again; without the bite of the tail-skid I could not steer . . . the speed was now too great to use the throttle. Round she went, one wing scraped the tarmac, the other, now exposed to the wind, lifted . . . and over went the Tiger. Up, around and over.

The propeller splintered as the spinner dug into the tarmac, and with a sickening crunch the rudder horn crumpled on the runway as the Tiger came to rest inverted.

The fire extinguisher and I executed a formation drop out of the cockpit, both our heads colliding simultaneously with the runway. This of course caused the extinguisher to foam at the mouth and I received a goodly dollop of foam in the face, and lost a shoe to boot!

I remember being obsessed with trying not to put my shoeless foot into what was now a river of rain flooding down the runway. What a comic sight I must have been, hopping around on one foot in the pouring rain, clutching my bruised head with one hand and wiping the foam from my face with the other.

The speed with which volunteer wingtip holders now appeared around the other aeroplanes had to be seen to be believed – my big mistake was being too quick off the mark.

After the storm had subsided and the excitement had died I felt utterly deflated, wet and miserable as I cycled back to my caravan, convinced that I had 'blown' my instructor's course and bent my favourite Tiger as well. Sometime later I learned that after my unhappy departure on the day of the line-squall much revelry had taken place and the CFI was to be seen astride the still-inverted Tiger, bedecked in hunting apparel complete with horn and feathered hat, and brandishing a shotgun.

This was not a good start. I spent a rotten night feeling sorry for myself. The following morning I reported to the Managing Director in his office upstairs in the white control tower, not knowing quite what to expect. I could never afford to pay for the damage to the Tiger, my pay was a mere £8 per week and my instructor's course, with NO staff reduction, cost £3 per hour. Fortunately my fears were exaggerated. No doubt the abundance of cheap Tiger spares helped, and after a reprimand to temper my enthusiasm with caution I was in the air again that day.

Much later and wiser I reckoned that since I was actually working at Thruxton as a draughtsman but was paid at less than mechanics' wages (which they took back, plus a lot more for my flying) they didn't lose a lot; not that I am complaining, even given this impossible chance I would not change a thing.

That autumn I was to see a test pilot from the Air Registration Board taxy out, prior to departure, on a certification flight in G-AOEX, the prototype Jackaroo, with a wider-track undercarriage but still no brakes. He lost control of the Jackaroo, in precisely the same place on the runway, and in only a slight breeze! After one groundloop he recovered the situation by opening the throttle and taking off downwind. This technique had crossed my mind too at the time, but as you may recall, I was not strapped in.

Now I felt a lot better.

Autumn days that year did not mellow the content or style of the flying activities at Thruxton; my sorties in the Tiger, aloft in the still air of the evenings, practising the not too difficult but wordful explanations of "The effect of controls" and battling over the problems of synchronisation of the spoken word with the spinning biplane, were just magic. Then suddenly, changing the mood, my log-book entry for 25th Sept.'57 reads: "G-ADTD MILES FALCON SIX. Army Co-op. VERY LOW flying with John.' He may have imagined he was back in the Western Desert in 1943, judging by the amount of time we spent below the tops of the dark green trees in the silver Falcon flashing over the muddy dunes on Salisbury's famous plain as we ostensibly flew for radar gun tracking, unofficially beating up numerous guns and tanks at next to nought feet. Nought feet? Our wheels were virtually IN the tank tracks. Officially an instructor training sortie, it was an experience that I will never forget.

As the Jackaroo took shape on my drawing board the first of the problems on the subject of weight arose again. Apparently when flying with all four passenger seats occupied the centre of gravity was still at or past the aft limit despite the attempts to cure the problem earlier during the year by moving the seats forward (not quite far enough it would now seem). As a result of this, the seat front under the pilot's knees restricted the aft movement of the joystick. The first method of overcoming this was to bend the joystick forward and up, but this proved unsatisfactory so a U-shaped indentation was cut in the seat front to allow the stick adequate aft movement.

The eventual solution to the C. of G. position now proved to be the fitting of a large-diameter metal propeller, its additional weight at the extreme forward position being just sufficient.

"Ginger, take up a pupil and demonstrate an 'ENGINE RESTART.'"

If John said "Go," I went, trying to appear nonchalant, which was difficult, to say the least, as we walked out to the Tiger. I don't know if the pupil guessed that I had never done this before but I went over the drill several times in the briefing hut, as much for my benefit as his, I hasten to add. I had also re-read the appropriate page in the then current gospel, *"The RAF Instructors' Handbook of Elementary Flying Training,"* a

269

priceless and virtually unobtainable volume which I had had the foresight to acquire previously. Its more pertinent advisory recommendations were repeatedly before my eyes:

'Raise the nose well above the horizon. Switch "off" and open the throttle fully. If this fails, try one turn of a spin.'

I found in practice that it is considerably more difficult to stop the propeller than expected.

Later it suggests: 'If a steep dive and recovery do not restart the engine, make a forced landing.'

"What else?" I ask. Interestingly the Tiger Moth glides much further with its prop stopped as I discovered on a later sortie when unable to restart; prudently I had already decided only to practise this exercise over the aerodrome.

John was now hinting at my readiness for the instructor's test and finished that evening's lesson with a circuit around the aerodrome perimeter track at the height of three feet; he had to climb before banking in the turns, even so how the wing did not scrape the tarmac I will never know.

"Have you taken the Tiger up and really thrown it about?" he asked as we roared past the black hangar.

"No," I croaked.

"Well, do it tomorrow . . . but NOT at this height."

Meanwhile, back at the drawing board the next hurdle on the Jackaroo's pathway to success in the skies loomed over the horizon. The brief document read: 'Before consideration can be given to the issue of the Certificate of Airworthiness the energy absorption capabilities of the (Tiger Moth) undercarriage must be increased in order to cope with the increased weight (of the Jackaroo with its four seats).

After looking into the possibilities of increasing the coefficient of friction of the sliding part inside the tubular members of the main undercarriage, the solution 'dreamt up' by the Thruxton team was much more simple: fit a new tail-skid with a longer arm and a STRONGER spring. One wonders whether this presupposes that all landings at maximum weight will or MUST be made on three points. Bizarre indeed, but it proved to be acceptable!

I passed my instructor's test at Hamble that autumn and I flew the prototype Jackaroo G-AOEX for the first time on the 1st of December. To the modern purist the Jackaroo is looked upon as some sort of mutation of the well-beloved Tiger but to one who has spent many hours trying to impart aerial wisdom whilst freezing in draughty open cockpits the advantages of the big wood and perspex canopy were very welcome, even without a heater. Compared to the Tiger Moth its warmth and sociability promoted easier communication and more intimate relations; after all we were not training fighter pilots and had several attractive lady students. Its handling was similar to its slimmer parent and it was not significantly slower, which is remarkable when considering the increased volume of the enclosed cabin with its ample space for maps and charts.

On the ground it was more stable due to the wider track of the undercarriage and for the same reason it was much easier to land cross-wind. I had great fun learning to teach cross-wind landings on the Jackaroo. We had the freedom of our own airfield with its three long runways and all the grass with NO RADIO or any other form of control. Many were the sorties on which I would use all six runway directions plus more landing directions on the grass. At that time I never knew what a utopian situation this was compared to today's over-regulated airspace and congested aerodromes, in the UK at least.

Not a lot else happened in December; it's the weather and the festivities, you know. Not so much dancing through sun-split clouds as creeping through the murk around the circuit, under a low and leaden ceiling, and the only laughter-silvered wings were on the fairies round the Xmas tree (apologies to John Gillespie Magee Junior and 'High Flight'). There would have been another movement but fate intervened. Having just authorised its pilot for a short local flight, I watched from my window in the white control tower as the prototype Jackaroo G-AOEX taxied away across the grass to the holding point for runway 27 on the far-off eastern perimeter.

Looking up some time later I was surprised to see that the Jackaroo had not yet departed, indeed it had turned away from the holding point and was taxying very slowly back up the hill towards the control tower. I knew the pilot well enough and I went out across the grass to meet him. If he had a problem, I guessed it would be imaginary, he was that sort of individual. I would not have recognised the white-faced aviator who climbed out from the Jackaroo's cockpit and staggered towards me.

"The stick's broken," croaked the day's luckiest pilot.

"What do you mean?" I asked.

"The stick," he repeated, "it's broken off!"

I looked with disbelief into the cockpit. Sure enough the front joystick was lying at a weird angle, held only by the leather gaiter at its waist. I clambered onto the wing and bent into the cockpit, where on undoing the gaiter, the joystick fell onto the floor. A obvious fatigue fracture of the cylindrical lower part of the joystick had occurred.

Due to the aft C. of G. problem a solo pilot in the Jackaroo sat in the front, reversing the situation to the original Tiger Moth which was flown solo from the *rear* cockpit. It was of course possible to turn round in your seat and grasp the rear control stick by reaching over the seat back,

271

but . . .! I leave you to ponder on the probable outcome should this stick have failed only seconds later, when airborne, with a SOLO pilot.

As I climbed to the office of the Managing Director upstairs in the white control tower I could see the headlines (in the aviation press at least): "ALL TIGER MOTHS GROUNDED"!

The MD was annoyed at being interrupted when with an important new client and he did not seem at all surprised or concerned, merely telling me to get an engineer to fit a new stick. There must be more to this than meets the eye, I mused, and it transpired that, after the first attempt to give the required aft stick movement by bending it forwards and upwards had been abandoned as unsatisfactory, the miserly motives of the Managing Director were revealed when he told them not to throw away the bent joystick but to "weld it straight again"! No wonder it subsequently failed.

On another day I was walking between the instructors' hut and the control tower, watching a Tiger Moth approaching to land on the grass far away at the eastern end of the field. It was approaching quite steeply, very steeply . . . The Tiger hit the ground very hard, bounced high in the air, the nose dropped, and it plunged straight into the ground. Flames burst out immediately. I was but a few yards from the fire truck, which distance I covered in no measurable time; the engine fired on the first few turns of the huge starting handle and several others who had witnessed the crash flung themselves on board as I drove the heavy truck straight out across the perimeter track and gathered speed downhill on the grass.

Fast as I was, my instructor John was faster. He emerged from a window in the office, upstairs in the white control tower, swung over the balcony rail and dropped to the ground below. His Austin Somerset passed the fire truck halfway across the airfield and when we reached the blazing Tiger he was already lifting the pilot out. We put the fire out with foam and had to consult the bookings sheet to identify the Tiger for there was no fabric left when we got to it, and the metal was too hot to find the registration plate. It was the last flight of the Tiger G-ANYX, but as I recall the pilot was not badly hurt, another instance of the ability of the Tiger to protect its pilot in a crash. This pilot had only made his first solo the previous week and should therefore have had a dual check this day.

Due to this lack of supervision Arthur the Chief Flying Instructor was told he would suffer some loss of pay, which he did not accept; he left, later to become the Chief Experimental Pilot for a crop-spraying company. He took off one foggy day some months later from an aerodrome on the Isle of Wight in a Miles Falcon Six, never to be seen again. One wooden wing from G-AECC was washed up later, somewhere in the Solent.

I was now considered to be experienced enough to take part in the Army Co-op flying for which, in addition to the Miles Falcon Six, the Wiltshire School of Flying had a fleet of seven Percival Proctors of various marks. I was first checked out in the dual-controlled Mark V G-AHBH, followed by a trip in G-AKZN (now resident in the RAF Museum at Hendon as Z7197 and incorrectly placarded 'G-AKNZ'), a Proctor III with another instructor, Jim. I cannot remember many details of the sortie which was over the Isle of Wight but equally I cannot forget the return flight.

The exercise, whatsoever it was, complete, Jim turned for home and let down to fly low over the waters of the Solent. One of Her Majesty's ships was returning to port. In the traditional manner the crew were standing atop the vessel in a line, in dress uniform. We passed very close and very low alongside and as we looked UP at the Captain on the bridge, he saluted as we passed his ship . . . it was a submarine!

In the following six months I subsequently flew many sorties solo in the Proctors G-AKWP, G-ANWA, G-ANWD, G-ANYP and G-ANYU. Other aircraft of interest that I flew during those halcyon days at Thruxton included Tiger Moths G-ACEZ, G-ALSH, G-AMBI, G-ANYX and G-ANFY (also when rebuilt later after a crash as a Jackaroo); and last, but not least, the delightful Dart Kitten G-AMJP.

The technical drawings of the Jackaroo complete and the instructor's rating stamped on my licence, the Isle of Wight and the West Country coast from Dorset to Bishop's Rock became my particular playground in the Jackaroo. Memorable flights were many; below the cliff tops we flew, and along the Chesil Beach, above the still water on its landward side often below the top of the sandbar . . . everybody waved in those days. Do not try it today, the penalty now is too severe to contemplate.

On reflection, the infectious happy-go-lucky atmosphere we enjoyed could easily lead to undisciplined behaviour and/or disregard of the rules and/or common sense which as we all know is undesirable in the world of aviation. Indeed there were several fatal accidents not long after the events described here, the causes of which could have had origins in a particular attitude to low-flying activities as a common denominator. I knew the pilots concerned well, some of them were far from inexperienced.

When I look back to my year (only a year!) at Thruxton, ever-mounting clouds of disbelief obscure the truth to discredit memory alone. Each and every month seemed to offer yet more and more excitement, not always sought after or indeed desirable, but nevertheless unforgettable. That I could have experienced so many significant events in such a short time would suggest that the fickle hand of fiction influenced my pen, were it not for my pilot's compulsory diary, the log-book.

Notwithstanding the above, the remarkably apt total of three hundred and sixty five sorties in my year, on the six Jackaroos (G-AOEX [68], G-AOIR [77], G-APAI [119], G-ANFY [44], G-AOIX [7] and G-APAJ [50]) decree that my unforgettable time at Thruxton can only be called "The Year of the Jackaroo."

CHAPTER 28

PROLOGUE AND EPILOGUE

by

John Pothecary

The fifties were an exciting time for me and lots of others concerned with light aeroplanes – and have been well recounted in the previous volumes. For my final contribution to this trilogy, I would first like to relate a prologue to the decade.

The dozen or so years before 1939 saw the growth of the Flying Club movement worldwide. Triggered by the emergence of Geoffrey de Havilland's Moth it was realized that the man in the street could at last afford to fly, a dream of many since the day of Icarus. The Director of Civil Aviation at the Air Ministry was Sir Sefton Brancker; his flying experience went back to the days of the Bristol School in 1910. Not content to run his department from Whitehall, he was present, complete with monocle, at the Light Aeroplane Trials at Lympne in 1923 and 1924, and it was at his instigation that subsidies were given to aero clubs near to large centres of population. This was a boost, albeit small, to the British Aircraft industry, which had to compete very hard for small orders from the Air Ministry.

De Havilland's were first in the field, followed by A.V. Roe's who had been converting their famous 504 trainer to a five-seater for pleasure-flying. Avro's rival to the Moth was their Avian. Phillips and Powis found a small market for the Hawk designs of the Miles family, and Robinson with his Redwing, at £100 more than a Moth, was but a minor player, as we shall see later.

In the latter part of the decade the first Piper Cubs were imported, and in 1939 Taylorcrafts were built under licence, bringing a significant impact to civil and military aviation for 30 years.

The average cost of flying was two pounds or less per hour, probably twice the current rate in real terms. As skies darkened in 1938 the Government produced their "Civil Air Guard" scheme. Suitable people could learn to fly for about £2 10s per hour and would be obliged to offer their services to the King in the event of hostilities. In the week before that event 210 pilots' 'A' licences were issued, and over 20,000 persons had become qualified civil pilots.

On the 1st of September private flying was banned and 81 flying clubs closed, with the majority of civil aeroplanes grounded. However our sorely-pressed Air Force needed all the help they could get, and in the following eighteen months 1,017 powered aircraft and 102 gliders were 'impressed' by the Ministry of Aircraft Production. Uses were varied; the

transport types went to National Air Communications, an internal, and –
until July 1940 – cross-channel air service. Fast private aircraft went to
communications flights. The club trainers continued their work in
uniform: for example, Bristol Flying Club Tiger Moths were sent to India.

Some Avro 504s found themselves towing gliders from High Post and
Christchurch on secret radar trials. Sadly many of the Gipsy Moths were
put to use as decoys on dummy airfields and just fell apart in the open
air. Others as a last resort were given to the Air Defence Cadet Corps
(later ATC), where many came to an ignominious end, although my
Comper Swift G-ABUU survived six years with the Newcastle Air
Training Corps.

For this the private owner was given £50 and a promise that he could
buy back something similar should the war be brought to a successful
conclusion. It was, and in 1945 thoughts turned again to private flying
and air taxi work. The larger 'airliner' market had been catered for by the
Brabazon Committee of 1943, which had proposed various specifications,
from "feeder liners" to the intercontinental Brabazon landplane and
Princess flying boat. But as for light aeroplanes, Percival was offering the
ultimate development of their prewar Vega Gull, the Proctor V – four
leather seats, folding wings, VP prop and 208 hp, but still wood and
fabric: expensive at £2,800. Miles were producing a civilianised
development of their 1943 AOP Messenger for not much less,
nevertheless with leather upholstery but inferior glueing. Taylorcraft
Aeroplanes, by now Auster Aircraft, were widely advertising the Mk. V
J/1 Autocrat for only £650.

Before these aeroplanes could be used the Air Ministry was offering
war-surplus aircraft back to those who lost their aeroplanes five years
earlier. The first postwar sale came up in December 1945. It was held in
one of the massive blister hangars at 5 MU Kemble. Included in the sale
were 3 Vega Gulls, 3 Hawks, 8 Taylorcrafts (including 'FTN, 'FUB, 'FUD,
'FVA and 'FZH), 2 Falcons, 2 Monarchs, 2 Envoys, Tipsy B.2 G-AGBM, 14
Moth Minors, Stinson Reliant G-AFVA, 3 Puss Moths, 3 Cygnets, the
Heston Phoenix, 4 Piper Cubs, Stinson Voyager G-AGZW, a Rapide and 3
Whitney Straights.

Eventually I worked on many of these ex-service aircraft and
remember a Miles Whitney Straight EM999. On stripping off layers of
camouflage we found the prewar owner's nameplate together with the
name he had given her, "Anky Sim," cut in aluminium letters and still
rivetted to the cowling.

The prewar owner had paid £50 to get his original aircraft back, but
at that time it was difficult to tie up prewar registrations with Service
serials, hence many acquired new registrations, e.g. G-AFVA became
G-AHAE, G-AFVD became G-AHBO and G-AFZH became G-AHEI.

When undergoing civilianization, it was almost impossible to remove evidence of the roundel and the only solution was to refabric that area. Another problem was gas warning paint. In early wartime days all aircraft carried a one-foot-square panel painted with a mixture that would change from green to yellow when contaminated by poison gas. It could never be painted over, so had to be removed. We even had a Taylorcraft in D-Day markings; G-AFVA was possibly the only prewar club aircraft to see service in France in 1944.

The 1st January 1946 saw the resumption of civil flying. Among flights taking place that day was a British South American Airways Lancastrian making the inaugural flight from the new airport at Heathrow and bound for Montevideo. On the lighter side Tiger Moth instruction started at Cambridge and the first air taxi flight was carried out by Hunting Air Travel with Proctor G-AGSX. A freight charter was flown from Cardiff to Filton in Auster V J/1 G AFWN. Flying clubs began work with their acquisitions from the surplus sales, together with a sprinkling of the new production machines available.

Bournemouth Flying Club at Christchurch had two Swallows and six Magisters; their Gipsy Moth G-AAHI had not been impressed but its fuselage had deteriorated beyond repair. The Wiltshire School of Flying at High Post had three Magisters, G-AHKP, 'IUA and 'IUB, and four Taylorcrafts G-AHKN, G-AHKO, G-AHAE and G-AHAF. The Royal Artillery Aero Club, also based at High Post, had G-AHUG and G-AHUH.

Sqdn. Ldr. James Doran Webb, owner of the Wiltshire School of Flying, decided on a new Autocrat, G-AGVP, as flagship for his fleet. A Salisbury garage, Anna Valley Motors, was agent for these machines. Spitfires had been built on their premises for the previous four years so they knew all about aeroplanes. They exhibited G-AGVP in their showrooms and it was this that inspired me to leave school and become an apprentice engineer, as RAF pilot recruiting was temporarily in abeyance.

JDW interviewed me and decided that I was a suitable candidate for apprenticeship. I would work weekends during the summer and on leaving school would be employed and paid the sum of 27/6d per week. This was in contrast to the prewar apprentices at High Post who had to pay a premium.

Ron Clear, the retired Airspeed and DH test pilot, was an early WSF apprentice, and Alan Grinter and Jim Stockdale from those days are still active in aviation locally.

When I started with the Wiltshire School of Flying I found a small hangar which had been Vickers' Flight shed; it contained Autocrat G-AGVP, 4 Taylorcrafts of the WSF, 2 Taylorcrafts of the RA Club, the "Maggie" G-AHKP and Cessna C.34 G-AFBY.

Enclosed in the hangar was the WSF office, and adjacent was the bar: "Dan" was the elderly barman. Bill Watts, an Australian, was an ex-WW I fitter and Chief Engineer, ably assisted by Ted Pepper, ex-20s-30s RAF with tales of DH.9s in Mesopotamia and the ghosts of Roman soldiers at nearby Old Sarum. My immediate superior was another local lad, recently ex-RAF, who ended his career as Head of AAIB at Farnborough – Geoffrey Feltham.

What an idyllic summer; I never left work until about 7 pm but was learning the hard way. I got dope in my eye whilst repairing the underside of a Taylorcraft and learned the explosive power of petrol when giving some encouragement to the hangar's boiler system. John Isaacs was flying our "Maggie"; neither of us understood the function of the ignition master switch and as a result the prop bit me, leaving scars I still carry.

Although flying was greatly reduced after the war almost every day produced some new excitement. Late-model Spitfires, Seafires, Spitefuls and Seafangs were still to be tested. Sea Otters and the Supermarine 322 variable-incidence machine were our neighbours.

The E.1/44 Attacker made its first flight from Boscombe Down towards the end of July. Situated as we were within 2 miles of Boscombe Down we witnessed many of their flights. Particularly impressive in early August was a low pass by the Tudor 2 G-AGSU. Perhaps it was on its return to Woodford where, after modification, it was destined to crash on August the 23rd, killing the designer Roy Chadwick and his senior test pilot Bill Thorn.

The CFI of the WSF was Ken Burt, ex-RAF of course, and he was assisted by "Bert" Hawkins, who had learned to fly with the Civil Air Guard whilst a bus driver with the Wilts & Dorset Bus Company. He became CFI at Thruxton and later joined me for a while at Christchurch, finally moving to the Royal Naval College Chipmunk flight at Plymouth until it closed. Also instructing were Wing Commander Pickford and Pat Shea-Simmonds, Vickers test pilots. On my days off I could put on my ATC uniform and go to RAF Old Sarum, to beg flights in their Ansons TX158 and TX184.

Many first solos took place that year and a delightful practice was that the lucky student bought a bottle of champagne to be consumed by the witnesses. A copy of the photograph required for the Royal Aero Club Aviators' Certificate was fixed to the bottle, which then graced the bar shelf.

The licence system was simple. The private pilot had an 'A' licence and the commercial pilot a 'B' licence. A navigator needed a First Class 'N' Certificate. To qualify for an 'A' licence a simple medical was required. Flying requirement was three hours solo and this could include the flying test; this was flown solo and comprised five figures-of-eight at 1,000 feet, followed by a climb to 2,000 feet and a glide landing to a designated spot on the airfield. There was no written exam but ten questions on Air Law were posed by a Royal Aero Club Observer. I suppose I am still valid as RAeC Observer No. 357.

By September 1939 approximately 24,000 licences had been issued – Lord Brabazon was pilot No. 1. The first two postwar years of civil flying saw another 3,500 licences issued. Flying meetings tended to be of a formal nature: 'Type Clubs' and 'Fly-Ins' were unknown.

To the detriment of new aircraft sales the Air Ministry continued to sell off war-surplus types. Wiltshire School of Flying purchased a further twelve Magisters which were in store at RAF Litchfield. Geoff and I were despatched to the care of the Sergeants' Mess at 51 MU at Litchfield, where in six weeks we assembled the twelve aircraft for Bert Hawkins to fly back to High Post. I travelled back in the last one, L8068, on the 15th December 1946 – my first introduction to open-cockpit powered flying.

Also at Litchfield at that time were a number of Miles Messengers awaiting disposal, including the third genuine ex-General Montgomery aircraft RH378. Oxfords by the hundred were on offer and, stored outside, the ex-coastal Fortresses and Liberators (lease-lend aircraft) were being broken up. Also present was the lone two-seat RAF Lockheed Lightning, still a subject of speculation.

Early 1947 saw the Wiltshire School of Flying move to Thruxton in the coldest winter this century. Footprints from the ghost of the Thunderbolt pilot who crashed near to the control tower were frequently plain to see in the snow. The weather affected aircraft production; glue would not set in the cold Miles factory; coal and fuel oil were rationed, as were bread, sweets and clothes. In the hangar at Thruxton we burned Horsa glider parts in 45-gallon drums in order to keep ourselves warm.

But 1947 brought a wonderful summer. 'Double Summer Time' meant flying up to 22.30 and exciting new types such as the Gemini and Newbury Eon made an appearance.

I learned to fly at the hands of Bert Hawkins and gained an 'A' licence. By now I was old enough to take the King's Shilling and was away to the delightful grass fields of Shellingford and Kelmscott in the lovely Vale of Uffington, where I was introduced to the Tiger Moth – not, I thought at the time, an easy transition from the Auster.

As we approached the fifties, club flying stabilized at an average figure of £3 per hour – in relation to average wages, higher than nowadays. Few aerodromes charged landing fees but MCA-controlled aerodromes such as Shoreham may have charged half a crown, i.e. 4% of the hourly rate: nowadays 15% is not unusual.

My story of the fifties was well covered in the previous volume. But as the decade ended so the Redwing came into my life. My partner in that venture was Ted Gould, whose provenance goes back to the Walsall Aero Club of 1937. In 1949 he brought Gipsy Moth G-AAWO out of semi-retirement in Scotland. Ted had heard about G-ABNX being stored in Frensham in 1959; she had been stored throughout the war, and a photo taken at Elstree in 1946 showed her very much dismantled. She was delivered by road to the College of Aeronautical Engineering at Redhill in April 1951 and was painted in a hideous blue and red colour scheme for the "50 Years of Flying Exhibition" at Croydon in 1952. There is evidence that unauthorised flight was made at about this time from Redhill, and at some time during this period 8" was broken from the tip of the propeller blade: this was carefully stuck back on and the break concealed with fabric. I discovered this much later when I first opened the throttle beyond 1,500 rpm; the tip came off and set up a terrific vibration. This was taking place on the lawn of my bungalow, much to the consternation of the neighbours. Three weeks later I found the tip 100 yards away.

However, I digress; 'NX went to Panshanger in the hands of V. Mitchell, and later to Frensham, from whence I rescued her. For a nominal sum she was mine, and arrived at Christchurch on the 18th December 1959; shortly afterwards I moved her to my garage at home, which had been designed to take a Tiger Moth-sized aeroplane. The engine at this time and for about five years previously had been in the hands of C. Humphries at Silverstone.

Airframe overhaul to full C. of A. standard was commenced: £1.10s for registration, £5 for C. of A. inspection fee, £5 for approval of mods etc. had to be paid out before we started. In the main the work consisted of removing corrosion, taking out sample bolts and cleaning off oil-based paint. One leading edge had to be renewed due to water soakage in storage. All flying wires were renewed by Bruntons and flexible pipes by Palmers. Since control cables were all straight runs with no fair leads or pulleys they only required reprotection. Generally, the internal structure, a ply box fuselage and box-spar mainplanes, was found to be in excellent condition, the inspector's stamp of 1931 being clearly visible in many places. Wing locking pins were renewed: the ARB wanted them made in S94 bar, which must, I am sure, be 10 times stronger than the original tube. Hugh Kendall was very helpful over this matter and he took the trouble to visit me and discuss this and many other airworthiness problems. An exhaust pipe had to be made with no patterns or original drawings to go by; I still suspect the collector ring's internal diameter is too small and is restricting rpm. Wiltshire School of Flying fitted stubs for their machines but nowadays we have our own noise abatement problems.

With the airframe almost complete attention was turned on the still-languishing engine. Due to oval cylinder bores and oversize little ends the engine could not be certified, but the PFA came to the rescue by increasing their AUW for a permit to include the Redwing at 1,500 lbs. Final assembly did not take very long. Mr S. Lane, managing director of Redwing Ltd, still at Croydon, helped with a rigging manual and, rather surprisingly, all the parts fitted together.

The manual contained a list of spares prices and it is interesting to compare 1932 prices with those I had to pay 30 years later:

Flying wires	new	£7.10s	I paid	£47
Interplane Strut Tube	new	£2	I paid	£5.10s
Wing Locking Pins	new	14/-	I paid	£7.14s

I also had to pay an additional £5 for design approval as no drawings existed. The exhaust pipe cost £24 against £8 new, and altogether the overhaul cost about £300 and took 800 hours of my time.

New, the machine cost £650, £660 with dual, rather more than the contemporary Moth! Surprisingly expensive extras were: compass £16, Turn and Slip Indicator £25.10s.

Two and a half years after first setting eyes on a Redwing the great day came. On the 3rd April 1962 I taxied beyond the end of the 1,600-yard runway at Christchurch and, tucking the tail well into the hedge and pointing the nose to the west, she was rapidly airborne, to my immense satisfaction and relief.

Whilst the Redwing saga was taking all my pocket money I still had to continue to earn a living. Summer 1960 saw plenty of activity in the flying club, and at Christchurch I was building up my Rapide time in charter flights, pleasure flights and parachute dropping.

I had been promised the first vacancy on Silver City's car ferry operation out of Bournemouth for the next season. But in the meanwhile I could not resist another winter in Sudan. With the help of a Piper Super Cub and a brand new Lycoming engine I was able to put in nearly 600 hours in four months. The most exciting moment of the season came when my windscreen disintegrated as a result of a bird strike, thus proving that a Cub will fly without a windscreen.

I returned to England at the end of January to find an offer from George Hogarth, the Chief Pilot of Silver City; I was to start on the 1st of February.

The technical exam on the Bristol Superfreighter required home study and the late mark Bristol Hercules engines were an improvement in power on those I had flown in the Viking and had worked on in Beaufighters and Halifaxes. Flying training consisted of six circuits and landings and one go-around; I was then a qualified co-pilot!

Just now I mentioned George Hogarth, a veteran of Silver City's earliest days in India. His deputy was New Zealander and ex-coastal Liberators Dick Besley; if one's landings were not of the best he would comment, as he removed his pipe from his mouth: "Pitch a little bumpy today!"

Of some of the other Captains, Brian Temple had been personal pilot to Winston Churchill. Charles Helliwell had recently returned from Silver City's oil exploration in Libya, when the fate of "Lady be Good" was discovered, as was the remains of a flight of three Blenheims. Derek Weetman joined from Aquila but left to fly one of the remaining Sandringham boats of RAI at Papeete in the Pacific Ocean, the last domain of big flying boat scheduled services.

A day's work at Silver City consisted of a respectable daylight start with three or four round trips carrying cars and freight between Bournemouth, Cherbourg and the Channel Islands, usually finishing somewhere 'in opening hours' for a drink on the way home. A great feature of the City was that first officers flew from the left-hand seat when it was their leg – hence hardly a need for command training when the time came. Silver City was brought into the BUA Group in 1962 along with Air Charter and Jersey Airlines; this opened a wonderful opportunity to convert to the DC-3. Training was the usual six circuits again from Hurn in G-AMYX and G-AMYV.

Later that year the Bournemouth base became responsible for the scheduled service between Hurn, Abingdon and Manchester for the Atomic Energy Authority. Dakotas in use at that time were G-AMZF, 'MZG, 'NTB, 'NTC, 'NTD, 'NEG and 'MYJ (still on the register with Air Atlantique). The worst weather this century taught me a healthy regard for icing and its effect on the DC-3 in particular.

On the lighter side at this time I managed to fly the Turbo Wot, a Currie Wot with a Rover gas turbine, and also to evaluate the Reid and Sigrist Desford now in East Fortune Museum.

Time to end my story! Flying clubs were discarding the Tigers and Austers and I had serious matters in hand such as my ATPL and subsequent first command on the Bristol Freighter.

To the present: now in my second retirement I hold the title of Chief Engineer at Old Sarum, and each day I walk over the spot where I first sat in a Hawker Audax 62 years ago. In addition to many modern aircraft, I frequently get to fly the Tigers and Austers of my earlier days.

Perhaps the most rewarding flight in recent years was in the DH Dragon G-AECZ that I worked on as an apprentice at Thruxton in the late forties – and indeed travelled in throughout Europe and the UK as "Flight Engineer," a polite euphemism for "prop swinger." She was eventually put on display in Dublin Airport to represent an example of

Aer Lingus' first equipment, and in 1996 I was invited by Aer Lingus to inspect the airframe and engines, and to advise on the airframe condition for continued airworthiness. This I very happily did, and as a reward I was allowed to fly her. With Aer Lingus top brass and restoration crew behind me, this was indeed a crowning satisfaction to a career in civil aviation.

CHAPTER 29

BY PEDAL POWER TO HORSE POWER
by
John Teasdale

Picture the scene. It is the summer of 1939, and the local team are enjoying their Saturday afternoon cricket match. Beyond the surrounding trees the sound of an approaching aircraft attracts the attention of players and spectators alike. Play stops and all eyes peer skywards as a large twin-engined aircraft flies directly overhead. No one had ever seen anything like it before. Eventually, I established that it was a Hampden, then only recently introduced into RAF service.

This event clearly had a significant impact on me, as I cannot recall seeing any aircraft prior to that time. Since then, however, I have never failed to look skyward whenever there was anything to be seen. Aircraft spotting, and the recording of sightings, must have been an unusual pastime prior to the second World War. The need to identify and record enemy aircraft sighted over UK airspace, however, led to the formation of the Royal Observer Corps and, additionally, numerous spotting posts were set up at factories, offices, and military locations to give immediate warning to their occupants of possible attack. There were three such posts in my home town of Stafford, and I was fortunate enough to have access to one of these, which was on the roof of the English Electric Company offices, where my father worked. From April 1942, I recorded my sightings in a similar way to the "professionals." I was twelve at the time, and must have felt quite grown-up listing aircraft by type, time, estimated height, direction and distance from the post. The expression "over post" remains for me part of the folk lore of the aviation enthusiast. My first log book carried the words "CONFEDENTIAL" (note spelling!) on the cover, in spite of the fact that its owner was a junior schoolboy using a purloined school book!

On numerous occasions, unknown types or modifications to familiar aircraft were sighted, and I produced sketches to illustrate these. One of the more notable was an aerial view of a single-engined aircraft, with a "greenhouse" cockpit and a yellow 'P' in a circle on the fuselage. This turned out to be the Fairey Firefly, but the space under the sketch reserved for the name remains unfilled to this day. On a later occasion, I did a drawing of the tail of a Wellington Mk. 11 in Training Command colours, which showed a bulbous extension in place of the rear gun turret, and from which "smoke" emanated. The accompanying note stated that the aircraft travelled faster than normal, and was assumed to be a smoke screen layer. Little did I know that I had seen one of the earliest jet engine testbed aircraft, which hailed from the Rolls Royce factory at Hucknall.

Most of us who grew up during the late 1930s and early 1940s must have had difficulties with identification, since there was so little reference material available. The increase in the number of types appearing during the war added to the problem. This made our hobby that much more challenging and the excitement of sighting the unknown remains with me to this day. The authorities, however, quickly realised that aircraft recognition was a matter of national importance for all, and so it was that I became a member of the newly-formed National Association of Spotters Clubs, and obtained my 1st, 2nd & 3rd class Recognition Certificates. This organisation was actively supported by the famous *"Aeroplane Spotter,"* published from January 1941 to July 1948.

The war years were an exceptionally exciting time from a young enthusiast's point of view. Seeing several hundred aircraft in a day is something unlikely to be experienced again, unless of course you happen to live next to an international airport. In 1943, I obtained an old bicycle which enabled me to visit the local airfields, and by the following year round trips of up to fifty miles were accomplished. I discovered airfields full of a great variety of aircraft types, including such rarities as Venturas, Turbinlite Havocs, and even a Brewster Bermuda.

When hostilities ceased in Europe, the number of aircraft seen in the air reduced dramatically. This was quickly forgotten as civil aviation rapidly expanded, and a whole new spotting experience presented itself. I resolved to venture further afield, and saved up for a brand-new Raleigh Superb cycle which, I subsequently discovered, was about the heaviest machine on the road! Undeterred, I exceeded twenty thousand miles on that bike, a good proportion of which involved visits to airfields. Having joined the Youth Hostel Association, overnight stops were possible when no relations were available on whom I could impose myself.

In the summer of 1947 I embarked on a tour of the airfields around London. This must have been prompted by the belief that all aviation venues in the Midlands had been fully explored. The challenge of a long-distance tour to unfamiliar airfields was an exciting prospect. An aunt of mine lived within two miles of Cambridge Airport, and the 120-mile ride seemed possible within a day. About halfway was Sywell, so what better place to stop for lunch? I was rarely refused access to civil airfields, and Sywell was no exception. Brooklands Aviation were in residence, with their colourful red, black and silver scheme brightening up Tiger Moths G-ADIA, G-AHML, G-AHMN, Taylorcraft Model D G-AHCI and Proctor 3 G-AIKJ. Also present were Messenger 2A G-AIEK, Piper L-4H G-AIIH and Monarch DJ714 being returned to civilian use. The use of colour applied to aircraft was always of great interest to me and from the earliest days I recorded this information. This included the production of side-view drawings in full colour and these, together with aviation artwork executed more recently, make an interesting collection.

After I had recovered from the previous day's marathon, a few hours were spent at Marshalls. Their substantial fleet of pale blue and silver Tiger Moths showed up well, as did the University Aero Club Taylorcraft Plus Model D G-AIIU, also in Marshalls' colours. There was a Hornet Moth G-ADOT in silver and green, and Gemini G-AISO in two shades of blue. Other aircraft included a Dakota of Air Contractors, Reading, G-AIWD, later to join BEA's fleet of "Pionair" Dakotas. Perhaps the most interesting type was Mosquito PR.XVI G-AIRT, the first to be civilianised since the war ended. Various RAF aircraft were on the airfield, so things haven't changed that much at Cambridge in over fifty years! Incidentally, Airspeed Horsa PF696 sported a prototype 'P,' for what reason I never knew. During my two-day stay at Cambridge I had a look at Meteor 4 RA418 where it had force-landed in a field near the airport. I also checked out Waterbeach, Oakington, and Duxford, but apart from a Meteor and some Yorks, I drew a blank – confirmation that I was right to turn my attention to civil aviation.

I then set out for Finchley, where I had an aunt and uncle, who were willing to provide me with bed and breakfast during my stay in London. In the four days that followed, I averaged around sixty miles a day and visited eight airfields. Northolt headed the list, where I enjoyed my first taste of foreign airlines. Besides eight Dakotas and three Vikings of BEA, the Scandinavians were represented by a Danish Viking OY-DLE, Norwegian Dakota LN-IAH and Swedish Skymaster SE-BBG. Swissair Dakota HB-IRA, Skymaster HB-ILE, Czech Dakota OK-WCR and Aer Lingus Dakota EI-ACT were also present. In retrospect, probably more interesting were two other Dakotas: one was RAF KJ874, coded YS-F (BBMF fans will recognise that squadron code) and the other was G-AHLY which was noted as having a dull pale blue fuselage graduated to dirty pink above. The letters UNRRA in red made clear its intended use.

During my visit to Northolt, I renewed my acquaintance with a fellow enthusiast who I had recently met at an air display, where he was accompanied by E.J. Riding. Known in the aeronautical press as L.T. Mason, he wrote in the *"Aeroplane Spotter"* what was probably the first article to describe the history and need for the Civil Aircraft Register. Having revealed in the article that he had been actively interested in aviation and the recording of aircraft for twenty-five years, he must surely be credited as being one of the original enthusiasts, if not having invented the pastime! As a result of our discussion, I attended a meeting somewhere in London (I cannot recall the exact location), when the possible formation of an organisation to cater for the interests and aspirations of the spotting fraternity was discussed. I suspect that the seeds of the Air-Britain organisation may have been sown on that occasion.

After seeing the heavy metal at Northolt, I chose to head north to Elstree for some smaller fare. The airfield was clearly an interesting and active venue, as confirmed by my records. Apart from the usual Austers, Proctors and Tiger Moths, other types included Aeronca C-3 G-AESP in silver and blue, Piper L-4Hs NC79819 and G-AJBE, Argus NC74315, Consul G-AIKP named "Silver Lady" and painted accordingly, Falcon Six G-AECC and the remains of BA Swallow G-AEOW. At opposite ends of the size scale were Martlet G-AAYX (illustrated in *"More Tails of the Fifties"*) in light blue and cream and Halifax Mk. 8 G-AHZM in blue and white. I returned well-satisfied to my hosts in Finchley after an eventful first day.

Next morning I set off for the embryo London Airport at Heathrow. I was pleased to find a visitors' enclosure provided, even in those early days. Admittedly it merely consisted of a roped-off area with odd seats scattered about, but during its existence it provided close views of some significant events in the history of commercial aviation. During my visit, I was delighted to see passengers emerging from Pan American Gold Plate Constellation NC86520 "Clipper America," following its trans-atlantic flight from the United States. BOAC was represented by the Yorks G-AGNB, G-AGNF, G-AGSN and Halton G-AHDX "Folkestone." British South American Airways produced Lancastrian G-AGWH and York G-AHFH "Star Glitter." Also there were South African Airways York ZS-BTT and Air France and Sabena Dakotas; the latter was OO-AWH, which was lost the following year.

There was always the temptation at any airfield to stay a little bit longer in the hope of seeing something even more exciting, but I had to depart if I was to make the two further visits I had planned for the day. The first of these was Heston which, unbeknown to me, was to close four months later after a comparatively short but historically significant existence. Present on that day were eleven Mk. 4 Fireflies in the VG970-980 range. With Fairey Aviation Stinson Reliant G-AFVT was Rapide G-AHJS: both were in silver and blue schemes. The most significant aircraft, however, was Fairey's communications and photographic mount, Fulmar G-AIBE, the only one of its type to appear on the British Civil Register. Its presence was entirely appropriate, parked as it was in silent tribute to Sidney Cotton and his work at Heston in the early war years on the development of photographic reconnaissance. This aircraft is now at the FAA Museum at Yeovilton.

My final visit was to Hanworth Air Park; clearly having seen better days, it too was about to pass into history. There was an air of solitude, even mystery, about the place. With only a few aircraft visible, I noted Anson G-AIRX, Rapides G-AHLU and G-AIWZ of North Sea Air Transport in the company scheme of chocolate and cream, Messenger G-AGPX and a Piper Cub Coupé G-AFTC.

The fact that the Comper Aircraft Co. was based at Hanworth before the war reminded me that twelve months earlier a cousin of mine from Spalding had shown me his aircraft, which was stored in a shed at the rear of his parents' house. It was the Comper Swift G-ABUU, painted at that time in cream with blue lettering. Not until recently did I discover that it still exists, although it will not be so easy to see now that it resides at the Cuatro Vientos Military Airfield Museum near Madrid. My cousin subsequently sold the Swift and purchased another rarity, the GAL Cygnet G-AFVR. In August 1969 he and his son, who was then in the RAF flying Dominies, were coming home in this aircraft from a rally in Geneva when they tragically lost their lives, as a result of a crash following engine failure. By coincidence, both aircraft were illustrated in Ian Allan's *"Civil Aircraft Markings 1966."*

Full of energy and with the weather holding, I set out the next day for Croydon and Gatwick. The direct route from Finchley seemed to me to be through the centre of London, and my records show that I went via Hyde Park. Even in those days there was a lot of traffic, and looking back, I wondered why the prospect of such a journey had held no fear for me. That was until I remembered my previous experience of cycling to school during the last years of the war. At that time, the English Electric Company were manufacturing Cromwell and Covenanter tanks, and these were taken out onto Cannock Chase for testing. Any cyclist who had been regularly overtaken by tanks on an ordinary main road with a long hill and canal and river bridges at the bottom had no fear of London traffic!

Croydon in the summer of 1947 was a hive of industry. Aircraft were seemingly occupying every available space but for the first and only time during my London visit, I was unable to view the main apron. It transpired that permission was required to gain access, and after an interview with uniformed officials, I was issued with a pass giving the necessary authority. I subsequently logged nearly sixty aircraft, and there must have been many more present in and around the hangars. There were five BOAC Yorks, two Lancastrians and four Dakotas, one BEA Dakota and two Rapides, three KLM Dakotas and two Rapides. Two Dakotas, ZS-AYK and ZS-AVM, were owned by PAAC Ltd, which was presumably the same company referred to as Peacock Private Air Charter on DH.86B Express G-AJNB. A second Express was registered SU-ACR.

No less than eleven Charter and Taxi companies were represented by a total of fourteen Consuls, nine Rapides and five Proctors. Individual aircraft of interest were a Lodestar ZS-BAJ, Dove G-AJBI of Hunting Air Travel, Goeland F-BCCB and two Leopard Moths G-ACLL and G-AIYS.

I had planned to cycle from Croydon to Gatwick, but time was running short and the hot humid air was accompanied by a gathering thunderstorm to the south. I did the unforgivable, and caught a Southern Electric train. In minutes, I was paying my one and only visit to the Gatwick Beehive and enjoying the sight of an exciting variety of aircraft. There were seven each of the expected Consuls and Proctors and no less than seventeen other types. The latter included two UNRRA Dakotas (G-AHLX and G-AHLZ), two DH.86Bs (G-ADUH and G-ADVJ) of Bond Air Services, Lodestar CF-TCM, Expeditor NC51830, Whitney Straight G-AERV, Argus G-AJPI, Benes Mraz Bibi G-AGSR, Q.6 Petrel G-AFIX, Beech D.17Ss G-AIHZ and G-AJJE, and Hornet Moth G-ADND. The Ministry of Civil Aviation had enough aircraft to run a sizeable airline of their own and the familiar colour scheme of black and silver appeared on four Avro XIXs, a Proctor, Auster V and two Tiger Moths. Two Geminis, including G-AIRS from Southend, were present as was Halifax G-AIOI of Bond Air Services together with Wayfarer G-AHJD, named "Pegasus" and operated by Air Contractors. Having recorded a selection of types sufficient to satisfy the most demanding of enthusiasts, I retraced my steps to Croydon and cycled back to Finchley in the warm, sticky evening air, looking forward to a cold bath.

Cycling in the London area involved an increased amount of gear-changing, so it was perhaps not surprising that the following day I was "grounded" whilst a new three-speed was fitted. Back on the road, I set out for the last destination of my tour, White Waltham. Once again I enjoyed easy access to the airfield, which is so symptomatic of the relaxed informality associated with private flying. Here I found twenty-one types, of which five, including a Bristol Brigand, were RAF aircraft. The West London Aero Club was evident with three Moth Minors (including G-AFNI), Taylorcraft Plus D G-AHXF and Tiger Moth G-AIRJ. Miss Naylor's Puss Moth G-ABYP was the oldest aircraft I came across, followed by Hornet Moth G-AEKY of the WLAC and Falcon Six G-ADTD, all of prewar origin. A rare Cierva Autogiro was present in the shape of G-AIOC. One of two Arguses included G-AIYO, operated by the National Association of Training Corps for Girls, and the Miles M.28 G-AHAA was also seen. Two Piper Cubs of the American Flying Club were appropriately registered NC79800 and NC79819.

Returning to Finchley via Maidenhead and Denham, where I took the wrong road and missed the airfield, I contrived to pass Northolt again. Lancastrian G-AHCC "Sky Chieftain" of Skyways and Halifax G-AIWL of

London Aero and Motor Services were present on this occasion, together with an RAF Mitchell and a USAF B-17 Fortress. It would seem that Northolt has enjoyed the patronage of interesting military aircraft for over half a century. My tour of London airfields was over, and I returned to Finchley before leaving for home the following day. It had taken nine days and over five hundred miles of pedalling. Looking back, I am surprised that the experience did not satisfy my enthusiasm for expending energy. In fact, it merely served as a test run for many future excursions.

It had never occurred to me that I might, as a result of my obvious interest in aviation, be offered a flight whilst on an airfield visit. Thus it happened that at Wolverhampton, I was taken up for my first flight by the thoughtful and generous owner of Autocrat G-AGYJ. On the second occasion, I was at Staverton admiring Cessna Airmaster G-AEAI and Cygnet G-AGBN when I was invited, for a small charge, to go aloft in "Dinah," Tiger Moth G-ADIH of the Gloucester Flying Club. Although my worldly wealth was only seven shillings and sixpence, that was enough to get me airborne and a magnificent twenty-minute flight followed, which offered wonderful views over the Severn estuary to the Welsh hills beyond. I can understand all those who over the last fifty years have derived so much pleasure from the Tiger Moth experience. Further flights followed in the fifties and early sixties which included trips in Dakotas, Heralds, Viscounts, and a Heron of Jersey Airlines. One such occasion was from Birmingham to Gatwick in Dakota G-ANEG of Don Everall Aviation, which was specially chartered for a visit to Crawley New Town.

I should at this point explain that instead of seeking a career in aviation I was encouraged, as a result of my ability to draw, to become an architect. Inevitably, my interest in aircraft gradually took second place to my commitment to architecture. Nevertheless, I still found time for cycling trips and airfield visits. During one of these, I attempted to take a photograph of the prototype Westland Wyvern TS375 as it taxied round the perimeter track at Merryfield in Somerset. The pilot, who may well have been Harald Penrose, brought the aircraft to a halt and signalled his disapproval – the net result, only a memory of the occasion. I recall a tour of Southern England, which included a visit to Southampton, where I was invited to view the interior of Sandringham 5 G-AHZE at the BOAC Marine Terminal. A member of the crew offered me a water melon but unfortunately my inability to carry extra items on a touring bicycle meant that I had to reluctantly decline.

My National Service was spent at the Royal Engineers HQ Gillingham, Kent, and in 1953 I cycled over to West Malling for their Battle of Britain display. I well recall a spirited performance by a

Vampire after which, instead of landing, it was held off in the distance by the pilot whilst the final items on the programme took place. As the public were departing, he made a low approach to the airfield and completed a perfect wheels-up landing beside the runway. No one had witnessed the most dramatic and well-executed display of airmanship that day.

Three air displays stand out in my mind. The Derby Corporation and Aero Club at Burnaston staged an International Air Display attended by some one hundred and forty aircraft. There were a number of foreign visitors, including an early Nord Noralpha F-BBJM, KZ.III Larks OY-SAI and OY-DKU, Electra OO-AFA, Cessna 120 HB-CAA and Hillson Praga Babies OK-BGA and OK-BGB. Ranald Porteous gave stunning performances in Sparrowhawk G-AGDL and Chilton G-AFSV. Rolls Royce produced their latest jet engines in the shape of a Nene-powered Vampire, TG280, and the Nene-Lancastrian, VH742, together with the world's first turbine-propeller aircraft, Trent-Meteor EE227. In fact, just about everything was on show, from the Blériot monoplane to the Meteor IV. At a display at Brough in Yorkshire, Blackburn B.2 G-AEBJ contrasted with some newer products in the shape of seven Firebrand TB.Mk. 5s from 813 Sqdn. Anthorn, a Mk. 5A EK769 fitted with power-boosted ailerons and the two prototype Firecrests RT651 and VF172. In the same year Wolverhampton Aero Club hosted a well-attended event which included Avro Avian G-ACKE, Hawk Speed Six G-ADGP, Aeronca G-AEXD, Cessna Airmaster G-AFBY and Monarchs G-AFCR and G-AFLW. The show was most notable, however, for the appearance of the Goodyear Duck NC5506M demonstrating how to taxi sideways and Ben Gunn flying the prototype Balliol VL892 round the airfield perimeter in a continuous low-level outside vertical bank.

A couple of events worthy of mention occurred much closer to home. I returned from work one day to discover a shiny aluminium-clad helicopter in the field at the back of the house. It was G-AMWG "Sir Gawain," one of BEA's two King Arthur-class Bristol 171 helicopters; I never did discover the purpose of its visit. In the late fifties, Boulton Paul Aircraft Ltd reactivated the disused airfield at Seighford for modification and experimental work on Canberras and a few Lightnings. The Company Oxford G-AHTW operated the taxi service to Wolverhampton but my main interest centred on the presence of the Tay-Viscount VX217. A photograph of this aircraft at Seighford appears in David Smith's book "Action Stations 3."

Battle of Britain displays usually attracted a few civil-registered aircraft. At Ternhill in 1956, Dragons G-ACIT and G-ADDI of the Air Navigation and Trading Co. provided the usual pleasure flights. There were at least seven civil aircraft at Gaydon for the 1959 event; they included the Rolls Royce Spitfire G-ALGT, Hurricane 2C G-AMAU piloted by Bill Bedford and Argosy prototype G-APRN. At the same venue the following year, Ken Wallis demonstrated his Gyrocopter G-APUD and Dart Herald G-APWD was present. Being the "V" bomber training base, it was perhaps not surprising to be treated to an early formation trio of Valiant, Victor and Vulcan.

Thirty-five years followed, during which a combination of career and family commitments kept my latent interest in aviation at bay. Since retirement, however, I have had the opportunity to seriously look to the skies once more. For the last nine years, I have filmed the West Midlands PFA Annual Fly-In at Tatenhill. It has given me much pleasure to record the great variety of light aircraft and their enthusiastic owners who regularly attend this event. This is especially so in the case of those who continue to operate aircraft that were flying in the fifties.

I also have another hobby involving flight. My interest in ornithology has led me to explore the possibilities of filming birds through the lens of a telescope; the results are astonishing! Extending this principle to filming high-flying aircraft enables me to obtain a visual record of the many planes that can be seen from my own garden. So once again I am spotting aircraft, as many of us used to, over half a century ago. This time however, the sightings are on video tape. The technique involves an image magnified around two hundred times; just how this is achieved, and just what interesting aircraft I have filmed as a result, is another story.

CHAPTER 30

I LEARNED A LOT AT AUSTERS

by

Ronald "Dickie" Bird

I joined Taylorcraft Aeroplanes (England) Ltd (subsequently Auster Aircraft) as Senior Stressman and Aerodynamicist in 1943. I later became Assistant Chief Designer and then Chief Designer in 1947.

During this period I was involved in a constantly-changing series of Auster versions, different engines, different configurations and changes affecting the handling characteristics. To reduce the time involved, I decided that when the changes involved flight tests of a technical nature I would be the Technical Observer.

There was one test I have never forgotten. We had some unusual engine installation features and for one purpose had to have an unusual test instrument. It was an American one and the only one available was in the care of the Napier Engine Company at Luton Aerodrome. We borrowed the instrument and had almost completed the tests when one morning I had a phone call from Napiers to say they must have the instrument returned that afternoon.

I found our test pilot, Geoffrey Edwards, and since there was one more flight to be made we decided to do it on the way to Luton after lunch at Rearsby in the works canteen. I finished lunch first and told Geoffrey that I would go to my office to collect the Test Schedule and the flight maps.

He looked at me and said: "Maps? To go to Luton? We don't need maps. We don't even need a compass!"

I returned to the Auster with my Test Schedule and got on board. The compass on that aircraft was an overhead type, viewed via a mirror hinged underneath it. Geoffrey closed the mirror and locked it.

The test involved a flight at cruising speed for about half an hour at an altitude of 3,000 feet. The cloud base was at about 4,000 feet and the cloud was solid. Not a bright spot anywhere. Anyway, we took off from Rearsby and all went well with the test run, finishing about 10 minutes from Luton.

As we landed there, Geoffrey said: "There you are. I told you we didn't need maps."

"True," I said, "but I see how it was done. At 3,000 feet I could see ahead to Market Harborough, Kettering, Bedford and Luton."

"If you think that's the way it's done," said Geoffrey, "when Napiers have removed the test instrument we'll go back a different way."

Luton aerodrome is on high ground near the edge of the town. When we took off we climbed only about ten feet high, just enough to clear the top of a small hedge at the aerodrome boundary. From there we went down the slope, over hedges, under telephone cables, around haystacks and farmhouses, and in and out among trees. Eventually we came to a long grass-covered steep slope ahead of us. Geoffrey opened up to full throttle to climb up and, as we reached the top, he pulled back the control column and closed the throttle. The Auster did a gentle stall and as the nose dropped, there was Rearsby aerodrome.

After we landed I asked Geoffrey how on earth he did that. He said that before the war he was in the Air Force Reserve. His Commanding Officer used to say that they had learned to fly at the tax-payers' expense and whilst they were enjoying their weekend trips they should remember that they were in the Air Force to defend the country in time of need.

"If we were at war," said the officer, "who would your enemy be? It would not be the Americans and, even if it was, they could not fly bombers across the Atlantic to attack us. Your enemy would be in Europe and would have to fly over the eastern half of England and particularly over East Anglia. Imagine if you are returning from a raid in Europe or had been fighting the enemy over England. You look at your fuel gauge and are almost out of petrol. You have only a few minutes to find an RAF airfield. I therefore want you to get to know every landmark over the area. Remember every railway line, every level crossing, every road junction and patch of woodland in relation to those airfields."

Geoffrey then reminded me: "I am not the only one who remembers these things. About half a dozen others could."

I still wonder how Geoffrey could do all this at an altitude of about ten feet! He and I did a few other 'mapless and compassless' technical flight tests over large areas later on.

One of these tests was made on a hot sunny day when we flew from Rearsby up to the north of Nottingham. As we passed over Nottingham on the return Geoffrey suddenly reduced the throttle setting and began a gentle descent in a tight left-hand turn. Puzzled, I asked him what had happened. He pointed to the ground below and as we went down much further there in the middle of the lawn in the back garden of a very nice house, lying on her back on a sunbed, was a young naked lady. When she realised what was happening the horrified young lady leapt up, and with both hands covering the strategic parts of her body, dashed into the house.

Other things, not only sunbathers, attracted Geoffrey's attention. Returning with him one day from a technical test flight, he saw a sheep lying on its back in a small field. He took me to Rearsby, took off again, landed on the field and put the sheep safely on its feet, and then returned to discuss the result of our tests.

In the late 1940s and the early 1950s the Auster company was changing from a military market to a mainly commercial one. An encouraging situation to contemplate, but under the conditions of the time, a company producing small private aircraft had to overcome a lot of problems.

At Austers there was a good demand for civil types but to begin with the only ones available were cleaned-up military types. Some customers wanted the Austers with American Lycoming or Continental engines, but these had been supplied during the war under the American "Lend/Lease" arrangements and at that time we did not have the 'hard' currency to buy them for civil use.

To make matters worse a lot of the Auster aircraft which became available to us for conversion to civil standards had no engines. Engine manufacturers were mostly involved in jet engines and the large piston engines for airliners etc. Austers had to await the release of batches of small engines from military stocks. These were often not of the exact model and horsepower that we needed and some had seen a lot of hard work.

The desire to produce completely new models of Austers had to be put off for a long time as we could not be certain that we could obtain a sufficient number of engines to justify the considerable costs of designing and tooling such a project: hence the large number of postwar types which came into existence to use up each limited supply of ex-military engines we could find.

The first Auster to be built for the civilian market was the J/1 Autocrat. It was developed from military components and became quite popular. The first one was built in late 1946 and a total of 414 were sold by 1953.

Between 1951 and 1953 we designed and built 250 of the Model B.3 Pilotless Target Aircraft and during this same period were involved in design tasks to meet the constantly changing requirements for the aircraft which subsequently became the military Mark 9, of which eventually 166 were built.

Mention of the Mark 9 may cause some people, and in particular members of the Army Air Corps who flew them in Malaya, to complain about their rate of climb in hot climates. There were a number of reasons for this.

As the Army's requirements for the Mark 9 were being finalised we were told that the engine was to be the Cirrus Bombardier, and I was sent copies of the installation drawings and the power/rpm data. These showed a power of 180 bhp and were used to finalise the design of the aircraft. When construction of the prototype was under way the first engine was delivered and I was shocked to see that the test-bed data for that engine was only 168 bhp!

Urgent meetings with the manufacturers and the military personnel gained us an assurance that the minimum acceptable test-bed power would be increased, and indeed it was.

Later on, a change was made for the Bombardier to run on M.T. fuel, as used in the Army's trucks and other vehicles. This I regarded as very sensible when arranging fuel deliveries to isolated places, but it reduced the maximum power of the engine to 173 bhp. This caused a big reduction in the Mark 9's rate of climb in all conditions, but coupled with the fact that the engine was now a fuel-injection type, in which the fuel/air mixture ratio could not be adjusted to improve the power available at altitude, the Mark 9 itself was blamed for it.

About a year before the Mark 9 began to be manufactured we had a request from New Zealand to go there to watch their superphosphate top-dressing operations on grassland to see if we could produce an efficient aircraft for the task.

As we considered this trip it became apparent that interest was growing in other parts of the world in aircraft in which we could become involved. It was decided that I should go to New Zealand as part of a round-the-world trip. And what a trip that was!

The journey began in a Lockheed Constellation at Heathrow at 9.30 am on the 25th October 1953. We were heading for Geneva but shortly after take-off we were advised that the weather there was very bad and were diverted to Paris (Le Bourget). About three hours later we were cleared to go to Geneva where we arrived round about 5 pm and were rushed through the procedures to get us away to Beyrouth. We arrived there the following day just before four o'clock in the morning.

We were taken to a hotel in the centre of the town and there alongside the bed in my room was a refrigerated bar full of a wide variety of bottles of alcohol. I had never seen or heard of these bars before, but I found the contents very soothing.

On the way from Beyrouth to Karachi I was invited to occupy the co-pilot's seat as we flew over the Persian Gulf. I had not expected to find that at 20,000 feet we would be flying in conditions of severe icing. I flew up front again on the journey to Calcutta but the Captain did not need my help from Calcutta to Singapore.

On the 28th October we set off for Djakarta, capital of Indonesia, where we arrived about midday, after I had crossed the equator for the first time. On board we had dozens of Australian soldiers who came on at Singapore.

After about an hour we set off for Darwin but after about 90 minutes the number three engine failed over Java so we had to jettison 1,450 gallons of fuel and returned to Djakarta. There we had to wait until a new Wright Cyclone engine had been flown out from Singapore and installed.

During this time the civilian passengers were provided with overnight accommodation in a nearby hotel. It was quite late in the evening and I was told that I would have to share a two-single-bedded room with a guest already there. I was told to go to the room along the outside of the building and into a door from the verandah. When I went in there were two beds with mosquito nets over them. In the bed nearest the door I could see through the net the back of a naked lady with long blonde hair almost down to her waist.

I was surprised about this and returned to the reception desk to sort it out. I was asked if I had gone into the correct room because the person booked in was a man. The receptionist sent an assistant back with me. The naked lady behind the mosquito netting *was* a man. I had been misled by the length of his hair, the like of which I had never seen before.

Eventually we left Djakarta for the second time at about half-past-ten at night and set off for Darwin where I was invited by the captain to "sit up front" for the landing.

After refuelling we took off again to go to Sydney. After a couple of hours the new number three engine failed, so this time 1,200 gallons of fuel were jettisoned and we returned to Darwin. By this time I felt that the name of the aircraft should be changed from Lockheed "Constellation" to "Consternation"!

At Darwin all passengers had to remain on board the aircraft except to visit the toilets in a nearby hangar. Simple meals were sent to the passengers and the soldiers did their best to increase the profits of the beer-brewing industry.

After 8 hours on the ground with the new number three engine problems finally sorted out, we left Darwin a few minutes after midnight and arrived safely at Mascot airport in Sydney 7½ hours later.

After four days of discussions on aircraft matters I left Rose Bay, Sydney, in a Short Bros. Solent flying boat to Evans Bay at Wellington, New Zealand. I spent three weeks there with the people who had asked me to go and discuss with them – and their equivalent of the British Air Registration Board – the design requirements for a specialised top-dressing and crop-spraying aircraft. I flew in a de Havilland Tiger Moth to examine about 20 different top-dressing areas to be sure that I understood the problems. This visit to New Zealand led eventually to the design of the Auster model B.8 Agricola.

I left New Zealand on the 24th November 1953 and flew across to the USA, where I had about half-a-dozen business meetings, and returned to

England on the 3rd of December. This was a day later than planned because the Boeing Stratocruiser from New York was diverted to Goose Bay, Labrador, due to severe headwinds across the Atlantic.

The first Auster Mark 9 Air Observation Post aircraft for the Army Air Corps was completed early in 1954. My own first flight in it was with test pilot Ranald Porteous on the 16th April. Several changes of equipment for the Mark 9 were made to enable it to be used in different types of operation but this unfortunately slowed the work programme for the Model B.8 Agricola. This brought about the reduction of the number of aircraft on order, and this was largely due to the fact that the Americans virtually flooded the New Zealand market with top-dressing versions of other aircraft.

The first Agricolas were delivered to New Zealand in 1956. In early 1957 I was to make a number of business visits around the world, so, of course, New Zealand was included. I was booked on a British Overseas Airways Company flight travelling first-class in a Bristol Britannia, which was just going into airline service.

My trip started from London Airport on the 29th April. The departure was delayed for an hour or so due to problems in persuading one of the engines to start. I began to wonder if my being one of the passengers activated a non-cooperative attitude among airline engines! We eventually took off and flew to Zurich where, because of late arrival, all passengers were taken to lunch in the airport restaurant. Afterwards we were put on board the Britannia and were taxying towards the runway when the captain announced that we had a problem and were returning to the terminal building. One of the essential pieces of equipment in the cockpit had failed and a replacement had to be flown out from England, with technicians to install it. We were told that the captain was trying to find overnight accommodation in the vicinity.

Late in the evening I and the other male and the one young lady first-class passengers were taken to a small hotel in the centre of Zurich. At the entrance hall the receptionist called the name of a man, who went forward, was given his key and told how to get to his room. The next call was for "Mr and Mrs Bird." I could not believe the coincidence. The names were called again, but no response, so I went and said that my name was Bird. The receptionist pointed at the lady and said: "There is Mrs Bird." Of course it was not her name but the receptionist said that the list of passengers showed Mr and Mrs Bird and as they had no other accommodation that night, the lady and I must share that room.

There was look of panic on the lady's face and a lot of muttering among the men, when a few seconds later an aircraft stewardess came down the stairs near to us, quickly realised what was going on and said:

"If the lady would share the double bed with me, Mr Bird could use my single room." So she solved the problem.

Next morning with the aircraft again serviceable, we set off again in the Bristol Britannia and I eventually reached New Zealand for my second visit.

I was in New Zealand for 76 days, making dozens of visits to top-dressing airstrips over the length and breadth of the country. One of these was to a field used by the man who bought the first Agricola, where there was a surprise barbecue party for me, attended by employees and their families.

I had a number of meetings with the airworthiness authorities on the subject of possible higher-powered versions of the Agricola when the engines became available. One of my special memories of the visit is my two hours of flying in the Agricola in the special conditions in which it was designed to work. I then went to my business contacts in Honolulu, Vancouver, etc. and returned home on the 25th of July.

It had became more obvious to me during my time overseas that light aircraft customers were becoming more keen on the new American ones rather than the steel tube, fabric-covered ones still produced by the Auster company. Austers were also affected by the money they had invested in the Agricola and which they had not been able to recover.

I prepared a technical document on my ideas for an all-metal aircraft of simplified construction which would be inexpensive to produce, but I could not persuade the company to go ahead.

In 1959 I joined the re-organised Miles Aircraft Company at Shoreham-by-Sea as the Special Projects Design Division Manager.

One Saturday morning in December George Miles and I had a visit by Peter Masefield (now Sir Peter) who wanted us to design and build the prototype of a twin-engined executive aircraft – to be known as the Beagle B.206X. Sir Peter said it had to be completed and certified in time to take part in the Farnborough Air Show in September.

He pointed at me and said: "You are going to be Chief Designer. How many design-man-hours do you need?"

I told him I did not pluck figures like that out of the air, but if we could meet again the next Saturday I would give him the figure. It was 82,000 man-hours, because to design it in a mad rush it could not be done efficiently. When it flew, 186 days after I began the design work, it was 405 hours over the estimate! But everyone was pleased and HRH The Duke of Edinburgh came to Shoreham to congratulate us.

Incidentally, a year or so after this the New Zealand top-dressing industry pleaded for the Auster B.8 Agricola to be put into production again. I still have a copy of their official report.

299

CHAPTER 31

IF ALL ELSE FAILS,
THEN TAKE UP BALLOONING

A TALE DEDICATED TO THOSE WHO ENJOY BOTH THE FREEDOM
OF THE SKIES AND A HIGH LEVEL OF PERSONAL DISCOMFORT

by

Arthur W.J.G. Ord-Hume

(Ballonautic Veteran and Survivor)

[The author was one of the first to take part in the revival of hot-air balloning during the 1950s. With primitive and largely home-made equipment, he claims to have single-handedly invented a new experience which he terms 'ballonautically constructive boredom.' Outside those elitist occupations such as astronaut, only ballooning offers you long spasms of absolutely nothing to do separated by moments of high adventure and considerable risk to limb and sanity. With the opportunity to end each flight in a pride-threatening crash, ballooning makes ordinary aeroplanes seem a shade on the tame side – he says . . . – Ed.]

I balloon! And before we go any further, let me make it clear that I use the word "balloon" as a verb, meaning in its active form, and not as a noun. In other words, when I say "I balloon" I do not mean to imply that I *am* a balloon as in, for example, "I bear, you Goldilocks."

No, "I balloon," meaning that I sail aloft gracefully into the gentle heavens in a bag full of hot air.

At least, I used to.

My introduction to the agonies of ballooning came about purely by chance. It happened when I realised that I had to prove myself by doing something to show that I could be as mad as the next chap. You see, as one of the founder-members of that most prestigious of immediate post-war luncheon clubs, SPUI (the Society for the Propagation of Useless Information), it was expected of me that I should get involved in some sort of Cracking Good Wheeze sooner or later. And, as the annual membership fees were waived for those Members who had proved their prowess at something original, the time of the year indicated that if I was to save my six guineas my Cunning Plan had better be demonstrated now rather than the other.

We were a whole group of youthful flyers and budding aviators. Comprising mostly ex-Royal Air Force wallahs and hence accustomed to terminal lunacy, we viewed life as a challenge. Part of that challenge was

TOP: A very rare visitor to Britain, a Martin Mariner of the Dutch Navy, seen at Blackbushe on the 4th September 1957. Photo: Peter Amos.
BOTTOM: The Dove G-AIWF (as in the title of Peter Amos' story), seen here in Dan-Air colours on the 18th April 1960.
Photo: Edwin Shackleton.

TOP: Two DH.86B Expresses (G-AJNB is in the foreground), seen at Croydon in the late forties.
BOTTOM: G-AIRT, the first Mosquito to be civilianised after the war, seen at Cambridge with John Teasdale's bicycle propping it up!
Photos: John Teasdale.

TOP: Ginger Bedggood preflights the Jackaroo G-APAI at St. Mary's, Scilly Isles, on the 8th April 1958. Photo: via Ginger Bedggood.
BOTTOM: Ginger flew the Zaunkoenig G-ALUA only once, at Fairoaks on the 13th July 1969; his seven-minute flight ended with his eighth engine failure! Photo: Ginger Bedggood.

TOP: By the flight test hangar at Christchurch in the early fifties: Ron Clear's Comper Swift G-ACTF is dwarfed by an Airspeed Ambassador. On summer days Clear used to entertain the Airspeed workforce at lunchtimes with spirited displays. Photo: courtesy of British Aerospace, via John de Uphaugh.
BOTTOM: Mamba-Marathon VX231 on the DH Propeller Co's apron at Hatfield, 1952. This was the third British type to be fitted with propeller turbines, and the first with reversible-pitch propellers.
Photo: John de Uphaugh.

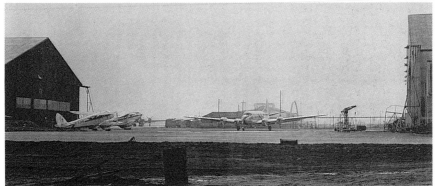

SCOTTISH SCENERY:
TOP: C-74 Globemaster 1 & C-124 Globemaster 2 at Prestwick, 1954.
MIDDLE: BEA's newly-delivered Heron G-ANXA (c.1954) with two of their Rapides (including G-AJXB).
BOTTOM: USAF F-86F Sabres seen at Prestwick during the mid-fifties. The 'palace' in the background, then Scottish Aviation Ltd's premises, was actually "The Palace of Engineering" at the 1938 Glasgow Empire Exhibition.
Photos: Dugald Cameron.

MORE SCOTTISH SCENERY:
TOP: The dump at Abbotsinch in 1958 contained Sea Mosquitoes and Avengers.
MIDDLE: PAA Stratocruiser N1036V at Prestwick in 1954.
BOTTOM: N711PA, one of the first Boeing 707-120s to visit Prestwick; this was in 1958.
Photos: Dugald Cameron.

to fly in the most unlikely – and cheapest – way possible. And to blazes with Red Tape!

I was already a member of the Kronfeld Club (housed in the basement of 74 Eccleston Square behind Victoria Station in London), so I knew all about gliding: I had taught Air Training Corps cadets to glide and what nobler challenge may the skies have than that! One learned that air was soft, earth was hard and the life expectancy of one of the primitive A-frame gliders was about half a dozen flights. It became too predictable and therefore boring!

It was back in the early 1950s when hot-air ballooning underwent its rebirth that, in company with several other lunatics, I began ballooning in the Chiltern Hills. After several ascents (and almost an equal number of descents), I considered that I had proved my point, saved my six guineas to SPUI – and went on flying powered aircraft. As amateur designer and builder of small aeroplanes, this seemed a more reliable means of flight. What was more, you could go places in an aeroplane with a fair degree of safety and a lot more certainty.

And then, just as I thought it was safe to fly, a friend built himself a balloon from Government Surplus bits and pieces, the key element being a large gas-burner ring. My friend insisted on ballooning at Cowes while other and more sober sporting types used the venue as a place to launch themselves onto the water in wooden boats.

Ballooning on the Isle of Wight became the pastime of several of us one fine summer. There was one drawback about that venue: the Isle of Wight is an island. As observations go, I'll grant that it's a bit basic, but what it meant was that once you were up you were conscious of the fact that all around was water and the Island tended to look precious small when you are in a basket at 1,500 feet scudding along at an impressive Mach 0.002.

After one evening when we narrowly avoided missing the Island altogether, and made landfall (*landfall*, indeed!) on the beach at Brighstone, from whose shingle we had to carry the balloon and oversized cat-basket along with miles of ever-more-knotted rope some vast uphill distance to the nearest place where a car could reach us, I gave up ballooning. This was, I hasten to add, no indication of weakness of personal spirit, merely a last straw. The week before we had landed in a stiffish breeze in a fresh cow-pasture. Over went the basket and we were dragged across the meadow nose downwards. When a colleague who was sane enough to restrict himself to motoring came with his car to collect us, he said we'd have to walk because we were in too objectionable a state to soil his leather upholstery. That, I think, was the penultimate straw. And hence I gave up ballooning.

Until, that is, some years ago when I was invited to experience the delights of modern hot-air ballooning at the Bristol Balloon Festival. In 25 years, I was told, ballooning has changed out of all proportion! I was given a condescending look. After all, I'd been in it in positively antediluvian days when it was just *so* primitive!

"You will not recognise it today when compared with those early days of loose camping-gas cylinders and the hotplate rescued from a gas-cooker found on the local dump," urged my youthful ballonautic pilot. He struck me as a bit young to have eaten much manure, let alone been dragged through some of the finest hawthorn hedges in Southern England.

I reckoned that as I was approaching dotage years I might as well abandon care and have one final fling. He repeated that I would relish the experience whereupon, feeling not unlike Bluebottle in "The Goons," I jumped up and down and said: "I *will* enjoy it, I *will*!"

But first, before going into detail about ballooning, a few observations upon the occupation of ballooning. I use the word "occupation" because while most ballonauts will tell you that ballooning is a hobby or spare-time pursuit, it is fairly obvious that it's a full-time business, for when not ballooning they are dashing all over the country either attending balloon festivals or undertaking that most delightful-sounding of all occupations – retrieving. No, this is not something which Man has learned from dogs and involving thrown sticks: it means finding your balloon after it has come back to Earth.

Perish the thought, though, of any sport or so-called spare-time pursuit which involves rising from the arms of Morpheus at 4.30 in the morning and then trudging about in very damp fields before sunrise (the sun itself never actually seems to appear). Call this a sport? Now my sports, such as they are, seldom begin before 10.30 in the morning and *never* involve such energetic endeavours as running about pulling on ropes or being blasted at by power-driven fans. No, sport is relaxation – and relaxation at this hour of the morning is unthinkable, unreasonable and probably in violent contravention of the Trades Description Act. Brussels, I should imagine, ought to have something to say about it.

Unlike the equally mad sport of sailing when at least you stand the odd chance of both survival and finding a suitable tide which allows you to lie in until a gentlemanly hour of the morning, all balloon flights take place desperately early in the day so, they say, that you have the benefit of calm air. Alternatively you do it late at night. The former has a definite advantage over the latter. With a dawn flight, the day gets lighter and the retrieval crew may actually manage to find you. If it's getting darker, well, you're probably on your own until the next morning.

Ballooning, then, is not a sport. It is a sufferance, it debilitates, it demeans the spirit, it taxes family life, it destroys relationships. Unless, of course, all that is your life comprises other ballonauts in which case you have group self-inflicted purgatory which is, presumably, more bearable.

It becomes apparent that all ballonauts (except this one) are young. They have yet to realise that, like other private youthful occupations which one grows out of, it can harm your well-being, probably make you go blind, render you impotent and, above all, infinitely poorer.

Let us observe for a moment the typical ballonaut and his *équipage*. Few appear to have wives but usually there are one or two hangers-on in tow, presumably in case there are any perks to be had other than a free breakfast and the unequivocal right to pull upon a rope before dawn while stumbling through wet grass, and mingling with other ballonauts, all charging around with their own ropes and shouting at each other.

Women, it must be said, add a certain flair, if not exactly colour, to a ballooning event. Most dress relatively sombrely while it is the men who dress in gaily-coloured overalls, coloured shirts, jackets with go-faster stripes, brightly-coloured shoes that will show up in the mud in case they land head-first – and fancy asbestos gloves.

The ballonaut is, like the golfer with his clubs, nothing without a balloon. Again like the golfer, he needs rather more in the way of vital accessories and accoutrements. First he needs a 'team' which can be made up of friends press-ganged into labouring free of charge. This team will do all the heavy work, all the objectionable stuff, and then, by way of recompense, can suffer the supreme indignity of being dragged along the ground on the end of a rope for a while.

Next is your vehicle. If you are a Skoda or Punto driver, forget it. You will never be accepted as a ballonaut by the elite Corps of Balloonists. To be a ballonaut you need at the very least a Volvo Estate (complete with roof-rack), or a long-wheelbase Landrover – and a large van. This is because a ballooning kit is of prodigious proportions when it comes to being packed up and put away. The sum of the parts becomes infinitely greater than the whole.

Then you need your clothing. Boots, gloves, tough, water-resistant flying overalls and, of course, those asbestos gloves so that you can handle flames without leaving skin behind. Oh! And yes: you require one of those things sold in the ironmongers for lighting the gas on the stove. This must at all times be kept in the top breast pocket and is needed because hot-air balloons survive with air under them by the simple process of lighting propane gas and if the pilot light goes out, then you come down.

303

Armed with that little lot, you are ready for the balloon. There is an element of disappointment when, having prepared for things large and bulky, you find this is zipped up into a large-sized weekend camping haversack and looks quite small. It is. By comparison, it is the basket which takes up the room. The basket is around four feet square and four feet high and the bottom of it is a piece of plywood. Note that there are no springs, no wheels and no skids. This is important when, later on, we come to the bit about the pain of making landfall.

Like all good laundry-baskets, this one is made of basket-weave or wickerwork. Built into the corners is a tubular socket. Into each of the four sockets is plugged a length of 3/4-inch diameter polypropylene rod – the stuff which they make chimney-sweeps' brush sticks out of these days. With the four corner uprights in place – in truth they lean inwards a bit – the burner assembly is fitted over the top of their upper ends. So that the whole integrity of the assembly is not totally dependent on purely the friction of a push-fit piece of plastic in a stainless steel tube, the tension load is resisted by a stainless steel cable clipped to the corner fitting of the basket and to the burner fitting at the top.

At this stage, there appears to be plenty of room in the basket for comfort and one could imagine leaning over the side of the balloon with your fellow ballonauts, observing at your comfortable leisure the passing of the ground beneath you and discussing the growth of the crops while eating ham sandwiches at 750 feet.

This feeling of spaciousness is, however, short-lived because, to the accompaniment of grunting and sweating, the helpers in the party are now seen to be approaching, staggering under the weight of four huge gas cylinders. These are tipped into the basket and tied into each corner with straps before being coupled up with a fuel hose. Room in the basket is now dramatically reduced and the ham sandwich bit has already entered the realms of improbability.

The basket, complete with its scent bottles, is now laid down on its side. The weekend bag has been produced and the balloon itself tipped out onto the grass. Rather like a parachute, it comprises a lot of pieces of string at one end, and a lot of rag at the other. It is important to get the string bits at the basket end because it is these which secure the balloon to the basket. The thing is now carefully unrolled onto the turf so that it stretches away from the basket.

Enter here a nifty piece of ground equipment which, one may safely assume, adds another couple of hundred quid onto the cost of getting your ballooning rig together. This looks like a suitcase trolley and on it is mounted a large wooden fan and a Honda petrol engine. To prevent children and sundry bits of clothing getting caught in the fast-spinning fan and thereby risking damage to it, the rotating parts are enclosed within a stiff wire frame.

With the balloon unfurled on the grass and the strings attached to the top of the burner frame which, along with the basket, is still lying on its side, the most gullible member of the support team is asked if he or she knows how to stand up and open the mouth of the balloon so that he is positioned, legs apart, hands stretched apart above his head, holding the maw in the aghast position. When the volunteer has agreed that he can do this and is in position demonstrating, the fan is started with a pull-cord and cold air blasted at this fellow so that it flows around him and into the balloon's envelope.

Gradually the thing comes to life as, now filled with air, it starts to heave itself into a lumpy shape as it lies on the field. At this stage there's something mildly erotic about all those bulges and curves wobbling around. Only the sheer size of it keeps a young man's thoughts pure.

As soon as the bag is partially inflated with cold air, the gullible chap jumps out of the way to get his breath back and two others leap forward either side of the maw holding it open.

Enter the balloon pilot. Unlike the captain of a Boeing seven-forty-seven who marches up to his flying machine with smart uniform, measured strides and dignity, our trusty ballonaut gets down on all fours and, with canine cunning, carefully negotiates the tangled bits of string and superstructure, and crawls feet first into the basket.

Once inside, he fires up the propane burner and great gusts of hot air, accompanied by a worrying quantity of vicious flame, blast into the bag. Hot air being lighter than cold, the balloon begins to wobble and take on strange shapes. As the thin cloth billows and riffles provocatively on the ground one is reminded of those days in one's youth when one admired sixth-form girls in school blouses as they ran to catch a bus.

Blasts of flame are carefully regulated so as not to burn the cloth and slowly the envelope starts to rise. It is at this point in the proceedings that it becomes abundantly clear to even the most non-aeronautical observer that as an instrument of flight the thing is already completely out of control. With the basket secured by an abundance of ropes to various fixed objects around the field such as the odd Range Rover or Volvo car tow-bar, the envelope starts to flap and swirl. Yet more ropes attached to its top and its sides are grabbed by helpers and here starts the fun.

In anything other than calm, the envelope swings about alarmingly despite the antics of the helpers who, resembling the losing team in the village tug o'war conflict, get dragged all over the place. All at once the balloon lifts itself clear of the ground and in so doing stands the basket upright. The pilot, kneeling on the side of the basket working the Regulo, quickly has to sort himself out so that he, too, is standing up, this time on the floor of the thing.

From now on, the balloon seems so hell-bent on ascending that every available body has to be roped in – good choice of words, that – to haul on the strings and drape themselves over the edge of the basket. The pilot uses his skill to blast in hot air in short bursts. It is the self-same skill as that used in the kitchen in trying to keep a pan of milk simmering on a gas-jet without actually boiling over. Too much hot air at this stage and the chances are that your helpers will gain experience of a balloon flight from the outside of the basket and learn first-hand the survival aspects attendant with hanging on for dear life.

Those who have drawn the short straw now clamber into the basket and adjust themselves as best as they can in juxtaposition with the pilot, the cylinders of gas and the assortment of strings, ropes, tubes and other objects, none of which are apparently involved in playing any part in keeping you secured to the thing. You now have a pretty good idea what it feels like to be an animal being taken in the cat-basket to see the vet.

Immediately above your head the burner roars masses of therms into the bag. Someone has called "Let Go!" You hope it really was your balloon pilot who said that and not the captain of that other balloon inflated a few yards away. I mean, you don't really want to be caught on the hop getting airborne before you are ready, now do you?

It is considered jolly bad form amongst ballonauts to pour in the heat so that the balloon goes up like a rocket. Not only does this strain the balloon and tend to shorten the legs and distend the stomachs of those in the basket, but it also risks taking along with you the odd helper who has been a bit slow in getting the "Let Go!" message. No, the right way to take off is to rise slowly in a stately, noble manner and, while so doing, stand erect in the basket and raise your hat at the watching crowds.

Balloons are quite uncontrollable. Every sane person understands that, but today, when adventurous members of the public are entreated to entrust their lives to the skills of the joyriding-balloon pilot, you dare not let on about this. It is for this reason that modern balloons are equipped with bits of coloured rope and string which dangle importantly from the canopy. The pilot can then be seen to pull at these occasionally during a flight, thereby giving his passengers the impression that all is under control. Real ballonauts, of which I can claim to be one, know these to be no more than placebo controls. There is only one piece of string which does anything at all and that is the piece which rips open the top of the canopy in an emergency. The purpose of this is to mask an ordinary emergency (such as making landfall) with one of even greater majesty.

Flight in a hot-air balloon is a charming and theoretically gentlemanly way of getting from Point A. Unlike normal flying machines, though, when you leave Point A there is no precise Point B to which you can hand-on-heart claim to be going. No, you go where the wind takes the balloon. Which is tough on the retrieval crew who at once climb into their car and head off at high speed to get to the place where they think you might be going to land.

One very important aspect of the sport of ballooning is to try to land somewhere where the retrieval crew can find you. A good retrieval is only a matter of an hour or so. A bad one can involve sandwiches and a night in a wet ditch discovering the hole in your groundsheet . . .

Because you fly with the wind, there is no slipstream, no sense of wind passing you and little sense of reality. The peace and tranquillity of the skies is periodically shattered by the roar from the burner above your head as your pilot, intent on avoiding things like steeples and power cables, greenhouses and sharp trees, pours on heat to give the balloon fresh lift.

Now one quirk of ballooning concerns the direction of the wind. Air travels in different directions at different altitudes and so it is quite possible to change the course of your flight by going higher or lower, so entering a different air mass. Sometimes it is by only a few points of the compass: occasionally you can alter course by up to 45 degrees.

This is a good test for the retrieval crew as, stuck in a traffic jam on the motorway below you, you promptly hare off in another direction leaving them frustrated and confused. This little variation on the sport can be practised a number of times if you are in a mean mood. Too much of it, though, and the sandwiches become essential since, in the final analysis, you do actually want the retrieval crew to find you and bring you back home safely. And if they get dejected and frustrated, you can't really blame them if they push off to the nearest pub and decide to make you wait or, even worse, if they forget you altogether.

Landing a balloon is an interesting experience. As hinted at earlier, the bit of plywood between you and infinity is generally strong enough to take your weight and tough enough to take the landing loads but, because it is unsprung, you can hit the ground with a spine-jarring bang which is likely to send teeth in all directions. You learn to bend the knees so that, when the ground does materialise, you collapse in a heap amidst the mud, dried cow-dung and propane gas bottles in the bottom of the basket.

First rule on landing is: do not jump out of the basket! Or fall out. If you get out too quickly, the balloon will immediately rise again and, deprived of your weight, disappear over the horizon. This makes it tough for you and hard for the retrieval crew who are looking for a balloon, not a bruised newly-ex-ballonaut stuck in a haystack ten miles from where his balloon has finally come to rest.

No, the technique is to stay with it regardless. In the early days when the basket was secured to the balloon purely by ropes, the basket could turn upside down so that you found yourself in a neat little wickerwork kennel with a pasture floor and a red-hot gas-burner resting in your lap. These days thanks to the semi-rigid superstructure supporting the burner, balloons only invert their baskets if the landing has been really, really terrible. This means about half of them.

Most of the time, you just fall over sideways and, unless you can deflate the balloon quickly by means of the inverted umbrella vent in the top of it, you can get dragged along the ground by the wind blowing on the canopy. This is an amusing experience since the edge of the basket can now act as a scoop picking up things from the ground as you travel sideways along the meadows. The odd small animal or flustered chicken is bad enough but the real problem arises when you have just landed as I used to in the 1950s in a fresh cow pasture. Since you are invariably face-down on the ground as well, the inevitable slurp as you scoop up a cow-pat with your nose can be a trifle unnerving. Now as before, this process also does not endear you to the retrieval crew who have to get you into their car later on.

One also learns never to take loose objects with you unless they are disposable. Hats, cameras and things in your pockets tend to spew out to form a sort of terminal moraine after such a landing. Now you begin to see why the pilot has zipped himself into his snazzy, whizz-kid track-suit-type overalls. Only raw novices fly in a grey three-piece pinstripe, bowler hat and white shirt.

In dead calm conditions, of course, it is possible to land without forward motion in which case the basket probably remains upright. An experienced pilot will, under such conditions, carefully keep just a little hot air going up into the balloon to maintain it partially inflated and in the air. This acts as a useful hint as to your location for the benefit of the retrieval crew as, with their binoculars, they scan the horizon from twenty miles away wondering where the dickens you are and, more to the point, where the blazes they are.

Failure to do this properly, though, has an unfortunate secondary result – the envelope slowly collapses about you turning day into night as several thousand square yards of cloth wrap themselves around your head. Trying to free yourself from the basket in the middle of this enforced night invariably means getting some of your feet caught in propane gas-bottle straps, snagging your buttons on the sundry wires and strings and generally making a pig's ear of it.

The person who balloons has to be possessed of several important characteristics which separate him very clearly from the normal air traveller. First he must never be in a hurry. And second he must not actually want to go anywhere specific. For him, the challenge of flight is going up from one place – and coming down again somewhere else.

Having risen before the lark, travelled in night-time darkness to your balloon, unpacked the thing, blown it up, flown an indeterminate distance and tried not to antagonise the farmers who don't like balloons or ballonauts, plunged into a cow meadow, survived, been retrieved, and got back to base, it is a sobering thought to look at your watch and, assuming it's still there on your wrist (and that your wrist's still intact), discover that it is still no more than ten past eight in the morning. Thus at a moment when you feel it just has to be mid-afternoon and you are all ready for lunch and that vital first large gin and tonic of the day, you have to make good with a large bacon-and-egg breakfast washed down with a mug of tea.

You can identify a ballonaut a mile off. He's the one who sleeps during the day. He's the one who thinks it's a late night if he's still up and about by seven in the evening. And he's the one in the Volvo with the large ungainly trailer.

After my brief experience of modern-day ballooning at the Bristol Festival, then, I reckoned that was it and I could continue into senility with dignity. I was wrong.

My wife and I took a few weeks to visit some relatives. We ended up in Queensland, Australia.

"There's a lot of ballooning in these parts," said Nick. "Great local sport. Thought you'd like to have a go so I've arranged us a trip tomorrow!"

We drove through the dark of a pre-dawn Brisbane and pulled into a park where four balloons were laid out, one being the famous Michelin Man doing a tour 'down under.' Ours, however, was a regular round one skippered by a large and friendly Yank who had found Aussies were a sucker for early-morning ballooning and had made himself a business out of it.

The eastern sky began to show that prescient glow as we watched him fire up his balloon. Nothing had changed. When he was ready, we climbed in. Nothing had changed. We blasted more hot air and finally rose into the lightening sky. Still nothing had changed.

Then suddenly it was all different. Modern technology had overtaken Montgolfier! Our pilot had a mobile telephone and was talking energetically to the three other balloons as we sailed over the yet-deserted high-rise buildings of the city.

The local breakfast radio station interviewed our fellow live from 800 feet all about balloons. It was an eye-opener! A live show from the basket of a balloon! Wow! Things *have* changed!

Being meteorologically inclined the way most flyers are, I was eyeing the ground and my wristwatch. As our pilot chirped on merrily about the fun of ballooning for the benefit of still sleepy toast-and-Vegemite-eating Brisbanites who probably couldn't give a damn, I noted with interest that our balloon was fairly zinging along towards the east.

From the perfect calm of our take-off we were now in an airstream which was picking up speed all the while. In forty minutes we had covered twenty-three kilometres, most of it in the past twenty minutes.

Having signed off his radio show and seen the other three balloons safely down in and around the city, our pilot said he was making for a field he knew way out the far side of town. It was a small meadow with high tension wires along the approach side. The field was small – and there was a lake in it which turned out to be a flooded quarry.

Interesting, I thought.

We crossed the electricity wires at a safe height and at about the speed you would cross electricity wires on finals in a DH.60 Moth, whereupon we had a pretty short stretch of meadow to contact if we were to steer clear of the lake and the wire fence at the far edge. Ten feet up, the captain pulled the vent rope.

With an enormous impact which surprised even me, the basket thumped into a tummock at a horizontal speed of quite a bit and then some. The basket crashed over on its side and, driven by the wind in the partially deflated canopy, proceeded like a ferret pursued by a dog towards the water. Hanging on for all we were worth, we watched grass and mud skimming past our ears as our crazy ship on the sea of earth skidded pell-mell in a series of sickening jerks and impacts on the crests of well-turfed waves. Ah! Now this was *just* like the old days!

Finally everything came to rest. We were rather close to the water, but not in it. Unfortunately, our pilot had unwisely allowed himself to be flung out on impact, thereby breaking all the rules of hot-air ballooning (*i.e.* stay with it and stick it out).

"That's the first time that's ever happened to me!" he exclaimed with the sort of pride which might, under different circumstances, earn a round of applause.

Another fellow had a gash on his forehead from where his glasses had broken and been driven into his flesh. The precious mobile telephone had disappeared (and was never found despite hunting the field and even calling up the number on another one to see if we could hear it ring in the grass).

The retrieval crew found us and, with the blood staunched and the cuts patched up, eventually we were packed up and set off back to base for breakfast in the big four-wheel-drive wagon. It was a Monday morning and it was Brisbane's rush-hour. We, the driving wounded, sat in the van, battered, bruised and caked in dried blood, enduring the worldwide slow traffic crawl. Other motorists stuck in the stationary traffic refused to notice us.

"But *look!*" we wanted to shout at them. "We've been *ballooning!*"

One could imagine the response such a statement might have earned.

Not one asked for our autograph – or a snapshot leaning against the basket the way they used to.

Yes, it's a strange business, this world of ballooning. As for me? Well, *I* balloon . . . but only as a non-believer.

CHAPTER 32
SOME THOUGHTS ON FLYING
by
Maurice Brett

On one of those dripping, melancholy, grey, overcast days we saw so often in the winter of 1978-9 (nowadays at any time of the year!), I was sitting at my desk in the office in the lunch-break, following a harrowing morning. In an attempt to cheer myself I visualised instead a warm sunny day with bright fluffy cumulus clouds contrasting to a backdrop of azure blue, then shut my eyes and was airborne once again in dear old Jackaroo 'OIR on a Vintage Aircraft Group Fly-In from Finmere, with three joyriding passengers up for their first-ever flight in an old biplane, a scenario associated with such meetings for very many years from the sixties through to the mid-eighties . . .

Then, for some reason, my mind flipped back to lunch – and tea-break – times when I was fifteen, working at Park Royal Coachworks, building Halifax wings in 1941. The Works Canteen overlooked an open space which at such times formed the battle-space for flocks of seagulls fighting for scraps from the kitchens – I spent long periods watching and envying the gulls and their easy, faultless flight, and dreaming . . .

Most of what follows just flowed onto the paper (the only time I have ever felt the slightest inclination to write anything in blank verse), though it took more time later to make it presentable. It cheered me up then, and has done on numerous occasions since; whether you enjoy vintage flying, or just dream of it, I hope dear reader, that it might do something for you.

It sums up exactly my perception, then and now, of vintage flying in the golden era; sadly alas such feelings of total freedom for most of us are now gone, never to return – ever-tightening bureaucracy and the airspace-grabbing pressures associated in this crowded island with the growth of high-speed and high-volume commercial and military aviation have unfortunately seen to that.

"When, as a wondering boy I watched the seagull's effortless flight,
The way in which they gracefully soared and wheeled,
Then, in a moment of flexing muscle swooped, headlong
For a proffered taking,
How unattainable did such easy grace appear,
The pinnacle of impossible dreams both sleeping and waking.

And yet, miraculously and half a lifetime on,
Those dreams have been, for long now, near reality.

At first each moment of flight was fiercely snatched as if,
And 'deed it was, too precious to allow slip by,
Unsavoured to the full.

But since those early days of exercising untried wings,
Faltering clumsily with hands and feet (and seat of pants),
And eyes and ears full at times beyond capacity
With a thousand new and awesome things,
A deftness, as of a comforting mantle,
Has smoothed out the unaccustomed fears,
And born of some practice, has crept upon the scene
Almost unnoticed in the passage of a few eventful years.

So now, when light of heart,
And time and pocket are not too pressing,
And machine is willing, and broken cloud
Only occasionally filters the friendly sun,
We all combine to set the balance redressing.

Back to those boyhood (and later) dreams,
Succumbing only too readily to the prompting words,
Of those riding within, we wheel and swing
In clumsy emulation of those graceful birds.

Then, with laden machine clambering breathlessly for height,
We top the silver clouds, and seemingly
Hold poised in space, with pure blue sky and golden orb above,
And clinical cloud white of dazzling Arctic scene
Stretching to each infinity.

At a moment's whim, the labouring clamour of full climb power
Is replaced by near-silence,
The winds sighing in the wires accompanied
Only by occasional popping of throttled-back exhaust.

Now our bird comes into her own,
With such height that we can twist and turn
And dive and zoom effortlessly, only the unwinding altimeter
Remorselessly grinding us back to earth.

To think is to act and, no sooner occurs a notion,
Than slight pressure on stick or rudder
Converts thought into flowing motion.
We dive, gaining speed and, with the wind rushing past
A back thought on the stick pulls us down in our seats,
As the high horizon slides down past the nose out of sight below.

The wind's roar gradually dies and in long, still, moments,
In which blades of the now slowly rotating prop

Can be snatched in momentary vision,
And through which the blinding sun mesmerically flickers,
We hang, kitebird dutifully waiting her next instruction,
Mindfully warning with sloppy controls
When the last moment of action is near.

We wheel to left or right,
Or push on over to save our height,
Or just lazily leave our dear old bird to gently stall
With no more than a reproachful shake until,
With nose pointing near vertically down,
She quickly gains a second wind
And waits impatient for her pilot's next call.

Fear now plays no part in such activity,
Just a nerve-tingling, deeply satisfying romanticism
Of sights and sounds and sensations,
Of which most earthbound mortals
Neither understand nor care.

With what wonderment do my joyriders first espy,
The perfect rainbow circle round our shadowy twin,
Steeplechasing over an undulating cloud floor of the sky.

Or on escaping through the eternal skin of brown haze
See, first-hand, the separation of clean blue air
From the dingy earth below.

Or discover, at somewhat greater height,
The liquid shimmering silver sea top of an overcast,
With iceberg cloud tips peeping through,
Brilliant and pure and white.

But all too soon the time comes to pass
For us to leave this private heaven, slipping off unwanted height,
Dropping ever hopeful of that last unequalled satisfaction
When all three points together lightly kiss the grass.

Then's the time to reflect, after switching off
When suddenly all is strangely still and quiet,
Save for faint whine of gyros running down
And tick-tick of cooling metal,
What beauty there is in the simple things of life."